English Poetry of the Sixteenth Century

Longman Literature in English Series

General Editors: David Carroll and Michael Wheeler
Lancaster University

For a complete list of titles see pages viii–ix

English Poetry
of the
Sixteenth Century

Second Edition

Gary Waller

Longman

London and New York

Longman Group UK Limited
Longman House, Burnt Mill,
Harlow, Essex CM20 2JE, England
and Associated Companies throughout the world.

*Published in the United States of America
by Longman Publishing, New York*

First published 1986
Second edition 1993

ISBN 0 582 09096 2 PPR

British Library Cataloguing-in-Publication Data

A catalogue record for this book is available from the British Library

Library of Congress Cataloging-in-Publication Data

Waller, Gary F. (Gary Francis), 1945–
    English poetry of the sixteenth century / Gary Waller.
    – 2nd ed. p. cm. – (Longman literature in English series)
    Includes bibliographical references and index.
    ISBN 0–582–09096–2
    1. English poetry–Early modern, 1500–1700–History and
    criticism.
    I. Title.   II. Series.
    PR531.W33   1993   92–41926
    821'.209–dc20   CIP

Set by 5L in 9½/11pt Bembo
Printed in Malaysia by PMS

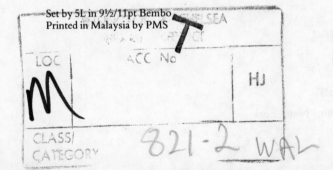

Contents

Editors' Preface

The multi-volume Longman Literature in English Series provides students of literature with a critical introduction to the major genres in their historical and cultural context. Each volume gives a coherent account of a clearly defined area, and the series, when complete, will offer a practical and comprehensive guide to literature written in English from Anglo-Saxon times to the present. The aim of the series as a whole is to show that the most valuable and stimulating approach to the study of literature is that based upon an awareness of the relations between literary forms and their historical contexts. Thus the areas covered by most of the separate volumes are defined by period and genre. Each volume offers new and informed ways of reading literary works, and provides guidance for further reading in an extensive reference section.

In recent years, the nature of English studies has been questioned in a number of increasingly radical ways. The very terms employed to define a series of this kind – period, genre, history, context, canon – have become the focus of extensive critical debate, which has necessarily influenced in varying degrees the successive volumes published since 1985. But however fierce the debate, it rages around the traditional terms and concepts.

As well as studies on all periods of English and American literature, the series includes books on criticism and literary theory, and on the intellectual and cultural context. A comprehensive series of this kind must of course include other literatures written in English, and therefore a group of volumes deals with Irish and Scottish literature, and the literatures of India, Africa, the Caribbean, Australia and Canada. The forty-seven volumes of the series cover the following areas: Pre-Renaissance English Literature, English Poetry, English Drama, English Fiction, English Prose, Criticism and Literary Theory, Intellectual and Cultural Context, American Literature, Other Literatures in English.

David Carroll
Michael Wheeler

Longman Literature in English Series
General Editors: David Carroll and Michael Wheeler
Lancaster University

Pre-Renaissance English Literature

★ English Literature before Chaucer *Michael Swanton*
English Literature in the Age of Chaucer
★ English Medieval Romance *W. R. J. Barron*

English Poetry

★ English Poetry of the Sixteenth Century (Second Edition) *Gary Waller*
★ English Poetry of the Seventeenth Century (Second Edition)
George Parfitt
English Poetry of the Eighteenth Century, 1700–1789
★ English Poetry of the Romantic Period, 1789–1830 (Second Edition)
J. R. Watson
★ English Poetry of the Victorian Period, 1830–1890 *Bernard Richards*
English Poetry of the Early Modern Period, 1890–1940
★ English Poetry since 1940 *Neil Corcoran*

English Drama

English Drama before Shakespeare
★ English Drama: Shakespeare to the Restoration, 1590–1660
Alexander Leggatt
★ English Drama: Restoration and Eighteenth Century, 1660–1789
Richard W. Bevis
English Drama: Romantic and Victorian, 1789–1890
English Drama of the Early Modern Period, 1890–1940
English Drama since 1940

English Fiction

★ English Fiction of the Eighteenth Century, 1700–1789
Clive T. Probyn
★ English Fiction of the Romantic Period, 1789–1830 *Gary Kelly*
★ English Fiction of the Victorian Period, 1830–1890 (Second Edition)
Michael Wheeler
★ English Fiction of the Early Modern Period, 1890–1940 *Douglas Hewitt*
English Fiction since 1940

English Prose

★ English Prose of the Seventeenth Century, 1590–1700 *Roger Pooley*
English Prose of the Eighteenth Century
English Prose of the Nineteenth Century

Criticism and Literary Theory

Criticism and Literary Theory from Sidney to Johnson
Criticism and Literary Theory from Wordsworth to Arnold
Criticism and Literary Theory from 1890 to the Present

The Intellectual and Cultural Context

The Sixteenth Century
★ The Seventeenth Century, 1603–1700 *Graham Parry*
★ The Eighteenth Century, 1700–1789 (Second Edition) *James Sambrook*
The Romantic Period, 1789–1830
★ The Victorian Period, 1830–1890 *Robin Gilmour*
The Twentieth Century, 1890 to the Present

American Literature

American Literature before 1880
★ American Poetry of the Twentieth Century *Richard Gray*
★ American Drama of the Twentieth Century *Gerald M. Berkowitz*
★ American Fiction 1865–1940 *Brian Lee*
★ American Fiction since 1940 *Tony Hilfer*
★ Twentieth-Century America *Douglas Tallack*

Other Literatures

Irish Literature since 1800
Scottish Literature since 1700

Australian Literature
★ Indian Literature in English *William Walsh*
African Literature in English: East and West
Southern African Literatures
Caribbean Literature in English
★ Canadian Literature in English *W. J. Keith*

★ *Already published*

Author's Preface to the Second Edition

Whether historians write history or critics criticism (even though never entirely in the ways they choose), or whether they are in some sense written by their subjects, will never be proved by a single volume, but the process by which this volume of the Longman Literature in English series, both in its first edition and in this substantial rewriting, has been written certainly supports what it tries to exemplify – that the disruptive and contradictory structures that erupt within writing are the product of the interactions of many discourses, not merely the product of the will of its 'author'. But as the scriptor of this study, I recognize many intellectual debts and personal obligations. When in 1979 Michael Wheeler, one of the General Editors of the series, originally asked me to undertake the volume, I had in process a study of the power of the Court over the poetry of the period. Much of that had grown from earlier work on the Sidney Circle, and especially from two studies of the Countess of Pembroke which convinced me (as usual, after they were published) that we needed to rethink our way of reading the period and its poetry. In order to let some of the answers to the questions that were arising find me, I had at times to stop reading sixteenth-century poetry, my ostensible subject, until I could find fit words by which it could speak through me. The preparation of the second edition has involved a not dissimilar process, not least because the questions we ask now are, inevitably, changing.

My specific debts (authors may not exist in quite the ways we once thought, but readers and friends certainly do) are many, and only the most important can be acknowledged here. I recall that as I read over the final stages of the first edition, I found myself drawn back to C. S. Lewis's *English Literature in the Sixteenth Century* and discovered myself agreeing, though from startlingly different perspectives, with many of his judgements: I commenced my teaching career in the rooms in which he had once taught at Magdalene College, Cambridge, and so my acknowledgement is a doubly appropriate one. His successors in the Chair of Medieval and Renaissance Literature, the late J. A. W. Bennett and John Stevens, both helped me greatly in those early days, and later, as did other teachers and mentors, including Peter Dane, Mike Doyle, L. C. Knights, and the late J. C. Reid. In writing the original edition, I learnt much from scholars such as Catherine Belsey, the late Diane Bornstein, Elizabeth Bieman, Jonathan Dollimore, Antony Easthope, Ian Donaldson, A. C. Hamilton, S. K. Heninger Jr, Bob Hodge, Ann Rosalind Jones, Roger Kuin, Richard Lanham, Ken Larsen, Jacqueline Miller, Louis A. Montrose, J. C. A. Rathmell, Jerry Rubio, William Sessions, Bernard Sharratt, Alan Sinfield, Peter Stallybrass and Frank Whigham. The second edition has benefited from the continued help of many of these, and especially from Curt Breight, Richard Dutton, Peggy Knapp, Mary Ellen Lamb, Naomi Miller, Janel Mueller, Josephine Roberts, Mary Beth Rose, Ann Shaver, Suzanne Woods, and many members of the congenial Spenser and Sidney groups at Kalamazoo, who'll know whom I mean and why. Among the students to whom in part this book is dedicated and with whom it was to a large extent written (in some cases giving me reason to break the Eighth Commandment) are: Andrew Brown, Andrea Clough, Craig Dionne, Margaret McLaren, Stacia Nagel, Michele Osherow and Susan Rudy Dorscht (who, for the first edition, served as my research assistant). Kathleen McCormick, my colleague and collaborator on other projects as well as an acute reader and 'onelie begetter' of some parts of this, is due especial thanks, not least for Philip. My colleagues at the University of Hartford bear some responsibility for the speed with which this second edition was finished. Humphrey Tonkin, himself no mean friend of sixteenth-century poetry, and Jonathan Lawson, a gamboler in the rural delights of the eighteenth century, deserve special thanks. I also thank Alan Hadad, Joel Kagan and Lynne Kelly. Michael Wheeler encouraged me by mixing indulgence and firmness.

Research for the first edition of this book was carried out over nearly ten years, with the help of research grants from the Canada Council, and the Social Sciences and Humanities Research Council, and short-term grants from Dalhousie and Wilfrid Laurier Universities. Parts of the second edition took shape in Cambridge in 1988, with the help of a fellowship from the John Simon Guggenheim Foundation, and in the congenial surroundings of the Newberry Library, Chicago, where I held a short-term fellowship in 1990–91. I wish to thank the Humanities Research Centre at the Australian National University for a fellowship in 1979 that helped me think through some of the beginnings of the first edition of the book.

Parts of this volume have appeared, in different form, as follows: portions of Chapter 1 in the *Dalhousie Review* (1981) and *Assays* (1982), different parts of the material on Philip and Robert Sidney, Ralegh and Shakespeare in *Short Fiction: Critical Views*, and *Poetry: Critical Views*, both published by Salem Press (1981 and 1982, respectively); much of the account of *Astrophil and Stella* in the special Sidney issue of *Studies In the Literary Imagination* (1982), edited by William A. Sessions. Some of the material on the Sidney Circle appeared first in *The Triumph of Death* and *Mary Sidney, Countess of Pembroke*, published by the University of Salzburg (1977, 1979); that on Petrarchism in Chapter 3 in *Sir Philip Sidney and the Interpretation of Renaissance Culture*, edited by Gary F. Waller and Michael D. Moore (Croom Helm, 1984), and parts of the new chapter on women's poetry in *Silent But for the Word*, edited by Margaret P. Hannay (Kent State University Press, 1985), in *Studies in Philology* (1991), *Reading Mary Wroth*, co-edited with Naomi J. Miller (University of Tennessee Press, 1991), and *The Sidney Family Romance: William Herbert, Mary Wroth and Gender Construction in Early Modern England* (Wayne State University Press, 1993). Throughout, ideas and occasional paragraphs have surfaced in comments and reviews in the *Sidney Newsletter*. In all cases, prior publication is acknowledged.

Nobody other than the author is responsible for the final product. But then, as some of my colleagues and friends say, nor am I, since, they say, it is discourse that creates us; we do not speak, we are spoken. Nonetheless, the world of scholarship is such that I will want to accept any praise for whatever stimulation this volume may produce in its readers, so I must accept all the blame for its shortcomings.

GFW
Carnegie Mellon University
December 1984

University of Hartford
December 1992

List of Abbreviations

The following common abbreviations of scholarly journals and series etc., have been used in this study:

ADE Bulletin	Association of Departments of English Bulletin
AUMLA	Australasian Universities Modern Languages Association
CQ	Critical Quarterly
EETS	Early English Texts Society
ELH	English Literary History
ELN	English Language Notes
ELR	English Literary Renaissance
ES	English Studies
HLQ	Huntingdon Library Quarterly
HMC	Historical Manuscripts Commission
JEGP	Journal of English and Germanic Philosophy
JMRS	Journal of Medieval and Renaissance Studies
JWCI	Journal of the Warburg and Courtauld Institutes
KR	Kenyon Review
MLN	Modern Language Notes
MLQ	Modern Languages Quarterly
MLR	Modern Language Review
NLH	New Literary History
OLR	Oxford Literary Review
PMLA	Publications of the Modern Languages Association
PQ	Philological Quarterly
RenQ	Renaissance Quarterly
Ren and Ref	Renaissance and Reformation
RES	Review of English Studies
SEL	Studies in English Literature, 1500–1900
SLitI	Studies in the Literary Imagination
SN	Shakespeare Newsletter
SNew	Sidney Newsletter
SP	Studies in Philosophy

This book is dedicated with gratitude to my students at Magdalene, Auckland, Dalhousie, Wilfrid Laurier, Carnegie Mellon and Hartford. The first edition was especially for Michael and Andrew; the second edition is, in addition, especially for Katie and Philip.

Acknowledgements

This book is indebted work pertaining to Maclaren, Aden and Dilmun, Ward, Lamber, Carnegie Mellon and Heerema. The information was already collected and Anthony, the second Britain ... especially ... of China.

Chapter 1
Reading the Poetry of the Sixteenth Century

Introduction

When a modern student, even a general reader, looks at a volume of sixteenth-century poetry, what is likely to be his or her impression? When I first started teaching the poetry of Wyatt and Sidney, even Shakespeare and Donne, there was a sense of their remoteness from most concerns we have in the twentieth century. Except as a kind of nostalgia, what do delicate love sonnets, songs with refrains like 'hey nonny nonny no', and seemingly artificial, conventional poems dealing with refined upper-class manners and the erotic anguish of long-dead high-born gentlemen (I mark the gender deliberately) have to say to us? Even if one were interested in the history of the time – with its stirring mixture of battles, beheadings, rebellions, and religious controversies – much of the poetry may seem pale and lifeless, or else crudely versified propaganda, monuments to dead ideas, especially to an unswerving sexism. Shakespeare and Donne are, perhaps, exceptions: as F. R. Leavis put it for us, only when we reach Donne after a century of dull poetry, can we 'read on as we read the living'.[1]

Today, all this has changed. The study of sixteenth-century poetry has become one of the most interesting fields in English literature. In part, it is because we have realized just how similar, in significant ways, our age is to the sixteenth century or what we now tend to call, significantly, the 'early modern' period. Despite real differences in the social, cultural, and ideological practices of the two ages in such issues as class, gender, and race or ethnicity, we seem to face either similar dilemmas and obsessions or else be able to trace the history of our dilemmas and obsessions to that period. In part this is because of a greater liveliness in the field of literary and cultural criticism in general. In the past two decades, we have asked different questions of our literature and even begun to question the nature and status of 'literature' altogether. This introduction to sixteenth-century poetry is written in the belief that the great advances in our understanding of the sixteenth century and its poetry – the work on canon, sources, traditions, conventions, rhetoric and poetics of the past century, all of which has given us access to the poems of the sixteenth century – will be wasted unless they are caught up into this new excitement about the ways we read literary and related texts. In order to make sixteenth-century poetry ours, to allow us to read it, to return to Leavis's words, not 'as students or as connoisseurs of anthology-pieces', but 'as we read the living', we must let it speak within the world we, its readers, inhabit.[2] By beginning with what appear to be urgent questions for us, we let the poems speak to us not only of our history but also of our present and of our possible futures.

Let me give one example – a poem to which I shall return in Chapter 4. Some years ago, some of my students were asked to read Sir Thomas Wyatt's best-known poem:

> They flee from me that sometime did me seek
>   With naked foot stalking in my chamber.
> I have seen them gentle, tame, and meek
>   That now are wild and do not remember
>   That sometime they put themselves in danger
> To take bread at my hand; and now they range
> Busily seeking with a continual change.
>
> Thanked be fortune it hath been otherwise
>   Twenty times better, but once in special
> In thin array after a pleasant guise,
>   When her loose gown from her shoulders did fall
>   And she me caught in her arms long and small,
> Therewithal sweetly did me kiss,
> And softly said, 'Dear heart, how like you this?'
>
> It was no dream; I lay broad waking.
>   But all is turned through my gentilness
> Into a strange fashion of forsaking.
>   And I have leave to go of her goodness,
>   And she also to use newfangleness.
> But since that I so kindly am served
> I would fain know what she hath deserved.

The students were asked to write one- or two-page 'response statements' to the poem in which they described in as much detail as possible the initial effect of the text upon them – whether it was confusion, suspense, interest, indignation or whatever. Then they were asked to try to account for why reading the poem had that effect. First, what was there in the repertoire of the text (its subject-matter, language, conventions, organization, themes, the gaps or indeterminacies which the reader has to fill in, and what is perhaps unstated but assumed by the writer of the poem and perhaps many of his original audiences)? Second, what was there in the repertoire of the reader that had contributed to that reading? What assumptions about subject matter, subjectivity, poetry, gender roles, class behaviour, was the reader bringing to his or her encounter with the text? How, in the act of reading, had reader and text co-operated? The results were fascinating. Most of the men in the class felt immediate identification with the wounded male ego that is seemingly articulated in the poem: he has been rejected by a woman with whom he has unexpectedly fallen in love only to be told by her that it was all enjoyable but superficial flirtation. Most of the women in the class were amusedly derisive of this attitude: what, they said, about the woman's viewpoint? In such a society, and within such a philosophy of love, both so male-centred, why should a woman not get what she could out of the game of sex? Girls just want to have fun. It should be added, perhaps, on a pedagogical note, that this course on sixteenth-century poetry traditionally culminates in a banquet using Elizabethan recipes prepared by the students themselves and accompanied by music and poetry readings. If we want the sixteenth-century poets to come alive, what better way than to combine poetry, music, and food!

More seriously, the students in the course were being introduced to a method of reading that this study will employ. The intention was to create strong readers of the poetry who would, as self-analytically as possible, bring their own most intense, often apparently very personal, questions to bear on their reading of Wyatt, or Sidney, or Shakespeare, or Donne. But, of course, they were asked to do more. As a means of intensifying their readings of Wyatt's poem, they were asked to read Roland Barthes's *A Lover's Discourse*, a remarkable anatomy of desire by a modern philosopher that seemed to many of the students, at this initial stage at least, to reflect uncannily on both the poetry they were reading and their own experiences. Barthes describes the lover, like the one in Wyatt's poem, remembering a love scene over and over 'in order to be unhappy/happy – not in order to understand'; and writes of how 'the ego discourses only when it is hurt'.[3] Barthes gave these student readers a powerful, contemporary vocabulary with which to articulate their questions about the text. He allowed them, too, to start to discover that his (and their) responses were not purely 'subjective', or 'personal', but rather constructed within a repertoire of common late-twentieth-century assumptions about love, desire, gender and sexuality. Readings, they were starting to learn, are never entirely 'personal' or 'subjective'.

The aim of this study is to introduce the poetry of the sixteenth century so that such confrontations, or dialogues – what I like to call 'polylogues' since many, often contradictory, voices are involved – can occur between today's readers and the texts that come to us from the sixteenth century. We need to realize that both texts and readers have vital parts to play in producing lively, informative, effective (and affective) readings. In a sense, the practice of 'polylogue' is not new: although without acknowledging (or perhaps even knowing) it, every age reads the poetry and other texts that come down to it from the past through its own concerns. If we look back a little further than our own time and study the history of the reception of sixteenth-century poetry, we can see how our understanding of it, and especially of the poems written in the two decades before 1600, has undergone quite distinct changes, especially over the past century. In 1861, Francis Palgrave's *Golden Treasury* established what became the basis for the modern canon of Elizabethan poetry. It provided a set of criteria for evaluating the poetry that was largely accepted for more than a century. It assumed that the best poetry had an immediacy that made it easily accessible to the educated reader. While the long, public poems of the period – *A Mirror for Magistrates*, Spenser's *Faerie Queene*, Harington's translation of Ariosto – clearly required some kind of historical understanding, Palgrave's selection suggested that the Elizabethan lyric poems could be immediately perceived as 'treasures which might lead us in higher and healthier ways than those of the world'.[4] They provided us with glimpses of an ideal order of love or harmony that the poets, all supposedly infatuated with the glories and buoyancy of the Elizabethan Age, celebrated in song just as they did in the pleasures, dances, and pageants of their lives at the Court. Even in modern times (in this case in the middle of the nineteenth century) we could have direct access to this magical world. Such poems were immediate in their appeal, and dealt directly with supposedly universal human experiences.

Such a reading has been increasingly questioned in our century, even though it underlies the most comprehensive anthology of the period's poetry, E. K. Chambers's *Oxford Book of Sixteenth-Century Verse* (1932). Eliot's championing of the highly intellectual 'Metaphysical' as opposed to the Elizabethan poets; Winters's construction of a native plain-style tradition that existed alongside the dominant 'golden' or 'aureate' court lyric in the sixteenth century; Lewis's division of the century's poetry into drab and golden (terms which he ingenuously asserted were not qualitative but descriptive); the articulation of the subtlety and richness of the Elizabethan poets' rhetorical training by such scholars as Lanham and Tuve – all these developments have made the *Golden Treasury* model of Elizabethan poetry less acceptable. Refinements upon Winters's approach have been especially influential, such as Peterson's influence of medieval rhetoric on both the plain and eloquent style and of the religious tradition of plain statement, Hunter's discussion of the division in the 1570s between moralistic, patriotic poems and courtly aestheticism, Inglis's or John Williams's reassertions of Winters's stress on the 'plain', moral-reflective, style and the claim that courtly Petrarchism is a deviation from the main English tradition. Valuable work, too, has been done on the canon of such poets as Wyatt, Googe, and Mary and Robert Sidney; Spenser has been rescued from disfavour (and even encyclopedized!) and most recently, the canon has been expanded by a significant amount of poetry written by women. As matters stand now, the reader of sixteenth-century poetry can find diverse approaches, all of which show that it offers very different kinds of interest. Nearly a century and a half after Palgrave, the dominant 'canon' of sixteenth-century poetry does not consist only of the golden lyrics and delicate songs of which he approved.[5]

There is one aspect of the *Golden Treasury*'s praise, however, which remained curiously untouched in the dominant evaluations of sixteenth-century poetry well into the 1980s, and indeed is still with us. Palgrave praised the Elizabethan poets for their ability to unify a variety of experience, asserting that their special excellence lay rather in the whole than in the parts, in their creation of unity, harmony and coherence. Most modern criticism – including the 'New Criticism', as well as 'Historicist' approaches that relate texts to their historical background – took for granted that a literary text is a unified, organic creation which 'reflects' or 'expresses' its author's views or vision, or the dominant philosophical assumptions of its age. What Tillyard termed the 'Elizabethan World Picture' – a philosophical conglomerate, supposedly believed by all Elizabethans, that the universe was a divinely created organism, characterized by unity, harmony and hierarchy – was widely seen as reflected in the age's poetry. In the last two decades, however (and if one traces its philosophical sources, at least as far back as Marx, Nietzsche and Freud) a new paradigm has arisen in our understanding of many of the human sciences, one that has drastically affected the way we read literary and related texts. Louis Althusser once suggested that our age would be looked back to as one in which the most fundamental human activities – perceiving, reading, writing – were radically revalued.[6] Perhaps not since the late eighteenth century have the roles and status of interpretation, history, reading and writing been put so fiercely and fundamentally into question. It is now difficult to approach literary history or criticism, the teaching of language, literature, culture – even the most fundamental human traits of perception and description – without being aware of radically different questions and to consider, however tentatively, new and disturbing answers.

It was not, however, until the late 1970s that such tremors started to affect sixteenth-century studies. They were first seen in print in such studies as Greenblatt's *Renaissance Self-Fashioning* (1980), Goldberg's *Endlesse Worke* (1981), and Sinfield's *Literature in Protestant England* (1983), which indicated that some of the major philosophical and cultural changes that had started to reconstruct literary criticism generally were having some impact upon sixteenth-century studies. As Patterson put it in 1980, 'the theorists' have at last 'got into the Renaissance'.[7] What did she mean? The assumption that underlay most criticism before the 1980s was that meanings – or what are still widely termed a text's *themes* – were not only inherently 'in' the text, but that they were accessible to close, empirical attention to the text itself. In Britain, the influence of Leavis, Richards and others enshrined 'practical criticism' as the dominant mode of reading, and similar in many respects was the American New Criticism. The fundamental reading strategy of both – the means by which a work's supposed 'themes' were elucidated – was 'close reading', by means of which texts were supposed somehow to yield up their hidden meanings. Rather than acknowledging the constructed nature of meaning, such an approach tended to be objectivist, assuming that meanings were independent of the historical or cultural context of the reader or critic. In an obvious sense close reading underlies all approaches to literature: it is important to pay careful attention to one's interactions with the text, and to the questions and issues one finds oneself asking to explain those interactions. The assumption that meanings are 'in' a text has, in recent years, been increasingly seen as naïve empiricism, ignoring what a reader brings to the text and what wider cultural pressures were on a text when it was written. In the late 1970s and early 1980s, a close reading technique of a particularly intense kind was fashionable in deconstruction, an approach to reading whereby a literary text is subjected to a rigorous – indeed, some would say perverse – close reading. The term 'deconstruction' has recently been applied loosely to any reading that refuses to take a text's surface or preferred meaning for granted, but in its heyday, a deconstructive reading focused primarily on the duplicity of rhetoric and, in particular, the power of figural language to create the illusion of a self-contained meaning seemingly contained 'in' the text. Deconstruction's influence on readings of sixteenth-century poetry was spasmodic, and never as powerful as upon readings of Romantic poems by leading deconstructive critics like Harold Bloom and Geoffrey Hartman.

In the 1980s, both in discussions of the Renaissance and in literary theory generally, both traditional formalism and deconstruction were attacked by a variety of critical approaches that focused more on the historical and cultural construction of texts and their readings. Today's readers of the poetry of this period will therefore encounter the methodological (and wider political) issues raised by New Historicism, Cultural Materialism and feminism.

All three have shown that a consideration of literary and related texts is inseparable from the locations and forms by which power and desire flow through society's dominant institutions, including the family, religion, and politics. Although much of the best current scholarship on the early modern period, including its poetry, is sufficiently eclectic to combine elements of all three so that to distinguish them may seem artificial, their different emphases are perhaps worthy of comment.

New Historicism, which was taking shape as the first edition of this book was written, has focused on texts as parts of a network of cultural forces, what Greenblatt terms 'a shared code, a set of interlocking tropes and similitudes that function not only as the objects but as the conditions of representations'. In the New Historicist view, a society is bound together, almost like a conspiracy within which individual texts and individual subjects alike are both imprisoned and legitimated. Like the various versions of 'old' Historicism – which it wants to supplant or supplement, although asking a wider range of questions, including many originating in the concerns of the present – New Historicism characteristically sees the past as 'other', and resists, not always successfully (or in my view, always wisely) the appropriation of earlier texts by those present concerns. It wants to put texts from the past back into their history. By contrast, Cultural Materialism has focused more on growing points and contradictions within a culture's ideological history, and so upon historical change: it endeavours to see texts as re-produced in *our* history rather than simply produced in their time of origination. Feminism, also characteristically reading the past as part of a project to change the future, has drawn our attention to the neglected and vital force of gender, characteristically arguing that gender assignments and relations between the sexes are 'a primary aspect of social organization', and therefore of the reading and writing of poetry. The most recent major anthologies of the period's poems, the revision of Chambers's collection, *The New Oxford Book of Sixteenth-Century Verse* (1991) and *The Penguin Book of Renaissance Verse* (1992) register the change. Both collections attempt to represent alternative, marginalized poetic voices; they include regional and women's poetry; they show how varied in political and theological outlook the poets were. The editors of the Penguin anthology, in particular, are aware of the revolution in criticism which has inevitably changed our ways of reading the period. Rather than presenting poems as 'timeless', they note that poems are 'social acts rather than isolated objects' and, responding to current critical debates, acknowledge that 'to recover the poetry of a past era is never simply a passive process; to recover is to become actively engaged, and to some extent to recreate'.[8]

I started this introduction talking about the fun of reading sixteenth-century poetry, of music, food and eager debate. And now, a few pages later, I am introducing readers to a somewhat abstract set of terms like 'deconstruction' and 'ideological', which might seem to take us very far from sitting back and simply enjoying Sidney's *Astrophil and Stella* or Donne's 'The Canonization'. But in any field of knowledge, as we discover we need to express or explain new experiences, we need to discover, invent, or adapt new terminology. Literary criticism has been traditionally weak in developing adequate terminology, probably because of a genteel reluctance to move beyond 'appreciation' or to offend the 'general' reader. One result of that reluctance has been the marginalization of literary studies, in terms at least of intellectual rigour and sophistication, among the other human sciences like information sciences, political theory or philosophy. Recent developments in cultural studies, initially in Britain and increasingly in America, have often been more forthright in adapting terms from the new theory, and so provide us with precedents for reading poems in terms of questions raised by psychoanalysis, feminism or cultural materialism.

At this point, I want to discuss a key term which has become increasingly central to both literary and cultural studies, and which is important to our understanding of sixteenth-century poetry. It is 'ideology'. In this book, the term is being used not to mean a set of false or partial ideas which lie behind and determine the meanings of texts, but rather a complex of distinctive practices and social relations which are characteristic of any society and which are inscribed in its language and other material practices. Ideology applies to all the largely unconscious assumptions and acts by which men and women relate to their world; it is the system of images, attitudes, feelings, myths and gestures which are peculiar to a society, which the members who make up that society habitually take for granted. In any society, especially in one as obsessed with order and control as Elizabethan England, one of the functions of ideology is, as far as possible, to define and limit the linguistic and cultural practices by which members of that society function. If, as usually happens, a society likes to think of itself as harmonious, coherent, and consensual, then it is ideology that enables this to occur. It tries to suggest that the existing order of things is permanent, natural, universally acknowledged, embodying truths we would all agree with – and in so far as it persuades us that such 'truths' are *not* ideology (ideology, as one of my students indignantly put it, is something other societies have, not ours), then it is successful. It gives us seemingly coherent representations and explanations of our lives, in particular by giving us the seemingly natural language by which we describe and thus try to understand them. Thus ideology acts as a kind of social glue, binding us all together.

It is important to be clear about the domain of ideology as a term for analysis. The immediate connotations of the term are political in the sense that it points to the machinery, overt and implicit, by which states police and even create the allegiances and assumptions of their subjects, as in the propaganda exalting the image of Elizabeth as the 'Virgin Queen'. However, ideology has a much broader relevance: it is concerned with issues as diverse as aesthetics and sexual feelings, family patterns and, indeed, with any area of experience in which a society needs to order and explain its beliefs, institutions and practices to itself. The various 'new' historicisms and feminism have done much to show just how far the seemingly most ordinary practices carry ideological value and interrelate: the establishment of sexual and gender identities are, for instance, intimately bound up with broader issues of order, the 'natural', authority and hierarchy. The value of the term 'ideology' as an analytical tool lies in making us think about the significance of contemporary assumptions about the world, about the constructed nature of those assumptions, their interrelationships, potential contradictions and tensions.

How does ideology affect the writing and reading of poetry? The impact of ideology upon the writings of a particular society – or, for that matter on the conventions and strategies by which those writings are read – is no different from the way it operates upon any other cultural practice. In no case, in Macherey's words, does a writer manufacture the materials with which he or she works. On the contrary, the power of ideology is inscribed within a text as, and indeed before, it is written. We might imagine ideology as a powerful force hovering over us as we read a text; even as we read, it reminds us of what is apparently correct, commonsensical, or 'natural'. When a text is written, ideology works to make some things more natural to write; when a text is read, it works to direct language into conveying only those meanings reinforced by the dominant forces of our society.[9]

With much sixteenth-century poetry, the above argument will have obvious force. Clearly, some works, like A Mirror for Magistrates or The Faerie Queene, defined themselves very explicitly in relation to dominant Elizabethan beliefs. With such texts, it becomes our role to call the bluff of ideology, so to speak, and to point out how it structured, or rather constructed, the text. To do so, we should therefore not be concerned just with the explicit 'ideas' that are 'reflected' by a poem, but rather on how and by what means and with what distortions the text has been subjected to the power of ideology. A 'public' poem like The Faerie Queene is clearly vulnerable to the most obvious kinds of ideological pressure because it deals explicitly with sensitive political issues. But, as we shall see, the seemingly innocent court lyrics so admired by Palgrave are also sites of ceaseless ideological interrogations and pressure. In the hands of a Campion, the lyric may seem lightweight entertainment; with Shakespeare it seems to become a moving articulation of a complex personality. Either way, the lyric no less than the epic is caught within the age's ideological struggles.

Throughout this study, however, I will be looking for ways in which the poems of the sixteenth century do not simply reflect the age's dominant ideology. I will suggest how oppositional voices are struggling to be heard and how we can help give them voice. *The Faerie Queene*, for instance, tries to be a celebration of the Elizabethan monarchy, ruling class, and court ideals, and yet it incorporates ideas and practices that call their dominance into question. Wyatt's lyrics contain scarcely veiled hints of rebellion and disgust with the dominant ideologies of power and desire. How conscious of these tensions were Spenser and Wyatt? To an extent, they probably knew what they were voicing. That kind of opposition clearly operates on the level of very explicit ideas. But there are other kinds of opposition more subtly and profoundly encoded in the poetry. One important function of the literary text – perhaps, it is often argued, what constitutes 'the greatness' of a work, and maybe the most important social function of art – is that of bringing out the contradictions and tensions that a dominant ideology tries to ignore or cover over. It does so not so much on the level of the explicit ideas to which a text points, but rather on the level of the text's 'unconscious', which we see both in the language and in the gaps and indeterminacies that accompany language. Poems are, after all, not ideas but words – words and spaces around words – and it is on the level of words that we can read the strains, oppositions, and struggles of an age. Language is a primary site of ideological struggle. It is our language where the struggles for meaning and power took place – and where they take place in our own reading and criticism.

Raymond Williams suggests that we should read literary texts as a means of probing an age's transitional nature, looking for signs of change not so much in their explicit ideas as within what can be termed a society's 'structures of feeling'. We do so, he argues, in order to stress the live, ever-changing, characteristics of a culture and, in particular, the generative and regenerative part that language plays within culture. Williams writes of a society consisting of archaic, residual, and emergent experiences, values, and practices.[10] The majority of any society's practices are inevitably residual, deriving from the past and closely identified with the historically dominant class of that society. A few are archaic, the residuum of, say, philosophical or religious ideas from a previous age: a key example in Elizabethan poetry would be chivalry, largely abandoned as a material practice by the end of the sixteenth century, but still very powerful in its cultural implications and as a source of ritual and initiation for the court poets. But within the inevitable flux and contradictions of any society, new experiences and practices are always emerging, always potential, and in periods of particular stress, like the 1590s, they may start to emerge more strongly. They are usually felt before they can be put into language, because there are no fully formed structures of discourse by which they can be expressed. It is at such points of strain that certain forms of writing and other cultural practices are most revealing. In the late sixteenth century we can look to the experimentation in the public theatre, the revival of verse satire, the unusual diversity of broken, mixed, unfinished works as indications of the sense that one often has in some of the age's poems that they are trying to articulate something which was already being felt but for which there were not yet adequate words. Williams terms 'pre-emergent' those cases where the structure of feeling that is tangible in particular writings points to an area of experience which still lies beyond us – the full significance of which may only become explicit years later as new language becomes available. All texts, in other words, are an articulation of more than they know and it is clear we must recognize that the texts we read are themselves unaware of their relation to ideology.[11]

What practical implications for the reader of sixteenth-century poetry do such considerations have? They suggest that we must concentrate on the 'dislocations' and 'disruptions' in poetic texts as well as on what they 'intend'. This advice may seem to conflict directly with notions of 'unity', 'order' and 'hierarchy' which have so long seemed inextricable from the discussions of the period's poetry and its 'world-vision'. I say 'seem' because it is, in fact, possible to interpret the sixteenth century itself as a period of surprising upsurges and dislocations. The whole age was, after all, one of extraordinary insecurity, quite deserving the title that Auden gave to the early twentieth century, the 'age of anxiety'. In other words, to insist that the textual practices of sixteenth-century poems operate in contradiction to their own intentions may, I hope, be seen less as a demolition of them then an appropriate way into understanding and enjoying them. We are dealing with a period where there was enormous pressure upon language to grapple with new experiences, new feelings, and new social patterns. It was a time in which (as many poets themselves noted) language itself seemed to be simultaneously inadequate and overflowing. Although the poems may attempt to efface the struggle that has produced them, that struggle none the less leaves its invisible but indelible marks. What is not in the text is just as important as what seems to be there.

The task of reading, therefore, becomes a very exciting one. It is that of bringing to life what has been blotted out, teasing out the conflicting discourses that fight within the text, that remain, in the metaphor that Derrida has made famous, 'active and stirring, inscribed in white ink, an invisible drawing covered over in the palimpsest'. We will watch, for instance, how in *The Faerie Queene* the surface text maintains an uneasy and shifting relationship with its apparent philosophical content. We will trace the movements by which a text falls short of or exceeds what it wants to say, the ways by which it is sidetracked, turned back on, or repeats itself. We will see how the period's best poems are full of eloquent silences and half silences. We will pose the question (the writings of the women poets of the period are excellent examples here) of what seem to be significant absences, silent or suppressed, in the texts. As Macherey puts it, there are times when not only do texts not speak but when they cannot speak, and it is in uncertainties and disruptions where they may speak most eloquently.[12]

Does such talk of looking for 'gaps', 'disruptions', 'uncertainties' and 'absences' in texts sound strange? One of my students once likened it to what a psychotherapist or analyst does with a patient, probing into the darkness of his or her repressed memories, and patterns of obsessions and habits. That is a good analogy. We are looking for the 'unconscious' of the texts we read, not just the hidden meanings but the suppressed or repressed meanings. To mention psychoanalysis is to be modern with a vengeance, but it is interesting how some Renaissance thinkers, notably Sidney, seem to have wrestled with such issues. As I will show in Chapter 2, in sixteenth-century poetic theory and practice, there are two contradictory views of language. One sees texts as communicating 'messages' or 'information', and is built upon a desire to extract conceptual statements from words. The other sees it as a means to escape into the endless play and self-indulgence of language. An interesting contrast exists between Sidney and Greville, one we will see in Chapters 4 and 5. On the one hand, there is a puritanical desire to see tropes, metre and rhyme as disciplined ornament, means for the presentation of ideas and, in Greville's case, to be used with great reluctance. On the other hand, we can see the overflowing productivity of language, its playing off of one mode of linguistic organization against another, as a means in itself of achieving genuine knowledge.

What differences do such considerations make to a study of poetry in the sixteenth century? They enable us to read Ralegh, Spenser or Shakespeare in most exciting ways. There are always wider struggles going on than a writer consciously knows – contradictions rooted in the history of which he or she is a part, covered over by the comforts of ideology and only visible, perhaps, to later readers. We read not only for the obvious surface meanings but for symptomatic absences in texts and so for the signs of those ideological pressures which the text has seemingly erased or covered over. Ideology's power forces texts to remain silent about or to marginalize questions on matters that go beyond or challenge the age's orthodoxy. In the terms much favoured by older modes of criticism, the 'intentions' of a text are the ways the ideology of the text tries to mobilize certain responses. But the text, we can learn to see, always has other 'intentions'. A careful reader of sixteenth-century poetry, therefore, must focus not merely on what a text seems to say, or what its author seems to want to be heard to say, nor even on what it does not say, but on what it cannot say, either at all or only with difficulty. The text's detours, silences, omissions, absences, faults and symptomatic dislocations are all part of what we focus on in addition to, and even at times in preference to, its surface. We look for the different languages, literary and social that hover in the vicinity of the text, trying to master and muffle it; in particular we focus on places where the seemingly unified surface of a work is contradicted or undermined, where the text 'momentarily misses a beat, thins out or loses intensity, or makes a false move – where the scars show, in the face of stress'. We ask in short not only what is there, but also what is not there and why, and who or what these seeming presences and omissions serve and what we, as their readers, might fill them with.[13]

The Court

This is a study of sixteenth-century poetry, and yet as I tell my own students, we have to read sixteenth-century poetry by means of something – ideas, desires, feelings and strategies for reading that embody these – and so I want them to read with as powerful a set of strategies as possible. Although they have over the past twenty years become relatively familiar in literary criticism, the issues raised in the last few pages may constitute an unfamiliar approach for many students. I hope they repay re-reading, and the discussion (here necessarily theoretical) will make much more particular sense, I hope, in ensuing chapters. In investigating the poetry of court poets like Dunbar, Wyatt, Ralegh or Greville, in Chapter 4, for instance, we shall have to look not merely to the ideas that can be abstracted from the age's commonplaces, or even those ideas of which the writer may have been aware, but to the events that have made the writer's history, and especially to ideas and feelings that play about (in the vicinity of) their writings. In many cases, the writer will have been unaware of them, as he or she struggled within the complex interplay of discursive structures, symbolic formations and ideological systems of representation that defined his or her cultural practices. We must try to relate the poetry we read – whether explicit public propaganda like *A Mirror for Magistrates* or lyrics like Wyatt's 'Blame Not My Lute' – to the hidden interplays of power that structured the society. A collection of 'private' lyrics like *Astrophil and Stella* no less than a massive 'public' poem like Daniel's *Civil Wars* or *The Faerie Queene* is culturally produced, coerced and compelled by political and wider cultural forces outside it, by networks of discourse in which it is caught or – to use Macherey's powerful metaphor – which haunt it, playing, encroaching, or teasing it from the edge of the text.[14]

I can make the foregoing discussion of 'ideology' more concrete by an explicit example of how it functioned in the sixteenth century. In his influential essay on 'Ideological State Apparatuses', Althusser discusses the very concrete practices by which any society structures, even in part creates, the allegiances by which its members feel they 'belong' to it – the system of education, characteristic lifestyle, patterns of religion, family organization and so forth. It is by means of such institutions and structures, what he called 'apparatuses', that ideology functions. Except that – and here we enter into a discussion of the dominant 'apparatuses' of this period – the poetry of the sixteenth century was not produced by 'ordinary people'. Or to put it differently, the received canon of sixteenth-century poetry is almost entirely the product of (written for, and almost always by) a small fraction of the population – the aristocracy, the gentry and those aspiring members of the 'middle' classes who had some pretensions to upward mobility, what Evans terms 'a new social phenomenon', the second generation of the new bourgeoisie going to university and abandoning their fathers' professions for a life of letters. He instances Donne, Peele, Harvey, Greene and Spenser, and points out that in fact, of the major poets of the century, only Surrey belongs to the old aristocracy.[15] Some exceptions to his generalization will be discussed in later chapters, notably in Chapters 8 and 9, when I comment on the poetry written by women and 'popular' poetry, but by and large it is an accurate statement.

The major institution or apparatus that dominates sixteenth-century poetry is the Court. In his famous history of the English Civil War, as he looked back at his youth and attempted to make sense of those years which we now recognize as one of the cataclysmic eras of English history, Edward Hyde, Earl of Clarendon, focused on the institution in which he had spent his youth. The Court, he wrote, was where 'as in a mirror, we may best see the face of that time, and the affections and temper of the people in general', for, he continued, 'the court measured the temper and affection of the country'.[16] Throughout the sixteenth century, 'Court' was a powerful word as well as a powerful institution; it accumulated round itself ideas and feelings that were often contradictory or confusing, but always compelling. Men and women 'swarmed' to the Court (the metaphor is a favourite one) for power, gain, gossip, titles, favours, rewards and entertainment. The Court was more than merely the seat of government, or wherever the monarch happened to be. All across Europe the idea of the Court, as well as its concrete existence, excited an intensity that indicates a rare concentration of power and cultural dominance. It is Gabriel Harvey's 'only mart of preferment and honour'; it is Spenser's 'seat of courtesy and civil conversation'; it is Donne's 'bladder of Vanitie'. What powers, real or reputed, did the Court have over the destinies, tastes and allegiances of men and women? What recurring anxieties or affirmations are associated with the Court? By whom are they voiced? With what special or covert interests? And with what degree of truth? What can they mediate to us of the Court's influence on the ongoing and deep-rooted cultural changes of the period – the complex struggles for political and social ascendancy, the fundamental changes of ideology and material practice?

How did the Court's power operate upon the particular details of life? How did the dominant 'apparatus' control the specifics of living, including the way poetry was thought of, written and received? I stress the word 'details' because, as Said explains, 'for power to work it must be able to manage, control, even create detail: the more detail, the more real power'. Power is felt more intimately in detail – in the particulars of our everyday lives, and in the particularities of poetry. The Court was one of the key places where, in Foucault's words, 'power reaches into the very grain of individuals, touches their bodies and inserts itself into their actions and attitudes, their discourses, learning processes and everyday lives'.[17] The Court produced, in all who came into contact with it, a set of expectations, anxieties, assumptions and habits, sometimes very explicitly, sometimes by unstated but very concrete pressures. And as we read the period's writings, we can see how writers and artists provide a kind of early-warning system for later historical developments.

What can the poetry of the age tell us about how it was to be exposed to, fostered by, or exploited by the Court? As Strong and others have shown, throughout the Renaissance, all European Courts attempted to use the arts to control and in a very real sense create the tastes, habits, beliefs and allegiances of their subjects. In some cases this attempt was carried out through overt state apparatuses – through control and censorship of the theatre, imprisonment of playwrights and the patronage and protection of particular literary forms and opinions, for example. 'Before the invention of the mechanical mass media of today', Strong writes, 'the creation of monarchs as an "image" to draw people's allegiance was the task of humanists, poets, writers and artists'.[18] Around the monarch was the Court, and all over Europe, it was to the Court that intellectuals, educators, artists, architects and poets were drawn. No less than the building of palaces or great houses, official state portraits, medallions or court fetes, poetry was part of what Strong terms 'the politics of spectacle'. It was part of the increasing attempt – culminating in England in the reigns of James I and Charles I – to propagate a belief in the sacredness of the monarchy and the role of the Court and mobility within a ritual of power. Just as 'the world of the court fete is an ideal one in which nature, ordered and controlled, has all dangerous potential removed', and in which the Court could celebrate its wisdom and control over the world, time, and change, so poetry too became, as John Donne's friend, Sir Henry Wotton, put it, 'an instrument of state'.[19]

In *Music and Poetry in the Early Tudor Court* (1961) Stevens showed how the sixteenth-century lyric loses much of its point when simply read as words on a page. Court poetry, he argued, is built of 'shades and nuances of meaning' which are social rather than literary. 'What distinguishes the individual from the type . . . arose from situation, not from words.'[20] Throughout the period, poetry is thought primarily of as action in and for the Court, as performance, even as production, not merely as written text. The poems are the visible edge of a whole complex social text, the centre of which, as Puttenham's potted history of the century's poetry (probably completed by the 1580s) put it, was a firm policy of binding poetry inextricably to the Court. When he focuses on the 'new company of courtly makers' who 'sprong up' at the end of Henry VIII's reign, and 'greatly polished our rude and homely maner of vulgar Poesie', Puttenham is articulating the Court's imprimatur upon not only a chosen number of poets but also upon a certain function for poetry in the Court. Briefly surveying the mid-Tudor poets, including Sternhold, Heywood and Golding, he then culminates his history by describing the courtly poets under Elizabeth I:

> And in her Majesties time that now is are sprong up an other crew of Courtly makers Noble men and Gentlemen of her Majesties owne servauntes, who have written excellently well as it would appeare if their doings could be found out and made publicke with the rest, of which number is first that noble Gentleman *Edward* Earle of Oxford. *Thomas* Lord of Bukhurst, when he was young, *Henry* Lord Paget, Sir *Philip Sydney*, Sir *Walter Rawleigh*, Master *Edward Dyar*, Maister *Fulke Grevell*, *Gascon, Britton, Turberville* and a great many other learned Gentlemen, whose names I do not omit for envie, but to avoyde tediousnesse, and who have deserved no little Commendation.[21]

Throughout his treatise, Puttenham links poetry to the favour of Courts and princes, repeatedly stressing the duty of the 'Civill Poet' to celebrate the values and acts of the Court in the way 'the embroderer' sets 'stone and perle or passements of gold upon the stuff of a Princely garment'.[22] While *The Arte of English Poesie* presents itself as a treatise on poetry, it is also setting out the ideal lifestyle of the courtier. Indirectness, even dissimulation (what Puttenham terms *Beau semblant*), ornament, calculated ostentation, are all characteristics that are simultaneously those of the poet and the courtier. The 'grace' displayed by the poet is inseparable from a training in the essential courtly characteristics of dissimulation and indirection. When he discusses the use of allegory, he describes it as the figure of 'false semblant' and 'the Courtier'; and at the conclusion of his treatise, he echoes Castiglione's advice that the courtier should strive above all else 'to give entertainment to Princes, Ladies of honour, Gentlewomen and Gentlemen', and to do so must 'dissemble' not only his 'countenances' and 'conceits' but also all 'his ordinary actions of behaviour . . . whereby the better' to 'winne his purposes and good advantages'.[23] The terms are exactly those he uses to describe the making of poetry.

The Court, then, as one of the dominant 'apparatuses' of the age, appropriated poetry as one of the practices by which it tried to exercise its political dominance. Within the Court, poetry was seen as entertainment by and for amateur gentleman poets of the Court; it was what Stevens calls 'idealised talk' performed and enjoyed along with what Lewis terms 'a little music after supper'. It was rarely designed to be published: as Puttenham notes, 'many notable Gentlemen in the Court . . . have written commendably, and suppressed it agayne, or else suffered it to be published without their own names to it'. Poetry was one of the means by which a Surrey, a Ralegh or an Essex displayed his desirability (along with dancing, music, and general self-display) and so advanced his political fortunes. It was part of a deliberate attempt to advance a new social order and not simply a 'literary' fashion. Sessions has traced the emergence in England to the self-conscious advancing of a 'cultural hegemony' in the poetry of Surrey in 1542, built on an unambiguous class bias: 'true' nobility and honour fashioning a new poetics and to some extent a new language, with the poet as a privileged voice of that nobility and honour. In aristocratic poets like Surrey, and then some time later, Sidney, Sessions argues there can be found an ideology of poetic virtue that is bound up with noble virtue.[24]

In a more democratic age, such assumptions about 'natural' nobility may seem unsupportable nonsense, and there was much else going on in the poetry of the time that undermined such class-bound theory of poetry. But there is no doubt that it was the theory of most of the dominant poets in the period before the end of the century. Ralegh's poetry, as we shall see in Chapter 4, was intended as a key to Elizabeth's political favour; Robert Sidney, as Chapter 5 will show, wrote most of his poetry while in exile in the Low Countries as an expression of his desire to be back in the centre of public affairs, while one of

Puttenham's 'crew of courtly makers',[25] the Earl of Oxford, was writing conventional erotic verse for over twenty years, which was clearly directed to his advancement in the Court. In many cases, of course, the poet was quite explicitly the spokesman for the Court – as panegyrist, as the celebrator of occasions of pageantry or of royal personages. Dunbar's 'The Thrissel and the Rois' or Ralegh's 'Praisd Be Dianas Faire and Harmles Light' are such celebrations of the Court's values and activities. On these occasions the poet finds a pattern of discourse already existing and a role waiting for him to fill. He inserts himself into it in order to establish his own place within a whole pattern of social discourse. As such, his writing operates within a very narrow register of themes and unusual linguistic coherence on the level of both general style and particular verbal details, what linguists term the 'ideologeme', the verbal unit that carries ideological detail at the level of syntax, grammar, and vocabulary.[26] Here Puttenham is once again our best spokesman. He writes of how the language of the poet must 'be naturall, pure, and the most usual of all of his country'. He identifies such language as 'that which is spoken in the kings Court' rather than in the 'peevish affection' of the universities, let alone that spoken by the 'poore rusticall or uncivill people' or any 'of the inferiour sort' or regional speech. The acceptable language of poetry is 'the usual speech of the Court, and that of London and the shires lying about london within ix myls, and not much above'.[27] Through such categorizations of exclusion and privilege, the dominant modes of poetry could be very precisely delimited. It thus became one of the regime's means of social stabilization and control. As Chapters 4 and 5 will show, poets like Robert Sidney and Ralegh record in their verse (and in ways they themselves could not have fully acknowledged) the power of the Court, the ways it created and controlled its subjects by exerting pressure upon their language. The 'social' text (the events under the pressure of which the poets wrote and of which they tried to be a part) and the 'literary' text (what they made of those events) are inseparable.

If the Court is the major cultural apparatus which controlled the creation of poetry, within its activities the particular apparatus that distributed or withheld approval was the system of patronage. However suspect in our time (the pejorative associations of 'patronizing' today registering the changes that have occurred), patronage was certainly one of the major apparatuses of cultural control in pre-industrial Europe. Patronage, specifically financial support, was what all authors sought – whether from monarch, lord, or rich man or woman. By 'patronage', however, we should understand not simply reward of money or a position given to an author: the term covers a huge variety of activities. Much patronage, especially for poetry, operated rather in the way 'public relations' works today. A writer might be directly commissioned to produce a work. Or he might simply decide out of gratitude or in hope of advancement to dedicate a work to an influential nobleman or woman. A dedication might be initiated by the author in the hope of just getting noticed. Either way, patronage formed a network of pressure, encouragement and exclusion, providing the powerful – and notably the monarch and the Court – with a system by which politically useful subjects could be either attached to or excluded from their presence and power.

Like today, poetry as such did not often command much reward. The cries often heard from poets about the scarcity of money and offices were numerous, poetry providing, in Ben Jonson's words, 'but a meane Mistress', her rewards being limited and unreliable. Still, there was, right through the period, even as far back as late fifteenth-century Scotland, and, in England from the time of Henry VII and VIII, an increasingly tightly organized system of patronage that exercised power over artists, musicians and writers, in an interaction of what Green has termed 'patrons and prince pleasers'. Directly utilitarian writing was what the sixteenth-century monarchs and Courts preferred to support. Throughout the century, many of the poets' complaints were caused by their awareness that while support was forthcoming to writers directly useful to patrons, it rarely seemed to percolate to poets as if, in Samuel Daniel's words, patrons did not realize 'how small/A portion' would 'turn the wheeles . . . to make their glory last'.[28]

Under Elizabeth I, the patronage system in England took a distinctive pattern. In many Renaissance courts, control of the arts became increasingly oppressive – or attractive, according to one's place and achievements within the system. At the centre of the society was the Queen, around whom there was concentrated a cult of extraordinary power by which she was celebrated – as the embodiment of power, beauty, justice, the imperium and, within the Court circles, as the quintessential, unapproachable yet alluring, Petrarchan mistress. While she flaunted her sexual power among her courtiers, her portraits and personal mottoes asserted her vaunted chastity before all else. Her admirers likewise responded by praising her 'cruelty' to them in tropes derived from Petrarchism and its neo-platonic trappings. But hers was not merely a convenient pose to encourage courtiers to turn graceful compliments or to spend huge proportions of their incomes in bedecking themselves to attract her approval, as Ralegh for one did. Rather, it had practical and direct political importance – and especially from the late 1570s until the end of the century. Interestingly enough, Elizabeth herself spent little on patronage, certainly less than either her father Henry VIII or her successor James I. Instead, she demanded that her nobles and courtiers themselves dispensed rewards, and she used her progresses through the country and visits to their great houses to encourage them to do so. In such ways, she would gain the glory while being spared the expense of the favours and perquisites that would bind her subjects more closely to her regime.

In the first twenty-five years of Elizabeth's reign, such a system worked almost exclusively to promote writers of religious, political, and generally utilitarian works. Hers was a regime that was unsure of its stability, afraid of religious and political enemies inside and out. Thus the patronage system was part of a concentrated effort to mould opinions and to direct writers to socially or politically approved goals. The tough-minded courtiers who surrounded Elizabeth – particularly Leicester and Cecil – supported writers who could be, primarily, propagandists. It was Sidney, in the late 1570s, who was the first of Elizabeth's courtiers to be actively interested in the patronage of poetry; Sidney and the Sidney Circle, especially his sister Mary, encouraged much of the renaissance of poetry in the last decade of the century.[29]

While patronage was the major apparatus by which the ideology of the Elizabethan Court was enforced, to glance at the typical form by which poetry circulated is to realize again the intimately detailed ways by which cultural power operated in the period. Typically, poetry was read during the sixteenth century not by means of publication (which would sometimes occur following an author's death and often without a family's permission, or even not at all) but rather by unpublished circulation, literally hand to hand. Poems would be copied, adapted, recopied, perhaps in a reader's own private anthologies or notebook collections or 'miscellanies'. Some of these might eventually be published but more often they remained simply the private note-books of their compilers. Some such books were often not exclusively devoted to poetry, but might include a variety of fashionable poems along with useful observations on manners. To survey some of these is to sense in most intriguing ways the control of the court's taste and values.

Bodleian Library Rawlinson MS C.813, for instance, comes from the early part of the period. Collected late in the fifteenth century, the manuscript is a typical collection of work popular and useful around the court of Henry VII. It includes a mixture of late medieval courtly poems – medieval rhyme royal, musical lyrics, popular rhymed political prophecies and the pseudo-Arthurian propaganda much favoured by the early Tudors. Other early Tudor songbooks which have come down to us similarly mix love and devotional songs, popular lyrics and political poems. Two slightly later miscellanies, the one published at the time, the other remaining unpublished until the eighteenth century, stand out as particularly significant examples. The first we know as *Tottel's Miscellany*. Perhaps the most important of all the Tudor miscellanies, it was published by William Tottel in 1557, and dedicated 'to the honor of the Englishe tong, and for profit of the studious of Englishe eloquence'. It not only brought together the bulk of Wyatt's and Surrey's verse; it shows openly the process by which the Court was starting to adapt, assimilate and control its poetry. Most of the additional poems chosen by Tottel seem to have been put into the collection for their ease of imitation for the aspiring courtier, who was advised by his rhetorical handbooks to exercise his poetic gifts according to such models. It went into nine editions by 1587, and became an essential guide to the kinds and modes of poetry that would deck out the aspiring courtier's taste.[30] It set the pattern, as well, for many later published miscellanies, including *The Paradise of Dainty Devices* (1576), *The Bowre of Daintie Delights* (1591), *The Phoenix Nest* (1593), *The Arbor of Amorous Devises* (1597), *England's Helicon* (1601), and *A Poetical Rhapsody* (1602).

A second collection of equivalent importance known as the Bannatyne Manuscript comes from Scotland. It is a compilation of poems from the reigns of James III (1460–88), James IV (1488–1513) and Mary Queen of Scots (1542–67). It includes work by Henryson, Douglas, Dunbar, Lindsay and Scott, and was put together around 1568. It reads as if it was collected as an act of homage to a century of Scottish written culture. It is a folio of some 800 pages and, set alongside its English equivalents, even Tottel, it shows, as Ramson and Hughes note, 'not only . . . the frivolity of English taste but its subservience to fashion'. It is carefully organized, dividing its poems into 'ballatis' (ballads) of theology, wisdom and morality, 'Mirry and Uther Solatius Consaittis', of love and, finally 'Fabillis Wyiss and Sapient'. The theological poems are mainly mediocre devotional lyrics and the 'Ballates Full of Wisdom' are likewise conventionally didactic, like the following:

> Prayer is the maist haly devyne service
> That man heir on erth unto God may present,
> Faith with repentance is the dew and perfect device
> That withstands the divill and his cursit entent.

Lighter material includes Lindsay's play *Ane Satyre of the Thrie Estaitis*, while the love-ballads are mainly those by Alexander Scott and the fables mainly those of Henryson. The Bannatyne collection is a rich compendium of what Ramson and Hughes have called the 'poetry of the Stewart Court'. Its poems are characterized by a wide variety of subject and style and yet together they are 'quite remarkably of a piece, belonging to a court culture' which is 'profoundly conscious of its own traditions'.[31]

Such miscellanies, published and unpublished, are thus important sources for ascertaining the Court's taste in, and control over, the development of poetry through the century. Utilitarian doggerel is mixed with aureate lyrics, moral tags with political allegory, musical ditties with erotic plaints. But it is noticeable how the miscellanies later in the century show much less interest in anything but specifically courtly forms of verse. The subtle but definite class basis of the Court's demands may be seen in the ways which popular poetry – ballads, satires, folk-tales – are excluded by or assimilated to court taste. Thus it is that the canon approved by modern 'courtly' interpretations of the age's poetry is being established. As part of the ceremony, ritual, and pattern of court life, poetry was viewed as a decorative, essentially harmless but useful diversion, a means by which a poet could be assimilated into the dominant class as part of the ongoing struggle to confirm and preserve the ideological structures of the Court. Not just a 'Court' poet, he is the Court's poet, controlled and in a real sense created by the Court. And yet although the power of the Court seemingly became irresistible, we can read, from our vantage point 400 years later, through the hesitations of the texts, the ideological struggles that were waged over language to gain such cultural ascendancy. Often, even unaware, the writings of the poets record the struggles by which they were made the Court's.

Courts and poetry in England and Scotland

It is now time to try to get a chronological overview of our topic. However differently their evaluations of sixteenth-century poetry, most modern historians of the period have generally agreed on the landmarks and the main subdivisions. Later I will suggest ways we might want to look again at the canon and question the usefulness of conventional periodization, and in particular, introduce the long excluded poetry written by women. But it seems sensible at the outset to construct the residual model. Sixteenth-century poetry has generally been seen by such diverse critics as Winters, Lewis and Evans much as follows. Coinciding with the consolidation of the English monarchy following the Wars of the Roses, the poetry of the late fifteenth and early sixteenth centuries gradually became more independent of the aureate and moralistic traditions of the later Middle Ages. By the 1530s, like English Court culture generally, it became more accessible to continental, especially Italian and French, influences, notably in the work of Wyatt and Surrey, who was in particular seen as the epitome of Renaissance nobility, shining as a poet and courtier alike. After thirty years of experimentation during which poetry was mainly subservient to the didacticism of humanist educators, a period of splendid achievement occurred, culminating in the work of Sidney, Spenser, and (slightly apart) Shakespeare and Donne. In Scotland a similar process of continental influence and achievement occurred somewhat earlier, in the works of Henryson or Dunbar, and again in the 'Castalian' poets of the late sixteenth century. An alternative view has highlighted a tradition of what it sees as plain, idiomatic verse, linking Skelton at the beginning of the century, Wyatt in the 1530s and (playing down the courtly line of Surrey, and Sidney, and upgrading the moralistic mid-century poets) culminating in the work of Greville and, in different ways, Donne and Shakespeare.

Most accounts, from Palgrave in the 1860s to the 1970s, of the sixteenth century's poetry resemble one or other of these models. The apparent strength of the 'courtly' interpretation is that it is rooted in some influential remarks made by poets and commentators late in the century, notably by Sidney and Puttenham. I have so far quoted Puttenham extensively, but Sidney's *Defence of Poesie* (also known as *An Apology for Poetry*, probably written by 1580) is more readable for today's students and no less revealingly partial. Sidney speaks scornfully of the state of English poetry, especially lyric poetry, marvelling that 'poesy, thus embraced in all other places, should only find in our time a hard welcome in England'. He singles out *A Mirror for Magistrates*, Surrey, and Spenser's *Shepherdes Calendar* for praise. About the same time, Puttenham was likewise trying to lay down what amounts to an authorized tradition of poetry, rejecting Skelton ('in King Henry th'eights time . . . I wot not for what great worthines . . . surnamed the Poet Laureat') and praising the 'new company of courtly makers', including Wyatt and Surrey, who adapted the 'sweete and stately measures and stile of the Italian Poesie', who 'greatly pollished our rude homely maner of vulgar Poesie', and who 'may justly be sayd' to be 'the first reformers of our English meetre and stile'.[32] Sidney's view is that of the young Protestant aristocrat, anxious to see the Elizabethan Court dominated by his own faction; The Sidneian literary revolution – the ideals, successes, and failures of which will be dealt with in Chapter 5 – climaxed in the 1580s and 1590s, with the spate of sonnet sequences, religious poetry, closet drama and the publication in 1598 of the authorized edition of Sidney's own works. The *Defence* thus can be seen as the initiating manifesto of a successful literary revolution.

But sixteenth-century poetry in Britain was not only written within, to revert to Puttenham's exclusionary terms, a few miles of the English Court. As Williams argued, many of the diverse minorities in Britain and even England itself are excluded by the dominant reading of this period. There is a long history of exclusion from standard poetical histories that reflects a longer history of cultural and political subordination.[33] This is especially true of Scotland. In 1603, with the accession of James VI of Scotland to his cousin Elizabeth's throne, the Courts of Edinburgh and Westminster were united. In the century before, the Scottish and English Courts had been quite separate with, at times, an uneasy and at times open hostility between them. The two Courts produced, as I have briefly indicated, similar kinds of poetry. Now I want to deal in a little more detail with the differences. They are especially interesting in that they highlight the early sophistication of Scottish court poetry and then the brilliance of English poetry of the late sixteenth century.

While Scotland shared much of the linguistic heritage of England, through most of the fourteenth and fifteenth centuries its literary culture was generally far more sophisticated than England's. If we glance beyond our period to the mid-seventeenth century, however, a strange phenomenon has occurred; the decline of Scottish aristocratic culture in the early seventeenth century is something more than the Europe-wide phenomenon of the ruling aristocratic caste upholding its values and power and adapting itself to a rapidly changing social substructure. While there are parallels with the English Court, such as an increasingly capitalistic economy and labour force and the dominance of an aggressive, nascent bourgeoisie, the crucial factor is the increasing pressure that was experienced in Scotland from its imperialist neighbour. By quite early in the seventeenth century, powerful, centralized court culture in Scotland has been dissipated as the Court was moved to England.

Back in the fifteenth century, however, Scottish court poetry had been much more diverse and more open to European influences than in England. As Lewis comments, to move from England to Scotland at that period is to pass from 'barbarism' to 'civilization', from dullness to the liveliness and complexity of a sophisticated court society.[34] James IV of Scotland was himself an accomplished poet, and the Scots Court included such fine poets as Henryson, Douglas and Dunbar. No English poetry of the period comes close to the variety, vigour, and insight of Henryson's *Fabillis* or (further into our period) the ease with which Dunbar's poetry shows an awareness of and uses European precedents of satire, lyric, epistle, classical translation, or the richness and technical skills of Douglas's translation of Virgil.

The major poets of the Scottish Court in the mid and late fifteenth century are often called the 'Scottish Chaucerians'. The term usually means those poets who, at some time after the reign of James I of Scotland (1394–1437), wrote supposedly with a Chaucerian style in mind. James I is usually singled out as the first Middle Scots poet who showed real

affinities with Chaucer, especially in *The Kingis Quair*, but the real
flowering of late medieval or early Renaissance Scots poetry occurs
in the reign of James III, some fifty years later. Krantzmann points
out that the *Quair* is a typical court poem, one which implies that it
was composed to be read aloud – in performance as well as privately.[35]
In that, it anticipated the dominant mode of sixteenth-century court
poetry, both trying to speak for a whole community and yet leaving
leeway for the interests, adaptations and (in a sense) rewriting by
its readers. It is a Boethian treatment of a lover, imprisoned, and
compensating for his captivity by dreaming of Venus, Minerva and
other deities who proffer good advice, always warning that the wheel
of fortune, in love or court affairs, is unpredictable.

The most important Scots poet of the century and, after Chaucer,
perhaps the most interesting English-language poet of the Middle Ages,
is Robert Henryson. A lawyer, teacher and an observer of court
fashions, he wrote fables, moral satire, and Chaucerian love tragedy.
His *Testament of Cresseid* is a continuation and darkening of Chaucer's
Troilus and Criseyde, and amounts to a grim moral commentary on
Chaucer's handling of the story of the Trojan lovers. He takes up the
question of Cressida's life among the Greek soldiers to show her moral
degeneration and then her realization of her crime and guilt. She turns
to warn her readers – 'Lovers be war and tak gude heid about/Quhome
that ye lufe, for quohoem yet suffer paine', and blames her own 'great
unstabilnes'. Though Henryson avoids any explicit Christian reference,
he moralizes over his heroine's behaviour. Integrity, stoicism, constraint
are the values that lovers need to survive in an untrustworthy world.
Henryson's other major work is *The Morall Fabillis of Esope the Phrygian*,
which, although often compared with the *Canterbury Tales*, is more
European than English in its affinities – a characteristic of Scottish
court culture in this period generally. As Krantzmann comments, there
is by contrast 'no English poetry of the late fifteenth century . . . which
approached the combination of stylistic variety, humour, moral rigour
and intellectual control illustrated by the *Fabillis*'.[36] They are witty,
varied, closely observed, sensitive to speech and idiom, and shrewdly
and complexly moral, the product of a confident, if relatively small,
court culture.

Dunbar's poetry will be looked at in some detail in Chapter 4.
Another of the poets of the late-fifteenth-century Scots Court who
justifies some attention is Gavin Douglas, a lawyer, priest, courtier,
one of the Lords in Council who was pro-English and was strongly
supported by Henry VIII to become Archbishop of St Andrews.
Douglas's poetry includes the elaborate allegory, 'The Palace of Honour',
the shorter verse tale 'King Hart', and a translation of the *Aeneid* into
heroic couplets, or 'Scottish metre' as the title calls it. This is the first

complete translation of Homer into either English or Scots, and it was praised by Ezra Pound in the twentieth century as being superior to the original. That is something of an exaggeration but it is a significant rewriting of the Greek. Its main characteristic is the varied diction which changes according to class and situation and idiom of the characters. Douglas's translation was a major influence upon Surrey's later, inferior, translation.

Surveying the Scots poets writing in the latter half of the fifteenth century, therefore, one is led to speculate on their greater sophistication, richness, and variety alongside their English counterparts. English poetry of the time is largely court doggerel, moral commonplace and turgid political allegory. When we go forward fifty or more years, and exclude Surrey and Wyatt, much the same observation might be made. Even during the mid-sixteenth century, while English verse was labouring to find appropriate forms and vocabulary, Scottish verse was still more varied and sophisticated. In the Bannatyne manuscript for instance, we get not only an anthology of the previous century's poetry, but also a solid body of poems of another fine Scots poet, active in the 1540s and 1550s. He is Alexander Scott, a courtier who studied in Paris, and wrote religious and erotic lyrics which, like Wyatt's or Ralegh's, are, as his modern editor argues, not simply expressions of a happy abandonment to the sensual power of love, but 'deeply brooding and disruptive' meditations on the self that has been created by the Court. While the traditional courtly apparatus – the Petrarchan balance of pain and pleasure, wit versus will, the 'manic-depressive alternation of rational and irrational which accompanies the passion' – are all present, there is a brittle edge to Scott's verse that anticipates the best English poetry later in the century.[37] The freedom that love makes possible is desperately dependent on political favour; the typical experiences are those of absence, wandering and loss, all experiences evoked in poems that can be read as simple (and superbly crafted) erotic lyrics but which have wider cultural connections. Courtly and Petrarchan love metaphors become, as in Wyatt, the accepted language for begging political favours.

As I have implied, one of the most fascinating aspects of sixteenth-century English court poetry is the socio-cultural fragility upon which its apparent confidence is built. Again a comparison with Scotland is useful here. We can sense the origins of this fragility by a detailed consideration of what occurred when the Scottish court emigrated to England in 1603–4. From the late 1580s, King James VI built around him a group of the so-called 'Castalian' poets, who were more vitally in touch with developments in France and Italy than the English poets – as Sidney was frustratingly to admit in his pejorative remarks on the state of English poetry. When James moved south in 1603, praised by the Scots poet William Alexander for joining 'this divided Isle', he took on his new responsibilities with some relief; but in doing so, James was not just depriving Scotland of a resident Court and thereby of a centre of culture, but indirectly depriving those Scottish courtier-poets who accompanied him of much of their native cultural independence and individuality. Shire asks the question which is also directly relevant to our understanding of English court poetry: on what terms could a 'Scottish Poesie' so dependent upon aristocratic culture 'continue to exist after the departure of the King and court?'[38] A generation of Scots poets was born and grew up in a Scotland without a Court, and Scottish literature had to wait for more than a century before a new class basis was established for a literature of a comparable quality. Once the Scots poets went south to their new, more dynamic and richer Court in England, Scottish court culture withered. Alexander's poetry, like that of his fellow Scots, relied for its appreciation on a special kind of audience; it is essentially poetry as delicate and intimate gesture, depending primarily for its impact on a closely knit group of peers, one which James's Court provided in Scotland and which his protégés hoped to find in England. Such an intimate relationship between social setting and literary expectation proved to be extremely fragile. It is paradoxically both the strength and the potential self-destructiveness of court literature that it relies so heavily on such a homogenous and ultimate social relationship. Scots court poetry became as peripheral as it had once been strong.

Now let us go back to England at the beginning of the century. Who are the English contemporaries of Dunbar? At times imitative of the Scots poet and, like him, looking to European models, we can find John Skelton, Stephen Hawes and William Barclay. Lewis simply comments that most of their verse has 'no intrinsic value'. It is only a slight exaggeration. Some of Skelton's verse is still accessible today. He is, Krantzmann comments, 'the first truly inventive English poet since Chaucer'. But the most interesting aspect of Skelton is the reputation that was constructed for him by the narrowly ideological outlook of later sixteenth-century commentators. Puttenham looked back to his work as 'rayling and scoffery', seeing his popular, seemingly disjointed, verse not merely as lacking the harmony of the court poetry he wanted to promote but, reprehensibly, allowing earthy, popular, and non-aristocratic class interests to enter it.[39] The buffoonery of his satiric 'flytings' grows out of a combination of the frank realism of popular medieval ballad with popular song. His 'Bouge of Court' reflects on the rewards and corruptions of court favour, and the three closely connected satires (1515–22), 'Colin Clout', 'Speake Parot', and 'Why Come Yet Not to Court', attack the abuses of the Church and the politicians of Henry VIII's Court. As with Dunbar, we can sense not merely a blend of traditions, but a style and political frankness antipathetic to later taste and political orthodoxy. Puttenham's hostility is politically motivated, based on class and religion, not simply on 'literary' considerations.

Other poetry written in the Court of Henry VII and early in the reign of Henry VIII that is worthy of note here includes Stephen Hawes's moral allegories *Exemple of Vertu* (1504) and *Pastyme of Pleasure* (1506), written to oppose 'vyce and the vycious to blame', by a glorification of the Christian Knight and the choice of the appropriate Christian life. Hawes was a member of Henry VII's Court, a groom of the Privy Council, who was employed (as were Skelton, Barclay, and Medwall) as a clerk and propagandist. Poetry was for him, as for other courtiers, an incidental accomplishment. His poems look back, to 'prudent Gower', 'noble Chaucer', and 'virtuouse Lydgate', as he puts it at the start of the *Exemple of Vertu*. But despite such ancestry, alongside the Scots poetry of the time his poems are weak, tedious and imitative. Likewise, Thomas Heywood's epigrams and his alliterative allegory 'The Spider and the Fly' are also tired reworkings of medieval concerns written in halting diction and rhyme. George Cavendish's poems are similarly – in his own words – 'stakerying in style, onsavery in sentence'. He was a member of Wolsey's household and wrote long moralistic complaints on historical and political themes. But, as Gordon Kipling has argued, even in such limping poetry, which is typical of the reigns of Henry VII and VIII, we can see how the Court is starting to use poetry systematically. Henry VII's laureates, he suggests, 'present themselves as orators rather than poets', and 'present Tudor policy', consciously modelling themselves on the more sophisticated Burgundian or Scottish Courts.[40]

The most compelling English poetry before the 1580s that shows us the growing presence of the Court on poetry, poet, and public and private experiences alike and which, incidentally, comes closest to the interest of the poetry written in Scotland, is that by Sir Thomas Wyatt, who will be discussed in detail in Chapter 4. Read in the printed versions first collected in Tottel's *Miscellany* (1557), Wyatt seemed sufficiently sophisticated and receptive to the 'false semblant' of Petrarchan fashion to allow Puttenham to list him among the approved courtly makers. Wyatt's poetry appears hospitable to the Court's domination even though it is shot through with an uneasiness about its growing power. It asks in effect a crucial question: what language is available to the poet who, by virtue of his position and even his very existence, is tied to the Court? To be not in the Court is to be not in the world, as a character in the Jacobean play *The Revenger's Tragedy* remarks. It is interesting how Wyatt, and after him, would-be dissident courtier-poets like Ralegh and Greville, fall back on the residual language of medieval religious renunciation. It provided them with the words of an oppositional culture, as they tried to articulate emergent forces that would eventually overthrow the Court's power but for which there was as yet no language – except that of a residual and increasingly archaic social formation.

We can see from reading the poetry of this period how a particular ideology is never totally dominant: any culture, even the most powerful, always contains the potential for opposition. From 1580 to the end of the century, the period for which Puttenham is most triumphantly the spokesman, the institutions, philosophical assumptions and systems of linguistic authority are under increasing pressure. The most interesting poetry of the whole period is written in the last twenty years of the century precisely because it is so torn by conflicting ideological pressures. The best poetry – that of Sidney, Greville, Ralegh, Spenser, the early Donne, Shakespeare – is that which reveals how the very act of writing itself generates forces that challenge and question the power of the dominant structures. Most of the poetry of the last twenty years of the century sets up tensions between the affirmations it is being forced to make and the negations which struggle into play. The conscious allegiances of Spenser or Ralegh grant unambiguous legitimacy to the dominant ideology of the Court as they celebrate Gloriana or Cynthia, but none the less their poetry articulates more disturbing counter discourses. The 1590s, in particular, see a struggle to establish a place for new and quite different kinds of poetry; it is a decade of frenetic experiment, the mixing of traditional genres, the attempted invention of new ones, a virulent if short-lived burst of satire, and the struggling emergence of a new class as a major consumer force. The new audiences are most radically seen in the development in the public theatres, but in poetry too – in the readership of Donne's erotic poetry and Shakespeare's sonnets, and in the growing and long repressed number of women poets – we can see the surge of new audiences and new social forces.

Struggle with and within the power of the Court, then, constitutes sixteenth-century poetry's most important single characteristic. It is not one we would sense to be of primary concern if we simply read the verse of the period through the perspective that a century of criticism since Palgrave has taught us to regard as 'natural', and which has been reinforced by an explicable but misguided attempt to restore seemingly 'true' Elizabethan readings. No reading is ever innocent, and the Elizabethan poets and – even more rigorously – the structures in which they served knew this. Institutions have power only as long as the words for them to retain power and exclude alternatives from it exist. Hence, Elizabethan poetry tried to create not only writers but readers who would respond with what Spenser termed 'right' reading.

But words are inaugural: they start us thinking, and writing, other (often unpredictable) words. Although they never free themselves from power, they in effect ask – 'to times in hope' as Shakespeare asserts in Sonnet 18 – for future readers not to reproduce but to extend into their own circumstances, the struggles that brought them into being. This is why we, their modern readers, might well feel a real sense of responsibility for them. We can help bring their struggles, and the ways they offer perspectives on our struggles, into the open.

I started this introductory chapter talking about the intensity with which some of my students took over some of the strategies I am using in this book to produce involved, interesting and individual readings of a famous Wyatt poem. What came through as they read their Barthes and put it alongside the Wyatt, or later as they were introduced to Althusser, Macherey or Williams on 'ideology' and saw just how powerful a concept it could be in probing Ralegh or Donne, or in asking whether there were any women poets writing at the time, was that added to the pleasure of the text, the music, the wine and the food was the need and the excitement of using contemporary 'ways into' the poetry of the sixteenth century. After the initial enjoyment came the hard work. And, thus, greater enjoyment. And that can be true, I think, for all readers of this poetry today.

I will conclude this opening chapter by posing again the question with which I started. From our perspective in the late twentieth century what is our picture of the sixteenth century? Perhaps the most vivid recreation in the media is that shown in the television series, *Elizabeth R*, starring Glenda Jackson. It is a picture that in some ways closely matches that of the poetry that will be presented in this study. It shows not a world of beauty, order, and natural (let alone supernatural) harmony, but a world of danger, intrigue, devious self-serving politicians, where the cunning and ruthless survive, and where beauty, aggression, ambition could open doors, windows, bedchamber drapes but also lead one into the Tower or to the gallows. It was a dangerous world where personal and political fortunes changed unpredictably and were fought over by a small, interrelated class of anxious, paranoid men and women. As we watch the re-creation of this world in the comfort of our living rooms, we can romanticize the heads of traitors on pikes outside the Tower, the disease and the danger, the plots, confessions, burnings, and manipulations – just as we have romanticized the poetry. But just as the colourful swirl of robes and dances covers the conflicts and plots of Elizabethan society, so the poetry of the period, with its beauty, confidence, music and order, also covered over struggles, repressions and silences. And this is where we make the period's poetry part of 'our' world. It is our privilege, as modern readers, to be able to tease out the tissues of the texts, to enjoy, to 'delight', in Sidney's term, as well as to understand something of the struggles that go into their making and remaking.

Notes

1. F. R. Leavis, *Revaluation* (London, 1936). p. 11.

2. Leavis, *Revaluation*, p. 11.

3. Roland Barthes, *A Lover's Discourse*, translated by Richard Howard (New York, 1978), p. 217.

4. Francis Palgrave, *The Golden Treasury*, edited by John Press (Oxford, 1968), p. xxi.

5. For the scholars and critics mentioned in this paragraph, see General Bibliographies pp. 290–4 below.

6. Louis Althusser and Etienne Balibar, *Reading Capital*, translated by Ben Brewster (London, 1970), pp. 15–16.

7. Annabel Patterson, 'Recent Studies in the English Renaissance', *SEL*, 20 (1980), 153–75 (p. 153). See also Michael McCanles, 'The Authentic Discourse of the Renaissance', *Diacritics*, 10 (March 1980), 77–87 (p. 77); Jonathan Goldberg, 'The Politics of Renaissance Literature: A Review Essay', *ELH*, 15 (1982), 514–42 (p. 516).

8. *The New Oxford Book of Sixteenth-Century Verse*, edited by Emrys Jones (Oxford, 1991); *The Penguin Book of Renaissance Verse*, edited by David Norbrook and H.R. Woudhuysen (Harmondsworth, 1992), pp. xxx, xxxiii.

9. The preceding three paragraphs draw on many sources. See the work already cited in n.6, plus the following: Pierre Macherey, *A Theory of Literary Production*, translated by Geoffrey Wall (London, 1978); Raymond Williams, *Marxism and Literature* (London, 1977); Stuart Hall *et al.*, *Culture, Media, Language* (London, 1980). See also Thomas E. Lewis, 'Notes Towards a Theory of the Referent', *PMLA*, 94 (1979), 459–75; Steve Burniston and Chris Weedon, 'Ideology, Subjectivity and the Artistic Text', *Working Papers in Cultural Studies*, 10 (1977), 203–33; Thomas Metscher, 'Literature and Art as Ideological Form', *NLH*, 11 (1979), 21 40 (p. 26); Jacques Ranciere, 'On the Theory of Ideology', *Radical Philosophy*, 7 (Spring 1976), 2–15; Tony Davies, 'Education, Ideology and Literature', *Red Letters*, 7 (1978), 415 (pp. 3–4); Terry Eagleton, *Ideology* (London, 1990).

10. Williams, *Marxism and Literature*, p. 121–27.

11. Williams, *Marxism and Literature*, p. 112; Macherey, *Literary Production*, pp. 41–42.

12. Jacques Derrida, 'White Mythology: Metaphor in the Text of Philosophy', *NLH*, 6 (1976), 5–74 (p. 11); Macherey, *Literary Production*, pp. 79–80.

13. See e.g. Colin Mercer, 'After Gramsci', *Screen Education*, 36 (1980), 5–15; Raymond Williams, *The Long Revolution* (London 1961), pp. 48–71, and 'Literature in Society', in *Contemporary Approaches to English Studies*, edited by Hilda Schiff (New York, 1977), pp. 36–7; Terry Eagleton, 'Text, Ideology, Realism', in *Literature and Society: Selected Papers from the English Institute*, edited by Edward W. Said (Baltimore, 1980), p. 156; James H. Kavanagh, '"Marks of Weakness": Ideology, Science and Textual Criticism', *Praxis*, 5, no. I (1982), 23–38 (p. 31).

14. Macherey, *Literary Production*, pp. 79–80.

15. Maurice Evans, *English Literature in the Sixteenth Century* (London, 1954), p. 23.

16. Edward Hyde, Earl of Clarendon, *The History of the Rebellion and Civil Wars in England* (Oxford, 1849), pp. 1,5,10.

17. Edward W. Said, 'Travelling Theory', *Raritan*, 1, no. 3 (1982), 41–67 (p. 62); Michael Foucault, 'Prison Talk', in *Power/Knowledge: Selected Interviews and Other Writings, 1972–77*, edited by Colin Gordon (New York, 1980), p. 39.

18. Roy Strong, *Splendour at Court* (London, 1973), pp. 19, 21.

19. Strong, pp. 19, 21, 76; Sir Henry Wotton, *The Elements of Architecture* (London, 1624), p. 6.

20. John Stevens, *Music and Poetry in the Early Tudor Court* (London, 1961), p. 208.

21. George Puttenham, *The Arte of English Poesie*, edited by Gladys Doidge Willcock and Alice Walker (Cambridge, 1936), pp. 60, 61.

22. Puttenham, pp. 50, 137–38.

23. Puttenham, pp. 186, 298–300. See Daniel Javitch, 'The Impure Modes of Elizabethan Poetry', *Genre*, 15 (1982), 225–38 (p. 225), and *Poetry and Courtliness in Renaissance England* (Princeton, 1978), p. 66.

24. Stevens, *Music and Poetry*, p. 160; C. S. Lewis, *English Literature in the Sixteenth Century Excluding Drama* (Oxford, 1954), p. 230; William A. Sessions, 'Surrey's Wyatt: Autumn 1542 and the New Poet,' in *Rethinking the Henrician Era: New Essays on Early Tudor Texts and Contexts*, edited by Peter Herman (Urbana, 1994), and *Henry Howard, the Earl of Surrey* (Boston, 1986).

25. Puttenham, p. 21. See also Frank Whigham, 'The Rhetoric of Elizabethan Suitors' Letters', *PMLA*, 96 (1981), 864–82 (p. 882), and the same author's longer study, *Ambition and Privilege: The Social Tropes of Elizabethan Courtesy Theory* (Berkeley, 1984).

26. Paul Zumthor, 'From the Universal to the Particular in Medieval Poetry', *MLN*, 85 (1970), 815–23 (p. 816); 'Registres Linguistiques et Posie aux XII–XIIe Siècles', *Cultura Neolatina*, 34 (1974), 151–61.

27. Puttenham, pp. 143–45.

28. Ben Jonson, *Discoveries*, in *Works*, edited by C. H. Herford and P. and E. Simpson, (London, 1947), VIII, 583; Richard Green, *Poets and Princepleasers*, (Toronto, 1980), p. 583; Samuel Daniel, prefatory verses to John Florio, *Queen Annas New Worlde of Words* (1611).

29. For a detailed account of the Countess of Pembroke's patronage, see Gary Waller, *Mary Sidney, Countess of Pembroke: A Critical Study of Her Writings and Literary Milieu* (Salzburg, 1979), chs 2, 3. For a more sceptical view, see Mary Ellen Lamb, 'The Countess of Pembroke's Patronage', *ELR*, 12 (1982), 162–79, and 'The Myth of the Countess of Pembroke', *YES*, 11 (1981), 194–202.

30. *English Poetry 1400–1580*, edited by William Tydeman (New York, 1970), p. 240.

31. Puttenham, p. 24; Wotton, p. 27.

32. Sir Philip Sidney, *A Defence of Poetry*, in *Miscellaneous Prose of Sir Philip Sidney*, edited by Katherine Duncan-Jones and Jan van Dorsten (Oxford, 1973), pp. 110, 116; Puttenham, p. 60.

33. Raymond Williams, 'Wales and England', *What I Came to Say*, edited by Neil Belton, Francis Mulhern and Jenny Taylor (1989), pp. 64–74 (pp. 67, 69).

34. Lewis, English Literature, p. 120.

35. Gregory Krantzmann, *Anglo-Scottish Literary Relations 1430–1550* (Cambridge, 1980), p. 33. See also *Poetry of the Stewart Court*, edited by Joan Hughes and W. S. Ramson (Canberra, 1982), pp. 185, vii.

36. Krantzmann, p. 31.

37. *Ballatis of Love*, edited by John MacQueen (Edinburgh, 1970), pp. xliv, lvi.

38. Helena M. Shire, *Song, Dance and Poetry of the Court of Scotland* (Cambridge, 1985), p. 228.

39. Lewis, *English Literature*, p. 129; Krantzmann, p. 31.

40. Gordon Kipling, 'Henry VIII and the Origins of Tudor Patronage', in *Patronage in the Renaissance*, edited by Guy Fitch Lytle and Stephen Orgel (Princeton, 1981), pp 117–64 (pp. 132–3). For Hawes see A. S. G. Edwards, *Stephen Hawes* (Boston, 1983); for Cavendish, see *Metrical Visions*, edited by A. S. G. Edwards (Columbia, South Carolina, 1980).

Chapter 2
Language, the Poet and the World

Sixteenth-century theories of poetry

Looking back at what Thomas Nashe, with exuberant exaggeration, called the era of 'Chaucer, Lydgate, Gower, with such like, that lived under the tyrannie of ignorance', Puttenham's *The Arte of Poesie* celebrated the triumph of the political and cultural apparatus which had become powerful enough to make many previously fashionable kinds of poetry seemingly socially contemptible. The barbarous ignorance of the previous age had, Puttenham asserts, neglected poesie, but now its ancient dignity was being revived by 'many notable Gentlemen in the Court'.[1] The kinds of poetry which Puttenham singles out for praise are significantly different from those that would have been familiar a century earlier, but the reasons are as much political as 'literary'.[2] Puttenham arranges both the subject-matter of poetry and its various kinds in a strict hierarchy. After the praise of the gods (or in a Christian country, matters of religion), the most important aim of poetry is to praise 'the worthy gests of noble Princes, the memorial and registry of all great fortunes'; this is followed by 'the praise of vertue and reproofe of vice, the instruction of morall doctrines, the revealing of sciences material and other profitable Arts, the redress of boisterous and sturdie courage'; finally, poetry is to be 'the common solace of mankind in all his travails and cares of this transitorie life'.[3] While he may talk of the 'sundry' or 'divers' forms of poetry, Puttenham's account is strictly hierarchical, and rigidly subordinates poetry to public or rather what are, more accurately, class-specific interests. His emphasis is on the public responsibility of poetry: it should praise the great, reprove vice, and 'show the mutabilities of fortune, and the just punishment of God in revenge of a vicious and evill life'. Even the lowly pastoral is rendered publicly useful by its aim 'under the vaile of homely persons and in rude speeches to insinuate and glaunce at greater matters'. 'In everie degree and sort of men', Puttenham notes blatantly, 'mens estates are unegall', so, by analogy, those kinds of poetry are preferred which serve the values and aims of the dominant power. It is a distinctively and unabashed appropriation of the 'divers' kinds of poetry into the centralizing hegemony of the Tudor court, a development we can trace back into the courts of King Henry VII and especially, when we think of Surrey and Wyatt, Henry VIII.[4]

The theory within which the practice of poetry in the sixteenth century was written is, therefore, far broader than what we might conventionally think. 'Poetic' or 'aesthetic' theory, at least as we have understood it since Kant, was unknown to the Renaissance, although there are signs in some Italian theorists and even in Sidney that what a post-romantic perspective might term as the autonomy of art was struggling to find voice. But the issues that Renaissance poetic theorists (often with titles like 'defence' or 'apology') raise are not often those which readers in the late twentieth century might consider seriously. Is poetry superior to history and philosophy? Does the good poet have to be a good man? What kinds of poetry best praise the gods and reinforce order in the State? What is genuine poetry inspired by? Is poetry the most ancient of the arts? Some of these questions may seem strange to us, especially since we assume that the marginalization of serious poetry today makes its political effects, except in rare cases, negligible. But one reason we study the past is to become aware of alternatives to our own histories – to be able to consider the options, possibilities, and cultural languages from which we have been cut off, is, potentially at least, to open more possibilities in our futures. Further, we necessarily interrogate our pasts from our places in history, and from within the languages we are afforded. It would, for instance, be absurdly antiquarian to try to approach sixteenth-century attitudes to love and sensuality and pretend that our history did not include de Sade, Freud, psychoanalysis, Lawrence or feminism, or that our understanding of the interaction of political thought and economic production, or the base of political power in the sixteenth century, should rely only on Hooker or Elyot and ignore Marx or Foucault. We cannot contract out of our places in history. We ask questions of our past precisely because we inhabit different presents.

So when we read either the systematic treatises, or the incidental accounts of poetry's nature and function written by sixteenth-century writers like Puttenham, Gascoigne or Sidney, inevitably we will encounter many issues that seem puzzlingly unimportant and irrelevant, even naive, to us. Renaissance criticism is both extraordinarily derivative and contradictory, an ahistorical mix of Neoaristotelianism, Neohoratianism and Neoplatonism.[5] Foucault notes how sixteenth-century learning generally was made up of an unstable mixture of rational knowledge, notions derived from magical practices, and the classical cultural heritage whose power and authority had been vastly increased by the rediscovery of Greek and Roman authors. It is 'clearly structurally weak: a common ground where fidelity to the Ancients, a taste for the supernatural, and an already awakened awareness of the sovereign rationality in which we recognize ourselves, confronted one another in equal freedom'. If we take Sidney's *Defence* as one of the central theoretical documents of the century, it is clear that it brings together a host of contradictory views of poetry. It is didactic and celebratory, often mixing neoplatonic, Calvinist, Horatian, Ovidian, Ramist, Aristotelian and other elements. It has also, at times, something of an opaque quality, as if poetic theory were a performative discipline rather than a truth-claiming one. Sidney often seems to play with his reader as much as his concepts of poetry. At times he seems to conform closely to logic in his argument; but occasionally he falls, perhaps deliberately, into inconsistencies and contradictions, often (almost) with a self-conscious chuckle. He shifts ground – on whether rhyme and verse are essential to poetry, on whether the golden world of poetry is referential, on the truth-value of poetry. Levao has argued persuasively that a central part of Sidney's argument is that it is 'feigned', that it is 'deliberately tangled and ambivalent', and that the discussion of poetic inspiration is 'at best metaphorical' and less a description of the poet's art than an account of its effect on the reader. Sidney, according to this argument, is really interested in poetry's work in the world, its practical manifestations; so his uses of neoplatonic cliché or philosophical commonplace are carefully chosen to develop a persuasive rather than 'truthful' theory of fiction.[6]

Didacticism and social utility

But the most obvious characteristic of sixteenth-century treatises on poetry is nothing so sophisticated. It is rather their blatant didacticism. Although later commentators have seen Sidney's *Defence* as advocating a potentially sophisticated distinction between 'fact' and 'fiction', the Romantic narrowing of literature to 'imaginative' writing had not yet been institutionalized. Sidney was aiming at a very utilitarian goal, that of justifying poetry as a valuable activity within a Protestant state. Sinfield terms it 'the most fully developed attempt to establish a puritan-humanist aesthetic', one that insists on the didactic function of poetry to 'move men to take goodness in hand'. What the 'goodness' consists of is explicitly defined for Sidney by the principles of the Elizabethan regime.[7]

The utility of poetry was an assumption that was widely taken for granted. The dominant medieval literary theory, as Montgomery puts it, 'seeks to explain or defend the value of fiction primarily in terms of the ends it gains in the mind of the reader and ultimately in his moral behaviour'.[8] In the sixteenth century, most arguments on poetry continue along such lines. All writers agreed that poetry's universal and ancient status is conceded by the best authorities; that because of its divine origins and social nature, poetry could (despite objections from some Protestants) be a moral force; and that it communicated its didactic aims with a pleasurableness that enhanced its power to change our lives. Poets, Sidney writes, 'do merely make to imitate, and imitate both to delight and teach; and delight, to move men to take that goodness in hand, without which delight they would fly as from a stranger, and teach, to make them know that goodness whereunto they are moved'. The conclusion of the *Defence* likewise stresses that poetry is not 'an art of lies, but of true doctrine', full of 'virtue-breeding delightfulness'. Can we see the beginnings of an 'aesthetic' approach to poetry, hints of the treasured Romantic and modernist notion of the autonomy of the work of art? If so, such elements are put alongside the more obvious moralizing or utilitarian sentiments. Sidney writes of the poet's 'high flying liberty of conceit', the 'vigour' of the poet's 'invention', and in one half of his most famous aphorism, he asserts that 'our erected wit maketh us know what perfection is'. But this ecstatic, neoplatonic celebration is immediately countermanded by the other half of the same sentence, that none the less, 'our infected will keepeth us from reaching unto it'.[9] 'Erected wit' and 'infected will': in those great opposites are epitomized the contradictory languages of sixteenth-century poetry.

Regardless of the kinds of poetry, then, didactic assumptions dominate most of the century's poetry. In the early part of the period, most of the work of the early Tudor humanist poets, like More, Barclay or Hawes, is stolidly didactic, and often painful to wade through. Often, however, Skelton's poetry is direct and energetically scurrilous, qualities that did not endear his poetry to later more courtly commentators like Puttenham. Likewise, Barclay brings to his *Ship of Fools* some attractive roughness as he attacks court corruption; while Hawes's *Example of Vertu* and *Pastyme of Pleasure* dimly anticipate *The Faerie Queene's* combination of chivalric romance, dream vision, and religious didacticism. The utilitarian tradition is epitomized in *A Mirror for Magistrates* (1559 and many subsequent editions) or in what was the century's most popular verse, Sternhold and Hopkins's versions of the *Psalms*. Lewis unabashedly blamed the bulk of this 'earnest, heavy-handed, commonplace' poetry on humanism, arguing that the pious, sober-minded educationalists of the first seventy years of the century saw poetry as requiring heavy moralizing, encyclopaedic scope and heavy-handed allegory, thus continuing the worst of medieval solemnity in its epigrammatic, halting, moral commonplaces. 'All the facts', he argues, 'seem consistent with the view that the great literature of the fifteen-eighties and nineties was something which humanism, with its unities and *Gorboducs* and English hexameters, would have prevented if it could, but failed to prevent because the high tide of native talent was then too strong for it.'[10] But the moralistic view of poetry does not disappear in the last decades. It is as prevalent in the 1590s, in the work of Greville or Chapman, say, as it had been earlier in the century. Nor, as we shall see, was it without its strengths, not the least of which was the seriousness with which it took its vocation to comment upon political, social and religious issues.

The poets, like Googe or Turberville, who are scorned in Sidney's *Defence* – and by the majority of modern commentators from Palgrave on – certainly saw poetry, as Lewis implies, as the natural outcome of the principles of humanist education. They wanted to influence public affairs. A poem for them is typically a well-modulated collection of *sententiae*, designed to show the universality of the human lot and, specifically, the moral and civic principles of the Tudor establishment. These poets writing in mid-century were largely highly trained statesmen, lawyers or scholars, concerned with the pacification and reform of society; and they directed their poetry (which was very much a minor part of their lives) towards a readership of similar men. They shared the belief that poetry should inculcate an obedience to authority and civic order. When we read their poetry today, it is useful to ask what kind of 'self' does it ask for and in a very real sense try to create? Or (another way of putting the same question): what role is the reader asked to occupy? It is usually that of a sober, primarily male, citizen, a member of a community linked together by unchanging moral virtues. The best of this poetry – some of Googe's or Gascoigne's – is distinguished by sonority, directness, and a stubborn dedication to the educational and moral ideals of humanism. Gascoigne's poetry, undoubtedly the most interesting written in England between Wyatt and Sidney, starts to articulate a little of the bind in which his poetry has been put as it wrestles to express something through, but not confined to, moral commonplaces. An eager seeker for court preferment, the dramatized speaker of Gascoigne's verse remains moralistic and his choice of the complaint form curiously medieval; but some of the contradictions of the age are starting to come through his solemn lines.

Before the last decades of the century, the quintessential didactic work of poetry, which combined both the general moralistic caste of late medieval public poetry and the distinctive role of the new Protestant regime – indeed the age's most ambitious poetical work before *The*

Faerie Queene – was *A Mirror for Magistrates*. This was a collection of versified tragic tales taken from English history, first compiled by Thomas Baldwin under the reign of Mary, but not printed until 1559. It was very popular – perhaps the second most popular work of poetry of the century – after Sternhold and Hopkins's lugubrious versifications of the *Psalms* (1559). It went through nine editions by 1610, most with newly added tragedies 'all to be oftener reade, and the better remembered' by 'the learned (for such all Magistrates are or should be)'. In the 1563 edition, an introduction was added, and the chronicle of tragedies was taken as far as the War of the Roses. In the 1587 edition, the editor, Thomas Blenerhasset, included a tale of Uther Pendragon and in his introduction described the additions as covering historical events 'from the conquest of Caeser unto the comying of Duke William the Conqueror'. The *Mirror's* authors included prominent nobles and courtiers, and the combination of medieval allegory, solemn moralistic tragedy, and public responsibility (all reinforced in a succession of additions) served the Elizabethan regime as a continually adapted reinforcement of its political aims. In the original introduction, written by one of Elizabeth's leading courtiers, Thomas Sackville, Earl of Dorset, the figure of Sorrow appears and invites the reader to 'leave the playning, and the byter bale/ of worthy men, by Fortune overthrowne', and after introducing a pageant of allegorical figures like Remorse, Maladie and Warre, the first of those whose tales are to be told in the ensuing tragedies is introduced with solemn melodrama:

> Next saw we Dread, all trembling how he shook,
>   With foot uncertain proffered here and there,
> Benumbed of speech, and with a ghastly look
>   His cap borne up with staring of his hair . . .

The *Mirror* thus was a secular equivalent of the homilies that were read in churches each Sunday, giving applications of its lessons, providing a 'mirror' for princes, governors and soldiers. The collection was widely imitated, its basic formula adapted to other material, its political intent reinforced by many similar works.[11]

It is worth underlining both the popularity and typicality of such poems. Despite our preference today for the period's lyrics, the bulk of the poetry extant from at least the first three-quarters of the sixteenth century is unremitting in the way it subordinated itself to the public needs of the regime. It is mainly such versified Protestant and civic propaganda – moral commonplaces, precepts, *encomia*, epitaphs, expostulations on patriotism, exposures of moral dangers, or on social evils, the dangers of life in Court, the shortness of life in general. It sets out the rules for responsible behaviour, usually reinforced by stern moralizations of theological commonplaces, like Googe's:

> Behold this fleeting world, how all things fade,
> How every thing doth pass and wear away;
> Each state of life, by common course and trade,
> Abides no time, but hath a passing day.

Such verse, as Sheidley comments on Googe (one of its most indefatigable producers), was designed to advance the general programme of the new regime, which included 'purging the realm of vice, papistry, and dissension, while educating the populace to the need for civil order, obedience, and a patriotism focused on the crown'. Even the period's satiric verse, such as Gascoigne's *The Steele Glas* (a typical continuation of the *Mirror* fashion), points out the social ills of the time in order to purge them, so that the Court might more fully emulate the pattern given, so the assumption was, by the Queen. Typical targets are the frivolity of courtiers and the corruption of foreigners, especially Italians. It is poetry in line with Ascham's requirement in *The Scholemaster* that literature 'gather examples' and 'give light and understanding' to good precepts. [12]

A particularly intriguing instance of the pervasive didacticism is pastoral poetry. 'Eclogues', Puttenham writes, are poems which 'in base and humble stile . . . uttered the private and familiar talke of the meanest sort of men', using 'the vaile of homely persons to insinuate and glaunce matters'. [13] The propagandist intent of a didactic poem like the *Mirror* is clear enough; much more discrete and yet as revealing is the use to which the Court put the seemingly harmless escapism of the pastoral eclogue and a range of poetry in which the pastoral mode permeated – prose romances, romantic drama, and (eventually, especially in the Jacobean Court) the court masque. To study the pastoral is, once again, to see how social tensions and ideological pressures operated in poetry. We may see this by concentrating precisely on a major absence in the pastoral. Ironically, what is *not* found in court pastorals are the real conditions of Elizabethan country life, which was, especially from mid-century on, passing through disruptive and painful transitions as land was appropriated and exploited by such great families as the Sidneys and the Herberts. In the placid, sophisticated world of Elizabethan pastoral such disturbances rarely occur, and require to be read back in by the modern reader. As Montrose comments, the pastoral's origins and connections are made presentable for service in the Court, and the shepherd-poet's plaints, however disguised, are the loyal expression of political aspirations. This is the case even when the pastoral is used for satire. In Spenser's *Colin Clouts Come Home Again*

(1591), the poet attacks court corruption, while praising the Queen and the noble ladies around her; within what he terms 'this simple pastorall' both sycophantic praise and stern moral satire coexist, and in this uneasy juxtaposition of flattery and satire we encounter pleas for advancement along with condemnation of those who seek 'with malice and with strife/To thrust downe other and himselfe to raise'. Returning to his plantation in Ireland, Spenser is looking back at England, and sternly rebukes and seemingly rejects the Court, but the whole poem is motivated by his desire to advance by means of its influence.[14] Such tensions are among those that typically dislocate much of the poetry of the 1590s, including the final books of Spenser's epic.

Didacticism, then, and of a distinctively civic and moral kind, is the predominant note of sixteenth-century theory, and it is borne out in the poetical practices of the age. Whether the emphases are Boethian, Augustinian, Horatian or Calvinist, most Renaissance pronouncements on poetry insist on the social, educational and moral responsibility of the poet. They also emphasize that poetry's role is to be subordinate to what they saw as the given meanings of the world – whether they were conceived as given by God's Word, the order of Nature, or the need for civic responsibility. Poetry was justified as supporting the establishment of the godly State. Poetry can help reform man's will: 'no learning is so good as that which teacheth and moveth to virtue', as Sidney writes.[15]

Poetry is not only a moral teacher, but it is the supreme moral teacher. It combines the conceptual advantages of philosophy with the concrete instances of history. Poetry will entice men into virtuous actions by imitating real virtue, not false illusion – by its imitation of what Sidney calls the 'golden' world, a world of moral inspiration of what may and should be. The poet, he argues, 'doth grown in effect another nature, in making things either better than nature bringeth forth, or, quite anew, forms such as never were in nature'. 'Poetry', therefore, he asserts, 'is an art of imitation, for so Aristotle termeth it in his word mimesis', not by simply reproducing the given world but by 'a representing, counterfeiting, or figuring forth to speak metaphorically'.[16] The main emphasis here is on metaphor as the primary way of speaking which brings about the effects of imitation and thus affecting the mind and the senses of the readers. Readers of poetry will thus be enticed towards the emulation of moral excellence by the power of poetry's mimesis, as it creates speaking pictures of how Nature might fulfil its potential. Even in the discussion of metaphors the final test of poetry is always in praxis – how it contributes to the moral improvement of its readers and to the wider society. The most triumphant creation of such a theory is unquestionably *The Faerie Queene*, perhaps the clearest and richest example of how the Elizabethan regime advanced its ideals through poetry. Political allegory, whether the clumsy moralization of the *Mirror* or the rich polyphony of *The Faerie Queene*, is built on a desire to subdue language to power, to make signification transparent to meaning and to prevent the potential promiscuity of language from spreading unwanted meanings too far.[17] Sixteenth-century poetry is, as Sinfield suggests, the poetry of a one-party state, and the closest parallels we find in our own time with both the theory and use of poetry in the sixteenth century are with the Soviet era; he points out the uncanny parallels between Sidney's sentiments and Leonid Brezhnev's address to the XXVI Congress of the Soviet Communist Party where it is argued the 'vivid images of our contemporaries move people, prompt debates, and make people think of the present and the future' by presenting a heroic ideal so that 'the reader or the viewer sees his own thoughts and feelings, and the embodiment of the finest qualities' of the national character. As Sinfield comments. 'some of the same virtues are absolutized in the *Defence*, and the same exemplary role is assigned to literature', thus covering up, 'in the interest of a particular view of culture and society', the range of possibilities poetry might and does, in fact, produce.[18]

But it would be a peculiarly partial reading of the *Defence* or the thinking about poetry in the period to see didacticism as totally dominant. It may be true, as Sinfield argues, that even Sidney handles the central issues of his treatise in distinctively Protestant ways and that we cannot understand him unless we see him as 'part of a faction committed to reinforcing the influence of Protestantism within the cultural apparatus and the state generally'.[19] But the *Defence*, and even some of the period's other treatises on poetry, are less absolute than this argument suggests. Like poetry, even a prose treatise brings into play contradictions and tensions it would consciously like to exclude. The *Defence* combines many contradictory strands which tend to unravel the hard-line Protestantism of parts of its argument, and I shall now proceed to tease out some of them.

Neoplatonism

The first we shall glance at is neoplatonism, a suggestive accretion of ideas derived, at some distance, from Plato, remixed from the late fifteenth century onwards by such thinkers as Ficino and Pico della Mirandola, and subsequently popularized in such works as Castiglione's *Il Cortegiano*. According to the neoplatonist view of the world, through his God-given power, the poet creates what Sidney terms 'another world', analogous to the way God himself created the world. The world is a rational universe created by a rational Creator who, in Heninger's words, followed the precepts of the Book of Wisdom, making the universe 'according to number, weight, and measure'.[20] As usual, Sidney's is the most elegant English formulation of the poetical application of such an optimistic doctrine. Although his idea that the poet creates a new Nature is not original – it is derived from the neoplatonic view of the artist as the vehicle of the Divine Ideas, popularized by such Italian critics as Landino or Scaliger – it is a most intriguing expression:

> Only the poet, disdaining to be tied to any such subjection,
> lifted up with the vigour of his own invention, doth grow
> in effect another nature, in making things either better than
> nature bringeth forth, or, quite anew, forms such as never
> were in nature . . . so as he goeth hand in hand with nature,
> not enclosed within the narrow warrant of her gifts, but freely
> ranging only within the zodiac of his own wit.

Here the poet is celebrated as an autonomous maker. He takes the miraculous creation of the world by God, the divine poet, as his model, and draws down the magical powers of the universe into his own mind; 'the zodiac of his own wit'. The superiority of the poet's world is unabashedly celebrated, since Nature's 'world is brazen, the poets only deliver a golden'. The poet's greatness is built upon his aspiring to encapsulate in his poem the beauty and splendour that shine in all natural things, and thus continuing God's divine creativity in his work. The poet is

> . . . set . . . beyond and over all the works of that second
> nature: which in nothing he showeth so much as in poetry,
> when with the force of a divine breath he bringeth things
> forth surpassing her doings – with no small argument to the
> credulous of that first accursed fall of Adam, since our erected
> wit maketh us know what perfection is, and yet our infected
> will keepeth us from reaching unto it.[21]

It is fascinating that here, at the end of this ecstatic sentence, Sidney comes back to didacticism, and most particularly, in the Calvinist emphasis on the 'infected will', to an inability to embody what the poet is inspired to perform. These contradictions (as we shall see in Chapter 5) surface in Sidney's own poetry as well. How did poets reconcile such oppositions? How do the erected wit and the infected will coexist?

The general neoplatonic caste of the so-called Elizabethan world picture is a particularly interesting phenomenon – and most relevant for the way poetry and poetic theory were rewritten by other cultural codes and so assimilated into the dominant understanding of cosmic and political order. As Quitslund has shown, most Elizabethan poets' interest in Platonism is little more than a reverent and convenient lip service, a 'dilution of serious thought', but it gave their work a distinctively aesthetic aura which undermines the otherwise ubiquitous grey utilitarianism.[22] Their primary interest was in raiding neo-platonism for compliments to the beauty of a mistress, or for tropes by which to express the enlightenment by which men might perceive God, or to make claims for the status of the poet as a prophetic articulator of truth, in Sidney's argument, as against the historian or philosopher or practical man of affairs. The philosopher has precepts, but is obscure, and abstract; the historian has access to the real, but is insufficiently theoretical: only the poet can combine particularity with general insight. The poet can thus be presented as a creator, mediating between the world of transcendent forms and the brazen world of Nature. Spenser's articulation of such a theory in the October Eclogue of *The Shepheardes Calender* or *The Tears of the Muses* combines neoplatonism and traditional Horatianism along with a Christian emphasis on divine inspiration. Another assimilation of neoplatonism found commonly in sixteenth-century discussions of poetry is the numerical coherence between the individual poem and that of the created world. It is often expressed by means of a musical analogy. Sidney mentions how the 'same exquisite observing of number and measure of words' has a 'divine force' in it, and thus introduces the close relationship of music to poetry. He speaks further of the 'planet-like music of Poetry'. 'Music' here includes far more than the modern term suggests. As Heninger argues, behind the phrase is the Boethian philosophy of the interconnection of the divinely ordained harmony of the universe (the *musica mundana*), the individual's harmony (the *musica humana*) and the expression of universal harmony in music (the *musica instrumentalis*). Sidney typically gives this theory a practical application: poetry's echo of the *musica mundana* leads to a therapeutic reorganization of the psyche towards cosmic harmony.[23]

What kinds of poetry did this less didactic theory favour? One kind attempted to unite its audience almost as a community of believers and so subordinated any possible irony or ethical conflict to the overall effect of participatory delight. 'It is the right harmony of lyric', asserts Dowland, which 'stirs men up to admiration and delight'; such effects are achieved by aspiring to the incantatory effects of music, with syntax and idea conceived of as parts of a musical whole, representing not so much a precise emotion as the morphology of emotion – not describing feeling so much as what it feels like to feel. To hear (always, we should remember, an important experience in studying the Elizabethan lyric) Dowland's settings of 'My Thoughts Are Winged with Hopes' or Sidney's 'Who Is It that this Darke Night' is, according to such a theory, to enter into an atmosphere of lyrical harmony and thereby to participate in an order that was not simply superficial pleasure nor direct and vulgar moralization. Such poems rarely attempt to arrest or obstruct the verse's flow to create a dislocation between sense and movement; the words are chosen to please the ear, to soothe the senses. There is, they seem to assert, no need to know anything more than the shimmering surface – to foreground any ambiguity, tension or urgent personal voice would dislocate the pattern. Light, harmony, proportion, and grace are meant to constitute the experience which the poem opens up in its readers, and it is our recognition of the poem's aptness, and our participation in its pattern of rich harmony, that Sidney includes in his key neoplatonic term, 'delight'. That, too, it is asserted, is a kind of knowledge. As Ralegh's celebration of the Queen puts it:

> In heaven Queene she is among the spheares;
> In ay she Mistres like makes all things pure,
> Eternitie in hir oft chaunge she beares;
> She beautie is, by hir the faire endure.

The Queen is not *like* Beauty; she *is* Beauty: she is above time, beyond criticism, and the courtiers around her do not question this. They just *know* it: 'A knowledge pure it is hir worth to kno,/With Circes let them dwell that thinke not so'. Anyone doubting that this is the case is cursed; more, is clearly sub-human. Such knowledge is 'natural': or, as we might now say, ideological! Lyrics like Ralegh's, or Campion's 'Rose-cheekt Lawra' or 'Come, O Come, my life's delight' attempt to create the experience of participating in a timeless world. Even given the necessarily sequential pattern of lines and stanzas, such poems try to fix us in a stasis, without any relation to the passing of time in the mutable world outside the experience of reading or hearing the poem. They are concerned with celebration, not discovery; they aim to be experiences of integration, not of alienation or stringent self-analysis.[24]

For a modern reader of sixteenth-century poetry, such a theory – more than a theory, since it was part of the ingrained assumptions of the age and so should be treated as one of the sixteenth-century's dominant ideological structures – can easily be pieced apart to show it merely to be an unstable accumulation of superstition, pseudo-magical practices, political obfuscation and ancient authority. But because such connections also affect the realm of language we must ask both how poetry fitted into the overall structure of discourse, and what effects the breakdown of the whole scheme from the late sixteenth century onwards had on poetry. As Foucault argues, until the end of the sixteenth century, 'the value of language lay in the fact that it was the sign of things. There is no difference between the visible marks that God has stamped upon the surface of the earth, so that we may know its inner secrets, and the legible words that the Scriptures, or the sages of Antiquity, have set down in the books preserved for us by tradition'.[25] Nature, the texts of antiquity, the Bible, society, and human nature were all linked, and the poet above all else was asked to relate and restore the invisible but unbroken links between humans and things. As this particular order broke down, the disruption and dislocation are mediated through the poetry. As part of a whole new division of discourse, we get a new poetry, and a new poetic theory.

Rhetorical theory

Didacticism and neoplatonism, then, were two major ingredients of the Renaissance potpourri of poetic theory; another was a strain of quasi-empirical Aristotelianism, which broadens as the century goes on to become the next century's dominant neoclassicism. As the works of classical philosophers and poets became available in England, many of the questions which had, much earlier, been raised in Italy and other parts of Europe came to interest and eventually to dominate English thinking about poetry; the debate over the status of the vernacular, the moral defence of poetry, the opposition of 'convention' to 'nature', and the emergence of neoclassical rules, thus adding to the forces that were relocating reality from an ontology based on a Platonic or Christian world of being to one based in the phenomena of physical nature. Poetry was put under increasing pressure by a new movement of humanist educators who, as Nashe put it late in the century, 'repurged the errors of Arte' expelled from their puritie, and set before our eyes a more perfect method of studie'. Texts like Cicero's *De Inventione*, the *Rhetorica ad Herennium*, Horace's *Ars Poetica*, and, especially, Aristotle's *Poetics* became increasingly quoted (often from Italian translations and commentaries) and discussed. As well, the influence of rhetorical handbooks by Cicero or Quintilian and, late in the century, the work of Ramus brought about major changes in the understanding of rhetoric, and therefore of poetry.[26]

For the sixteenth century, 'rhetoric' meant the theory and practice of the uses of language in concrete social practices. It was the means by which citizens (predominantly men) could enter civic and political life. Studying the classical masters of eloquent language was primarily utilitarian: it was the necessary preparation for court and political service. During the sixteenth century, we can trace changes in the theory and practice of rhetoric which are illuminating for our understanding of the poetry – in particular the gradual separation of 'invention' and logic from decoration or rhetoric. What became seen pejoratively as 'eloquence' became criticized as an unnecessary intrusion between the speaker of 'truth' and its reception. Throughout the sixteenth century, in fact, two rival views of rhetoric coexist uneasily and by the end are breaking into clear conflict. There is, on the one hand, what Lanham has termed *homo rhetoricus*, the man who plays freely with language, devising rather than merely discovering truth, indulging in the copiousness and richness of rhetoric; on the other hand, there is *homo seriosus*, seen in the Protestant or Ramist view of language, whereby rhetoric is seen merely as appropriately chosen devices of persuasion.[27] Is logic an inventive process or merely the mirror of what nature provides? Where Erasmus, following Quintilian, argues for the variety and pleasure of *copia*, with logic and rhetoric in equal balance, both Ramism and Protestantism were suspicious of the self-indulgence of the humanist exaltation of language. Logic is aligned with nature, rhetoric with convention, artifice and embellishment. By rigidly separating logic from rhetoric, Ramism implied that the 'truth' was a matter of the given objects-in-nature which were to be 'discovered' rather than 'invented', while the arts of language were merely the necessary clothing of those truths. 'More matter and less art' asks Shakespeare's (at least momentarily) Ramist Queen Gertrude in *Hamlet*. By the end of the century, ornament is increasingly suspect, moderation and clarity admired for both prose and poetry. As Eagleton summarizes the process, 'a vigorous division of labour was gradually instituted between thought and speech, language and discourse, science and poetry'.[28]

If 'rhetoric' was at issue in the sixteenth century, so too was the key Aristotelian term, *mimesis*, or 'imitation'. Every art, argues Sidney, has 'the works of nature for his principal object' and so poetry is to be defined as 'an art of imitation', and the poet by 'that feigning' of 'notable images of virtues, vices, or what else'. The poet 'imitates' to teach and delight.[29] One of the questions Sidney raises is: what is the object of mimesis? What does the poet imitate? In his *Republic*, Plato has the arts expelled since they are based on deception, merely counterfeiting the appearances of things; in the *Timaeus* and *Sophist* he modifies the harshness of his criticism, but it was left to Aristotle to redefine mimesis as a presentation of the universal or characteristic mode of existence, a 'conveniency to nature', as Sidney puts it.[30] During the Renaissance, the contradictory interpretations of the concept included the neoplatonic valorization of the poets' access to the world of forms, an adaptation of Aristotelian 'universals' into the reproduction of local particularities, and a pedagogical view of it as the careful, even mechanical following of a literary model. If we glance ahead, for Jonson early in the next century, 'imitation' has become simply the reasoned, judicious use of the thoughts, words and examples of approved authors.[31] Jonson's difference from Sidney is important here. For Sidney, the essence of the poetic act was the art of 'figuring forth to speake Metaphorically'. Metaphor is a means of extending knowledge by the use of words to make visual (not merely conceptual) its meanings: 'it is that feigning notable images . . . which must be the right describing note to know a poet by'. It is a process best characterized by *enargeia*, force, power, not merely by a mere manipulation of words. As Heninger notes, when Sidney is writing the *Defence*, ' "metaphor" is still a prominent term in the critical lexicon with a rich history and wide applicability'.[32] But for Jonson, as for Bacon or Hobbes, metaphor is merely ornamentation, a device to illustrate pre-existent matter. From Sidney to Jonson is one generation but the difference in poetic theory and the understanding of language and/as reality is immense.

Discussions of such issues, as with so many that are important to the period's poetry, should not be oversimplified or too quickly harmonized. The age's views of 'imitation' betray ideological conflicts as surely as the rest of the poetical theory does. Too often, as Miller has shown, modern accounts of imitation in the Renaissance try to show that just as that which is 'imitated' is supposed to be transformed into a new creation, so the heterogeneity of the various writings that are woven together in the theory can be harmonized. On the one hand, Sidney argues that poets are different from arithmeticians or philosophers who follow Nature, or grammarians and rhetoricians who follow rules, since 'only the poet . . . doth grow in effect another nature . . . not enclosed within the narrow warrant of her gifts'.[33] On the other hand, he repeatedly stresses the need to follow artificial rules, models and ancient masters. It is not only the disparity between such views, but the attempt to pair such recognizably discordant ideas that seems to be most representative of the period's thinking about poetry. Inherently contradictory concepts are brought together, held only by the writer's desire to set them side-by-side, and not by any kind of achieved harmony.

In speaking of poetry as an art of *mimesis*, or imitation, the art of 'figuring forth to speak metaphorically', Sidney is voicing the commonplace that the poet is closely allied to the orator. His remark combines a description of the orator as he who masters the figures of rhetoric, and the poet as he who imitates the actions of men. Both share the same goal of persuasion. The Ciceronian and Horatian emphasis on the teaching function of poetry and the humanist emphasis on language's persuasion all assumed that certain tropes would produce certain effects. Erasmus's *De Copia*, widely used as a school text, concentrated on the orator's effects on an audience and inculcated a view of poetry as an art of conscious choice and calculated effect. A number of handbooks were translated into English the precepts of classical oratory. These included Leonard Cox's *The Arte or Crafte of Rhethoryke* (1528), Thomas Wilson's *Art of Rhetoric* (1553), and Abraham Fraunce's *Arcadian Rhetoric* (1589). Parts of Puttenham's treatise are also in this vein.

From such works, all dealing in immense detail with grammar, rhetoric and logic, we can piece together an extremely complicated system of language as persuasion, one that was to be acquired by 'studie & discipline or exercise' in schools and universities, and then applied to the various arts of discourse, including poetry. It involved selecting and developing a subject ('invention') and then elaborating or 'amplifying' it according to approved structures and illustrations by schemes and tropes. Many sixteenth-century poems read as if they are handbook exercises; others, more subtle and complex, like Sidney's, grow from the same training and assumptions. The seemingly endless exercises in translation, imitation and adaptation focused the poet's skill upon the appropriate rhetorical devices. Lanham's *homo seriosus* and *homo rhetoricus* were thus both served by such study. The former – most poets of the mid-century period – saw the goal of poetry as communicating given truths. Language must be chosen to be transparent, self-effacing, and to highlight the apparent referential reality. The latter saw language itself as central, not the truths to which it points – the poet conceived as a player, a master of roles, in effect what Plato had sternly rejected as sophistry and what rhetorically inclined Elizabethans lauded as the production of *copia*, copious matter. The 'method' (otherwise called 'disposition' or 'arrangement') of the organization of a poem or poetic sequence would be chosen in order to influence the anticipated reader response most effectively – for instance, in Ramus's influential scheme, by simplicity and directness (the 'natural' disposition), or by digression and complication (the 'prudential').[34] Poets wishing to instruct would be likely to choose the former; poets seeking to write poetry as display, entertainment or provocation, the latter – although it is fair to point out that in the most interesting poems of the period, the characteristics of the so-called plain and eloquent styles are inevitably mixed.

The mid-century period was a muddled but finally useful period of experiments in finding ways by which words could be used to serve poetic eloquence of many kinds. Tottel's *Miscellany* may be seen as Shakespeare's Slender saw it – as a model handbook of rhetorical exercises, giving subsequent poets models for their own verse, 'a full scale attempt', as Peterson puts it, 'to extend the possibilities of the short poem by adapting the various themes and modes of *dispositio* that are outlined and illustrated in the handbooks of rhetoric currently in the use of schools'.[35] Poets were encouraged to note such models, to consult rhetorical handbooks, and to model their work on them. Turberville is obviously and carefully following handbook patterns in his verse, and Gascoigne's best poems adapt a decorously plain style straight from the models provided by the rhetorical handbooks. As Ringler points out, the most valuable part of Sidney's training was the grounding he received in logic and rhetoric; by the time he wrote, the lessons of the period of experiment in mid century had been absorbed. Puttenham's *Arte* is, on this as on much else, central in the linking of poetry and oratory. After a first book dealing with poetry in general, he devotes a second to 'proportion poeticall'. Poetry involves the 'skill to speake and write harmonically'; it is a kind of 'Musicall utterence', based on stanzaic form, metre, rhyme and figure. The twenty-five chapters of the third book classify the 'flowers and figurative speaches' of rhetoric, the 'instruments of ornament'.[36]

Puttenham pays special attention to the writer's sense of audience. Although Elizabethan rhetorical theory pays detailed attention to the writing process, it is also intriguingly audience or reader orientated. Part of a poet's training was to be aware that the power of poetry resided in the forcefulness of the image that was presented to what Cicero termed the mind's eye of the reader. Sidney's *Defence* emphasizes how poetry aims to produce visible images in order to move a reader in the way that an orator does. Peacham's *Garden of Eloquence* (1577) sets out in a rigid hierarchy appropriate rhetorical figures, beginning with metaphor, and emphasizes how the reader or hearer must seem to see 'a lively image . . . then a reporte expressed with the tongue'.[37] The writer-centred theory of poetry, whether 'imitative' or 'inspirational', was, in other words, complemented by a strongly affective theory. The true poet, writes Sidney, 'holdeth children from play, and old men from the chimney corner'; he adds that poetry was a more effective teacher than history or philosophy because its power is rooted in its ability to 'move', in Sidney's key term. True poets, he asserts, 'imitate both to delight and teach' and, he goes on, 'delight, to move men to take that goodness in hand, which without delight they would fly as from a stranger; and teach, to make them know that goodness whereunto they are moved'. Here the discussion of mimesis is joined with the standard Horatian formula of delighting and teaching, pleasure and profit, overlaid by the Protestant insistence that knowledge alone is never sufficient to change the will and produce effective action. 'Delight' captivates a reader; 'moving' produces an effect on the will, since, Sidney argues, switching back to an Aristotelian dictum, 'as Aristotle saith', it is not *gnosis* but *praxis* which 'must be the fruit' of teaching. He talks further of the poet's powers to move readers by arguing that 'truly I have known men that even with reading Amadis de Gaule . . . have found their hearts moved to the exercise of courtesy, liberality, and especially courage'.[38]

Such statements still seem to preserve the determinative nature of the writer's intention – that the 'great' poet, say, communicates a 'message' to an essentially passive audience. But in fact something much more interesting is going on here. Sidney confesses that poetry's ability to move its readers is not predictable or automatic; readers may not be moved at all, or may not translate vision into praxis. Poetic power is, as Ferguson has argued, 'viewed as a circuit of energy which goes from author to work to reader', and that energy can be diverted, adapted or resisted, as well as used for direct illumination. Poetry directs us to self-study; it opens the possibility of discovering virtue in ourselves, of becoming the way we might extend or explore the self, but it also opens the possibility of error. When we read, we temporarily adopt a new 'self', one suggested by the poem and our experience of reading it. The play between that flickering self, the self with which we started to read the poem, and the reconstituted self we have when we finish reading it is, as Sharratt has argued, part of the essential value of reading poetry.[39]

Reading and introspection, then, are closely linked in some theoretical discussions; they are also prominent in the poetry. In *Astrophil and Stella*, for instance, we are watching the early stages in England of what is to become the striking 'open form' of baroque art – dynamic, stressing indeterminacy of effect, disruption and broken surfaces, dilated space, illusory and relativistic effects, inducing the spectator to shift viewpoint continually, thus emphasizing how the work's meanings are partial, kinetic and continually metamorphosing. The emphasis is increasingly on the active, inventive role of the spectator who becomes an actor, a participant in the work's meanings. The result, as Barthes puts it, is to make the reader no longer merely a consumer, but 'a producer' of the text.[40] The best poetry of this whole period is characterized by this kind of rich and subtle sense of audience. Dunbar's poems to the Queen of Scotland play to and with his anticipated primary audience of her court ladies and their aristocratic friends. Wyatt's 'Who So List to Hunt' creates a world where love and its uneasy place in Court are self-consciously described in general terms, with the poem inviting the members of its audience to read their own individual and collective experiences into the lines they hear.

It has often been argued that one of the major technological break-throughs of the Renaissance was the printing press. Speech was accorded an apparent permanence and audiences given an accessibility to writing in ways that revolutionized the spread of ideas and the comprehension of writing. Yet, for all its obvious manifestations such as the encouragement to poets to publish rather than have their works circulate in manuscript, the printing of poetry only gradually changed the ways poets thought about language itself. Part of the strength of sixteenth-century poetry remains its closeness to the oral tradition. We are not dealing with monumentalized texts but with texts (even, in a sense, scripts) for performance, not with an authoritative authorial voice but with performative writing. Writing is inaugural, open, and therefore often (in the eyes of *homo seriosus*, like Fulke Greville) dangerous. This is something of which the editor of Tottel's *Miscellany* was aware when he created, by adding titles to the poems he collected, the persona of 'the lover' through whose authorized words we are meant to read the poems. As Kamholtz notes, 'the very act of titling – asserting the presence of a speaker and frequently proposing moral *sententiae* imposes some distinction on the courtly lyrics, as does the change from manuscript to printed word. The printed poem belongs to a different political context and a different literary tradition'.[41] The oral-acoustic primacy of language, marked in the closeness of poetry and oratory, does gradually become replaced by a more intentionalist and instrumentalist view based on the primacy of authorial will, but it is a transition that does not take place overnight and, indeed, perhaps has never been fully completed in that the strongest modern poetry remains closest to the speaking voice. And it is perhaps only in recent years that we have once again started to take seriously a reader-centred understanding of literary cognition. Now we know that when we read we assimilate information and make associations in relation to an already existing and always changing view of the world. It is the reader's cognitive processes that create the reading, not the author's intentions. Even though sixteenth-century poets were indeed worried about that realization – someone like Greville, for instance, would have viewed it as one more instance of man's sinfulness – they were, oddly enough, more aware of the issues involved in reading than any theorists before the twentieth century. In developing a reader-centred cognitive model or pedagogy, today's educational theorists are returning to something of which the sixteenth-century poets were, at least, dimly aware.

My discussion of the close and fruitful connections between poetry and oratory, intention and reception, has brought another important issue into sight. The very power of language was becoming a matter of both celebration and fear. Many Elizabethan theorists praised language that was copious (*copia*); the ability to create multiple meaning from language was seen as one of its distinctive features. The various possibilities of language differentiated it from the 'brazen' world of Nature in that language's central characteristic was such multiplicity. Its pleasure was in variation, copiousness, in the transgressions of daily speech. Although *periphrasis* was one of the rhetorical devices by which a poem might be composed, such a 'paraphrase' was certainly not seen as identical with the poem. One of the defining characteristics of the rhetorical mode of writing was that 'one fable could not only yield many glosses, but that it was expected to do so'. Words generated other words and other matter.[42]

Hence the mixture of celebration and anxiety that many Elizabethan scholars and educators showed towards their language. Some complained that the Latin and Greek languages were too 'copious and plentiful', or criticized their 'inkhorn terms', just as they did dialect or archaism. Yet other writers perceived that the inrush of new experiences in the age meant, in Ralph Lever's plaintive but revealing phrase, that there were 'more things, then there are words to express things by', or in Richard Mulcaster's more reasoned judgement, that 'new occasions' bring 'furth new words'.[43] Such a bountiful overflowing of new language had immense consequences for poetry. But there was often a sense of alarm that language's multiplicity might get out of hand, and a desire that it should be disciplined and controlled, and so cleansed, as Nashe put it, 'from barbarisme'. To make the language 'gorgeous and delectable' was one thing; to make it a hodgepodge was plainly unacceptable, especially in a society where political and cultural control was paramount. Language, in the words of Tottel's preface, should be 'to the honor of the Englishe tong, and for profit of the studious of Englishe eloquence'.[44] Social order might be threatened by a language run riot. It is not merely a literary argument being advanced when Puttenham insists that the language of poetry is that of the Court and its environs.

In short, once again, we distort the significance of poetry and poetical theory if we isolate them from their socio-cultural contexts. As Eagleton has pointed out, the systematic literary and rhetorical treatises of the age analyse not merely the 'literary' value of figures and schemes, tropes and arrangement, but the material effects of particular use of language within broader cultural contexts. What we call 'criticism' or 'literary theory', they called 'rhetoric' and saw it explicitly as the instrument of training the governors and members of the ruling class in the techniques of political domination. Puttenham's book is, as Javitch, Montrose and others have shown, a guide to the procedures of gaining and maintaining political power by the means of controlling language: 'rhetoric emerged as a discourse theory utterly inseparable from the social relations' of the Elizabethan ruling class, the members of which, orator, poet and courtier alike, shared not only common political but stylistic characteristics. The decorum of which Puttenham and others repeatedly speak is consistently identified with proper conduct, a sense of disciplined grace in social situations, in which 'the good maker or

poet . . . ought to know the comeliness of an action as well as of
a word'. Puttenham's discussion of rhetorical figures concentrates on
what he terms 'sensible' figures, which 'alter and affect the mind by
alteration of sense', and in particular the quintessential court figure,
Allegoria, 'which is when we speake one thing and thinke another'.
Any courtier who cannot employ such a 'figure of false semblant or
dissimulation' is 'sure never or seldome to thrive and prosper in the
world', and Puttenham speaks likewise of the poet as a dissembler,
a 'counterfeiter', paralleling the different kinds of poetry to court
practices, and to what Spenser calls 'the use of these days'.[45]

Metre, vernacular, language

I have looked at some of the diverse traditions of thought that feed into
the sixteenth-century discussions of poetry. I want now to illustrate one
or two particular issues that preoccupied theorists and poets during the
century. The first is whether classical prosody could be adapted into
English verse. Throughout the century, there were attempts, made
notably by academics and some members of the Sidney Circle, to adapt
classical metres to English. Classically trained scholars found syllabic
and rhyming verse barbarous; Spenser noted that Sidney had devised a
set of rules and observations on the principles of the art. But although
Sidney, the Countess of Pembroke, Fraunce, Campion and others
produced workmanlike examples, the rapid changes in spelling, idiom,
and flexibility that English was undergoing would simply not conform
to any academic's desire to discipline a living language. In the *Defence*
Sidney had argued that 'ryming and versing' did not make a poet, and
in the *Arcadia*, the shepherds Dicus and Lalus argued along lines that
would have been familiar to Sidney and his Circle. Dicus speaks of the
'secret music' and constant variety of poetry which can be achieved by
appropriately measured words; Lalus argues that poetry must appeal to
the intellect as well as the musical sense and 'he that rhymes observes
something the measure but much the rhyme, whereas the other attends
only measure without all respect of rhyme; besides the accent which the
rhymer regardeth, of which the former hath little or none'. Hamilton
comments 'the history of English poetry shows Lalus wins the debate.
Quantitative verse failed because the English language is strongly and
stubbornly stressed.' Sidney likewise said that 'though we doo not
observe quantitie, yet wee observe the Accent verie precisely'.[46]
   Like Senecan closet drama, a literary experiment that the Sidneys
also supported, quantitative verse was one of the dead ends of late

Elizabethan cultural development. Yet in the 1570s and through the 1590s, quantitative experimentation was widely seen as one possible way of creating an independent and learned literature in England. As part of the humanists' reforms, Elizabethan schoolchildren were brought up to accept and respond to quantity in scanning classical verse, to recognize the harmony of quantitative metres from the way a poet manipulated the lines' oral qualities. From Ascham onwards, pedagogues and poets attempted to wrestle the unco-operative vernacular into quantitative verse, finding, as classically trained scholars, the mere counting of syllables and the barbarity of rhyme somewhat simple alongside the sophistication of Latin verse, which appealed to the learned mind because of its difficulty and the technical skills required for its composition. Consequently, as Attridge remarks in the most comprehensive and sympathetic recent treatment of the Elizabethan Quantifiers, 'the experiments were the natural result of the attitudes to verse and metre inculcated by the grammar schools', and were thus a typical expression of the age's beliefs in the value of education.[47] Classical versification was one of the major interests of the European humanist movement, and Sturm, Ramus, Baif, Estienne and Lipsius, among others, had written quantitative verse. Given the distinctly pedagogical orientation of English humanism, it was an experiment that was inevitably going to be made, even if, with rare exceptions, it turned out to be a dead end. It also, one might charitably concede, represents the willingness to experiment that characterizes so much of the Elizabethan poetic revolution.

In October 1579 Spenser wrote to Harvey that 'the twoo worthy Gentlemen, Master SIDNEY and Master DYER' have proclaimed 'a generall surceasing and silence of balde Rymers . . . in steade whereof, they have, by autho[ri]tie of their whole Senate, prescribed certaine Lawes and rules of Quantities of English sillables for English Verse'. Later the same month he writes again requesting these 'Rules and Precepts of Arte' which Harvey has devised, or requesting his friend to 'followe mine, that M. Philip Sidney gave me, being the very same which M. Drant devised, but enlarged with M. Sidneys own judgement, and augmented with my Observations'.[48] As the correspondence proceeded, Spenser came to have more doubts on the practicality of the scheme. The document to which Spenser referred is preserved in the St John's College, Cambridge, manuscript of the *Old Arcadia*. It is a brief guide to the determination of English syllabic quantities, based upon recognizable classical rules, while attempting throughout to allow for the idiom of ordinary English speech. In his own verse, too, Sidney seems to have followed the general rule of a prosody modelled on Latin but, as far as possible, considered common English pronunciation. Many of the eclogues in the *Arcadia* use quantitative verse, phaleuciacs for instance, in 'Reason, tell me thy mind, if here be reason' and irregular asclepiads in 'O sweet woods the delight of solitariness' (Eclogues 33 and 34). Some poems in Davison's *Poetical Rhapsody* used phaleuciacs; and Campion's 'Rose-cheeked Laura' is probably the one acknowledged masterpiece of the movement.[49]

What were the Quantifiers attempting to do? The fundamental metrical pattern of classical scansion is based upon the duration of syllables, which were divided into short and long, and which were combined in different measures. The basic problem for the experimenters in England – as in Italy or France – was to adapt fixed syllabic rules to a language without established punctuation or spelling. Another crucial problem involved the adaptation of the movement of a line to ensure forceful and idiomatic movement. Hence the caesura was crucial in the handling of a line, permitting rhythmical breaks in the quantitative structure. The successful versifier thus had to be extraordinarily sensitive not only to a highly intellectual structure but to the cadence of his lines. Campion comments that ditties and odes may be 'compounded' in 'simple numbers' and yet still maintain the rules of scansion. But Campion, Davis notes, is 'the last champion of that Quixotic attempt Sidney had inaugurated . . . to adapt the accentual language to the quantitative scansion and verse forms of Latin poetry'.[50]

Directly contrary to the quantifying movement was the movement towards the gradual regularization and developing cultural dominance of the iambic pentameter. Easthope likens the development of pentameter to that of linear perspective in art and harmony in music: it is a historical creation, naturalized by the buoyant court culture of the century as the dominant metre of English poetry. It is well established by the time of Tottel's *Miscellany* and Puttenham's praise of Wyatt and Surrey as the first reformers of English verse is the culmination of a deliberate promotion of 'the "properly" poetic from the "improperly" poetic, poetry from verse'. The pentameter came through as the dominant representation of the poet's 'real' voice. It became identified with the 'I' of the poem and attempted to interpellate, or construct, a 'natural' representation of the reader who is asked to identify with the poet's apparent voice. Stevens sees both Tottel and the *Mirror* as crucial in such a development. The metrical revolution of the sixteenth century, the ' "Tottelization" of English metre', he argues, involved a 'verbal individualism' that no longer represented a common speech, but emphasized the 'voice of performance'.[51]

What we sense in such struggles and contradictions are tensions far beyond the 'literary'. On the one hand, this is a culture of image-makers, of the promiscuous multiplication of signs, of *copia*. Perhaps for the first time in Western culture, as Foucault has argued, we find

revealed the absolutely open dimension of a language no longer able
to halt itself, because, never being enclosed in a definite statement, it
can express its truth only in some future discourse which 'does not
have the power to halt the progression, and what it says is enclosed
within it like a promise, a bequest to yet another discourse'.[52] But then,
on the other hand, alongside such celebration of textuality, we must
note as well the growing tide of hostility to Renaissance logophilia.
The promiscuity of language is continually confronted by an anxiety
to find ways of limiting its meanings and power. The tireless repetition
of commonplaces, the search for gnomic utterance, the popularity of
emblem and referential allusion in allegory are also features of the age.
It is as if a plethora of expression were constantly being bullied into
knots of meaning, much in the way that the Protestant propagandist
marked the margins of his text by 'Mark ye this, ye hogges and dogges'
or 'Here be sound doctrine'. What is at stake in Protestant attacks on
poetry, romance, images, is ultimately a deep suspicion of writing.
Words let loose meaning, and as Protestantism tended to read the
Bible, the word, preached, proclaimed and valorized in the authorized
Word of the living God is acceptable only in that it is (if received by
the Elect) unvarying and closed. But human words, overflowing in the
materiality of signs into history, let loose a promiscuity of writing that
ends in damnation. By what miracle can words, black marks on a white
page, become bearers of truths? It is a question that haunts Protestant
intellectuals and poets, like Spenser and Greville. In *Caelica* and *The
Faerie Queene* there is a problematic relationship between words and
meaning, writing and representation: every attempt to approximate
truth is necessary yet feared because it will inevitably dissolve into an
infinity of random signifiers.

It is often argued that the first signs of the autonomy of fiction arise
from the sixteenth century's anxiety about writing. As we have seen,
the conventional defences of poetry – that it is an ancient art praised by the
greatest authorities, that it has a moral force more powerful than related
arts – betray some uneasiness about the intersection between language
and history. Where Protestants insisted that human powers be accorded
as little access to truth as possible, Sidney insists that the poet, 'freely
ranging only within the zodiac of his own wit' creates his own world.
Yet, uneasily, contradictorily, he none the less insists on the power of
poetry to refer to and influence our world. He argues that 'the poet . . .
nothing affirms, and therefore never lieth'; he 'never affirmeth . . . never
maketh any circles about your imagination, to conjure you to believe for
true what he writes'. If the essential feature of poetry is its 'feigning',
then its cultural site is a distinctive one, neither referential like history
nor abstract and disconnected from the particular, like philosophy. As
Levao argues, Sidney does not explicitly argue for 'fiction' over 'fact';

but he suggests that any attempt to make sense out of the world is based on illusion, and that poetry is thus a special instance of the fictionality that pervades all discourse.[53] Thus humanity's only access to understanding is through fiction. It is this *copia*, this open-endedness of both writing and reading, which Sidney's friend Fulke Greville so distrusted, which constitutes one essential characteristic of poetry in the *Defence*.

Class, race, gender, agency

In reading sixteenth-century poetry today, we become aware of such striking historical differences: even when the language has seemingly changed little, the range of meanings and especially the dominant meanings to which words point may well have changed radically. When we look at the material practices of sixteenth-century society (as distinct from the dominant and conflicting ideas), we find even more radical differences. Yet we may find some intriguing continuities that are also registered in the language of the poems: as Norbrook and Woudhuysen note, for instance, Renaissance humanists 'have something in common with post-modern and feminist writers who have tried to reaffirm rhetorical play against philosophical asceticism', attacking the 'aridities of metaphysics' and breaking down the 'clear-cut distinctions between philosophy, rhetoric and poetry'.[54] I want briefly to consider the interconnection of historical difference and continuity in our reading of the period, and to do so by concentrating on four categories of analysis that make up elements of any period's ideology, the matters of class, race, gender and agency.

The class basis of the age's dominant poetry is blatant. In *The Arte of Poesie*, Puttenham wrote about a century after Caxton printed the *Morte d'Arthur*, a collection of prose tales based on Arthurian legends, and incorporating much folk or popular material, and he poured scorn on all popular ballads and narratives, what he called 'stories of old time . . . old Romances or historical rimes, made purposely for recreation of the common people at Christmasse diners and brideales, and in taverns and alehouses, and such other places of base resort', as well as 'Carols and rounds and such light or lascivious Poemes'. The key phrase here is 'common people'. Puttenham's theory of poetry makes no secret of its class interests. All these, he scornfully concludes, 'in our courtly maker we banish . . . utterly'.[55] His agenda, and Sidney's less aggressive but clearly class-biased goal have, by and large, triumphed, at least until recently, in what subsequent literary history has regarded as the canonical works from this period. The names of the poets and the kinds of poetry that have been reprinted, anthologized and taught from this period may not exactly be those praised by Puttenham, but they would largely have met with his approval. Most of the poetry that has survived is poetry that was in some way connected with the Court, predominantly written by or for or in imitation of the aristocracy. Some alternatives to this canon will be offered in Chapters 8 and 9.

In regard to race, the sixteenth century sees, although belatedly on a European scale, the rise of a vigorous nationalism in England. Among other matters, it affected the choice of language for poetry. The question of the appropriateness of the vernacular had been raised much earlier by poets and politicians in the Courts of Italy and France; it surfaces in English from about the middle of the century onwards. Puttenham's patriotic ideal of 'an Art of our English Poesie, as well as there is of the Latine and Greeke'[56] is a belated echo of Dante and Petrarch, Boccaccio or Ariosto. 'Our national tong is rude . . . our language is so rusty' bewailed Skelton, early in the century; in English, unlike Latin and Greek, everything is expressed in 'a manner so meanly, bothe for the matter and handelynge, that no man can do worse', is Ascham's similar opinion fifty years later. In *The Elementarie* (1582), Mulcaster asks that the English develop 'the verie same treasur in our own tung', noting 'I love the *Latin* but I worship the *English*'. The doubts about English were partly caused by its supposed lack of dignity. It was 'symple and rude' – again, we should note the class bias – and lacking the 'gaye termes of rethoryk', as Caxton noted late in the previous century. And there were seemingly practical considerations. There was no standard form of English. Where Latin was the language of the learned, the vernacular was subject to change and variation, and was therefore deemed appropriate only for vulgar usage. Many writers felt acutely that English lacked an aureate diction suitable for ceremonial or complimentary poetry since, as Hawes put it in *The Pastyme of Pleasure*, 'elocucyon/doth ryght wel clarify/The dulcet speche/frome the language rude', thereby making explicit the class bias of courtly diction. Nationalistic, political and religious pressures over the century brought more and more educationalists and writers to try to improve the language – by adopting archaisms, dialect words, or by imitating classical or Italian syntax – in short by augmenting vocabulary and syntax to make English more dignified.[57]

Such matters preoccupied English poets throughout the century. Indeed, most of the century's poetry may be seen as a workshop in which the poets fumbled, under socio-cultural pressures they did not fully comprehend, for acceptable language and form. Wyatt's innovations in adapting Petrarchan modes are less important than his struggles in forging a flexible syntax and a sparse, effective vocabulary; Grimald's verse, which was also collected by Tottel, was written in part to see whether latinisms, archaisms, and compounds could augment the language. However dull much mid-century poetry seems – consider E. K.'s protest in his notes to Spenser's *Shepheardes Calendar* against the 'rakehellye route of our ragged rhymers' and the attacks on those who have 'made our English tongue a gallimaufray or hodgepodge of all other speeches'[58] – for fifty and more years, English was buoyantly expanded, polished, augmented, and thus made more flexible for poetry. Being 'English' was starting to acquire some distinctive ideological resonance. The consolidation of national states, part of the long-term political developments in the Renaissance, took a distinctive pattern in Britain. The union of England and Wales had been achieved by the establishment of administrative units called 'marches' and the establishment of a lord deputy. The Welsh language and its tribal culture was progressively marginalized in what Raymond Williams termed a series of 'forced and acquired discontinuities', which relate not to some submerged essence but to the material 'realities of subordination'. Successive generations of a Welsh landowning class were Anglicized and the Welsh language was made the 'object of systematic discrimination and, where necessary, repression'.[59] The union of Scotland was celebrated but not completed in law under James (Sixth of Scotland and First of England), but – as Spenser was to discover – Ireland was a different matter. Spenser lived most of his adult life in Ireland. He became not merely the apologist for a monarch and a Court that, after 1580, he was rarely to visit, and then with a sense of bewilderment and betrayal, but for a policy of such racist brutality that even Lewis, Ulsterman and admirer of Spenser, summed up his views in remarkably strong terms: 'Spenser was the instrument of detestable policy in Ireland, and in his fifth book [of *The Faerie Queene*] the wickedness he had shared begins to corrupt his imagination'.[60] Like *The Tempest*, Spenser's epic registers some of the great contradictions that characterized imperialism; unlike Shakespeare, Spenser had a direct material stake in the racism that motivated the imperial enterprise.

The matter of being 'English' became, then, an important dimension of writing poetry. It becomes caught up in what was for some three hundred years a narrowing to the politically and socially dominant conception of 'Englishness': as Williams points out, before about 1550 and after 1900, we must think more of the varieties of dialect and languages and a wider spectrum of social and political voices than those that are covered by the exclusive title of being 'English'. Spenser is arguably the first poet of the new English imperialism that was to reach its dominance in the Empire of the late nineteenth and early twentieth centuries.

Race, and what we call today 'ethnicity', then, provide an emerging dimension of the age's poetics. Gender is the most complex, perhaps, of the cultural dimensions of the period's thinking about poetry. The majority of the poets of this period were men. That seeming triviality is in fact fundamental to our understanding of the kinds of poetry they wrote and a great deal besides in the period. The impact of feminism upon our rewritings of our pasts has been, in recent years, profound: gender, we have learnt, is not a characteristic with which one is born, nor a stable mode of categorization, either across history or within the life of an individual subject. Nor is it neutral to the writing or reading of poetry. Our gender assignments are a fundamental factor in the ways we conceive of our lives. It is all the more important, therefore, in writing of an age in which gender assignments were rigidly conceived, that we should ask what difference did it make, not least to his poetry, that most of the poets whose writings have survived were men.

'Being' a man is a question-begging phrase, in fact. We need rather to ask: What was it for Spenser or Sidney, say, to be born and socialized into assumptions and practices that were labelled as male? Most critical and scholarly treatments of the period, at least until very recently, have assumed that questions of gender are not relevant. Shepherd further points out that most of the critics, too, have been men: writing on *The Faerie Queene*, he argues that overwhelmingly a 'male-authored poem is serviced by' male editors and critics 'for a male readership'.[61] Gender roles can, of course, theoretically be organized by any number of categories, even though in many societies they may be identified with the presence or absence of supposedly fixed biological characteristics. What are assumed to be the 'essential' values of being a man in the sixteenth century? And how do they affect being a poet? The first characteristic is the assumption of the naturalness, indeed the virtue, of masculine dominance and aggression, most obviously seen in, though by no means confined to, military aggression. *The Faerie Queene* is one of the major monuments in our cultural history of such an ethos. Paglia argues that 'Spenser is history's first theorist of aggression', with his questing knights embodying an Appollonian hostility to Nature, and conquering the ever-threatening female urges of an unruly Nature. The knights' armour is, she argues, 'a male exoskeleton', the embodiment of 'the hardness of western will'. Her argument is an intriguing, even alarming, one, not least because it is put forward by a woman explicitly in the face of feminism's critique of western patriarchal gender stereotypes: 'feminists', asserts Paglia, 'seeking to drive power relations out of sex, have set themselves against nature. Sex is power. Identity is power. In western culture, there are no nonexploitative relationships'.

She celebrates the intimate link between the Western male psyche and ideologies of virility and domination, seeing the 'testing and purification of the male will' through struggle, control, and the violent imposition of intellect upon nature, especially as (literally) embodied in the female, as the triumph of our cultural history. For many of us today, men and women, this will seem unsupportable nonsense, but it may be persuasive to some, since the assumption that men are more naturally aggressive is deeply rooted in our culture, and the 'naturalness' of aggression is clearly a major ingredient of the age's poetry.[62] In sixteenth-century England, there was a multitude of cultural experiences in which male aggression was reified as a seemingly natural process, and not only in the most obvious manifestations of war and politics. The structuring of a vast range of experience by a pattern of rivalry and conquest points to the dominant ideology from which, of course, today we are hardly immune.

The code of chivalry, flourishing long after its military and political relevance were gone, is most certainly directly relevant to the age's poetry. Throughout the sixteenth century, English political organization and military technology altered drastically, rendering most of the specifically military aspects of chivalry obsolete; yet the trappings of chivalry, most visibly in the form of tournaments, like the annual Accession Day tilts, greatly intensified. The chivalry of *The Faerie Queene* may have seemed archaic to many of its original readers, but the ideology of masculinity and personal honour that it enacted were far from dead, not least in formulating the allegiances into which both men and women were indoctrinated. Tournaments were, in Elizabethan society, a major institution designed to display what was seen as the essence of nobility, the ritualized expression of violence in the service of an ideal cause. As Shakespeare's *Troilus and Cressida* dramatizes so effectively, the early seventeenth-century may have seen the growing dominance of newer technologies of war and different strategies of mass destruction from those of chivalry, but the traditional view of the aristocratic male warrior as an innocent, idealistic (and humanistically educated) youth lived on as both an individual and collective fantasy. By the time Sidney, Greville and other noblemen were taking part in chivalric rituals, they had become means to assert a man's commitment to martial violence and to allow him to display himself to advantage within the usually less overtly physical aggression of the Court's political and social rivalries. In *The Booke of Honor and Armes* (1590), Sir William Segar noted the continued dominance of at least the ideology of chivalric combat: 'each particular Gentleman or other person professing Honor and Armes, ought sufficientlie bee moued thereunto for defence of his owne particular reputation'. As McCoy points out, by the time Segar is writing the goal is clearly 'the regulation and containment of violence', so that the tourney becomes a form of 'conflict negotiation'. But the underlying ideology of masculinity as aggression is untouched. When an embassy from England visited the Landgrave of Hesse in 1596, for instance, a combat 'betwixt jest and earnest' was arranged, with the knights of Hesse announcing that they desired 'not to make devises, but to show their manhood'.[63]

The knights, tourneys, challenges, and skirmishes which make up such a overwhelming part of The Faerie Queene and which are referred to in many of Sidney's sonnets, therefore require to be read not merely as a part of the background of the age's poetry, but as a revelation of the gender politics of the poetry. The chivalric ideal of the age is epitomized in the Penshurst portrait of Philip Sidney, in partial armour, one hand on hip, the other holding a sword, the essential hero, 'untrammeled', as Quilligan points out, 'by any social context', as if the values he represents were absolute, unalterable by historical accident or even death. He embodies the ideology (though Paglia would not accept that distancing phrase) of what she terms 'the hardness of western will'.[64]

Margaret Mahler suggests that behind such masculinist values lies what she terms the phenomenon of 'the not-fully-born', a recurring masculine pattern by which many men achieve ego stability only in relation to the demands of outside authorities. Such men are violent and frequently destructive, and what impels their violence and destruction – however it may be transferred into socially approved activities like war – is a childhood failure fully to differentiate, and a consequent 'fear and longing for fusion' with some greater, authoritative power that might prevent their fragmentation. What such a personality has to fall back on for its stability are fantasies of incorporation into larger bodies. These bodies represent mother surrogates, idealized authority figures to represent the mothering figures they both want to return to and separate from. Chivalry and the monarchistic state, so strongly celebrated in Spenser, and so dominant in the ideologies of the age, clearly provided such a structure for men in early modern England.[65]

The poetry of the sixteenth century is also populated by women. In asking the question, 'what was it to be a man?' we cannot neglect the question 'what was it to be a woman?' – and ask it both from a woman's point of view, and a man's. What were (and, for that matter, are) the 'male fantasies', to refer to the title of Theweleit's suggestive analysis of western masculinity, by which men deal with the women in their lives?[66] The poems of the age, especially in the Petrarchan tradition, which will be the major focus of Chapter 3, reveal that just as women learn to disguise their forbidden masculine wishes behind a stereotype of female innocence, weakness and self-sacrifice, so men learn to disguise their forbidden feminine wishes behind a stereotype of male virility. Such fears of otherness underlie much of Petrarchism: fear, mastery, distaste, attitudes which express a need but which seem unable to recognize women as different but like subjects.

The consequence of such a pattern may be the early idealization of women as all-powerful objects to whom the boy looks for nurture and protection at the same time as he seeks to differentiate himself from them and becomes aware that what constitutes him as a man involves rejecting what Shakespeare terms the 'woman's part' in himself. In adult life, a pattern may be established whereby he continually tries to recreate this primitive maternal bond, and yet seeks continually to break from it: 'what boys seem to need most from the mother and continue to need and, as lovers and husbands, go on to get from other women is an all-present but unobtrusive Mother who is willing to stand by in the wings ready to rescue the mighty acrobat as he recklessly hurls his body through the open spaces', thus becoming one of Paglia's 'questing knights, isolated against empty panoramas' that she sees in *The Faerie Queene* and throughout western history, replaying the male's primitive struggle to tame (female) Nature.[67] As she puts it, 'Men know they are sexual exiles. They wander the earth seeking satisfaction, craving and despising, never content. There is nothing in that anguished motion to envy'. In this pattern of repudiation and return – a pattern we shall observe repeatedly in Petrarchan poetry – men's search for that ambivalent lost object will frequently be 'represented by an endless series of substitutive objects none of which, however, brings full satisfaction'. Are these contradictions inherent in being male? Or in being male within patriarchal society? At the very least there is such continuity in western history in the male fantasies about women that we can continue to observe that the conjunctions of attraction/repulsion, fascination/abhorrence and dependence/dominance have an uncanny historical continuance. As Freud put it in his essay on the Mona Lisa, men fear women's sexuality as 'ruthlessly demanding – consuming men as if they were alien beings'.[68] As we shall see when we look at Books 3 and 4 of *The Faerie Queene*, much of the eroticization of women in the Elizabethan court – its caste of erotic titillation, the language of Petrarchism, the casting of political rituals in terms of the erotic, its fear of the devouring promiscuity attributed to women's sexual powers – can be linked to this fascination for and fear of women.

The chivalric atmosphere of so much sixteenth-century poetry, then, represents not only fantasies of class, but also fantasies of gender. The stereotypes of love and war, the traditional subjects of epic poetry, have traditionally been male; the quests, adventures, battles and heroic loves displayed the prototypical wish fulfilments of what Theweleit terms the 'soldier-males' of the feudal and post-feudal aristocracy. The passionate celebration of ritual violence were rituals of maturity, spiritual as well as physical rites of passage to establish a gender identity whose destructive effects remain with us today.

The final social characteristic of the sixteenth century's understanding of poetry is 'agency', by which I mean those social practices that human subjects view as means by which they can act in the world, with more or less autonomy, and so gain a sense of their own empowerment. What such acts are will vary from one historical period to the next. To what extent was poetry such an act in the sixteenth century? Sidney makes enormous claims for the transcendent power of the poet's mind – but, good Protestant that he is, qualifies his enthusiasm by reference to fallen human nature. A more material claim on behalf of the poet is made by Spenser, who self-consciously tried to construct a role for the professional poet within the State, as the Queen's and the State's most faithful servant. It is a view of the poet that is – for reasons that could not be foreseen – a major development in both English cultural history and in the history of attempts to define 'literature' and the shifting relations between it and other social practices.

As I will further explain in Chapter 6, Spenser is relatively unusual in the period in that the question of the vocation of a poet was, quite explicitly, a central one for the whole of his literary career. Most of his writings not only imply, but argue for, distinctive attributes for, and the social importance of, the poet. Today, living in a culture where the writing and reading of poetry are highly marginal cultural practices but in which our dominant educational structures still insist that poetry (along with novels, plays and other 'literary' forms) remain important, we might be intrigued to find just how seriously Spenser insisted he and his audience should take the function – one could almost say, using the religious term, the vocation – of being a poet. And yet it is clear from reading his writings and those of others who comment upon him that however certain Spenser may have been about the importance of poets and poetry to society (and we can widen the discussion and talk about artists and art generally), the detailed articulations of that importance not only change but contradict each other. At times Spenser appears uncompromising and confident; at others, uncertain or defensive. However marginal an activity it may be in any particular social formation, art usually constitutes a major site of ideological and material struggle, which may suggest that there is something worth struggling for. It is also an indication of the real, material marginality of poetry in the absolutist state. If human agency is to be expressed, it may perhaps be aided by poetry. But can it do more? The sixteenth-century poets remained very uneasy, and in Spenser's case, finally disillusioned by such a possibility.

Notes

1. Thomas Nashe, 'Preface to Greene's Menaphon', in *Elizabethan Critical Essays*, edited by G. Gregory Smith, 2 vols (Oxford, 1904),1, 318; George Puttenham, *The Arte of English Poesie*, edited by Gladys Doidge Willcock and Alice Walker (Cambridge, 1936), p. 21.

2. Compare Fredric Jameson: Genres are complex 'sociosymbolic messages or narrative constructs imbued with the [ideological] charge of a lived reality'. See *The Political Unconscious* (Princeton, 1980), p. 40.

3. Puttenham, p. 24.

4. Puttenham, pp. 25, 38, 42.

5. Miner, 'Assaying the Golden World', p. 7; S. K. Heninger, Jr, 'Speaking Pictures: Sidney's Rapprochement between Poetry and Painting', in *Sir Philip Sidney and the Interpretation of Renaissance Culture*, edited by Gary F. Waller and Michael D. Moore (London, 1984), pp. 3–16 (p. 15); and ' "Metaphor" and Sidney's Defence of Poesie', *John Donne Journal*, 1 (1982), 117–49 (p. 119); Michel Foucault, *The Order of Things* (New York, 1970), p. 32.

6. Ronald Levao, 'Sidney's Feigned Apology', *PMLA*, 94 (1979), 223–33 (pp. 223, 232).

7. Terry Eagleton, *Literary Theory. An Introduction* (Oxford, 1983), p. 18; Alan Sinfield, *Literature in Protestant England* (London, 1983), pp. 23, 270.

8. Robert Montgomery, *The Reader's Eye: Studies in Didactic Literary Theory from Dante to Tasso* (Berkeley, 1979), p. 1.

9. Sidney, *A Defence of Poetry*, in *Miscellaneous Prose of Sir Philip Sidney*, edited by Katherine Duncan-Jones and Jan van Dorsten (Oxford, 1973), pp. 81, 109, 120, 77, 78, 79.

10. C. S. Lewis, *English Literature in the Sixteenth Century excluding Drama* (Oxford, 1954), pp. 1, 2, 20, 28, 19.

11. For the *Mirror*, see *The Mirror for Magistrates*, edited by Lily B. Campbell (Cambridge, 1938).

12. Barnabe Googe, 'An Epitaph on the Death of Nicholas Grimald', in *English Renaissance Poetry*, edited by John Williams (New York, 1963), p. 96; William E. Sheidley, *Barnabe Googe* (Boston, 1981), p. 18; Roger Ascham, *The Scholemaster*, in *Elizabethan Critical Essays*, 1, 20.

13. Puttenham, pp. 26, 38.

14. Edmund Spenser, 'Colin Clouts Come Home Again', in *Spenser's Minor Poems*, edited by Ernest de Selincourt (Oxford, 1910), pp. 308, 327; Louis Adrian Montrose, 'Of Gentlemen and Shepherds: The Politics of Elizabethan Pastoral Form', *ELH*, 50 (1983), 415.

15. Sidney, *Defence*, p. 102.

16. Sidney, *Defence*, pp. 78, 79–80. Here I have, following Heninger, preferred Ponsonby's reading of 'imitation'; see ' "Metaphor"', pp. 120–29.

17. Terry Eagleton, *Walter Benjamin or Towards a Revolutionary Criticism* (London, 1981), p. 5.

18. Sinfield, *Literature in Protestant England*, p. 3; Sinfield, 'The Cultural Politics of the Defence of Poetry', in Waller and Moore, pp. 124–43 (p. 140).

19. Sinfield, 'Cultural Politics', p. 127.

20. S. K. Heninger Jr, *Touches of Sweet Harmony: Pythagorean Cosmology and Renaissance Poetics* (San Marino, 1974), p. 382.

21. Sidney, *Defence*, pp. 78, 79.

22. Jon A. Quitslund, 'Spenser's *Amoretti* VIII and Platonic Commentaries on Petrarch', *JWCI*, 36 (1973), 256–76 (p. 258).

23. Sidney, *Defence*, pp. 109, 119, 121; Heninger, 'Speaking Pictures', p. 9.

24. Sidney, *Defence*, p. 92. This paragraph draws on 'Critical Puritanism and the Elizabethan Lyric Poets', *English*, 21 (1972), 83–88.

25. Foucault, *Order of Things*, p. 33

26. Heninger, 'Speaking Pictures', p. 3; Thomas Nashe, *Works*, edited by R. B. McKerrow, revised by F. P. Wilson and W. W. Greg (revised edition, Oxford, 1958), 5 vols, III, 307.

27. Richard Lanham, *Motives of Eloquence: Literary Rhetoric in the Renaissance* (New Haven, 1976), p. 4.

28. Eagleton, *Benjamin*, p. 105.

29. Sidney, *Defence*, pp. 78, 81, 92.

30. Sidney, *Defence*, p. 78. See also O. B. Hardison Jr, 'The Two Voices of Sidney's Apologie for Poetrie', *ELR*, 2 (1972), 83–99 (p. 97).

31. Richard S. Peterson, *Imitation and Praise in the Poems of Ben Jonson* (New Haven, 1981), p. 4.

32. Heninger, ' "Metaphor" ', p. 144.

33. Jacqueline T. Miller, 'New Readings of Sidney', *SNew*, 3, no. 2 (1982), 12–15.

34. John Webster, ' "The Methode of a Poet": An Inquiry into Tudor Conceptions of Poetic Sequence', *ELR*, 11 (1981), 22–43.

35. Douglas L. Peterson, *The English Lyric from Wyatt to Donne* (Princeton, 1967), p. 51.

36. *The Poems of Sir Philip Sidney*, edited by William A. Ringler Jr (Oxford, 1962), p. xix; Puttenham, pp. 64, 137–38, 262; Marion Trousdale, *Shakespeare and the Rhetoricians* (London, 1982), p. 94.

37. Henry Peacham, *The Garden of Eloquence* (London, 1577), sig. A[3].

38. Sidney, *Defence*, pp. 92, 81, 91; Miner, 'Assaying the Golden World', p. 13.

39. A. Leigh De Neef, 'Rereading Sidney's Apology', *JMRS*, 10 (1980), 155–91 (p. 186); Margaret W. Ferguson, *Trials of Desire* (New Haven, 1983), p. 146; Bernard Sharratt, *Reading Relations* (London, 1983), pp. 16–24.

40. Cathleen M. Bauschatz, 'Montaigne's Conception of Reading in the Context of Renaissance Poetics and Modern Criticism', in *The Reader in the Text*, edited by Susan R. Suleiman and Inge Crosman (Princeton, 1980), pp. 266–91; Roland Barthes, *S/Z*, translated by Richard Miller (New York, 1974), pp. 15–16.

41. Jerome Z. Kamholtz, 'Thomas Wyatt's Poetry: The Politics of Love', *Criticism*, 20 (1978), 349–65 (p. 351).

42. Puttenham, p. 8; Trousdale, pp. 117, 125.

43. Ralph Lever, *The Arte of Reason* (London, 1573), foreword; Richard Mulcaster, *The First Part of the Elementarie*, edited by E. T. Campagnac (London, 1925), p. 172.

44. Nashe, *Works*, II, p.61; Francis Meres, in Smith, *Elizabethan Critical Essays*, II, 310; Richard Foster Jones, *The Triumph of the English Language* (Stanford, 1953), p. 5; *Tottel's Miscellany*, edited by Hyder Edward Rollins, revised edition (Cambridge, Mass., 1965), I, p. 28.

45. Eagleton, *Benjamin*, p. 101; Puttenham, pp. 276, 186; Sidney, *Defence*, p. 92; Puttenham, pp. 3, 298; Edmund Spenser, 'A Letter of the Authors', *The Faerie Queene*, edited by A. C. Hamilton (London, 1977), p. 737.

46. Sidney, *Works*, III, 10; *The Countess of Pembroke's Arcadia (the Old Arcadia)*, edited by Jean Robertson (Oxford, 1973), pp. 189, 90; Hamilton, Sidney, p. 63; Sidney, *Works*, III, 44.

47. Derek Attridge, *Well-Weighed Syllables: Elizabethan Verse in Classical Metres* (Cambridge, 1974), p. 113.

48. *Elizabethan Critical Essays*, I, 89, 99. For more detailed discussion, see G. L. Hendrickson, 'Elizabethan Quantitative Hexameters', *PQ*, 28 (1949), 237–6; Mary E. I. Underdown, 'Sir Philip Sidney's "Arcadian" Eclogues: A Study of his Quantitative Verse' (unpublished doctoral dissertation, Yale, 1961); William A. Ringler Jr, 'Master Drant's Rules', *PQ*, 29 (1950), 70–74.

49. *The Works of Thomas Campion*, edited by Walter R. Davis (London, 1969), pp. 309–10.

50. Campion, *Works*, p. xix.

51. Antony Easthope, *Poetry as Discourse* (London, 1983), pp. 65, 74; John Stevens, *The Old Sound and the New* (Cambridge, 1982), pp. 11, 15, 16, 17.

52. Foucault, *Order of Things*, pp. 38, 40.

53. Lewis, p. 319; Sidney, *Defence*, pp. 78, 102; Levao, p. 28.

54. Norbrook and Woudhuysen, *Renaissance Poetry*, p. 54.

55. Puttenham, p. 21.

56. Puttenham, p. 4.

57. John Skelton, 'Phyllyp Sparrow', *The Complete English Poems*, edited by John Scattergood (Harmondsworth, 1983), p. 91; Roger Ascham, Preface to *Toxophilus*, edited by Edward Asker (Westminster, 1895), p. 14; William Caxton, quoted by Vere L. Rubel, *Poetic Diction in the English Renaissance*

from Skelton through Spenser (New York, 1941), p. 1; William Hawes, *The Pastyme of Pleasure*, edited by W. E. Mead, *EETS*, 6, n. s. 73 (London, 1928), pp. 917–18; *English Poetry 1400–1580*, edited by William Tydeman (New York, 1970), p. 5; Tottel, p. 2.

58. Spenser, *Minor Poems*, pp. 5, 6.

59. Williams, *What I Came to Say*, pp. 59, 65–69.

60. Lewis, *English Poetry of the Sixteenth Century*, pp. 378–9.

61. Simon Shepherd, *Spenser* (London, 1989), pp. 60–1.

62. Camille Paglia, *Sexual Personae: Art and Decadence from Nefertiti to Emily Dickinson* (New York, 1991), pp. 173, 19, 10.

63. See e.g. Roy Strong, *Splendor at Court* (Boston, 1973), chs. 2, 6; Richard C. McCoy, *The Rites of Knighthood: the Literature and Politics of Elizabethan Chivalry* (Berkeley, 1990), pp. 23–24; William Segar, *The Booke of Honor and Armes*, ed. Diane Bornstein (Delmar, 1975), pp. 89–90; John Nichols, *The Progresses, Processions, and Magnificent Festivities, of King James the First* (London, 1828), 3, pp. 392–93.

64. Maureen Quilligan, 'Lady Mary Wroth: Female Authority and the Family Romance', in *Unfolded Tales: Essays on the Renaissance Romance*, edited by Gordon M. Logan and Gordon Teskey (Ithaca, 1989), pp. 274-98 (p. 276). Paglia, *Sexual Personae*, p. 173.

65. See Robert J. Stoller, *Perversion: The Erotic Form of Hatred* (London, 1975), p. 99; Klaus Theweleit, *Male Fantasies, Volume I: Women, Floods, Bodies, History*, trans. Stephen Conway (Minneapolis, 1987), I, p. 213; Jessica Benjamin, *The Bonds of Love: Psychoanalysis, Feminism, and the Problem of Domination* (New York, 1988), p. 135.

66. See Klaus Theweleit, *Male Fantasies, Volume I: Women, Floods, Bodies, History*, trans. Stephen Conway, Volume II: *Male Bodies: Psychoanalyzing the White Terror*, trans. Erica Carter and Chris Turner (Minneapolis: University of Minnesota Press, 1987, 1988).

67. Kaplan, *Female Perversions*, p. 107; Paglia, *Sexual Personae*, p. 173.

68. Paglia, *Sexual Personae*, pp. 19, 10; Freud, 'On the Universal Tendency to Debasement in Love', *The Standard Edition of the Works of Sigmund Freud*, ed. and trans. James Strachey *et al.* (London, 1952–66), XI, pp. 181, 189; 'Leonardo da Vinci and a Memory of his Childhood', *Standard Edition*, XI, p. 108.

Chapter 3
Erected Wit and Infected Will: Cultural Contradiction in the Lyric

The lyric

At the bottom of Puttenham's hierarchy of poetical kinds is the sixteenth-century poetry that today we tend to find most interesting, the lyric. We may want to describe it in less florid ways than Palgrave did more than a century ago, but it is Puttenham's 'meanest sort' which is to be 'used for recreation only' that has most excited readers over the last century or more. When Puttenham writes of how such poetry deals with 'the common solace of mankind in all his travails and cares of this transitorie life', he is referring to what we have come to see as perceptive, moving, 'individual' poems, especially the love poems of Wyatt, Sidney, Shakespeare and Donne. When we browse through an anthology of the age's poetry, we may find ourselves agreeing with Puttenham when he writes of how love 'of all other humane affections is the most puissant and passionate, and most general to all sortes and ages of men and women'. But we do not see poetry dealing with such subjects to be 'mean'. To be be fair, Puttenham does acknowledge that such subjects require special skills, 'a Poesie variable, inconstant, curious, and most witty of any others', whereby the 'many moodes and pangs of lovers' might 'thoroughly . . . be discovered'.[1] Here at last, we may surmise, is the stuff of which real poetry is made.

The reasons for the twentieth century's preference for the lyric are less a conscious repudiation of Elizabethan presuppositions about the superiority of longer, more prestigious forms like the epic than our own dominant literary and broader cultural ideologies. Within universities and colleges, Practical Criticism and New Criticism were demonstrably most successful with the short lyric which can (seemingly) easily be detached from history, read as an autonomous 'aesthetic' structure and subjected to formalist analysis. But deeper than that, the enormous prestige since the Romantics of the short lyric as the apparent revelation of sincere personal feeling (Wordsworth's 'spontaneous overflow of powerful feelings') helps modern readers to respond more easily to lyrics which can be very easily read as the expressions of direct personal feelings. Any teacher who has tried to disentangle the ideological strands from Ralegh's or Donne's lyrics knows the scepticism or disappointment of students indoctrinated with the potent if contradictory combination of New Critical formalism and naive Romanticism. Why should they look at what is 'not' there? Are not Sidney or Donne 'sincere'? Why not just enjoy (or laugh at) Astrophil and his rehearsing of 'poore Petrarch's long deceased woes'? Why not simply indulge themselves voyeuristically with Donne and his devious seductions of diverse women? Such poetry seems to resist what Richard Howard calls 'the prudency of ideological analysis': it seems to be attempting to create a 'site of bliss', not of contradiction (how strange that Barthes, the master semiotician of our time, can sound so close to Palgrave!) which reaches us 'across the centuries, out of certain texts that were . . . written to the glory of the dreariest, of the most sinister, philosophy'. Such poems seem to speak of 'all the pleasures which societies object to or renounce'.[2]

Unquestionably, an enthusiastic and sensitive teacher today should encourage in students of sixteenth-century lyric poetry manifold pleasures that go beyond either rapid consumption or extended academic analysis. There is no reason to feel ashamed to look up from the final lines of *Astrophil and Stella*, Sonnet 108 –

> So strangely (alas) thy works in me prevaile,
> That in my woes for thee thou art my joy,
> And in my joyes for thee my only annoy.

– and recognize that we have been there, we have wept with Astrophil, and laughed with Sidney, and learnt to see the conflicts and contradictions of love in our own experiences. Life, we may say, is often like that, and it is the function of poetry to illuminate such experiences for us. We are tempted to use generalizations about 'life' or the 'human condition' or 'love' in part because such powerful poems may push or seduce us into doing so – even if, intellectually, we are aware that such claims are ahistorical and all too readily ignore the material realities and contradictions of gender or class or race. Our time is, I suspect, especially vulnerable to the affectivity of the lyric: it seduces us much more easily than a long poem like *The Faerie Queene*, not only because it is easier to read, or at least takes a shorter time, but because its fragmentariness seems to answer to our own. Thus we have made Puttenham's least prestigious kind of poetry the kind by which we most appreciate sixteenth-century poetry.

It is not my desire to do anything but enhance the pleasure we get from reading sixteenth-century poetry, lyric or other. Lewis once remarked that 'if we are ever to "enter into the life of our ancestors" we must try to appreciate the *Arcadia* as well as the *Astrophil and Stella* (as if somehow we could 'enter into the life of our ancestors').[3] Likewise, modern readers may indeed come to enjoy *The Faerie Queene*, although it is difficult to imagine *A Mirror for Magistrates* producing what Barthes calls bliss except in the most sado-masochistic circumstances! But there is, in fact, a strong case to be made for the cultural centrality of the short poem in our understanding of the sixteenth century; and it is a case that can be made precisely because the lyric is Puttenham's least regarded form of poetry. But it is not the case which has traditionally been made.

The case starts by conceding that this lowly kind of poetry is apparently less significant in the public world than the celebration of the deeds of kings, the death of great men, and the moral virtues of public servants, which Puttenham argues should be the prime concerns of poets. Moreover, we need to acknowledge that despite the growing professionalization of writing towards the end of the century, much of the typical lyric poetry of the age is the work of amateurs, of part-time poets. Primarily courtiers or statesmen, they wrote occasionally, merely as a pastime, as part of the plumage of being a courtier. They disparaged the work for which we revere them. Yet it is precisely because sixteenth-century poets did not take their roles as poets as seriously as, say, Wordsworth, that their lyrics can be seen as central to our readings of the age. We can ask about how the public roles in fact overflowed into their poetry. Did it represent an escape for them from the pressures of the public world? Was poetry a kind of therapy? Or private revelation? Are Sidney or Ralegh pre-Romantics, acknowledging that the world is 'too much with us'? Or, if the poetry seems often deliberately to exclude the public role of the poet, what is the significance of that exclusion? Certainly, some poems in *Astrophil and Stella* and in other lyric collections do seem to be asserting that love is a private refuge, an escape from pressure and anguish. Such a view is taken to its extreme in the songs of the period, where a timeless world of music and harmony is evoked, where the individual human experience becomes uplifted into a realm of ideal celebration and beauty. It is seen quintessentially in the work of the poet-musicians Dowland or Campion in their melodious combination of the harmony of word and sound, calling, even as we read, for the sound of the lute, the swirl of court ladies' dresses, and the polite ripple of civilized courtly conversation. It is the lyric that one of my students described as 'upper-class musak'.

But, as Marvell was to write in the middle of the next century, 'at my back, I always hear/Time's winged chariot hurrying near'. Why, we might ask, is history, the material conditions of real existence, so politely (though no less ruthlessly for that) excluded from such poems? To what extent does the seeming absence of the historical distort or limit our readings of a seemingly innocuous lyric apparently written for sheer enjoyment? In fact – and here I begin the construction of a different case for the centrality of the lyric – the poet can be seen as a demystifier of the public order he serves precisely because of that innocuousness. He works on the seemingly innocent boundary between private and public languages, caught between conflicting cultural discourses which we can see struggling and rewriting one another. Because loss or absence seems to be the primary subject of the lyric, the form with all its variations and possibilities was able to articulate loss or absence of other experiences than love. Despite its apparent superficiality and marginal social role the lyric was uncannily able to articulate the significance of the complex relations between language and power, literary text and social text. What gives the sixteenth-century lyric its particular importance is the way in which even a literary kind which seems so culturally peripheral becomes a site of intense cultural struggles.

To demonstrate these assertions, in this chapter I am going to tease out two major discursive structures which wrestle within the age's lyric poems. They are Petrarchism and Protestantism. They are not the only structures of discourse which we can locate in the poetry, nor is the lyric the only literary form in which they can be found, but they provide us with a fascinating and far-reaching set of interactions and contradictions which are very useful for understanding, and enjoying, the poetry of the age.

The Englishing of Petrarch

'O Petrarke hed and prince of Poets all': thus Tottel's *Miscellany* introduces what for the whole period, especially in the last quarter of the century, became an increasingly powerful literary space. English lyric poetry in the sixteenth century is made up of the traces and struggles of many texts, but the single name that stands above them all is that of Petrarch, who gave not just Renaissance poetry, but Western discourse, one of the most hospitable conceptual schemes by which we have discussed sexual desire and its relationship with language. Francesco Petrarch (1304–74) is one of western Europe's seminal figures. His poems had, as Trinkaus puts it, a 'special relationship to the new mode of philosophical consciousness that was emerging in the Renaissance'.[4] Although regarded in his lifetime primarily as a historian, humanist and man of letters, it is through his vernacular poetry – the *Trionfi*, and in particular his lyric poetry, the *Canzoniere* – that much of Petrarch's impact was transmitted to later ages. His collection of lyrics written to Laura was started in the 1340s and given a definite shape almost twenty years later, a decade after the death (6 April 1348) of the woman whom Petrarch probably only knew slightly. By his death the *Canzonieri* had undergone some modifications, finally consisting of 366 sonnets, divided in two parts: 1–263 before Laura's death, 264–366 afterwards.

For three centuries the emergence of what Foucault has termed writing 'the truth of man's sex'[5] was mediated through Petrarch – or, more accurately, through what became known as Petrarchism. Generations of commentators and imitators elaborated a collective (mis)reading of his poetry of such potency that it was impossible to locate oneself within the discourse of writing sexuality into poetry outside the complex and inclusive code of Petrarchism. Commentaries on the poems abounded throughout the fifteenth century; major imitations of the poems were appearing in Italian at the same time, in Spanish in the late fifteenth century, and in French shortly after. By the time the English poets started to read him seriously, Petrarch had already been mediated by nearly 200 years of imitation and commentary. His poems were rewritten variously – as a diary of sexual desire, as a handbook of rhetorical ornamentation, as a systematic exposition of love. Petrarchism was adapted to other rival systems: to neoplatonism, Stoicism, Ovidian, and different versions of Christianity. Petrarchan poetry could be solemn, witty or blasphemous; Petrarch could be imitated slavishly or scurrilously mocked. Laura herself could be interpreted by neoplatonist commentators as an earthly lover drawing the soul towards Good, or towards God (as in Spenser's *Amoretti*); she could be presented as an erotically enticing yet tantalizingly frustrating court lady to be wooed, complained at, or scorned. What modern commentators have termed 'anti-Petrarchist' sentiments are as much a part of the Petrarchan mode as the more obviously serious poems for which Petrarch is revered as philosopher, psychologist, and master rhetorician: Shakespeare's seemingly anti–Petrarchan Sonnet 130 is a dramatic tribute to the power of Petrarchan commonplaces as the inevitable language within which poet and lover alike necessarily had to struggle:

> My mistress' eyes are nothing like the sun
> Coral is far more red than her lips' red
> If snow be white, why then her breasts are dun
> If hairs be wires, black wires grow on her head.

Donne's 'The Canonization' stands out in English poetry for its bravado and irreverence towards Petrarchan conventions, but it is not at all unusual alongside Italian poems of more than a century before which display similar panache.[6]

Let us first, then, look at Petrarchism as a flexible rhetoric of erotic desire. It rests on a series, even a system, of conventions about how love should be described. It sees love as a frustrating though inspiring experience, characterized by a melancholy yet obsessive balance between desire and hopelessness, possibility and frustration. Its fundamental characteristic is conflict, or – the key term in Petrarchism – 'paradox', usually expressed as a balance of powerful opposites, forces in or outside the lover which simultaneously move him on and hold him back. As Forster explains, 'later generations were less interested in the balance than in the antitheses' and it is 'this elaboration and exploitation which is the essence of Petrarchism'. While Forster warns us against describing Petrarchist poets as being conscious of working within a system – it was 'for them a natural mode of conventional utterance and conventional behaviour in certain circumstances'[7] – nonetheless, from our perspective, we can see Petrarchism as just that: a systematic ordering of the discourse of erotic desire. Today, even when we recognize frustration and contradiction as recurring parts of love, we tend to see Petrarchism as artificial, and finally (as I shall suggest soon) even destructive and exploitative. But that it seemed natural in the sixteenth century only goes to show how ideology, the social glue of a particular culture, works.

Now to the particulars of the system. Petrarchan poetry is written predominantly in the subject position of a suffering male lover contemplating a beloved's, usually (though not exclusively) a woman's, effects on him. From thousands of poems, a composite beloved can be readily composed, her physical parts described or modestly alluded to. She might have, in the conventional conceits of Ralegh's 'Nature that washt her hands in milk', such features as 'eyes of light', 'violet breath', 'lips of jelly'; typically her hair would be likened to wires, 'crisped', in the words of another Ralegh poem, her breasts compared to young does, and so forth. Such charms would often be set forth, either rapturously or satirically, in a catalogue poem (or 'blazon') listing the ravishing physical characteristics of the Petrarchan mistress, with her 'fayre golden hayres', her doe-like breasts, rosy cheeks, and other physical charms.[8] The most crucial characteristic is the contrast between her fair appearance and her icy or stony heart which inevitably causes the lover suffering. In the words of Ralegh's poem:

> At Loves entreaty, such a one
> Nature made, but with her beauty
> She hath framed a heart of stone,
> So as love by ill destiny
> Must dye for her whom nature gave him
> Because her darling would not save him.

Petrarchism focuses on physical characteristics less than their effect on the lover. Typically, the effect is expressed as what (I will soon suggest) we might fairly term masochism, as cruelty, distress, and pain. The lady's effects upon the lover are like fire, ice, blindness, torture, and yet the lover is inevitably drawn to her, even though he is puzzled and anguished over his self-torture. It is the combination of such effects which characterize the peculiar impasse of Petrarchan love. Sexual desire is at once repetition (and thus produces frustration) and transcendent (and thus produces hope) – and all at once. Frustration is balanced by hope, the love of God by the love of the world, humility by fame, passivity by restlessness, public by private, icy coldness by the fire of passion. Absence is a seeming necessity; presence is not conducive to poetry. Words arise only in absence and if the hoped for correspondence between word and desire occurs, usually the sequence closes.[9]

In describing the Petrarchan mistress and the love relationship thus, it can be seen how the mistress is entirely the product of the discourse in which she is placed. The second major characteristic of the Petrarchan poem is, therefore, that it is not just a rhetoric for declaring passionate but frustrated love which seems to focus on the depicting and idealizing of the beloved and to offer her patient, unrewarded service. It is rather a theatre of the lover's desires alone. Rarely are the beloved's desires accorded autonomy; rarely is there a desire for mutuality or negotiation. The beloved is the subject of the lover's anguish, manipulation and struggles of conscience. What does Petrarch's Laura reply to him? What does Stella reply to Astrophil's earnest self-regarding pleas for favour? We are told, occasionally, but her words are given to her by the poet. She is located within a discourse in which she is predominantly a focus of his gaze, obsessions and insecurities. The Petrarchan poet, then, could focus on the beloved's external beauties, her surroundings, even on the object of fetishization like her favourite pet, her handkerchief or other accoutrements; or her spiritual qualities of chastity, unapproachability, wisdom or virtue could be the objects of similar obsession. But the real focus is on her effects on the poet himself; she is the means by which his autonomy and identity can be established.

The world of Petrarchism is, then, unpredictable and threatening. All the mistress's characteristics, and the events of their relationship, appear in a state of deliciously anxious fluidity which forms a rhetoric for the construction of a remarkably fluid self: love at first sight (or its alternative, Astrophil's 'with a dribbed shot'), the lover's obsessive yearnings, the stimulation of frustration and rejection, the intensity of insecurity and occasional brief achievements. Petrarchan love is claustrophobic, self-conscious and introverted, obsessed with the contradiction between external image and internal effect. The 'self' or the sense of being a 'subject' that emerges from such poetry is likewise an especially insecure one. The poem is often presented as a reluctant confession. Yet the subject that speaks is also the subject under investigation: the poem is articulated in the presence of readers, who variously listen, judge, intervene or forgive. The result is a highly unstable subjectivity. Perhaps, as modern philosophers, from Nietzsche to Lacan, argue, the traditional sense we may have of possessing a fixed or stable identity is always a fiction. But in the highly artificial world of the sixteenth-century Court, the 'self' of the courtier, blown this way and that by the winds of fortune, is blatantly, at times brutally, the creation of conflicting codes of behaviour and action.[10] The poem is thus an attempt to achieve some momentary stability. A theme of Petrarch's own poetry is, as Forster notes, the incomprehensible changeability of the self in love, which is so violent as to call its very identity into question.[11] Such a discovery is especially disruptive because of the clash with the age's dominant belief in the stability of a person's inner spiritual and moral self, traditionally isolated as the soul. The Petrarchan 'I' is a device that looks as if it is likewise stable, but in fact it puts into discourse a radically decentred self. By 'self' here, of course, we should not understand the comfortable eighteenth-century belief in a real, stable 'self' with an autonomous inner life. As Ferry points out, the terms available to sixteenth-century poets to discuss such issues were crude. But they are still revealing. Such phrases as 'the closet of the heart', 'secrets', the juxtaposition of 'inward' and 'outward', Polonius's 'own self', all point to the grappling with a phenomenon that the poetry bears out – that the received language and its residual philosophical contexts were being outstripped by the emergent experiences that we can perceive in the poetry.

Petrarchism provided a perfect language for the aspiring courtier in that it created a discourse in which his restless anxious self could be temporarily located. Fumerton points out the correlation between the sixteenth-century sonnet in England and the distinctive art of the miniature portrait. Miniatures were often kept in the most private room of an owner's house, where they could be gazed at, brooded over and used to reveal something of the 'true' self of the beholder. Sonnets likewise look as if, through artifice, they reveal the inner life of lover or poet or reader. Greenblatt has written of the habit thus engendered of 'self-fashioning' by the Renaissance courtier, but the phrase perhaps implies too much conscious control. As we follow through a collection of courtly lyrics, we discover that the self that writes is continually rewritten and the more it writes, the more words interpose themselves as frustration, as negative mediations between the desperate subject and its object of desire, or between, in Vance's words, 'the spoken signifier and its signified, dispossessing both into a centerless, unending productivity'. Hence the longer the self of the Petrarchan sequence pursues its goals the less likely it will be materialized – 'the less its signifiers point to some expressive or referential context: they point, instead, only to the discourse in which they begin and end'.[12] The desired object constantly recedes: its primary function is merely to frustrate the final, unreachable guarantee of the identity of the self which pursues it.

When we move from considering the individual sonnet to the larger structure of the sonnet sequence, the way individual sonnets are organized by the poet or an editor, a similar unresolvability presents itself. The sonnet form accretes obsessively minute and often seemingly random details. We come to the unresolved end of one sonnet and then are pressured to go on. Many readers attempt to deal with this impasse by looking for narrative continuity. Should a sonnet sequence be read as a narrative? That is, cumulatively rather than randomly? The temptation may be to read a collection of sonnets as a story. But typically, the method of composition used in a collection of poems makes each one a variation on a conventional theme, often making reference to earlier collections (notably, of course, Petrarch's). Freccero has shown how the *Canzoniere* are 'fragments strung together like pearls on an invisible strand', discontinuous, open to a multiplicity of juxtapositions and combinations, and so insisting upon a self that is fragmented, dislocated, self-questioning. Linkages may be suggested by the poet, or the lover, even (at times) the lady, but such hints of a plot are invited rather than imposed. Neely has argued that in a typical Petrarchan collection, fragmentary composition, reflecting the randomness and unpredictability of the experiences, might be followed by a careful rearrangement by author or editor to suggest the outlines of a general sequence. A common arrangement would be an introductory sonnet, setting forth the starting-point of the attraction of lover to beloved, praising her, and often discussing the need to express himself in poetry; this would typically be followed by a poems showing the ebb and flow of the lover's suit; a set of concluding poems might detail his loss of her. But some sequences (e.g. Drayton's *Idea*, with its six editions) changed radically over their lifetime, with each new arrangement allowing for modifications of the sequence. Warkentin notes that the 'collectivity' of Petrarchan sonnet sequences is built on the concept of *varatio*, variety, 'a simple but flexible structural concept: that of a work exhibiting the variety of the moods of the lover, set forth in *rime sparse* or separate lyrics', a principle which, she adds, English sixteenth-century poets tended to imitate more and more loosely.[13]

Petrarchism, then, offered both authors and readers an intensely complex discursive space in which to play. It afforded a suggestive mixture of poetic workshop and psychological encounter session. It provided a space in which the poet could experiment, trying out figure and form; it offered a psycho-erotic model in which ideological and social tensions were acted out. The sonnet itself is such a model space – a stanza, a small room, like those, no doubt, of study or closet in which it would be written or read; 'much excellentcie ordred in a small room' as Daniel put it.[14]

The rhetoric of dramatic introversion marks an interesting difference between the sixteenth-century English court poet and the majority of his medieval predecessors. The medieval poet's dominant role was that of the announcer, as or 'herald', Zumthor claims. For the medieval courtly 'maker' poetry was part of a social game which expressed the Court's sense of collective identity. The poet's writings were contributions not to a self-contained autonomous category of 'literature' but primarily to 'social life and, especially, to the delicate fiction of courtly love which helped to sustain the life and interest of social relations'. The relationship between this kind of poetry and the social reality that lay within the Court and beyond is an extremely problematic one. Rather than providing a direct mirror of social realities, medieval court poetry is distinctive in that it is unusually self referential – a subtle arrangement of words, topics, tropes from a narrow range of possibilities. Moreover, what is so important in the sixteenth century, what Zumthor terms the *je du poete* (i.e. the notion of individual voice mediated through the language and structure of the poem) is less pronounced than it became in the later period. 'Although creation as such is indubitably individual', he argues, it is true of all medieval literary works that they appear 'less as individual creation . . . than as a mimetic activity, derived from a need for collective participation, comparable to choral song or dance'.[15] What differentiates this medieval structure from that characteristic of the sixteenth century is an increasing sensitivity to and uneasiness about the nature of the 'self', the 'individual', and the 'individual voice' of the poet within the discourse that spoke through him.

It has often argued that through the course of the sixteenth century, there is a distinctive English adaption of Petrarchism. It is seen, the argument goes, most especially in Wyatt's or Sidney's unusual emphasis on the moral dilemmas of erotic experience, and in the relative neglect by English poets of the spiritual dimension of Petrarch's love for Laura. Certainly, what the English poets seized upon particularly was the mechanism of the Petrarchan conceit, and such techniques as the isolation of the oxymoron, the employment of natural or landscape settings as representational of the movements of the mind, and specifically concrete courtly settings and activities such as the hunt, battlefield, public roles and responsibilities. One of the earliest Petrarchan pieces in England is Wyatt's workshop poem, 'I Find No Peace', where the poet can be perceived as simply experimenting, attempting to reproduce mechanically the tricks of his original. Closely based on Petrarch's 'Pace non trove e non o da far guerra', with its easily imitable oxymoron of peace/war, this poem provided a model for more than a dozen sixteenth-century English poets to try their hand at the techniques. The play on the logical impossibilities codified in the war and peace oxymoron, like the equally ubiquitous fire and ice paradox, show one especially important way the Elizabethans saw Petrarchism: as a rhetorical master-text, adaptable to the increasingly self-conscious rhetorical world of the Elizabethan Court, where display and self-aggrandizement were expressed with becoming humility, and were thus the means of acquiring place and, if not power, at least the possibility of power.

Petrarchism was therefore, and in many ways, far more than a poetic rhetoric. It was adapted to very precise political purposes, especially in England, where the fact of a Virgin Queen on the throne produced an extraordinary transference of the Petrarchan manner to politics. Elizabeth systematically encouraged her (male) courtiers to relate to her in the role of Petrarchan lovers, always in hope, caught between desire for advancement and fear of losing their places, single-mindedly devoted to the hopeless attainment of her favour, and grateful for any token. So Petrarchism was not simply a charming and sophisticated fashion for court entertainment or for fictionalizing love affairs. It became, especially in the last twenty years of the century, part of public policy. Many poems written to Elizabeth, or to an unnamed but obviously identifiable royal lady, are transparently pleas for political favours. We will see some examples when we look at Ralegh (Chapter 4) and Robert Sidney (Chapter 5). In Petrarch's own work, the relationship between the poet and his beloved seems to reflect the uneasy reorganization of feudal class relations: Laura is the suzerain, her poet a vassal, eager to follow her yet aware of his unworthiness and the hopelessness of attaining her. In the same way, the political relations of the Elizabethan Court were articulated through Petrarchism. The Queen's encouragement to her courtiers to display themselves in the trappings of Petrarchism is a clear instance of the blatant political manipulation of language in the interests of a dominant ideology. As Forster notes, inheriting the shakiest throne in Europe, with a populace divided by religion, faced with a 'ruling class composed of energetic, violent and ruthless men', Elizabeth turned her position as a woman to advantage by encouraging her courtiers to adopt the Petrarchan roles of 'men irresistibly attracted, preferring the light of her eyes and her favour' to other, lesser and less dangerous lights. They are what they dare not say they are: pleas for political favour not erotic satisfaction.[16]

The first major impact on English poetry of Petrarchism, then, comes with Wyatt and Surrey. Both faced the problem of adapting the sonnet, the main form in Petrarch's *Rime*, to English. Lewis speaks of Wyatt as 'a man who was escaping from the late medieval swamp',[17] and his technical achievements are less impressive than Surrey's. Wyatt's basic technical challenge was to get the sonnet to fit the English iambic pattern. He breaks it into two uneven units, octave and sextet, and then struggles to find enough rhymes in English to match the flexibility and flow of Italian. The English sonnet eventually becomes much more structured and logical than its Italian model and it was in fact Surrey who introduced the most important technical innovation – the so-called Shakespearean sonnet form, consisting of three quatrains and a concluding couplet. Later in the century Thomas Watson wrote some eighteen-line 'sonnets', three quatrains each followed by a couplet, and later too, we find the so-called Spenserian sonnet, the three quatrains linked by internal couplets and a concluding couplet. These metrical experiments make the later English Petrarchan sonnet a more flexible and idiomatic poetic unit than the form of some of Wyatt's experiments, and than the muddle and controversy over English verse forms in the mid-century decades might have promised.

When in 1557 Tottel published his collection of Wyatt's and Surrey's poetry, along with some other verses by various other poets, the most influential collection of secular verse before the 1580s was available for five decades of readers. Tottel's *Miscellany* went through nine editions by 1587 and its part in forming the consciousness of aristocrats and those aspiring to gentility alike may be grasped by Shallow's reference in *The Merry Wives of Windsor* to his constant need for his 'book of songs and sonnets'. It is also interesting to see the particular way Petrarchism was assimilated. While Sidney found little to praise in his predecessors, it is obvious he had read them carefully. There are a significant number of mid-Tudor collections which use Tottel as their model, but consistently stress the moral and civic virtues rather than metaphysical or psychological aspects. They were intended, as Turberville puts it, to warn us 'to flee that fonde and filthie affection of poysoned unlawful love', thus combining Petrarchan rhetoric with the moralistic public poem of the *Mirror* tradition. Such collections include Turberville's *Epitaphes, Epigrams, Songs and Sonets* (published 1567), Googe's *Eclogs Epytaphes and Sonnettes* (1563), and Gascoigne's *A Hundredth Sundrie Flowres* (1573). These mid-Tudor poets with their determinedly utilitarian view of the public responsibility of poetry were suspicious of the frivolity evoked by many Petrarchan sonnets and songs.[18] They used their poetry primarily to display their humanist ideals and oratorical capacities in the hope they would find court employment. Turberville writes love lyrics as if they were a frivolous task, purportedly for others who indulge themselves in vanities. Posturing as one who 'never came where any beautie lay', his role is that of the unwilling hired servant: 'I had my hire, so he mought purchase grace.' In the preface to his poems, he argues against 'any youthlie head' following 'such fragile affections' as the 'meere fiction of these Fantasies'. Only Gascoigne, in the 1570s, attempts to create an atmosphere of levity, indulgence and play, and a rhetoric to match it. Like Sidney, he wrote a treatise on poetry in which he attacks the 'playne and simple maner of writing . . . we are fallen into', and in his own poetry he brings a sense of dramatic situation and an awareness of audience into the lyric that had been lost since Wyatt.[19]

To explain the changes that we can see coming over the short courtly lyric in the 1570s and, in particular, the seemingly sudden upsurge of Petrarchan love sonnets in the 1580s, simply as a discovery or revival of Petrarchism is far too simple. To ask the traditional literary history questions – to what extent English lyric poetry of the 1580s and 1590s is best seen in the Petrarchan mode? Or is Petrarchism an aberration, a swerving from the native plain style tradition? – is to raise incompletely formulated questions. Petrarchism was rewritten by too many conflicting, subverting and modifying discourses for us to accept such simplistic formulations. One complicating factor is the life of the Court itself. The growing rhetorical flexibility and prestige of the vernacular, the Court's role for poetry as a political instrument, and the internalized mix of possibility and frustration experienced by an ambitious, highly educated generation of men like Sidney, Greville, Ralegh, and Essex – all are major factors in the so-called 'Renaissance' of the 1580s which Sidney and Puttenham praise so highly.

The year 1579, the date of publication of Spenser's *Shepheardes Calender*, the likely date when Sidney was writing the *Defence*, starting the *Arcadia* and also contemplating what later became 'Certain Sonnets' and *Astrophil and Stella*, coincided closely with the date when his sister, the Countess of Pembroke, was settled into Wilton House, later the centre of an attempt to continue her dead brother's literary, political and broader cultural ideals. The last years of the 1570s are then a landmark of fundamental importance. The 1580s and 1590s see an explosion of literary experiments, among which are conventionally listed the increased number of Petrarchan sonnet sequences – by Daniel, Smith, Drayton, Spenser, Lodge, Philip and Robert Sidney, Barnes, Barnfield and others. There are also many miscellanies of verse, most especially *The Phoenix Nest* (1593), and, perhaps the most representative collection, *A Poetical Rhapsody* (1602). This is what we have usually seen as the so-called golden age of Elizabethan poetry. It is the era of Ralegh's gallantry, Sidney's noble death, Spenser's celebration of Gloriana, Marlowe's celebration of sensuality, Donne's buoyant flippancy, Southwell's Catholic meditations, the mellifluous sensitivity of Shakespeare's sonnets, the easy-flowing melancholy of

Drayton or Daniel of whose sequence Lewis aptly remarked it has 'no ideas, no psychology, and of course no story: it is simply a masterpiece of phrasing and melody'.[20] But there is not a simple transition from lugubrious, halting moralistic verse by earnest civic-minded fumbling poets like Googe or Turberville to the sophisticated aestheticism of a Sidney or Daniel. The amount and energy of the poetry increase dramatically, but there is no abandonment of the 'drab' style and its replacement by a 'golden' one. Moralistic verse continues in Spenser's Christianized Petrarchism in the *Amoretti*, in Greville, Ralegh, and others. Even *Astrophil and Stella*, supposedly the zenith of the 'golden' style, is deeply concerned with moral questions raised by Protestantism.

Petrarchism as perversion

Petrarchism helped, then, to articulate a cultural crisis over the nature of the 'self' or the 'subject' far broader than just the emergence of a 'personal' voice in poetry. It also spoke to the emerging consciousness of the 'self' as constructed by gender and sexuality. Petrarchism is one of the four or five great systematizations of sexual desire in Western history. For over three hundred years, it provided men and women with some of their basic assumptions about how desire operates within and between them. To have that longevity it needed to have been more than a literary fashion, and to have seized upon something very deep-rooted in the culture's inner life.

Why should this have been? Here, with some changes that I will discuss below, is a stimulating recent account of the inner life of Petrarchism, which may help to explain:

> Petrarchism is theater, the production of a scenario, for
> which characters – in the form of people, parts of people,
> and nonhuman (including inanimate) objects are cast. The
> performance is played before an audience, the crucial member
> of which is the Petrarchan lover himself viewing [himself]
> performing . . . Petrarchism is a detour that, at best, leads
> asymptotically to intimacy: it never arrives . . . Petrarchism is
> centered not upon the partner, but upon the lover . . . The pain
> and frustration of earlier times live on unresolved, carried within,
> always a potential threatening force motivating one to resolutions
> that never quite work, to an undoing never quite done.[21]

This probably would be accepted by contemporary scholars as an accurate, though incomplete, account of the major dynamics of Petrarchism. The writer, however, would not easily be recognized as an expert in the field – although he was certainly a world authority in his own field. In quoting his opinion, I have cheated, but only slightly: apart from a few brief elisions, and substituting the words 'Petrarchism' or 'Petrarchan lover' for the words the writer used. What I have given is a quotation from Stoller's study of perversion, *Observing the Erotic Imagination*. The words he uses are not 'Petrarchism' and 'the Petrarchan lover', but 'perversion' and 'perverse person'. He goes on to draw conclusions that would also be acceptable (were we not now alerted) as a description of other aspects of Petrarchism. The perverse situation (I restore Stoller's terms, though I invite the reader to substitute for it as the discussion moves along) is scripted to help the lover to deal with the overwhelming power of the object of his desire. Since her full reality cannot be faced, she can be accommodated by the lover's mind only if she is accorded less than full personhood. He therefore depicts her as the 'possessor of selected parts or qualities only. He anatomizes them either in a list (a blazon) or singly. And if even that is 'too intimate', he turns from human to 'inanimate objects, such as garments, granting them a certain amount of humanness'. The careful scripting of these erotic scenarios is, Stoller writes, seen as an 'aesthetic task', undertaken in the spirit of the *sprezzatura* of which Castiglione and Puttenham write: the perverse scene is 'most pleasing when it is seamless, when it does not give hints that it was constructed, when it looks as if it sprang full-blown from unconscious depths. If not created spontaneously . . . then it should look as if it was.'[22]

My argument is not that Petrarchism ought to be added to the list of common paraphilia along with copraphilia, kleptomania or exhibitionism, but rather that as a poetic discourse its longevity was based on the uncanny extent to which it incorporated the major fantasies of patriarchal gender assignments and sexual pathologies. Beyond the rhetorical conventions of Petrarchism men (and to an alarming extent the women who were interpellated into it), played far more than a set of rhetorical scripts. They were acting out patterns of perversely repetitive strategies that were the outcome of the dominant western gender assignments. Petrarchism was, historically, predominantly a male discourse and its central psychocultural trope is the quintessential male perversion, fetishism. It characteristically incorporates other characteristic male perversions, including aspects of both sadism and masochism, exhibitionism, voyeurism and, at times, catering for more specialist tastes such as transvestism, paedophilia and necrophilia. When, in Chapter 8, I discuss the poems of Mary Wroth, I also raise the question of what happens when a woman poet enters this largely male discourse. Are there signs of what Kaplan terms the 'characteristic female perversions'? The central one, extreme submissiveness, is clearly relevant to Wroth, as is – at least in the sense of 'stealing' the Petrarchan mode of writing – kleptomania. Whether there is space even in as hospitable a discourse for self-mutilation (including self-cutting, surgical addiction and trichotillomania), female impersonation, homovestism, anorexia, and 'the incest wife' is a matter for more specialized investigations.[23]

In part I joke, and yet I am deadly serious. We all, even today, carry with us and enact at the very least the remnants of discursive systems we inherit from our cultural pasts and of which we often have little conscious knowledge or control. In our attempts to make sense of our desires, their unpredictabilities, joys, losses, repressions and returns, we have recourse to these remnants. The erotic stories we construct, or have constructed about us, are all the products of pasts we did not create, worlds we did not know. But to know more of at least some of the specific contradictions in which we are caught is to at least open the possibility of agency, perhaps to some extent of choosing our strategies. Real men and women, not merely fictional figures, have suffered from, as well as been transfigured by, their own and others' compulsions, needs and lacks, and it behoves us to understand what languages our cultural pasts have given us, and denied us, to cope with our desires. More than a fashionable literary mode or set of moral commonplaces is at stake here.

In Petrarchan poetry, the idealization of the beloved is characteristically accompanied by fear of her. Erotic idealization, as has often been pointed out, is a form of 'oppression through exaltation', in which the object of idealization rarely exists in a relationship of mutuality or as the subject of her own desire. She is 'overvalued', as Freud put it, in order that she can be, the lover hopes, exclusively the subject of his desires. Whenever she does act in relation to her own wishes – predominantly by rejecting him – she is castigated by him as cruel, causing him 'violent distress'; she is accused of having a beauteous exterior framing a heart of stone, or in psychoanalytic terms, of being the punishing mother figure from whom it is so difficult to differentiate.[24] It is as if she compensates for a deficiency, a lack, in the wholeness of the male lover, thereby putting into question that wholeness and its apparent power. The Petrarchan lyric traditionally presented itself as a man's appeal for mercy based on an acknowledgement of fear of discontinuity and helplessness before (or even in the absence of) the cruel, hard-hearted, alluringly yet frustratingly chaste mistress. When she does respond, the male lover typically finds some way not just to express gratitude and dependence, but to assert his further power. Her effects on him are, in short, like those the child feels in the process of birth, weaning and, separation/individuation, when he must leave the comfort of the mother, and finds himself thrown alone into the world – and yet is inevitably drawn, in fantasy, back to her, puzzled yet reassured by the contradictions of his pleasurable tortures. She is the all-powerful mother, simultaneously loved and hated, on whose nurturance the male child is totally dependent, and yet from whom he must break if he is to achieve his individuation. However much the beloved's absence may be bewailed, it is therefore, paradoxically, both welcome and necessary. The typical Petrarchan poem cannot be written in the beloved's presence, and therefore absence becomes a precondition for writing of the miseries of her absence. That works as a clever and recurrent trope. But on the psychological level, it indicates something more deeply rooted in male gender construction: the lover cannot bear the full presence of the beloved because her claims seem so overwhelming, and moreover he must ultimately reject her if he is to assert his male autonomy.

If the beloved embodies both the alluring necessity and the threat of the mother (whom the male desires) must reject, and yet to whom he is inevitably drawn back, he needs to construct a satisfying narrative of this struggle. This is where Petrarchism embodied an enormously powerful appeal. The presence/absence paradox in Petrarchism is an adult narrativization of Freud's fort/da game, in which the child pushes the toy away in order to have the pleasure of having it come back (and also, as the game accumulates more potent fantasies, to punish the object for its power over him): the vicissitudes of the male in his sexualization lead him to fight to escape the temptation of returning to his former fusion with the maternal image, the holder of primitive power, the phallic as well as the great nurturing mother. In such circumstances, the lover argues that it is her, the beloved's cruelty, not his desires, that is depriving him of fulfilment. Since he may not possess her, he constructs the easier and more sinister course of constructing narratives about her mental image or picture. She thus becomes his creation, and her autonomy consists in being constant, holding still, as it were, so he might fix the image of her which he desires. Her desires are rarely considered, although the effects of this obsessive male scopophilia (the pleasure gained by viewing objects of desire) are angrily and contradictorily explored in some of the rare poems in the tradition written by women, as I shall show in Chapter 8.

This brings me to another of the long acknowledged characteristics of Petrarchism: the predominance it affords to sight, specifically to the male gaze. Scopophilia is, Stoller argues, predominantly a gendered strategy (that is, a disorder in the development of masculinity and femininity) constructed out of a tradition of hostility: rage at giving up one's earliest bliss and identification with the mother, fear of not succeeding in escaping out of her orbit, and a need for revenge for her putting one in this predicament. In Petrarchism, the lover's admiring eye attempts to fix the mistress not just as a beautiful object that he wishes to possess, but often as a guarantee against the threat she represents. Psychoanalytic studies of scopophilia have seen the gaze embodying a 'pre-oedipal fear . . . of merging and fixing with the mother', which may be guarded against only by incessant watching. Stoller argues that 'sexual excitement will occur at the moment when adult reality resembles the childhood trauma – the anxiety being re-experienced as excitement'. The viewed object is thereby rendered less threatening, thereby relieving the voyeur of his fear, either directly or by being projected upon and so shared with another. The viewer thus enjoys closeness without the fear of engulfment. Scopophilic pleasure can be secretive or the woman may know she is being seen and apparently involved in his fears, in which case her knowledge represents his superego giving permission for his own look/show impulses.[25]

How do these characteristic male strategies for dealing with these fears that seem so basic to our culture's construction of gender become encoded in Petrarchan poems? The male gaze is predominantly directed, most obviously in the blazon, at a woman as the sum of separable parts. Vickers points out that the distinction between a woman's 'beauty' and her 'beauties' is a feature of the whole Petrarchan tradition. The 'whole body' of Petrarch's Laura appears to him at times 'less than some of its parts, and the technique of describing the mistress through the isolation of those parts became universal. . . . When late-Renaissance theorists, poets and painters represented woman's body, Petrarch's verse justified their aesthetic choices'.[26] The beloved is partitioned, each of her features accorded object status separate from her totality. Thus she is rendered passive and (in the sense Shakespeare puns in Sonnet 126) passively rendered. Many of the descriptions of women in Petrarchan poems, especially the so-called 'witty' Petrarchists (Donne comes to mind here) are a fictional construct of male fantasies that could fit any woman, and are directed less to any woman than to an implied primary audience of the poet's male friends. Beneath the jocularity on the surface and the easy cynicism of male bonding, there are serious and disturbing issues of gender politics. Why this fixation on avoiding direct and intimate contact with women? Or the unwillingness to accept the equality of another's desires? In agonal relationships, in order to keep the forces of frustrated infantile rage from being turned back on the self, women have served the role of scapegoat for men's insecurity and awareness and fear of separation, individuation and contingency. Petrarchism is one of the most compelling systematizations of these fears.

Petrarchism is also intimately bound up with the premier male perversion that seeks to come to control this overwhelming fear of the beloved's overwhelming power, fetishism. The fetishist is usually not trying to victimize or control the beloved, since fetishism is, like Petrarchism itself, directed at the effects of the beloved upon the lover, not the reverse. His goal is rather to find just the right intensity of her power that he can, for the moment, deal with. If her effects on him become too overwhelming, how much, he asks, can he bear, without actually banishing her? The fetish is the attempted answer to that question. A sexual fetish, notes Kaplan, is 'significantly more reliable than a living person . . . when the full sexual identity of the woman is alive, threatening, dangerous, unpredictable, the desire she arouses must be invested in the fetish . . . fetish objects are relatively safe, easily available, undemanding of reciprocity'. The fetishistic narrative is designed to divert attention away from the 'whole story by focusing attention on the detail'.[27] Unlike the real, complex woman, who has desires of her own, and therefore within patriarchal society can be even more threatening to the supposedly autonomous male, the fetish can be commanded, assigned multiple or contradictory parts and (except in the masochistic scenario, a special case to which I come soon) not make demands of its own. Fetishes are created as nodes of meaning within the earliest narrativizations of what Freud termed family romances, the desires to emulate, replace or seduce our parents. They acquire their magical power as part of the primitive fantasy structure of the child and may be reactivated and often enormously elaborated in adulthood, their origins long lost under the accretions of later narratives. The classic fetishistic move in Petrarchist poetry is to focus on a bodily characteristic, to lock it up in the heart, or the memory, or in the poem. There it is easier to deal with and miss the overwhelming power of the beloved when one is alone, when the lover has the beloved in fantasy rather than in the flesh, than it is to face the whole complexity of her. After all she is always more complex than the fetish: she may be married (or the poet may be) or unavailable, or have, as people do, changing moods, or her own desires. Hence the preference for the fetish. To reverse Orlando's desire for the real in *As You Like It*, the fetishist prefers to try to live by 'thinking'.

Fetishes, of course, may be anything that the erotic imagination imbues with metonymic power – shoes, clothing, pets, portraits, locks of hair, odours, sounds. The clinical literature is full of stories of the bizarre, banal, outrageous and ordinary in this most widespread of male paraphilia, as is the Petrarchan canon. The beloved's very absence may be fetishized. Sight, and by extension rational visualization, is what is used to conjure up the power of the woman, even when she is absent. The lover freezes the beloved into an image, a statue, a picture, at a moment of his choice. Indeed, it is as if he can deal with a woman best – as he puts it, when he most admires her – only when he aestheticizes her, when the power of her physical presence is no longer a threat. He uses a freeze-frame, capturing her for all time, not as true to life, but true to what he can bear.

I turn now to yet another standard characteristic of Petrarchism. The Petrarchan lover's tone is overwhelmingly one of complaint. He has been rejected; his mistress is absent, unkind, loves another, has a cold heart that denies her fair exterior, he himself has no peace and yet is continually at war; he burns and freezes. There is, in short, a strong strain of male masochism involved in the Petrarchist pose. In this case, the scripts are subtly different from the struggle to assert male dominance and independence and yet retain a way back to the love object that I have so far discussed. Masochism, according to Freud and much popular parlance, is bound up with sadism, and there are no doubt cases where the same person is caught up in both perversions. But the partner of a masochist does not have to be a sadist. The peculiar script of masochism is that it requires only a co-operator, who need not even be aware that he or she has been co-opted into the masochistic narrative. The essence of masochism is the pleasure taken in delayed gratification, in the pain of denial and waiting: the masochist 'waits for pleasure as something that is bound to be late, and expects pain as the condition that will finally ensure (both physically and morally) the advent of pleasure'. Masochism involves assigning to the other the absolute power of forbiddance of pleasure, in the case of male masochism, giving the all-powerful mother the power of the Law to rule over him. 'Masochism', writes Deleuze, 'is a story that relates how the superego was destroyed and by whom, and what was the sequel to this destruction'. Such a description is found throughout Petrarchan poetry. It is found in the serious rather than the witty Petrarchists, where love is a substitute for or pathway to God, and self-denial and delayed gratification are means to what Sidney terms 'heavenly bliss'. It is ubiquitous in Petrarch, in Sidney, in Shakespeare.[28]

This leads to a crucial question for our understanding of Petrarchan poetry. What place does a woman occupy in Petrarchism, which is so obviously a predominantly male discourse? To answer that, one might initially focus on the degree of autonomy a male poet allows the woman in his verse. She (and the personal pronoun is hardly appropriate since 'she' is so completely 'his' creation) is entirely a product of the discourse that she supposedly shares. She controls her lover's destiny, and yet can operate only within his domination. She is the object by means of which he can indulge his anguish, his pleas, his manipulations. Either way, in no sense is she ever an agent: she has no choice but to be sexualized, and is not accorded reciprocal power. Today, we are rightly attuned to looking at social mobility as a major factor in the construction of a sense of agency. But physical mobility is a crucial material reality as well, one that in this period had significant gendered differences. Movement is denied to women within this discourse. If she 'moves,' she is fickle; if he does so, it is part of the necessity of being male, as Donne argues at the end of 'A Valediction: Forbidding Mourning'. A number of Petrarchan poems assume that a woman is blameworthy if she is inconstant, but a man can always justify his leaving. Such a view is unselfconsciously and benevolently masculinist. Often, the only acknowledgement of a female role in the production of desire comes from male bewilderment and fear. Reflecting this male fear, women must be kept on display, their each movement and habit sexualized not merely for the benefit but the protection of the male onlooker. Laces, fabric, hair, eyes, all are constructed to be evaluated by the controlling spectator. That the impression of women on the speaker is so overwhelming is less attributable, therefore, to anything inherent in particular women than to the discourse that is producing Woman, either as ideal or threat. Either way, in no sense is she ever an agent: she has no choice but to be sexualized, and is not accorded reciprocal power.

This whole poetic tradition, I am suggesting, betrays a vast and powerful set of cultural assumptions. How could we, it might be asked, continue to enjoy the poems of Petrarch, or Sidney, or Donne? Is it not heavy-handed to condemn a whole tradition of poetry, even the gender politics of a whole culture, for what has been an overwhelmingly 'natural' practice? Can we acknowledge the residual pleasure afforded by particular practices while at the same time culturally situate them – and examine the cultural conflict set up by these two, ideologically at odds, forms of enjoyment. That may constitute a less innocent, less 'natural' form of enjoying the poetry of the sixteenth century, but the closer we look at any form of pleasure we have, the more we learn how deeply involved in matters of gender, class and race it invariably is. When reading Petrarchan poetry, therefore, the mixture of pleasure and pain it affords is, as I have suggested, closely akin to some of our most deep-seated and (dare I say it?) most enjoyable perversions.

Protestantism

In the final section of this chapter, I will introduce the major disruptive discursive structure of the age – one that did not only invade Petrarchism but the whole socio-cultural framework. It is Protestantism. In western society, the many varieties of Protestantism retain great power today. One way of engaging the interests of some contemporary students may be with the socio-cultural as well as the theological roots of the religious beliefs they profess or have been brought up with. It is often a revelation to see either the fierce, intellectual rigour of Calvin and the revolutionary writings and acts of Cranmer in the students of today, or to realize how like the more bizarre reaches of modern American evangelism some of the theology of the sixteenth century sounds. Like most successful revolutionary movements, Protestantism combined an impatient elitism with an energetic populism. It articulated not just intellectual changes, but complex and confusing deep-rooted shifts in religious allegiance and, indeed, the whole social formation. An Englishman or woman born in the reign of Henry VIII could, with some affluence and a lot of good luck, have lived through the reign of five other monarchs – and five changes in official religion. Between the 1540s and the 1620s, such a person would have seen the last stages of the Henrician reformation, the uneasy Protestantism of the Edwardian protectorate, the short-lived radical Protestantism of the abortive reign of Lady Jane Grey, the about-face of Marian Catholicism with its burnings of Protestants, well publicized by Foxe and later controversialists like Thomas Beard, the return to a deviously politic Protestantism under Elizabeth, the growing religious split of the 1580s and 1590s which saw both a Catholic revival and the growing disaffection of separatist sects, and finally, (beyond our period) the highly theocratic Anglicanism which developed under James I and was intensified under Charles I. Religious controversy was the most prolific literary form of the whole age: More against Tyndale, the Genevan exiles under Mary, Catholic and dissenting controversialists, Hooker and his great adversary Perkins, and many popular controversialists including those who produced the so-called *Marprelate Tracts* of the late 1580s.

What was a revolutionary allegiance for many young radicals of the 1540s and 1550s became a conventional set of assumptions for the generation of intellectuals, courtiers and poets born (as were Sidney, Greville and Shakespeare) in the 1550s and 1560s. Calvinism, usually in a moderate, hazily doctrinal version, provided the dynamic of much sixteenth-century poetry and hardly any major literary figure is untouched by its power. The Calvinist doctrine of God's Providence struck a deep chord in the lives of sixteenth-century men and women. Much Elizabethan writing, Sinfield notes, represents 'a confident and elaborate attempt to render coherent, persuasive and effective' a set of doctrines which are for the most part alien to us today. He argues that 'strong Protestantism' (i.e. Calvinism) was 'hardly disputed in the English Church before 1600' and, however, remote from modern experience it may be, 'if we are to comprehend the literature written during the period of its dominance we must attempt to see why many found it helpful and comforting at the time'.[29]

We should not ignore, however, the strong and continuing influence of Catholic Christianity on sixteenth-century poetry. In England, Catholics were fighting (often literally) for their lives, and there is a strong tradition of devotional poetry late in the century in the work of such poets as Alabaster, Gurney and Southwell, the 'recusant' poets. Not only was Protestantism the emerging religious force in England, but Protestantism also 'defined the first problem of English criticism' by making poets and poetic theorists justify or 'defend' poetry. The Protestant reformers themselves were neither exclusively negative nor monolithic in their views of poetry, but writers like Puttenham, Harington, Webbe and Sidney found a need to defend poetry against certain 'Puritans' because of the earnest, angry or well-intentioned zeal of Protestant (mainly, though not exclusively, Puritan) polemicists. The early Protestant reformers attacked the Catholic Church for, in Tyndale's phrase, giving 'themselves only unto poetry', and shutting 'up the scripture'. But such a moralistic defence of poetry against even more moralistic Puritans is not really the central issue. Most of the poets of the century were, in any case, themselves pious Protestants. In fact, from Protestant theology, devotional practices and biblical commentaries, we can piece together what Lewalski terms 'a substantial and complex poetics', which we can see articulated in an interesting phenomenon developing from the middle of the century – a body of Protestant devotional poetry.[30]

For Protestants of the sixteenth century, poetry was not something that could be separated from the godly pursuit of a Protestant State. As part of the Reformation dynamic, there grew up a body of devotional, propagandist, and polemical writing that helped spread the theological arguments that were the intellectual meat of the movement. What Protestant poetry there was was fiercely utilitarian. Under Edward VI, for instance, there was a strong biblical poetry movement, whose authors combined reverence for biblical themes and what they perceived as an appropriately unadorned populist poetic style. King terms the poetic theory implied by this movement a 'major shift in mimetic theory', and points out how the prolific 'gospellers' who wrote on biblical or devotional subjects in a variety of popular forms – ballads, fourteeners, poulter's measure – were deliberately rejecting the Italianate courtly forms like the sonnet and *ottava rima*.[31] He argues that the Protestant Court of Edward VI was thus far more eclectic than under Elizabeth in that 'Italianate' and 'native' forms and fashions co-existed. Such a division is to oversimplify the way the court poetry itself was permeated by Protestantism. The miscellanies from this period jam together contradictory strands of taste and allegiance. Perhaps the most accessible for a modern reader is the Arundel Harington Manuscript, which was begun by John Harington the elder in the 1550s, and then continued until late in the century by his son, the Elizabethan courtier, John Harington the younger.[32] It includes some Petrarchan lyrics, but (at least from this early period) more brief, moralistic lyrics on fortune, penitence, sin, and other Protestant themes.

The poets King singles out as important in this early Protestant poetry are hardly household (or even lecture-room) names: Luke Shepherd, a popular gospeller and satirist, who wrote in rough Skeltonic verses and rambling alliterative verse, and Robert Crowley, a printer and propagandist, who saw Langland's *Piers Plowman* (which he printed) as prophetic of the religious revolution of the time. His verse is awkward, as in 'The Voyce of the Last Trumpet' which in thumping doggerel admonishes the godly:

> Give easy awhyle
> And marke my style
> You that hath wyt in stove
> For wyth wordes bare
> I wyll declare
> Thyngs done long time before.[33]

In addition to such examples we should not forget the age's most popular work of poetry, the versification of the Psalms prepared for use in church by Sternhold and Hopkins, often known as the 'Old Version', the most famous of which is still to be heard in churches:

> Oh God our help in ages past
> Our help in years to come:
> Our shelter from the stormy blast
> And our eternal home.
> (Psalm 100)

In thumping broken-backed adaptations of fourteeners (alternating lines of eight and six syllables) the delicacy and emotional riches of the Psalms are hammered into unmemorable (though memorizable!) shape. As Freer puts it, 'the Sternhold-Hopkins psalter was a public joke as poetry' and the chief problem in discussing it is to keep it 'from seeming a comic anthology'. Its syntax is wrenched, its idioms distorted, and its rhymes forced, in such masterpieces of bad taste as:

> Leave off therefore (saythe he) and know
> I am a God most stout:
> Among the heathen hye and low,
> And all the earth throughout.
> (Psalm 46)[34]

With such poetry to choose from, it is not difficult to see why Protestant poetry, at least that written before the end of the century, has been neglected by modern readers. Its outstanding products do not appear until the seventeenth century in the devotional verse of Donne, Herbert, or Vaughan. In our period, the one minor masterpiece of the movement is the Sidney *Psalms*, which will be looked at in Chapters 5 and 8.

But Protestantism did far more than produce a quantity of mediocre verse. Its most important impact can, in fact, be seen in the secular poetry it scorned. First, it provided a model of both poetry – those parts of the Bible which were seen as poetic, notably the Psalms – and of the poet. Sidney, following Calvin, Beza and others, describes King David as the approved mirror of the Christian poet:

> . . . he maketh you, as it were, see God coming in His majesty, his telling of the beasts' joyfulness and hills leaping, [is nothing else] but a heavenly poesy, wherein almost he showeth himself a passionate lover of that unspeakable and everlasting beauty to be seen by the eyes of the mind, only cleared by faith.[35]

When we penetrate beneath both the thundering attacks on the vanity of poetry and the pomposity of the pious arguments about the use of poetry by Crowley or Sternhold, many intriguing implications emerge. In their theological treatises, when the Reformers discussed the nature of man, they thought little of what we might term 'imagination,' but they would defend artifice or images if truth was served. Hence much sixteenth-century Protestant discussion of art and poetry focuses on the means of discriminating between true and false images. We see it, for instance, in the vivid way Spenser deals with the question in the first book of *The Faerie Queene*, where Red Cross cannot distinguish between Una and the dream produced by the malevolent Archimago, the 'source of images'. At stake is the question that, as we shall see in succeeding chapters, all the poets of the age who professed strong religious allegiances – Sidney, Spenser, Donne, Greville, in particular – had to face: how can one trust the products of the distorting human mind? Is not, to use Sidney's famous phrase, the 'erected wit' always undercut by the degraded 'infected will'? Can a poet at once embrace Calvin and Castiglione? These are the contradictions which, as we shall see, create much of the energy in the poetry of Sidney (Chapter 5) and Spenser (Chapter 6).

Second, Protestantism set up a series of major ideological conflicts within the everyday material lives of sixteenth-century men and women, not only to poets. As Sinfield notes, Protestantism created a universe of strife and tension, and demanded total allegiance in every aspect of life; it challenged the humanist belief in the educability of man; it created a stern, wrathful, and determining God whose power reached into every moment of a man's life; and it focused relentlessly upon the inner coherence (or disparateness) of a person's sense of self.

Protestantism reinforced what we have already noted as a major anxiety of Petrarchism – the uneasiness about the relationship of the 'I' of a poem and the 'I' of the poem's author. To what extent and through what mediating structures does language articulate private, 'individual' feelings or thoughts? To what extent is poetry mimetic of the poet's inner states of feeling or of its readers? And what is the relationship between the state of salvation of the poet and the poem's 'truth' or integrity? Must the poet be a good man? One of the most powerful contradictions thrown up by Protestantism is the privilege extended to the subject on the one hand and the precariousness of that subject before God on the other. Whether chosen or rejected, saved or reprobate, the individual is isolated before God. He was constantly exhorted to look at the signs of salvation within, while he knew that his inward nature was evil. He was constantly called upon to witness to God's truth while his very nature was totally corrupt. He called upon God with his innermost being, while knowing that inner voice was able to call on God only by grace. Alongside such contradictions, the Petrarchan paradoxes of ice and fire, war and peace, seem petty.

When the Protestant turned to poetry, then, especially given its use in the Bible, and most notably in the Psalms, he could find a powerful model for articulating the paradoxes of individuality. The Protestant self, curiously analogous to the Petrarchan self, is always in flux, always changing even while it articulates an ideal of stasis. So the Protestant poet, whether he was as obsessive as Greville or as ambitious as Spenser, would inevitably find himself writing out his contradictions and anguish into his poetry, at once fascinated by words and aware of their untrustworthiness and suspicious of their promiscuous materiality.

A third issue also has curious affinities with one special trait of Petrarchism. It concerns the Protestant concern with language, specifically the relationship between God's Word and men's words, between divine intentionality and the medium of expression. In the work of Greville, especially, a matter central to the Protestant poetic becomes the extent to which the black marks on a white page of a written text can become bearers of meaning. For Greville, and with other Protestant poets such as Spenser, there is a problematic and (given that a man's salvation, not merely his literary reputation, was at stake) fearful question of the relationship between word and representation, when it is perceived that every attempt at representing meaning might dissolve into an infinity of random signifiers. Half a century later, Milton was to deal with the problem by imperiously invoking the

Holy Spirit as his muse; Greville is more tentative and anguished; Spenser, as *The Faerie Queene* becomes more and more beyond his capacities to finish, is increasingly more despairing until he rejects his own poetic creation as an example of the mistrustful promiscuity of worldly signification.

With all of these issues, it can be seen how the dominant drives of Protestant theology and devotion variously overlap with, contradict, or reinforce the merely 'literary' structures of Petrarchism. In particular, what this potent combination brought under scrutiny in the sixteenth century was the issue I have just mentioned – the overlapping concepts of 'self,' 'individual', 'personality' or the 'subject'.

Ideological struggles are always fought out within a shared code that may disguise the real issues at stake. These struggles inevitably operate within residual rather than emergent terms, and so in order to find out exactly what was going on, it is important not to be trapped into describing it strictly within the dominant ideologies of the age. Renaissance 'individualism' is an especially complex phenomenon. It was identified by Burckhardt a century ago as central to the period – and that is a view that remains largely unchallenged, even if we now tend to speak of the 'subject' rather than the 'individual'.

One widespread concern in the age's poetry that impacts on the sense of being a 'subject' in this period is a concern with time and mutability. Time is, on the one hand, an abstract category of experience, as when Sidney's friend, the Huguenot theologian Philippe de Mornay, writes, 'what greater contraries can there be, than time and eternitie', thus pointing to the residual medieval view by which time is created by and ultimately guided by God.[36] On the other hand, there is time experienced by the self, as the passing of moments, the experience the Elizabethans characteristically described as 'mutability'. It is evoked in Spenser's 'Mutability' Cantos or in Shakespeare's Sonnet 60: 'Like as the waves make towards the pebbled shore,/So do our minutes hasten to their end'. For most sixteenth-century writers, time is still a religious notion, marked by the transience of human life, the inevitability of death, the transcendent eternity of God and His constant guiding of time towards His own mysterious ends. But what is interestingly observable in late sixteenth-century poetry is a growing uneasiness about the traditional understanding of, and language for, time. Where the scholastic doctrine of God's providential control of time stressed what John Veron called the 'general ruledom' of God, Protestant theologians saw time much more in terms of God's intervention in particular moments of time. Calvinist theology and popular devotion are distinctive for their simultaneous avoidance of a general doctrine of Providence and yet a rejection of any possible fortuitousness. The result is a view of time that is under God's control and yet is, from the human viewpoint, absolutely unpredictable. 'What if this present were the world's last night?' is the way one of Donne's religious sonnets opens – and it is a common cry of anxiety. Before each moment lies, for all we know, the abyss. The overall control of our lives may be in God's hands, but we cannot see, from moment to moment, where that control will take us. Each moment of human existence is therefore radically dependent on God: 'every yere, moneth and day is governed by a new and speciall Providence of God', wrote Calvin. Donne's sermons are full of such emphases. 'Upon every minute of this life, depend millions of years in the next', he writes and is echoed in many religious writers. A recurring phrase in the sermons and tracts of the age is the Pauline exhortation to 'redeem the time', to seize each moment's opportunity. A widespread nervousness about the discrete moments of man's life permeates the writing of the age. George Poulet has observed that 'the religions of the seventeenth century are all religions of continued grace', in the sense that God is felt to be holding up each moment of each man's life.[37]

The self that is created by Reformation theology and devotion and in the Protestant poetry takes a most distinct form. The Protestant self is one that is anxious, obsessed with its own state of salvation. It is the self that is created by the reading of the Geneva Bible, the poring over handbooks of self-knowledge, of searching for signs of election. It is the self that is articulated in the theological works of Perkins, Ames or Downame, and by the crude propaganda of Foxe or Beard. It is the decentred self of Greville's or Donne's religious poems. Greville asserted that we should see 'God's revenging as put upon every particular sin, to the despair, or confusion of morality'[38]; the pious believer was exhorted to look inwards – to look in his heart and write, to adapt Sidney's phrase – to see if there were signs of belonging to the covenant of grace. The self that is found is one radically subject to time. In each changing moment there might be new signs, as well as new opportunities for temptation, sin and damnation. Or it might provide unpredictably, the opportunity for God's grace arbitrarily to appear. In the words of Greville's Caelica, 'down in the depth of mine iniquity/Depriv'd of human graces, and divine,/Even there appears this saving God of mine'. The Protestant 'I', like the Petrarchan 'I', is an anxious, self-obsessed and above all time-bound 'I'. Its poetry is likewise 'self'-obsessed and that obsession often emerges in a concern with time, mutability, and flux – as we will in particular see with Shakespeare's sonnets in Chapter 7. The Reformation world is what Foucault terms a 'confessing society',[39] one obsessed with self-examination and with developing means to produce some fixed truth about the self. The lyric 'I' is invested with a keen anxiety about identity, a longing for a stable centre; it is what Zumthor speaks of as a 'hollow I', needing to be filled and yet never satisfied.

Neither theological certainties, nor the ritual of the Court, nor even the willed physical presence of the beloved can satisfy this anxiety. As Greenblatt has argued, a desperate faith in such a central core informs Wyatt's poetry, but what emerges is the artificiality and constraints with which the self is constructed. A mobility and restlessness of desire likewise haunts the poetry of Sidney, Ralegh, Donne and Shakespeare and – observable in the stern way by which it is repressed – in Spenser's and Greville's. What Greenblatt has termed 'unresolved and continuing conflict'[40] is a distinctive characteristic of the age's poetry and of much of its richly complex and problematic life.

The problematic nature of the self and its languages is thus not only a central concern in the age's secular poetry – it is a concern into which the age's theological contradictions feed. We can see the curious phenomenon of conflicting discursive structures – here, Protestantism and Petrarchism – crossing and rewriting each other. And it is fascinating seeing the contradictions between the official language – of theology or philosophy – with the articulated experience in writing. While the assumption of a unifying, fixed self remains fundamental to the religious and philosophical commonplaces of the age, the poetry continually exposes the fragility of the self – its artificiality, its temporality and vulnerability, its uneasy place within the age's ideological struggles. Throughout the age's poetry, we can see how the world of the sixteenth-century self is one of arbitrary events, unpredictable moments. It is a world dominated by change and un-predictability. Shakespeare's sonnets are among the greatest articulation of the inescapable determinism of time in the language. But the presence of time the destroyer, the corrupter that continually disrupts love, beauty and the security of the self, saturates late sixteenth-century verse.

Why were the late Elizabethans so obsessed with time? Another, more pertinent, way of putting that question is to ask what was this residual language – time, mutability, decay – really pointing to in the material contradictions of the age? Are there any senses that such a vocabulary was adequate? Are there signs of an alternative discourse arising?

There were, in fact, a few signs in the late sixteenth century, especially, that some writers were indeed sensing the inadequacy of the residual vocabulary for speaking of the 'nature' of human beings and of mattters traditionally controlled, often under pain of death, by orthodox religion (however 'orthodox' happened to be defined). There was undoubtedly more 'freethinking' in the period than the dominant ideology of religious conformity suggests, and some of it percolates into the poetry: into the sexual licentiousness of Marlowe's Ovidian narratives, for instance, or even indirectly in the repressed voices of heretics, like the one we hear condemned in Thomas Gilbart's moralistic doggerel about the death of the 'detestable and obstinate heretic', John Lewes, who was executed for heresy and who, under threat and intimidation, refused to conform:

Quoth he, 'Thou liest', and no more words
  At all this caitiff said
Nor no repentant sign would show,
  Which made us all dismayed.[41]

An especially important figure is the Italian philosopher and poet Giordano Bruno, who spent two years at Oxford (1583–85), published six books in England, had close contacts with the Sidney Circle, and dedicated his sonnet sequence *Gli Heroici Furore* to Sidney. Among Bruno's many heretical philosophical speculations – he saw God as a variable being, inseparable from the created universe, speculated on the infinitude of the universe, and saw Fortune, not Providence, as the highest power of the world – was a rapturous celebration of the mutability of the self. Typically he couches it in metaphysical terms, but often as if reaching towards some future epistemology. The typical sixteenth-century attitude to temporality is one of anxiety, with the self uncertainly caught between a desire for permanence and a fear of change. But for Bruno – and there are, as we shall see, intriguing echoes in some of Shakespeare's and Donne's sonnets – the self is defined precisely by its changeableness. Men, Bruno writes, 'are fools' if they 'dread the menace of death and of destiny, for all things in the stream of Time are subject to change and are unconquered by it; and this thy body, neither as a whole nor in its parts, is identical with yesterday'. In the ever-changing world, the self is always decentred: 'if in bodies, matter and entity there were not mutation, variety and vicissitude, there would be nothing agreeable, nothing good, nothing pleasurable'. In a spirit very different from traditional Christian theologians and preachers he exhorts his readers to accept their destiny as mutable beings and not to 'waste time, whose speed is infinite, on things superfluous and vain; for with astonishing speed the present slips by and the future approaches with equal rapidity'. Montaigne, widely read in England – not least by Shakespeare and Donne – was another writer obsessed by the mystery of the self and its dissolving: 'I describe not the essence, but the passage', and 'not a passage from age to age . . . but from day to day, from minute to minute'. Because, he argues, man's life is 'but a twinkling in the infinit course of an eternall night', men must 'tooth and naile retaine this use of this lives pleasure, which our yeares snatch from us, one after another'.[42]

The lyric 'I', then, is intimately bound up with major historical transitions. They include that from medieval thought to the self-conscious subjectivity of the late Renaissance; the Protestant obsession with the self decomposing before eternity or held together only in each new moment by God's grace; the emergent strains of speculative libertine philosophy like Bruno's or Montaigne's; the powerful insistence in the Court on *beau semblant*; and interacting with all, the last stage of the breakdown of the feudal mode of production. These contradictions leave their marks on the poetry of the age. It is time to turn more closely to the details of some of that poetry.

Notes

1. George Puttenham, *The Arte of English Poesie*, edited by Gladys Doidge Willcock and Alice Walker (Cambridge, 1936), pp. 24, 45.

2. Christopher Marlowe, *The Complete Poems and Translations*, edited by Stephen Orgel (Harmondsworth, 1971), p. 209; Roland Barthes, *The Pleasure of the Text*, translated by Richard Howard (New York, 1975), pp. vii, 7, 39, 46, 67.

3. C. S. Lewis, *English Literature in the Sixteenth Century, excluding Drama* (Oxford, 1954), p. 380.

4. *Tottel's Miscellany*, edited by Hyder Edward Rollins, revised edition (Cambridge, Mass., 1965), p. 28; Charles Trinkaus, *The Poet as Philosopher* (New Haven, 1979), p. 2.

5. Michel Foucault, 'The History of Sexuality: Interview', *OLR*, 4, no.2 (1980), 3–14 (p. 3).

6. See Malcolm Evans, ' "In Love with Curious Words": Signification and Sexuality in English Petrarchism', in *Jacobean Poetry and Prose: Rhetoric, Representation and the Popular Imagination*, edited by Clive Bloom (London, 1988), 119–50.

7. Leonard Forster, *The Icy Fire* (Cambridge, 1969), pp. 4, 5, 22.

8. Spenser, *Amoretti*, p. 81; *The Poems of Sir Walter Ralegh*, edited by Agnes M. C. Latham (London, 1951), p. 21.

9. William Shullenburger, 'Lacan and the Play of Desire in Poetry', *Massachusetts Studies in English*, 7 (1978), 33–40 (pp. 34–35).

10. Stephen Greenblatt, *Renaissance Self-Fashioning* (New Haven, 1980).

11. Forster, p. 27.

12. Patricia Fumerton, 'Secret Arts: Elizabethan Miniatures and Sonnets', *Representations*, 15 (Summer, 1986), 57–97; Anne Ferry, *The 'Inward' Language: Sonnets of Wyatt, Sidney, Shakespeare, Donne* (Chicago, 1983); Eugene Vance, 'Love's Concordance: The Poetics of Desire and Joy of the Text', *Diacritics*, 5 (Spring 1975), 40–52 (p. 49).

13. John Freccero, 'The Fig Tree and the Laurel: Petrarch's Poetics', *Diacritics*, 5 (Spring 1975), 3440 (p. 34). See also Germaine Warkentin, 'The Meeting of the Muses: Sidney and the Mid-Tudor Poets', in *Sir Philip Sidney and the Interpretation of Renaissance Culture*, edited by Gary F. Waller and Michael D. Moore (London, 1984), pp. 17–33 (p. 18); Carol Thomas Neely, 'The Structure of English Renaissance Sonnet Sequences', *ELH*, 45 (1978), 359–89; Germaine Warkentin. ' "Love's Sweetest Part, Variety": Petrarch and the Curious Frame of the Renaissance Sonnet Sequence', *Ren. and Ref.*, 11 (1975), 14–23.

14. Samuel Daniel, 'A Defence of Rhyme', in *Elizabethan Critical Essays*, edited by G. Gregory Smith (Oxford, 1904), p. 366.

15. Paul Zumthor, 'From Hi(story) or the Paths of the Pun: The Grand Rhetoriquers of Fifteenth-Century France', *NLH*, 10 (1979), 231–65; 'From the Universal to the Particular in Medieval Poetry ', *MLN*, 85 (1970), 816; *Essai de Poétique Medievale* (Paris, 1972), pp.189f; John Stevens, *Music and Poetry in the Early Tudor Court*, (London, 1961), p. 206. For the impact of printing on the interiorization of the poetic voice, see William J. Kennedy, 'Petrarchan Audiences and Print Technology', *JMRS*, 14 (1984), 1–20.

16. Forster, pp. 128, 131–32.

17. Lewis, p. 225.

18. Warkentin, 'Meeting of the Muses', p. 21; Richard J. Panofsky, 'A Descriptive Study of English Mid-Tudor Short Poetry, 1557–1577' (unpublished Ph.D. dissertation, University of California, Santa Barbara, 1975), p. 182.

19. George Turberville, *Epitaphs, Epigrams, Songs and Sonnets* (1567) and *Epitaphes and Sonnetes* (1576), edited by Richard J. Panofsky (New York, 1977), pp. ix, 119; George Gascoigne, *Certayne Notes on Instruction*, in *Elizabethan Critical Essays*, 1, 150.

20. Lewis, p. 49.

21. Robert Stoller, *The Dynamics of Sexual Attraction* (New York, 1979), p. 31.

22. Stoller, *Dynamics*, p. 32.

23. Paglia, *Sexual Personae*, p. 189; see also Louise Kaplan, *Female Perversions: The Temptations of Emma Bovary* (New York, 1991).

24. Freud, 'Three Essays on Sexuality,' *Standard Edition* VII, p. 156.

25. Robert Stoller, *Perversion* (1975), pp. 99, 105. See also Charles W. Socarides, 'The Demonified Mother: A Study of Voyeurism and Sexual Sadism', *International Review of Psycho-Analysis*, 1 (1974), 192–93; David W. Allen, *The Fear of Looking or Scopophilic-Exhibitionist Conflicts* (Bristol, 1974), especially pp. 40–41.

26. Nancy J. Vickers, 'Diana Described: Scattered Woman and Scattered Rhyme,' *Critical Inquiry*, 8 (1981–82), 265–79 (p. 265).

27. Kaplan, *Female Perversions*, pp. 125, 35.

28. See Gilles Deleuze and Felix Guattari, *Anti-Oedipus: Capitalism and Schizophrenia*, trans. Robert Hurley, Mark Seem, and Helen R. Lane (Minneapolis, 1983).

29. Alan Sinfield, *Literature in Protestant England* (Brighton, 1983), pp. 14, 19.

30. William Tyndale, *The Practice of Prelates*, ed. Henry Walter (Cambridge: The Parker Society, 1849), p. 12; *Elizabethan Critical Essays*, I, xiv; Barbara K. Lewalski, *Protestant Poetics and the Seventeenth Century Religious Lyric* (Princeton, 1979), p. ix.

31. John N. King, *English Reformation Literature: The Tudor Origins of the Protestant Tradition* (Princeton, 1982), pp. 16, 209.

32. See Ruth Hughey, *John Harington of Stepney, Tudor Gentleman: His Life and Works* (Columbus, 1971).

33. King, p. 319.

34. Coburn Freer, *Music for a King: George Herbert's Style and the Metrical Psalms* (Baltimore, 1972), p. 60.

35. Sidney, *A Defence of Poetry*, in *Miscellaneous Prose*, edited by Katherine Duncan-Jones and Jan van Dorsten (Oxford, 1973), p. 77.

36. Philippe de Mornay, *A Worke Concerning the Truenesse of the Christian Religion*, translated by Sir Philip Sidney and Arthur Golding (London, 1587), p. 139.

37. John Veron, *A Fruteful Treatise of Predestination* (London, 1563), fol. 85; John Calvin, *The Institutes of the Christian Religion*, translated by Thomas Norton (London, 1561), p. 1, xvi, 4; *The Sermons of John Donne*, edited by G. R. Potter and Evelyn M. Simpson (Berkeley, 1953–62), III, p. 288; René Descartes, *Principles of Philosophy, A Discourse on Method, etc.*, translated by John Veitch (London, 1912), p. 173; Georges Poulet, *Studies in Human Time*, translated by Elliott Coleman (Baltimore, 1956), p. 18.

38. 'An Edition of Fulke Greville's Life of Sir Philip Sidney', edited by J. C. Kuhn (unpublished doctoral dissertation, Yale University, 1973), p. 163.

39. Michel Foucault, *The History of Sexuality, Volume 1, An Introduction*, translated by Robert Hurley (New York, 1978), p. 59.

40. Zumthor, 'From the Universal', p. 816; Greenblatt, *Renaissance Self-Fashioning*, p. 8.

41. Jones, *New Oxford Book*, pp. 339–42 (p. 342).

42. Giordano Bruno, *The Expulsion of the Triumphant Beast*, translated by Arthur D. Imerti (New Brunswick, 1964), p. 89; *Giordano Bruno's The Heroic Frenzies*, translated by P. E. Memmo Jr (Chapel Hill, 1966), pp. 175, 219–20; *The Essays of Michael Lord of Montaigne*, translated by John Florio, introduced by A. R. Waller (London, 1910), Vol 2. p. 232; Vol 1. pp. 261, 25.

Chapter 4

A Century of Court Poets: Dunbar, Wyatt, Ralegh, Greville

Poets and audiences

Every society has its dominant cultural apparatuses which both make possible and control its cultural practices, including poetry. For the sixteenth century it was the Court. The Court nurtured, encouraged (and discouraged) particular kinds of poetry. In this chapter I will examine the poetry of four poets whose careers, over some 150 years, were moulded and defined by royal courts in England and Scotland. The first, William Dunbar, was a poet in the Scottish Courts of James IV and V, in the late fifteenth century. The second is Sir Thomas Wyatt, whose poetry was seen by Sidney, fifty years after, as marking a radical poetical breakthrough. From the Court of Henry VIII we will go forward to two contrasting figures who wrote under both Elizabeth and James I, under whose reign the crowns and courts of England and Scotland were united: Sir Walter Ralegh, one of the most flamboyant of Elizabethan courtiers, an incidental but extraordinarily powerful poet; and Fulke Greville, second Lord Brooke, who was a close friend of Sidney, and whose poems continue and in significant ways intensify the Protestant ambivalence about the value of poetry.

Puttenham's *The Arte of English Poesie*, from which I have already quoted extensively, is a particularly intriguing guide to the power of the Court if only because its author was very much on the Court's margins. Married to a baroness, Lady Windsor, Puttenham himself had no court status, and the only comment on his skill in poetry by a courtier, Sir John Harington, is scornful. But his views are those of an observer who saw the Court's influence over far more than those men and women who are clasified as 'courtier poets' in a recent study, 'the ranking officeholders' and 'that relatively permanent group of courtiers' who 'spent an appreciable amount of time, often traceable for weeks or months per year, attending court'. Beyond that small and often intensely anxious group, who certainly included all four of the poets in this chapter, were many aspiring gentlemen, like Puttenham, or Donne, or Spenser, who wished to be part of that magic circle. Beyond that again was a further circle, that included a poet like Shakespeare, whose living was made in activities that were on a social level below the Court but which were still subject to its surveillance and sometimes direct intervention. Furthest of all from the Court's power are some of the poems, songs and ballads that grow from marginal regions and dialects, from the dispossessed and poor, many of which were appropriated by poets closer to the Court (as the old 'Walsingham' ballad is by both Ralegh and Sidney). These are the relatively voiceless poets, whose compositions and, very occasionally, whose writings echo across our history in their eloquent silences and half-silences.[1]

With all four of the poets discussed in this chapter, the direct connections with the Court are unmistakable. The poetry they wrote and the social formations by which they were themselves, in a very direct sense, written are inseparable. All four were taken into the Court's attempt to control poetry as a means of articulating its values, to make it an 'art of state'. For them all, poetry was something incidental, merely a small part of their public careers. All were glittering public successes and yet also suffered frustration, failure (and in two, almost three, cases) execution. All four used poetry as a means of becoming noticed at Court: to entertain, advance their political careers, or to cope with political defeat or disillusion.

The Court provided all these poets with their primary audience, and at this point it is worth stressing in less theoretical terms than were possible in Chapter 2, the way 'audience' is important in our understanding of sixteenth-century poetry. There are some poems in this period written primarily for their authors, almost like entries in a diary – many of Greville's *Caelica* poems, for instance. But most of the poetry, whether an epic like *The Faerie Queene* or the myriad of seemingly more private lyric poems, are directed at a multiplicity of audiences. The lyrics, in particular, were often 'performed' rather than read among audiences of friends at Court or in courtiers' country houses. Many of the love poems of the period must have meant very different things according to these different audiences. Even (perhaps especially) those poems written originally as expressions of love for a particular woman would have been adapted to different occasions (or women!), and were variously understood by different members of their audiences. Some very particular references – to black eyes, boating on the Thames, or special tokens or words, for instance – may have acted as a kind of secret, even confessional, code for the apparent addressee of the poem, but in general such poems are deliberately designed to be as indeterminate as possible, so that different audiences could relate to them. Likewise, today as we read or listen to them, we fill in the gaps and indeterminacies we encounter in the text: we bring our own experiences to bear on the poems and so in a real sense their meanings become ours.

We can very readily deduce the ways by which many of the period's lyric poems assume a multiplicity of audiences by looking at the choice and variety of rhetorical techniques, especially in the way the lyric 'I' invites a reader or hearer to become part of the poem's experience. Part of the 'delight' of poetry, to use Sidney's term, is the way that when we read we become part of a 'suture' effect, as we oscillate between the 'self' the poem asks us to participate in as we read and the 'self' we (think we) are. As Sharratt explains it, it is as if ' "I" were both present and absent, looking over my own shoulder rather than simply identified with myself, yet unable to be seen even in the mirror I hold up to myself'. The 'mirror' of course is the poem: the particular *frisson* we get from the poem is the experience of reading, rather like the participation we get from love, and as Sharratt puts it nicely, 'the "primal scene" of literature is always an act of a reader rather than a mysterious attribute of a text'.[2] It is we – the successive 'I's of the poem's readings – who make the poem's meanings. The 'I' of the poet is just one of the 'I's that are contained by the poem in its successive readings. Like a crystal held up to the light, the poem refracts light from many different angles. Today, we read much contemporary poetry as 'confessional', directly reflecting the intimacies of the poet's self sorting out the complexities of his or her experiences. But, no less than with sixteenth-century poems, the 'self' of contemporary poetry is likewise made up of a tissue of languages, and many modern philosophers have argued that our age will be looked back to as one when the notion of the 'self' was finally dissolved (after 400 years of trying!) back into the languages which make it up. Just as Einstein saw the notion of an 'object' as 'one of the most primitive concepts' of human thinking, so the notion of a fixed 'I' is less the guarantee of our identity than a figure or metaphor whereby we focus our desires upon the world.[3]

But what about the poet's 'intention'? Did he not have a special audience or even a special meaning in mind? Often a special audience is indeed named, as we shall see in a moment with Dunbar. But there are occasions when even the primary audience will change, as a poet might decide to change the colour of the eyes of the lady 'in' his poems as a compliment to his new-found love – or else to disguise that fact! And there are many, perhaps most, poems where the audience is deliberately left indeterminate. In his autobiography, the (extremely) minor poet Thomas Whythorne explained how, in an exchange of love verses with a noble lady by whom he was employed, he deliberately left his verses ambiguous and open-ended so that his audiences, both the lady and other later readers, might fill out the lines with their own meanings. 'A man', he writes, 'cannott alway speak in prynt' and so, he says, 'I mad this song sumwhat dark and dowtfull of sens bekawz I know not serteinly how shee wold tak it, nor to whoz handz it miht kumen after that she had read it.' His own interpretation of the poems he prints in the autobiography is, to say the least, ambiguous, as if the friend he is addressing needs to have the whole affair explained away! Poets not only change their minds about poems; they change their minds about love. To adopt the ironical advice of Greville's *Caelica* 22, 'no man' should 'print a kiss, lines may deceive'.[4] With such considerations about audience and the performative nature of sixteenth-century poetry in mind, let us turn to a sample of four court poets.

Dunbar and Wyatt

Dunbar's poetry shows the relative backwardness of the English Renaissance upon which Sidney was to comment in the *Defence*. Long before the English monarchy had consolidated its power and started to use poetry as an 'instrument of State', the Scottish Court, notably under James III and IV, was showing the powerful hold over poetry and poets exercised by many other European courts. Even more than Sidney's or Ralegh's a century later, Dunbar's poetry shows how confident he is in his inheritance of both a native Scots tradition of courtly poetry and a whole European tradition, from which English poetry at the time and for much later was relatively isolated. Dunbar is self-consciously the servant and the panegyrist of a system upon which his living depends. 'The Thrissell and the Rois', for instance, is a typical public court poem, an epithalamion celebrating the marriage of James IV and Margaret Tudor. Written in rhyme royal and taking the form of a dream allegory, it presents an idealized picture of the Court and the monarch on whom its life centres as models of stability, much as a Ralegh's 'Praisd Be Dianas Faire and Harmless Light' does nearly a century later. Dunbar's verse has a confidence in its significant place in its society, conveyed in part in a lightness of touch not found in England before Surrey and Sidney. He presents the Court itself as harmonious and sophisticated, the embodiment of a golden age as replete and aureate as the language in which its celebrations are expressed. Like many of Ralegh's, Dunbar's poems are essentially pieces of reassuring propaganda, full of stylized and dehistoricized landscapes decked out in courtly garments – the May morning, rose gardens, birds singing, ladies dreaming and goddesses visiting the humble poet, who then wakes and tries to tell his vision. In such poems, Dunbar is flattering, light, even occasionally lascivious and flirtatious. As Scott notes, there is often a 'homeliness' about his poems, 'almost a cosiness as of the pater familias at his own fireside'. In 'Of a Dance in the Quenis Chalmer', there is a warm, idealized picture of the Queen's room. It is a place of good company, cheerfulness, where the poet is welcomed as an entertainer and even asked to be a helpful critic.

Dunbar has a particularly strong sense of an audience, most of whom were probably such court ladies. His rhetoric of address moves slyly between direct identification of a primary audience (without excluding others) and a sophisticated nonspecificity. His idealized pictures of his specified courtly audience, in such poems as 'The Goldyn Targe', create an atmosphere of dignity, hierarchy and order while a similarly directly focused poem, 'Sweet Rois of Vertew and of Gentilnes', is one of the most moving lyrics in the period, a celebration of sensitivity and beauty as fine as most of Wyatt's fifty years later. Likewise, 'Of a Dance in the Quenis Chalmer' is the confident work of a courtier favoured for his skill and usefulness to the Court, slyly adding sexual innuendo to the traditional role of court wit and favourite. In such poems, using the pose of the speaking bard, Dunbar's verse is notable for its confident dramatization of a multiplicity of court voices, but always keeping a particular audience, even particular kinds of social occasions, in mind. In such poems, he will address his audience collectively or individually and will sometimes include their possible responses in the poems, which are designed to evoke a distinctively congenial, communal, atmosphere. In 'Tua mariit Wemen and the Wedo' he presents a witty account of three forthright women's differing views of men, and invites his audience to choose among them, putting the question 'Quhilk wald ye waill to you wif, gif ye suld wed one?' It is a nice device to include his courtly audience in the poem, even if it sweeps questions of gender politics aside in its unselfconscious masculinist assumptions. Similarly, with 'Of a Dance', where the fun and harmony are paramount: the poem is a light-hearted account of how the lead dancer can never keep his feet in time, and so sets the pattern for the rest of the dancers:

> Than cam in Maistir Robert Scha
> He leuket as he culd lern tham a;
> Bot ay his ane futt did waver,
> He stackeret Iyk ane strummall aver
> That hopscchackellt war aboin the kne:
> To seik fra Sterling to Stranaver,
> A mirrear daunce mycht na man see.[5]

The 'man' who stands out (apart, that is, from the women) is 'Dunbar the Mackar' himself, who leaps about in the 'dirrye dantoun' so enthusiastically that he loses a shoe. Such poems – often enlivened

by some fairly coarse humour – show the place of poetry in the late
fifteenth-century Scottish Court. But Dunbar's poetry also introduces
us to a darker side of court poetry – to the power relationship between
poetry and Court. The Court of James IV of Scotland generated a myth
of itself much like that of the Court of Elizabeth I of England – that
it was the embodiment of a golden age of harmony, stasis and order.
Even in Dunbar's most apparently celebratory verse there emerge hints
of a darker side, incongruities that occur on the level of idiom or syntax,
and that suggest the strain and dislocation of subduing poetry to the
Court. In the long poem 'The Flyting of Dunbar and Kennedie', a
satiric account of a sustained argument between poets (which, of course,
Dunbar wins), the comic invective cannot hide a darker insecurity over
status, not only of the person of the poet, but of poetry itself.

In short, reading Dunbar – situated as he is as a late 'Scottish
Chaucerian' at the beginning of our period, we become aware not
just of his skill as a 'makar' but of the rich and powerful court culture,
for which he is the spokesman and panegyrist, and yet of which he is
also the product and victim. Not unlike Wyatt's or Ralegh's, Dunbar's
poems reveal a darker underside than the light-hearted courtly game
or witty flytings. For his world is inherently fragmentary. As Scott
comments, 'disintegrated and bitty, its proper form [is] the short
poem, for there is no wholeness to sustain a long one'. That is
a remark worth pondering with all these 'occasional' court poets.
Perhaps the short poem predominated throughout the age not just
because it usually took less time to write but because it was the
best record of the felt fragmentariness and arbitrariness of court life.
Certainly in Dunbar's short lyrics, beneath the dominant fantasy of the
Court's benevolent and harmonious power, is a sense of it as watchful,
plotting, controlling. In 'Schir, Ye Have Mony Servitouris' we see the
typical anxious self produced by the Court: we sense it as a world of
time-serving professional entertainers, divines and anxious courtiers, all
surrounding and dependent upon the King. Celebration is undercut by
what it tries to exorcize – the anxiety of separate selves created by and at
the mercy of the Court. Dunbar, Scott suggests persuasively, is a 'poet of
revolution before the time for revolution is ripe'.[6] His poetry articulates
a frustration through and despite the Court's language, the energy of his
verse beating against the Court's desire to master it. This is an anxiety
that as yet has not found alternative language; it emerges, therefore, as
a coarseness or an intrusion of moral outrage or frustration in the way
a century later it erupts into the poetry of Ralegh or Robert Sidney.

The second of the four poets in this chapter is Sir Thomas Wyatt.
Like Sidney, fifty years later, Wyatt has some claim to be seen as an
all-round Renaissance man. He was a soldier, statesman, diplomat,
linguist and courtier. Although later in the century his reputation as a

poet fell below that of the Earl of Surrey (especially in Puttenham's and Sidney's versions of the triumph of courtly poetry and the embodiment of 'true' aristocratic nobility in Surrey), in our time he has been generally seen as the more interesting, largely because of what is perceived as his anticipation of the vigorous, idiomatic and dramatic style of Donne. Wyatt was, like Sidney, and unlike Surrey, not born into an aristocratic, but certainly a 'Court' family. His father was a Privy Councillor, and before he was twenty, Wyatt was active at Court. His life – which likely included an affair with Ann Boleyn, daring diplomacy, an interest in Italian fashions and poetry – was, as Starkey puts it, 'though dramatic . . . in no way unusual. Every major aspect of it could be paralleled in the biographies of a dozen or more of his contemporaries at the court of Henry VIII'.[7] What sets him apart is his poetry. Wyatt's is certainly the most compelling English poetry written before the 1580s. It articulates brilliantly the growing pressures of an increasingly centralized Court upon poetry and poet, upon public and private experiences alike. First collected after his death in Tottel's *Miscellany*, Wyatt seemed, forty years later, to be sufficiently sophisticated and attuned to the 'false semblant' of Petrarchan fashion to allow Puttenham to list him among the 'new company of courtly makers'. But struggling to be heard in his poetry are other contradictory voices – those of the puzzled or indignant lover, the frustrated or anxious courtier, and the humanist moralist whose wisdom was rooted in a tradition to which the ostentatious, paranoid Court of Henry VIII was at once paying lip-service and ignoring. What emerges in the gaps, absences and repression of his verse are the strains of a late medieval moralism adrift in a new, seemingly amoral world which is intent on using traditional moral commonplaces to justify a ruthless *realpolitik*. Caught among these contradictory discourses, Wyatt's poetry articulates a losing battle against a collective power determined to control access to and forbid participation in the dominant discourse except on terms dictated by itself.[8]

Like Dunbar, Wyatt is a typical courtly 'maker'. He was not only a prominent diplomat and courtier but an accomplished court entertainer. Most of his poems are conventionally elegant, clear, impersonal, speaking with the voice of the collective, directed at his audience rather than to his own experiences. It is largely occasional verse, simply elegant dramatizations of courtly values, contributions to the games of love, preferment, and intrigue in the Court. It is poetry (as Stevens puts it) as stylized talk, but it is unusually intelligent, taking advantage of the new interest in humanist rhetorical theory, especially the Ciceronian ideals of directness and concentrating on the emotional effects of language upon an audience. Greenblatt has argued that the court lyric in Wyatt's circle was like the diplomatic mission, 'sent forth to perform the bidding of its creator, to manifest and enhance his power at the expense of someone else': just as 'Wyatt was sent, on behalf of Henry VIII, to entice, to threaten, to complain of ingratitude, to circumvent attack, so Wyatt's own lyrics circulated through the court on their author's behalf'.[9]

What makes Wyatt's poetry different is the vigour and flexibility of the voice, and the uncertainties and contradictions that emerge through that voice. Unlike the verse of most of his contemporaries, there is in his poetry little aureate diction, and although, read together, his poems tend to be monolithic in tone, when he starts to experiment, especially by adapting the complex use of the verse paragraph as a unit of argument, Wyatt's courtly songs become complex and evocative, like the haunting and quietly witty 'Blame Not My Lute', which uses the strength of the late medieval court poetry – a plain, muscular line, a direct voice, a sense of a shared community – out of which a self-analytic self is struggling for definition. In other poems, some of the less felicitous characteristics of late medieval verse can be seen: lumbering, broken, heavily end-stopped lines, the hints of aureate diction, heavy allegory. But alongside the bulk of earlier sixteenth-century verse, Wyatt's poetry makes a marked movement away from the copious, aureate diction towards the rhetoric and systematization of desire offered by the Petrarchism that had been a predominant fashion in much of Europe for well over a century but which had never taken hold in England. In Wyatt's poems, we can see sixteenth-century English poetry catching up with the rest of Europe in one enormous step.

But Wyatt is of even more interest to us as an early (in English, not European terms) Petrarchan experimenter. His is the first substantial body of work in the period in England through which the power of the Court speaks as the controller and creator not only of the dominant discourse but of alternatives to it, which however dimly apprehended and unable to find a place within it except by negation, none the less radically disrupt it. Poetry is thus linked not merely to courtly dalliance or personal desire, but to the increasingly ruthless and desperate need to find a place within power. Responding to Stevens's remark that poetry in Henry's Court was 'a little music after supper', Greenblatt comments ironically, 'I tend to think of it more as a little small talk with Stalin'.[10] Wyatt's satires have frequently been seen in such a context but as we saw with Dunbar, and will see with Ralegh, where a writer is deliberately attacking the Court, his arguments tend to be couched in archaic and moralistic terms. Wyatt's satires, however stringent, still operate within the dominant discourse. In his third satire, addressed to Sir Francis Brian, a fellow flamboyant and outspoken courtier, for example, he ironically considers the principles by which courtly success is determined. One manuscript is submitted: 'How to Use the Court': . .': 'Thou know'st well, first whoso can seek to please/Shall purchase friends where truth shall but offend'. It is vigorous but finally commonplace satire, nothing but sound moral advice without hope of shaking what already in Wyatt's time was seemingly unshakeable, the power of the Court itself. Wyatt's other two long verse epistles also satirize, in a similar moralizing manner, the abuses of the Court, where one must learn 'to cloak away the vice' and 'press the virtue that it may not rise'.

But nowhere in the satires is there the means explicitly to call into question the structure that holds the whole together. The emergence of cultural alternatives and, eventually, a new social formation is always uneven and outpaces the available discursive structures. Wyatt may raise the question of where the honest man finds succour at Court – but it is the typical question of one who has lost, or is anxious about losing, his place and is not able to conceive of cultural alternatives. Something more interesting, however, is going on in the poems found in Wyatt's personal manuscript, known as the Devonshire Manuscript. There we find poems that, ostensibly less political, provide more subtle, indirect references to the ways in which the Court created and controlled its members. Many adapt for political ends as well as erotic ones – for the first time in any extensive way in English – the Petrarchan conventions. In origin these poems look like *vers de société*, pleas designed to titillate and amuse a closely knit yet nervously anxious social group. But, often, speaking through the poetry, where it is, as it were, off its guard, are the fragments or anticipations of alternative discourses. Many of these poems are disrupted by a discomfort with the game that is more than conventional erotic disillusion. Even songs like 'My Lute, Awake!' and 'My Pen, Take Pain', as Kamholtz comments, 'hint at an artistic mode on the verge of collapse, for they are lyrics which end symbolically in the silence of the court artist'.[11] In other poems, the fear behind this repression becomes very specific – at least as some of the poems might have been read by Wyatt himself. 'Ye old Mule' is in origin, perhaps, a 'private joke' at Anne Boleyn[12]; 'Whoso List to Hunt' is a fine piece of wistful irony, a graceful withdrawal from erotic and political entanglements. But although such poems may have had specific erotic occasions, and however much they look like conventional love poetry, they are less erotic than political lyrics: their 'I' is written not merely by literary languages but by the language of political power. Paradox – 'I my self my self always to hate' – becomes a language of cultural paralysis: the repeated 'I' is insistent, urgent, yet still controlled by the codes in which it must function even while it struggles unsuccessfully to articulate something beyond them. New modes of articulation, 'active and pressing but not yet fully articulated', in Williams's terms, are crying out to be heard, but there are as yet no words for them.[13]

Wyatt's most celebrated lyric, 'They flee from me', may stand as a prime example not just of the complexity, verbal sensitivity, and increasing metrical dexterity of his poetry (as it is conventionally, and I think, justly, seen) but also of the multiple anxieties articulated by his poems and about the power that both brings them and the values they explore into existence and controls them. In Chapter 1, I mentioned the variety of readings the poem can provide today. It can certainly be read as a fictional dramatization of erotic anguish, or (if we put it back within Henrician society) within the Renaissance tradition of debating questions about love, here raising specifically the question of fickleness ('new fangleness') and desert ('what she hath deserved'). It is thus a communal lyric: the 'you' in the final lines contains a genuine question, as the speaker turns to his audience in puzzlement: 'But since that I so kindly am served,/I would fain know what she hath deserved.' The undecidability of 'kind' and 'kindly' comes from its meanings as 'according to kind', 'with kindness'. But which kind? The lover has carefully played by the rules of the courtly game, only to find them undermined by a disturbing and unique experience of love, 'once in special', for which his training as a courtier in *fals semblant* has not prepared him, but with which the lady in question remains content. She might even (as some of my women students say) gloat over it.

Thomas Whythorne, occupying a similar role in relation to his lady, writes that 'her joy waz to hav men to bee in loov with her, and to brag sumtyms how shee kowld handl such az wer so, az how shee kowld fetch them in, and then how shee kould with a frown mak them look pal, and how with a mery look shee kowld mak them to joy again'. He also gives the male members of Wyatt's audience a possible answer: 'to dissembull with A dissembler waz no dissimulation, and to play with her az the hunter doth, who hunteth A hart, as much to see her subtyl skips and leaps az for to get her karkas'.[14] In such remarks we come very close to the material realities of the time and to poetry's place in it. But Wyatt's lover cannot yet perhaps rise to such bravado. Ostracized by those he once hunted, whether women or all those who, like timid and eager animals, hunt and are hunted in the Court, the poem's speaker cannot choose which language – courtly, political, individualistic – deals best with his emotional complications, and his 'gentleness' (like 'kindness', a key undecidable word, torn apart by the conflicting discursive systems that float and eddy around it) has proved inadequate before this new complexity.

And what (as my students insisted) about the woman? Can we imagine that she has a voice in such a world? In Dunbar's poetry, the women are reduced to an admiring audience, to be praised, flattered, idealized, and – in certain genres – reviled as sexually voracious. All these roles are part of both a courtly game and indications of a gender ideology so seemingly unshakeable as almost to constitute a permanent part of the Western psyche. Can the same be said of Wyatt's poem? It is clear that it can be read as embodying a typical male fantasy, wanting, even with the best, most idealistic intentions, to fix a woman as a possession – tamed, overcome, part of what as a male and a courtier, he deserved. But what political force does that taming try to repress?

The hurt and puzzlement of this poem, evocative and perplexing, contain, therefore, more than just the anxiety produced by the conflicting codes of erotic desire. The implied question at the poem's end is more than a sophisticated plea for sympathy by the hurt male ego, and the questions it raises go far beyond erotic and social role playing in the Court of Henry VIII. Like the best of Wyatt's poems, 'They Flee from Me' is the product of conflicting discursive structures that point to crises in the whole social formation. Greenblatt points out parallels in the language of diplomatic dispatches, including Wyatt's own, to the language of love poetry, and his point can be extended. Political power is expressed in terms of personal allegiance and pressure; erotic power is expressed in the codes of political domination. What is at issue in the relationship is simply (or complexly) power, the same preoccupation with domination and submission, in which 'the options are to enforce submission or to submit, to be the aggressor or to be the victim'.[15] The pain of a poem like 'They Flee from Me' arises not only from thwarted power but from an inability to formulate any more creative alternative to that permitted by the Court, either on the erotic or the political level. The lyric poem, seemingly a socially marginal cultural form, is being put under pressure and registering far beyond what its author consciously intended – what Williams terms emergent 'structures of feeling'. 'They Flee from Me' and many of Wyatt's other lyrics are struggling to articulate not just 'individual' but far broader socio-cultural experiences for which there are not, at least for the writer, and perhaps for society at large, words in which they can be voiced.

Ralegh

For the third and fourth examples of court poets in this chapter, we move on some fifty years or more where, in the poetry of the last twenty years of the century, we can see emerging much more noticeably the conflicts that haunt Dunbar's and Wyatt's. Part of the interest of late sixteenth-century poetry arises from the way we can see the increasing emergence of alternatives to the power that brought it into being. Let us start by looking back from the very end of the era. The succession of Elizabeth by her 'cousin of Scotland' in 1603 was chiefly manoeuvred by a man whose family had manipulated many of the routine aspects of English politics for four decades, Sir Robert Cecil. In the anxious shuffling for court influence and position that accompanied James's accession two men's careers were thwarted by Cecil's craft and power. Each had served the Queen, though in very different roles; each was an occasional, though fine, poet; and a comparison of their careers shows both the lure and unpredictability of the power of the Court and the place of poetry within it. The two poets are Sir Walter Ralegh and Fulke Greville, later first Baron Brooke.

In 1601, Ralegh and Greville were associated, probably for the only time in their careers, in their joint arrest of some of the followers of the Earl of Essex who had supposedly plotted to overthrow the Queen. Greville had long been a cautious supporter of Essex, and in the 1601 crisis fought carefully to save the Earl's life while always maintaining his overall loyalty to the Queen. Ralegh had, for a decade, made no secrecy of his jealousy of Essex, the man with whom he had fought for the favours of the ageing Elizabeth. Over twenty years earlier, both men had entered the Court without spectacular advantages: but whereas the flamboyant Ralegh became a favourite of the Queen, Greville later recalled his own 'misplaced endeavours'[16] in Elizabeth's Court, though his caution and circumspection did earn him a series of responsible positions. The fall of Ralegh in 1603 and his sentencing to death for treason were spectacular events, as was his eventual execution in 1617; the fall of Greville, as part of Cecil's prudent policy of eliminating supporters of Essex, went virtually unnoticed. In 1615 Greville, an embittered sixty-year-old, returned to high public office; in 1617, after a fruitless voyage to find the supposedly fabulous wealth of El Dorado, Ralegh perished on the scaffold. During their years of exclusion, each wrote a major prose work which meditated on the monarch and the Court in which they had served: in Greville's case, a life of the man whose memory and friendship he carried to the grave, Sir Philip Sidney; in Ralegh's, a book which belies its title by being one of the most revealingly subjective works of the age, the great unfinished *History of the World*. Greville, hiding his revulsion from the Jacobean Court, never published his; Ralegh brazenly published his as an affront to King James.

Ralegh accepted and chose to live out the myth of the Elizabethan Court, conceiving his life as a flamboyant epic, and his handful of poems are part of that myth. As one lyric puts it, its naked request for favour appropriately disguised in the gentility of Petrarchan plaint, 'Then must I needes advaunce my self by Skyll/And Iyve to serve, in hope of your goodwyll' ('Sweete ar the thoughtes'). Advancing himself by skill meant, in Ralegh's case, accepting the Court as an arena of self-assertion, or (in another of the metaphors that recurs in his work) as a new world to be conquered. Both are recurring motifs. In Thomas Pynchon's metaphor, Ralegh 'yo-yos' between the roles of the courtier, politician, explorer, free-thinker, poet, amateur philosopher and lover. Greenblatt has suggested that Ralegh saw his life as a work of art, and that the Court was, in another of his favourite metaphors, a great theatre in which the boldest actor was the most successful. He argues that Ralegh's role-playing incorporates two contradictory Renaissance traditions – one seeing life as a series of required roles, the other seeing life itself as a play that is empty, futile, and unreal.[17] But was Ralegh that much in control of his roles? Was the multiplicity of his life the product of his personal choice? If he were to succeed in the glittering and dangerous world of the Elizabethan Court, he needed to take on and excel at whatever roles the Court thrust upon him. But unlike someone like Sidney, who was a courtier by birth and training, Ralegh became one because his survival depended upon it. He had to commit himself absolutely to each role forced upon him in a world that was was dangerous, unpredictable and changing; the wonder was that he survived so brilliantly for so long. The roles he played, including the poet, were like the explorations, the geographical 'discoveries' he made: short, tactical essays, opportunistic and pragmatic, impositions of his will upon the world into which he found himself thrust.

What makes Ralegh so interesting is, first, that the 'selves' he lived out were not, in fact, self-created, and second, that his poetry registers his struggle to accept his positioning within the Court's power. Unlike Dunbar and Wyatt, he was a poet because poetry was an approved and effective way of advancing himself. Puttenham mentions Ralegh as one of the 'crew of courtly makers, Noble men and Gentlemen' of the Court. 'Blown this way and that (and sometimes lifted into real poetry)', as Lewis condescendingly put it (the parentheses revealing his own ideological positioning), Ralegh's poetry, like his life, articulates with fearful clarity not merely the gaudy surface of the late sixteenth-century Court, but something of the process by which its subjects were moulded.[18] Ralegh's career as a poet and a courtier (the two are almost inseparable, literary and social text repeatedly writing and rewriting each other throughout his life) should not be simply seen as the daring, wilful assertion of the gentleman adventurer who strode into the Queen's favour with a graceful and opportune sweep of his cloak and who wrote a handful of charming lyrics. That would be to take at least some of his poems and the power they hoped to participate in too much for granted.

Puttenham mentions Ralegh's poetry approvingly as 'most lofty, insolent and passionate', and by the mid-1580s, Ralegh already had the reputation of a fine craftsman. 'The course and quality of men's lives serving in the Court is of all others the most uncertain and dangerous', wrote Ralegh,[19] and like every courtier-poet of the age he used his verse as one of the means by which he clambered for position. He is the lover, poor in words, but rich in affection; his passions are likened to 'floudes and stremes'; the lover prays 'in vayne' to 'blinde fortune' and resolves none the less 'but love, farewell, thoughe fortune conquer thee, /No fortune base nor frayle shall alter mee'. Much of Ralegh's poetry looks like typical Petrarchan love poetry. It can be, and no doubt was by many members of his original audiences, read as such. Skimming over the surface of Ralegh's verse, we encounter the typical paraphernalia of the Petrarchan lyric – hope and despair, pleasure and fortune, false love, frail beauty, fond shepherds, coy mistresses, deceitful time. For those, then and now, wanting to register the *frisson* of mingling noble language and feelings of unrequited love, 'As You Came from the Holy Land' and 'The Nymph's Reply to the Shepherd' read marvellously in a modern classroom. With the stanzas read alternatively by 'lover' and 'pilgrim', 'As You Came', in particular, conveys the dialogic nature of the poetry, drawing its audience into the debate, especially in the final stanzas (who exactly speaks each one is debatable; they can be made to work well in different ways) about the nature, even the possibility, of 'true' love. 'As You Came' can be read not only as a superbly melancholy affirmation of love, but also as a political poem, praising the impossibly inaccessible ideal offered the courtiers by the Queen: 'Nature that washt her hands in milke' takes the reader through a witty blazon of the perfect mistress's charms, her outside made of 'snow and silke', her 'inside . . . only of wantonesse and witt'. But like all Petrarchan mistresses, she has 'a heart of stone' and so the lover is poised, in perpetual frustration before his ideal. In the second half of the poem, Ralegh ruthlessly tears down all of the ideals he has built. What gives the poem its power is the unusually savage use of the Elizabethan commonplace of time the destroyer or thief – lying, rusting and annihilating, as it 'turnes snow, and silke, and milke to dust'. What was to the lover the 'food of Joyes' is ceaselessly fed into the maw of death, and the lovers' liquid wantonness is rendered dry and repulsive.

Likewise, the ruthlessly demystifying reply to Marlowe's delicate 'The Passionate Shepherd' (if it is by Ralegh) is an impressively terse expression of the conventional *carpe diem* motif. What is stressed is the solemn, logical, emphatic brooding over moral wisdom, not the light, celebratory escapism of the court idyll:

> The flowers doe fade, and wanton fieldes,
> To wayward winter reckoning yeeldes,

A honny tongue, a hart of gall,
In fancies spring, but sorrowes fall.

Thy gownes, thy shooes, thy beds of Roses,
Thy cap, thy kirtle, and thy poesies,
Soone breake, soone wither, soone forgotten:
In follie ripe, in reason rotten.

('The Nimphs Reply to the Sheepheard')

Typically, Ralegh's poetry has superb control of mood, movement, voice modulation and an appropriately direct rhetoric. Like Wyatt, he pares down the ornate tropes of the courtly tradition, chooses syntactical and logical patterns which emphasize rationality and urgent, emphatic movements of mind. Ralegh's poems are quintessentially those of the gifted amateur: a seemingly casual compliment, occasional verses typically dropped, as the manuscript title of another poem possibly by him has it, 'Into My Lady Laiton's Pocket'. But his poetry does more than put sexuality into discourse: inevitably the language of erotic compliment and complaint is inseparable from the language of power. Despite their seemingly trivial, light, or occasional nature – epitaphs on Sidney's death, 'A Farewell to False Love', dedicatory poems to works by Gascoigne or Spenser, poems directly or indirectly written to the Queen – their significance reverberates far beyond their stock metaphors and gracefully logical structure.

It will have been noted how I am repeatedly using 'possibly' about the authorship of many of Ralegh's poems. We do not, in fact, know whether many of the poems attributed to him in the manuscripts and miscellanies in which Elizabethan court poetry typically appears are his. Although we have access to more autograph writing for Ralegh than for any other major Elizabethan poet except Wyatt and Robert Sidney, we can only speculate about the authorship of many of the best poems attributed to him. In one important sense, however, it does not matter: Elizabethan court poetry often speaks with the voice of a collectivity and its authors are scriptors or spokesmen for the values of a dominant class and its ideology. An author's relationship to the languages that traverse him are much more complex than allowed for by the sentimental nineteenth-century biographical criticism which has held sway in Ralegh scholarship until very recently. In any court lyric, there is an illimitable series of pre-texts, subtexts, and post-texts which call into question any concept of its author as a free, autonomous individual. Like those by other court poets, Ralegh's poems, like those of Wyatt, are sites of struggle, attempts by Ralegh (or whatever court poet may have written them) to write himself into the world. Hence there is a sense in which we might speak of 'Ralegh' and 'his' poems alike as texts that require always to be read against what they seem to articulate, since they often speak out as much in their silences, in what they cannot or dare not say, as in what they are ostensibly about.

Some of the poems are, however, very explicit about their ideological allegiances. They are explicitly propagandist art. 'Praisd Be Dianas Faire and Harmles Light' is a poem (again only possibly by Ralegh) which reifies the ideals of the Court in a hymn of celebration, demanding absolute allegiance to the magical, timeless world of the Elizabethan Court in which no challenge to the replete atmosphere can be admitted and in which the readers are permitted to share only so long as they acknowledge the beauty of the goddess the poem celebrates:

> Praisd be Dianas faire and harmles light,
> Praisd be the dewes, wherwith she moists the ground;
> Praisd be hir beames, the glorie of the night,
> Praisd be hir powre, by which all powres abound.

The poem's atmosphere is incantatory, its movement designed, like so much court music, to inculcate acquiescence through a harmony that, it is assumed, is not simply aesthetic. Only the subhuman (including any reader foolish, or treasonous, enough to dissent from its vision) are excluded from the charm and the power it celebrates: 'A knowledge pure it is hir worth to know,/With Circes let them dwell that thinke not so.'

The typical pose of the poems is that of the worshipper, devoted to the unapproachable mistress or of the idealizing devotee with the Queen as the wavering star, the chaste goddess, the imperial embodiment of justice, the timeless principle on which the universe turns. In the way that Ben Jonson's masques came to embody the dominant ideology of James's court, Ralegh's poems evoke the collective fantasy of Elizabeth's – a world that is harmonious, static, and from which all change has been exorcized. However seemingly depoliticized, these poems are the product of the allurement and dominance of the Court, their confidence less that of the poet himself than of the power of the structures in which he struggled to locate himself.

As well as this miscellany (sometimes startlingly evocative, invariably competent and provoking) of poems, there are four closely connected and important poems, all undoubtedly Ralegh's, which are found in his own handwriting among the Cecil Papers at Hatfield House, north of London, the family home of his great enemy Robert Cecil. They are 'If Synthia be a Queene, a Princes, and Supreame', 'My Boddy in the Walls Captived', 'Sufficeth it to Yow, My Joyes Interred', and 'My Dayes Delights . . .'. The third of these, a poem of 522 lines, is headed 'The 11th: and last booke of the Ocean to Scinthia' and the fourth is headed 'The end of the bookes, of the Oceans love to Scinthia and

the beginninge of the 12 Boock, entreatinge of Sorrow'. The existence
of one or more closely connected poems written to the Queen and
entitled something like 'Cynthia' seems to be mentioned by Spenser
in *The Faerie Queene*, and is usually identified with these two poems.
The second, usually called 'Ocean to Scinthia', is the most important
of the group. It appears to be the barely revised draft of an appeal,
if not to the Queen herself, at least to that part of Ralegh's mind he
knew to be occupied by her power. It lacks many narrative links; its
four-line stanzas are often imperfect, with repetitions and gaps which
presumably might have been revised later. But its unfinished state
makes it not only a fascinating revelation of Ralegh's personal and
poetic anguish; in its very fragmentariness it is perhaps the clearest
example in Elizabethan court poetry of the way the dynamics and the
contradictions of power speak through a poetic text. Indeed, nowhere
in Elizabethan poetry is a poem so obviously constitutive of ideological
struggle felt by a writer as personal. 'Ocean to Scinthia' registers cultural
contradiction as intense and confused feeling and as fragmentary form:
it repeatedly deconstructs the philosophy to which it gives allegiance:
its incoherences, gaps, uncertainties and repetitions at once affirm the
dominant Elizabethan court ideology and articulate a desire to oppose
it. What in Ralegh's other poems is simply ignored or repressed is here
starting to emerge in the fractures and symptomatic maladjustments of
the text.

The poem is addressed to a patently transparent female figure, who
has withdrawn her favour from the faithful lover. Ralegh projects
himself as a despairing lover fearful (and tearfully) aware that his
service has been swept into oblivion, simultaneously acknowledging
that honours inevitably corrupt and yet that he cannot withdraw from
pursuing them. The 'love' he has seemingly won includes favours that
open doors to glory, but also to ruin and death. Yet even knowing this,
it is as if he cannot help himself. He must 'seeke new worlds, for golde,
for prayse, for glory', with the tragic result that he bewails:

> Twelve yeares intire I wasted in this warr,
> Twelve yeares of my most happy younger dayes,
> Butt I in them, and they now wasted ar,
> Of all which past the sorrow only stayes.

The result of his 'twelve yeares' dedication has been imprisonment and
disgrace. Yet he is helpless before his own inability to abandon the
glories of office. 'Trew reason' shows power to be worthless. Yet
even while he knows that 'all droopes, all dyes, all troden under dust',
he knows also that the only stability in the world of power is the
necessity of instability and emulation. The Petrarchan commonplace

with which the successful courtier has played so effectively, almost on demand – the helpless lover wooing the unapproachable mistress who is the unattainable goal of desire – has suddenly and savagely been literalized. The role Ralegh has played has become actualized in a way that explodes his habitual adaptability. He cannot protest that the game of the despairing lover is only a game; it has now become real. In 1592 he wrote to Cecil: 'My heart was never broken till this day, that I hear the Queen goes away so far off – Whom I have followed so many years with so great love and desire, in so many journeys, and am now left behind her in a great prison alone.'[20] The letter is an obvious echo of the lines from Ralegh's adaptation of the Walsingham ballad, 'As You Came from the Holy Land':

> She hath lefte me here all alone,
> All allone as unknowne,
> Who somtymes did me lead with her selfe,
> And me lovde as her owne.

Whether Ralegh wrote these haunting lines is almost beside the point: the courtly game to which they gesture, and yet transcend, is that played by and through all courtiers. But in Ralegh's life the contradictions which were now given voice had been repressed and silenced. Now they are revealed as terrifyingly real. Ralegh himself has ceased to play Elizabeth's game by marrying; he has thus found the role of masochistic victim he cast himself in for political advantage has been taken literally and he has become an outcast. 'Ocean to Scinthia' expresses the agony of a man whose choices and commitments have been built on the myth of a changeless past in an ever-moving power struggle. The very unfinished quality of Ralegh's poem is the perfect formal expression of the disruptiveness that has overwhelmed him.

We are fortunate that another key poem of this period is among the Hatfield Manuscripts. 'The Lie' is an ejaculation of explicit anger, a struggle to find form for deep frustration in finding no alternative to renunciation and repulsion. It is a statement of deeply felt impotence, written, it is often suggested, after Ralegh's release from prison in 1592, but before he was restored to favour. Ralegh's poem is seemingly total in its rejection of the ideology by which he has lived: natural law, universal harmony, love, court artifice are all rejected in a mood of total condemnation. And yet Ralegh's poem is neither philosophically nihilistic nor politically radical: his revulsion from the Court does not allow for any alternative to it. What 'dies' is the 'I' of the poem, as he gives the lie to the world, and takes refuge in a bitter *contemptus mundi*. 'The Lie' is an explosion of the frustration that throughout the century has underlain the Court's ideological confidence. In such poems the ideology of the Elizabethan Court is betrayed by the very writing it controlled: the poem constantly releases an anxiety to find unknown realities, which challenges the surface harmonies, even if the struggle cannot be heard against the dominant language of the court poetic mode. Ralegh's melancholic formulation of the persistence of 'woe' or pain as the very mark of human self-consciousness is the special tell-tale sign of his texts as sites of struggle and repression: 'The life expires, the woe remains' is a refrain echoed elsewhere as is 'Of all which past, the sorrowe onely staies' ('like truthless dreams'). It is also echoed in phrases throughout the *History*. Such recurring motifs create more than a characteristic tone to Ralegh's writing. They point to the thwarted insurrection of subjugated experience struggling to find expression, knowing that there are no words permitted or seemingly possible for Ralegh's poems, then, are haunted by what they try to exorcize. The fragility and uncertainties of court life in the 1580s and 1590s undermine his poetry's announced role as the spokesman of a replete court ideology.

Despite their confident surfaces, his poems are less celebrations of the power of the Queen and Court than a conspiracy to remain within their protection. The Petrarchan cliches of 'Like truthless dreams, so are my joys expired' or (if we accept it as Ralegh's) the neoplatonic commonplaces of the Walsingham ballad become desperate pleas for favour, projections into lyric poems of political machinations. 'Conceipt begotten by the eyes' (if it is Ralegh's) also starts out as a stereotypical contrast between 'desire' and 'woe', and emerges as a poignant ejaculation of radical insecurity – a powerless acknowledgement that the self of the court poet is a creation of the discourses he has uneasily inhabited and from which he now feels expelled. Above all, the Hatfield poems show us what all Elizabethan court poetry tries to repress, that however the poet asserts his autonomy, he is constituted through ideology, that he has no existence outside the social formation and the signifying practices legitimized by the power of the Court. Ralegh, like every other poet who wrestled within the Court, does not speak so much as he is spoken.

More than twenty years after his fall from favour and after ten years of imprisonment under James, Ralegh published his incomplete *History of the World*. Pious in at least part of its intention, the work (like so much of his poetry) articulates a philosophy that radically undercuts orthodox sentiments. It reveals a view of history with no final eschatological goal, no ultimate consummation. History consists only of the continual vengeance of an angry God until 'the long day of mankind . . . and the world's Tragedie and time near at an end'. A few years later, on the eve of his execution, Ralegh took up the last lines of one of his early lyrics:

> Even such is tyme which takes in trust
> Our yowth, our Joyes, and all we have,
> And payes us butt with age and dust:
> Who in the darke and silent grave
> When we have wandred all our wayes
> Shutts up the storye of our dayes.

- and appended to it, in two new lines, the only hope he could conceive of, a *deus ex machina* to rescue him, in a way neither Queen nor King had, from the grip of time's power: 'And from which earth and grave and dust/The Lord shall rayse me up I trust.' It is a cry of desperation, not a transformation of 'the consuming disease of time', as he puts it in the *History*.[21] What is finally triumphant over Ralegh is the power of that world of which his poems are an extraordinarily moving acknowledgement and testament.

Ralegh's importance, then, belies the slimness of his poetic output. The author of perhaps two dozen extant poems, mostly short lyrics, plus a number of brief verse translations in the *History*, he is none the less one of the most important of the Elizabethan courtly 'makers', articulating with fearful clarity not merely the gaudy surface and fashions of the late Elizabethan age, but much of the felt pressure of the Court upon the lives and sensibilities of those caught in it. Ralegh described himself towards the end of his life as 'a sea-faring man, a Souldior and a courtier', and his poetry articulates much of what drove him to those vocations. He knew, deeply and bitterly that, as he puts it in the *History*, there is nothing more 'becoming a wise man' than 'to retire himself from the Court'. Yet the Court was his stage and it was, he wrote, where he 'exercised in the service of the world'.[22] The achievement of his poetry is that it gives reverberating words to the struggles of those who lived in and were controlled by the Court. Most of his poems look, on the surface, like delicate, even trivial, songs, complaints, or compliments typical of the most superficial kind of Petrarchism. In fact they are constituted as rich, confused responses to the complex and powerful set of discourses, symbolic formations and systems of representation that made up the Elizabethan Court. They try to carve out a private space in a public world and find only that privacy is in turn produced by the very public structures it tries to exclude. Ralegh's poems thus offer us a unique way into the interplay between the social text of Elizabethan society (the events that made Ralegh's history) and the literary text (the poems that he made of those events). Ralegh is, in many ways, the quintessential court poet of the Elizabethan period in that his poems are determined by, and finally silenced by, the power of the Court.

Greville

Ralegh's poetry articulates, more explicitly than Wyatt's, but still at a pre-formative stage, oppositional cultural forces that were already challenging the Court. Of course, as well, he is an alluringly tragic figure and his boldness and defiance make a striking contrast with Greville's more sombre and calculated career. More clear-sightedly than Ralegh, Greville brooded over the nature of the Court that he entered along with the man he admired all his life, Philip Sidney. One of Greville's Jacobean acquaintances wrote that he had 'the longest lease and the smoothest time without rub', of any of 'the Queen's favorites', and in that alone it can be seen how Greville's achievements were very different from Ralegh's. The substance of a remark he made in 1598 – 'she in her princely nature knoweth that I have commanded mine own genius, and left all courses in the world that advance other men only for her sake'[23] – could have been spoken by Ralegh, but like Greville's achievements at court, it is more prudent and calculated than most of Ralegh's actions. Greville's remark also has a characteristically deep pessimism about his ability to change the course of events at Court. Under Elizabeth, he achieved some modest advancement: he held a series of minor positions including, in 1598, Treasurer of the Navy. During the Essex crisis of 1599–1601, he seems to have been unable to commit himself absolutely either way, perhaps seeing Essex as the inheritor of Sidney's ideals and yet disturbed by the flamboyance of the Earl's methods. His caution and fear endeared him to neither faction but he survived and was, probably, on the verge of becoming a Privy Councillor when the Queen died.

Like Wyatt and Ralegh, Greville was a politician before he was a poet, but his poetry was kept at a greater distance from his public career. Greville's earliest poems are known to have circulated among members of the Sidney Circle from the 1570s on. Puttenham also mentions him as one of the 'crew of courtly makers', but though some of *Caelica* was set to music later in the seventeenth century, none was published in his lifetime and very few of Greville's poems are found in manuscript collections. *Caelica* is a collection of 108 sonnets and songs; it was continually revised by Greville in a manuscript and only published some thirty years after his death. It is therefore even more miscellaneous than most collections of sixteenth-century lyrics: although many are addressed to a mistress, named variously as Caelica, Myra or Cynthia, there are no narrative links, and their most insistent focus is not on love so much as politics and theology. They are often tortuously compressed and crammed with tight philosophical argument. Throughout, Greville is grappling to overcome the seductiveness of Sidney's rhetoric, trying to pare it down, attempting to get it closer to what he sees as truth unadorned by the deceptiveness of human language. The obscurity of his poetry is a consequence of a deep-seated and probably increasing scepticism about poetry and its place in a culture which he found degraded, alien and corrupt but to which he could conceive no alternative. He tries to use poetry as a weapon against much that his friend Sidney had advocated.

Warkentin argues that the poems 'reveal Greville's boredom with the intense focus on the self of the poet'[24] which I have indicated is so central to the tradition in which he was writing. That is particularly the case with the later, explicitly religious poems. But his revulsion from poetry has deeper roots. Very often, Greville seems to write poetry as a man who distrusts it, and his distrust spreads beyond the surface rhetoric to the world to which it is reacting. The impact of many of the poems, therefore, is to call into question not merely a poetic style, but a whole style of life. There are a few poems that Greville would presumably have felt safe about circulating. Some are moralistic, grimmer versions of the subject matter of Wyatt's satires: Sonnets 91 and 92 are conventional attacks on false nobility, 81 praises Elizabeth triumphing over Fortune, and 83 is a plea for favour which uses the conventional motifs of being exiled from paradise, withering in anguish and loneliness. It concludes with an effective but disarming play on his own name: 'Let no man ask my name, nor what else I should be;/For Greive-ill, paine, forlorn estate do best decipher me'. More interesting, however (and far more challenging to Elizabethan orthodoxies had they been circulated, and – not a trivial note – comprehended) are the poems where he broods over the ways the Court creates (or, in Greville's usual terms, exalts and so corrupts) the self. In the early poems, Greville may start from the conventional Petrarchist stance, but he injects it with an unusual bitterness, as in 5:

> Who trusts for trust, or hopes of love for love,
> Or who belov'd in Cupids lawes doth glory;
> Or joyes in vowes, or vowes not to remove,
> Who by this light God, hath not beene made sorry;
>   Let him see me eclipsed from my Sunne,
>   With shadowes of an Earth quite over-runne.

To hope for access to any kind of reality through the conventional courtly paraphernalia, to 'trust for trust', or to seek divine love through human agency is not merely rhetorical affectation – it is self-deceptive folly. The poems in *Caelica* often take as their starting-point the commonplace stance which Ralegh took so seriously, that the forlorn lover is the required rhetorical role of the courtier. Such a role, in

Greville's view, is appropriate for men only because their fallen nature, epitomized in the courtier's, is 'restlesse', 'wandring' and basically self-deceptive. In Sonnet 10, the lover, 'invited' to see 'Vertues and beauties' in the 'glory of those faire eyes', may view his mistress as a divine goddess, but the poem tries to get its readers to reject such blasphemous theologizing as fraudulent, self-deceptive, and irrational. The poem asks an ironical question – 'Then tell me Love what glory you divine/Your selfe can find within this soule of mine' – which not only demands an inevitable negative reply, but also undermines the possibility that courtly idealizations are anything but unreal and self-deceptive. Throughout *Caelica*, such terms as 'love', 'delight', 'beauties riches', 'glory', 'hope', 'desires affinity' – all the talismanic phrases of the courtly poet – are invested not with their felt sense of security, but with fragility. They are not simply deceptive or erotically threatening, but rather evidence of mankind's fall into self-deception. Sonnet 22 paints the whole courtly game of love as a self-deceptive farce; 24 goes further and depicts courtly art, 'painting, the eloquence of dumbe conceipt', as deception; 49, with grim facetiousness, makes very explicit Greville's rejection of the deceptiveness of courtly love, courtly rhetoric and the court ethos. Some poems, especially Sonnets 1 and 3, do assert a belief in the transcendence of one, singular, figure – some idealized mistress, perhaps the Queen – but even here (presumably when Greville is writing most under the influence of Sidney) a deep scepticism enters. If love, delight, virtue and reason 'are from the world by Natures power bereft', and only in 'one' creature, 'for her glory, left' (Sonnet 1), then the possibility of even greater disillusion occurs should such an ideal fail.

Dunbar's poems are the product of a Court that is still essentially feudal; Wyatt's of a buoyant if paranoid Renaissance Court; Ralegh's poems are part of a campaign for an impossible autonomy within a Court that had evolved into a complex cultural machine. But all are the products of similar struggles and of the repression of alternatives to the ideology that has brought them into being. Greville's poems are slightly different. Because they are deliberately cast as private meditations, his poems seem to allow a scepticism about the Court to appear more clearly than the others. When we compare his more public poetry, the verse-treatises and poetic dramas, we can see him brooding cryptically over the great issues of the years after Sidney's death and being able to give a more explicit treatment of the issues. *Mustapha* was written in the 1590s, and includes a series of debates on matters Greville must have thought much about at the time of Essex's fall. *Alaham* and the early drafts of the *Treatise on Monarchy* were probably written at the end of the 1590s: their dominant political philosophy is one of non-resistance, even to a tyrannical monarch, and when we consider them alongside the deep-rooted scepticism of *Caelica*, a fascinating paradox is revealed. Unlike Ralegh, who was told at his final trial that 'he had lived like a star, and like a star he must fall, when it troubled the firmament', Greville made no attempt to blaze forth his rebellion. Yet it is clear that his rejection of the Court and its values was much more radical and clear-sighted than Ralegh's. He sees the courtier called by God to a passivity before the unrelieved evil around him, observing how 'when evill strives, the worst have greatest name . . . Those mischiefes prosper that exceed the rest.' Politics shows that it is, indeed, the tyrants, atheists, and the ruthless who triumph, 'as if the earth . . . were to the worst left free'. In *Mustapha*, the question 'is Providence of no . . . use to power?' seems to be necessarily given a disturbingly negative answer. What the faithful courtier must do, it seems, is to accept a grim Calvinist paradox – that while man's salvation depends not on his works but only on God's predestinate will, yet his election is nevertheless tested by his activity within the world where he must survive in ways his creed abhors. The courtier must accept the secular ethic that he must 'first judge your Ends, and then your Meanes', leaving judgement 'to His will that governs the blind prosperities of Chance; and so works out His own ends by the erring frailties of human reason and affection'. In Greville's grim Calvinist scheme, there seems to be no way of knowing the divine will since 'when each of us, in his owne heart lookes/He finds the God there, fame unlike his Bookes'.

A similar dualism characterizes Greville's meditations on public policy elsewhere: 'The world doth built without, our God within;/He traffiques goodnesse, and she traffiques sinne' or 'Fly unto God: For in humanity/Hope there is none' are typical sentiments. True fame may be afforded to the elect, whereas those – presumably like Ralegh, whom Greville referred to as being possessed by 'pride' in 1603 – who seek earthly fame 'Make Men their God, *Fortune*, and *Time* their worth,/Forme, but reforme not; meer hypocrisie,/By shadowes, only shadowes, bringing forth'. What differentiates Greville's from Dunbar's, Wyatt's, and Ralegh's poetry – and it is an indication of how the strains of late sixteenth-century court poetry are becoming more evident – is this deeply ingrained Calvinist pessimism. The increasing power of Calvinism is a major factor in changing the tenor of sixteenth-century poetry. Dunbar was a Catholic, Wyatt an uneasy Protestant, but in different ways Ralegh and Greville are deeply scarred by the Protestant dynamic. Yet where Ralegh took refuge in a deterministic scepticism, Greville's radical Protestantism produces something much more disruptive, even if in his writings as in his life it was never translated into concrete political action.

The contradictions involved in holding together Protestant and courtly, Calvin and Petrarch, with which we shall see Sidney also struggled, are what give Greville's poetry its distinctive strength. His work is situated at the intersection of vast contradictory cultural claims which are all the more powerful because Greville struggles to be as rational and as untouched by sin as he can, even while he believes that rationality and truth are denied him.

Greville's starting-point seems invariably to be his detailed observations of the society around him. Like the other three poets we have considered in this chapter, he gained first-hand insight into the workings of power and his picture of sixteenth-century court society is a grim one. The virtuous man must either opt out of society, or else accept the necessity of craft and policy as the 'base instrument of humane frailtie' (*A Treatise of Monarchy*, 284). Protestant activism makes the first of these alternatives unacceptable. Greville praised Sidney as 'a man fit for conquest, Plantation, Reformation, or what action soever is greatest and hardest among men'; a noble nature like Sidney's could not escape the responsibility of public duty, even in an unredeemable world. It followed from the Calvinist ethic that man's salvation depends not on works but on God's predestinate will and yet, paradoxically, continual activity in the world is still stressed to be the test of a man's election. So, argues Greville, even the godly must employ the very means they abhor, since God, as he puts it, 'made all for use'.[25]

Among some late sixteenth-century Calvinists, politics come to be regarded as the consequence of man's fall. Yet although secular life is outside the realm of grace, it is none the less necessary for the proper ordering and disciplining of men. The Christian must still live in these two spheres of life, and so his life will necessarily be contradictory and tragically corrupt. In special cases of remarkable virtue, like Sidney, some limited achievement seems possible – though one might sense in Greville's praise of Sidney a belief that his ideals were never adequately tested. But the Christian is forced by his own sinfulness to acknowledge that craft, deviousness and seeking advantage are the means of survival in society. To face up to one's inner corruption means that one learns 'first [to] judge your Ends, and then your Means', leaving the outcome 'to His will that governs the blind prosperities of chance'.[26] Coming through Greville's writings is a deeply troubled awareness of contradiction – God cannot err and yet events seem to display only the triumph of evil. In *Mustapha* he asks 'is Providence of no . . . use to power?' His faith answers yes, his experience of politics, no. *Alaham* echoes Greville's troubled scepticism when he writes 'that God of whom you crave/is deaf, and only gives men what they have'.

Compelling in their logic, Greville's poetic dramas mull over such questions. He, of course, blames man's depraved nature, seeing men, as the first chorus in *Mustapha* puts it, as 'a crazed soule, unfix'd'; Man is 'borne under one Law, to another bound:/Vainely begot, and yet forbidden vanity'. In the end only Eternity can redeem the inadequacies of time: 'Fly unto God: For in humanity/Hope there is none', argues Alaham.

There are some experiences which look as if they offer hope within the world. Greville was acutely conscious that his friend Sidney saw human love at least tantalizing us with that possibility. But Greville's stern Calvinism dares not accept any state less than perfect, and the disillusion inherent in human idealizations of love is a pressing theme in *Caelica*. The poems constantly stress both the transience of love and its underlying cause: 'For lest Man should thinke flesh a seat of blisse,/God workes that his joy mixt with sorrow is' (*Caelica*, 94). In love, as in politics, Greville looks for God's approval in vain in the world and in himself, and concludes in *A Treatise of Religion*, 7, that 'Nature contains him not, Art cannot show him.' The world is merely a testing-ground for men's perseverance. The faithful can only combine their determination to obey with a humble awareness of the ultimate incompatibility of the world which is 'made for use', whereas God is made only 'for love' (*A Treatise of Religion*, 114).

Calvinism seems to have given Greville a rigorous context to settle many of the issues that haunted him. Nevertheless, a frustrated idealism keeps forcing its way through the surface of his poetry. As opposed to Sidney, whose idealism seems to have fed on the disillusions and failures it perceived in love – witness the seventh song of *Astrophil and Stella*, Greville works through a kind of *realpolitik* of love. Love and human aspiration seem inevitably associated with guilt and mistrust, which is projected on to the formerly peerless mistress, and love itself thereby corrupted:

> Whence I conceav'd you of some heavenly mould,
> Since Love, and Vertue, noble Fame and Pleasure,
> Containe in one no earthly metall could,
> Such enemies are flesh, and blood to measure.

The disillusion in the last line is strongly wrought through the concrete, agonized imagery, and then is put into the inevitable theological context:

> And since my fall, through I now onely see
> Youre backe, while all the world beholds your face,
> This shadow still shewes miracles to me,
> And still I thinke your heart a heavenly place:
>   For what before was fill'd by me alone,
>   I now discerne hath roome for every one.

(Caelica, 64)

The mistress is still the desired paradise: but the limitations and jealous demands of fallen humanity have corrupted the vision so that the largesse of heaven becomes equated with the hell of promiscuity.

The later sonnets in *Caelica* show Greville fleeing the deceptive and damnable show of earthly love, but he is grimly aware that he cannot escape the bonds of earthly existence. Even man's deepest, most sincere cries for salvation are interwoven with guilt and sin. Some of the most striking of the later sonnets show Greville looking within his own guilt and depravity, and finding in his deepest isolation, the presence of God, as in 99:

> And in this fatall mirrour of transgression,
> Shewes man as fruit of his degeneration,
> The errours ugly infinite impression,
> Which beares the faithlesse down to desperation;
>> Depriv'd of humane graces and divine,
>> Even there appeares this *saving* God of mine.

The last phrase is an oddly grasping one, the product of a faith that demands that the believer look for certain signs of assurance and yet denies the possibility of finding such signs. The strength of Greville's best poetry is that it articulates his struggle to accept what is clearly antipathetic to much of his life. As Thom Gunn finely puts it, 'the body cries out in pain at the rejections it is forced to make, and in the note of the cry we recognize the very humanity it is a cry against'.[27]

Greville's poetry is clearly distinct from the other court poets we have looked at in its foregrounding of Calvinist theology and the contradictions it raised for courtier and poet alike. It is fortunate, therefore, that we have a document of his – the life of Sidney – written at the end of the first decade of the new century, as he looks back at his youth and maturity in the Court. He chooses his dead friend as the focus of his own frustrations. He sees Sidney as the embodiment of ideals the Court has abandoned. 'I am', he says, 'enforced to bring poignant evidences from the dead, amongst whom I have founde more liberall contribution to the honor of true worthe, then amongst those which now live.' Greville's life of Sidney is thus a key document in our understanding of the ways in which the Court and its power operated. Greville is able to look at the Court he has been rejected by. He sees it from the perspective of a man who remembers nostalgically how the Court had once promoted virtue, piety and goodness. He presents himself as an admirer of the man who in his 'too short scene of his life' exemplified a phoenix-like 'greatness of heart'. [28]

Greville's admiration for Sidney was something from which he never wavered. But writing the life of his friend, and especially in revising it, was a process that brought out more and more contradictions in his own commitments to the court. Whenever Greville points to a characteristic of Elizabeth's policies, he does so in order to criticize James and his Court. Elizabeth, he notes, was opposed to extra-parliamentary proclamations of new taxes; she saw how the 'Court it selfe' might become 'like a farm'. He points, by contrast, to James's 'monopolouse use of Favourites', and the endangering by royal power by what he calls 'selfe-prerogatives' such as the selling of honours. Where Elizabeth 'kept awe stirring over all her Countes and other Chiefe imployments', James's lackadaisical manners and his 'Princely licentioussnesse in behaviour' is blamed as a 'fashioner of Atheisme among . . . Subjects'.[29] In such remarks, we sense Greville's distaste for the manners and entertainments of the Stuart court. Even though he sought employment under James he must have found the characteristic lifestyle of that Court most disagreeable. From *A Treatise of Monarchy*, it is clear he regarded the use of illusionistic art in masques and pageants as dangerous and self-deceiving; in the account of Sidney he is derisive of Kings who 'suffer or rather force their Wives and daughters to descend from the inequallitie and reservedness of Princely education into the Contemptible familiarity' of shepherds and pastoral disguises. Like the throne they support, the courtiers of the Jacobean Court live by pride and self-ignorant deception.[30]

Such observations clearly constitute a radical revulsion from the Jacobean Court, from its policies, its ethos, its use of art as propaganda, and its degeneration from the Elizabethan era. Yet Greville's strong belief in non-resistance, even to tyrants, puts him into further contra-diction. In Chapter 6, we shall see how Spenser tried to disassociate Elizabeth from the Corruption he perceived in her Court; so Greville uneasily disassociated King James from the criticism he makes. He describes James as 'that chief and best of *Princes*' and 'amongst the most eminent Monarchs of that time'. What he focuses upon is, most significantly, 'the Courte it self ', the institution which he himself had entered with such hopes and served with such faithfulness. He sees it, from his exile, 'becoming like a farme, manured by drawing up not the sweate but even the brows of the humble subjects'. What, like the most virulent anti-court satirist of the 1590s, he terms 'the catching Court ayres' are the sign of an infection that is destroying England.[31] His is as wholesale a rejection of the Court as any in the writings of Webster, or Tourneur, or Shakespeare, and his is all the more significant because it was voiced by a man who, like Dunbar, More, Wyatt, and Ralegh, knew the Court intimately, from years of service.

Yet there is another aspect of Greville's condemnation of the Court in the life of Sidney which helps us see how his poetry is distinctive.

Feeling for the difference between Sidney and the new world of 1610, Greville predictably sees it in Sidney's piety. Unlike the Jacobean courtiers, Greville argues, Sidney combined his exemplary 'image of quiet and action' with a sense of his own unworthiness before God. Yet Greville must face an awkward question here. While he praises Sidney's greatness of mind, he cannot but ponder the 'secret judgements' of God who 'cut off this Gentleman's life, and so much of our hope'. He is uneasily aware that the God Sidney served chose to permit his death, and that the ideals Sidney represented had failed. Sidney had been called to a life in the world – he was 'a man fit for Conquest, Plantation, Reformation, or what action soever is greatest and hardest among men' – yet even he was merely the sinful instrument of God's will. All men, even Sidney, must accept 'what our owne creation bindes us to' – the absolute incompatibility of man's actions with God's will.[32] Greville's Calvinism reads Sidney's death as God's harsh but just judgment on England. Indeed, as Greville revised the life, an increasing scepticism about his own memories of Sidney's ideals came through. As Greville contemplates the world before him, more and more of his friend's idealism receded into self-delusion.

In this chapter, I have looked at four poets whose commitments to their poetic vocation were formed by the pressures and demands of their being situated in or subject to the Court. Each struggled to locate his writing within the complex socio-cultural text of his society; each articulated both the excitement and the anxiety of living, entertaining and striving for prestige in the Court. By placing them together, we can see certain apparent continuities in the dominant mode of sixteenth-century poetry. But we can also see, as we try to account for some of the differences among the four poets, more than the usual factors – like the impact of Petrarchism, growing stylistic sophistication, and so forth – that are traditionally ascribed to the 'maturity' or 'continuity' of sixteenth-century poetry. What emerges are the growing ideological strains within the Court. In particular, there is the richly disruptive presence of Protestantism within court poetry.

It has been persuasively argued by Sinfield that a fundamental strand of literature in England between 1550 and 1650 is the working out of the contradictions inherent in Protestantism, so that cultural practices seemingly impossible early in the sixteenth century were increasingly able to find space and plausibility and eventually to transform the whole society.[33] Such a view omits a consideration of the continuation of Catholic ways of thinking, the rich substructure of popular superstition and local devotion, some of which is adapted, as in Spenser, in Protestant poetry, some of which emerges directly in Catholic poets like Alabaster or Southwell. But Sinfield's overall thesis is a useful one: it was the revolutionary dynamic of Protestantism that became, often violently, the dominant ideology of sixteenth-century England, and what we can observe in the four court poets studied in this chapter is something of the first phase of this process. All four are marked by a frustrated search for oppositional or counter-dominant voices. They are all court poets committed to the values and practices of an increasingly powerful ideology which held them seemingly totally and reinforced their bondage with religious, moral and material practices, and yet frustrated their search for any alternative. For Dunbar, the buoyancy and hierarchical order the Court embodies cannot hide the uneasiness and dislocations of experience for which he and his fellows had, as yet, no words to express. For Wyatt, the lack of an alternative voice is also seen in his falling back on medieval moral commonplaces, or on the puzzled silences of some of his lyrics. For Ralegh, fifty years later, such frustration is expressed in bitterness, revulsion and once again a recourse to increasingly archaic moralism. With Greville, what had been a part of the dynamic of the early sixteenth-century Court has become a plausible alternative to it. As Protestantism gradually rewrote the languages of the Court, while, as it were, Calvin and Castiglione battled in the discourses of Elizabethan poetry, alternative models of poetry, Court behaviour and wider social practices gradually became possible. The poet whose work, life and reputation best illustrate this process is the major subject of Chapter 5.

Notes

1. Steven W. May, *The Elizabethan Courtier Poets: The Poems and their Contexts* (Columbia, 1990), p. 20.

2. Bernard Sharratt, *Reading Relations* (London, 1983), p. 31.

3. Gary Waller, 'I and Ideology: Demystifying the Self of Contemporary Poetry', *Denver Quarterly*, 18, no. 3 (Autumn 1983), 123–38 (p. 125).

4. *The Autobiography of Thomas Whythorne*, edited by James M. Osborn (Oxford, 1961), pp. 3, 41. I owe this reference to Dr Bernard Sharratt of the University of Kent at Canterbury.

5. Tom Scott, *Dunbar: A Critical Exposition of the Poems* (Edinburgh, 1966), p. 160. Quotations from Dunbar's poems are taken from *The Poems of William Dunbar*, edited by James Kinsley (Oxford, 1959).

6. Scott, pp. 19, 210.

7. David Starkey, 'The Age of the Household: Politics, Society and the Arts *c.* 1350–*c.* 1550', in *The Later Middle Ages*, edited by Stephen Medcalf (New

York, 1981), p. 278. Quotations from Wyatt's poems are taken from *Collected Poems*, edited by Richard Rebholz (1978).

8. George Puttenham, *The Arte of English Poesie*, edited by Gladys Doidge Willcock and Alice Walker (Cambridge, 1936) p. 61; Raymond Southall, *The Courtly Maker* (London, 1964), p. 23.

9. John Stevens, *Music and Poetry in the Early Tudor Court* (London, 1961), chapter 9; H. A. Mason, *Humanism and Poetry in the Early Tudor Period: An Essay* (London, 1959), p. 171; Stephen Greenblatt, 'The Resonance of Renaissance Poetry', *ADE Bulletin*, 64 (May 1980), 7–10 (p. 8).

10. Greenblatt, 'Resonance', p. 9.

11. Jerome K. Kamholtz, 'Thomas Wyatt's Poetry: The Politics of Love', *Criticism*, 20 (1978), 349–65 (p. 354),

12. Raymond Southall, 'Wyatt's "Ye Old Mule"', *ELN* (1967), 5–11 (p. 5).

13. Raymond Williams, *Marxism and Literature* (London, 1977), p. 126.

14. *Autobiography of Whythorne*, pp. 36, 40.

15. Greenblatt, 'Resonance', pp. 8, 9.

16. Greville, *Life*, p. 127.

17. Stephen Greenblatt, *Sir Walter Ralegh: The Renaissance Man and his Roles* (New Haven, 1973), p. 44. Quotations from Ralegh's poems are taken from *The Poems of Sir Walter Ralegh*, edited by Agnes Latham (London, 1952). See, however, the more rigorous though still unpublished edition by Michael Rudick, 'The Poems of Sir Walter Ralegh: An Edition' (unpublished doctoral dissertation, University of Chicago, 1970).

18. Puttenham, p. 61; C. S. Lewis, *English Literature in the Sixteenth Century excluding Drama* (Oxford, 1954), p. 519.

19. Sir Walter Ralegh, *The Cabinet Council*, in *Works* (London, 1829), 8 vols, VIII, pp. 113–14.

20. HMC, Salisbury, IV, 220.

21. Ralegh, *History*, II, vi, 9, in *Works*, II, 97; *Poems*, p. 72.

22. Quoted by Greenblatt, *Ralegh*, p. ix; Ralegh, *Works*, VIII, 114; *History*, Preface, in *Works*, II, xxxii.

23. Sir Robert Naunton, *Fragmenta Regalia* (London, 1641), p. 50. Quotations from Greville's poems are taken from *Poems and Dramas of Fulke Greville, Lord Brooke*, edited by Geoffrey Bullough (Edinburgh, 1938–39).

24. Charles Larsen, *Fulke Greville* (Boston, 1980), p. 31; Germaine Warkentin, 'Greville's Caelica and the Fullness of Time', *English Studies in Canada*, 6 (1980), 398–408 (p. 400).

25. Greville, *Works*, edited by A. B. Grosart (London, 1870), IV, 37, 32.

26. Greville, *Works*, IV, 32.

27. *Selected Poems of Fulke Greville*, introduced by Thom Gunn (London, 1968), p. 61.

28. Greville, *Life*, pp. 119, 116.

29. Greville, *Life*, pp. 177,161,160,171, 46.

30. Greville, *Life*, pp. 28,177,139.

31. Greville, *Life*, pp. 131,105, 29.

32. Greville, *Life*, pp. 105, 126, 2, 198, 98, 45.

33. Alan Sinfield, *Literature in Protestant England* (Brighton, 1983), pp. 129, 134.

Chapter 5
The Sidneys and Their Circle

Philip Sidney

One of the most intriguing figures of the sixteenth century, one whose fascination has lasted to the present, is the courtier, politician and poet Sir Philip Sidney. He has been the focus of many myths. One has been alluded to while discussing Greville – Sidney the lost leader, whose tragic death signalled the death of Elizabethan idealism. Part of Sidney's fascination is the ways in which both his own and succeeding ages have appropriated him: as the lost leader of the golden Elizabethan age to Greville and some other Jacobeans; in later centuries, the Victorian gentleman; the anguished Edwardian, caught between contradictory moral worlds; the committed existentialist; the apolitical quietist, even (most recently) a member of the Moral Majority. And most recently, as scholars have become more attuned to both the linguistic and ideological complexity of Renaissance literature generally and to the new possibilities of reading it by means of contemporary critical methods, Sidney's writings have been seen, both in their apparent confidence and their symptomatic gaps and absences, as central to our understanding of Elizabethan literature and culture. The 1980s and 1990s have seen a major re-evaluation of Sidney.

How did Sidney's contemporaries see his poetry? In the words of one courtier, he was 'our English Petrarke' who 'often conforteth him selfe in his sonnets of Stella, though dispairing to attain his desire . . .' Thus Sir John Harington in 1591, and subsequent generations of readers have similarly sighed and sympathized with *Astrophil and Stella's* tragi-comic enactment of 'poor Petrarch's long deceased woes', and have often likewise identified Astrophil with Sidney himself. As depicted in conventional literary history, *Astrophil and Stella* marks a poetical revolution no less than Wordsworth's *Lyrical Ballads* or Eliot's *The Waste Land*: Sidney is seen as a young, ambitious poet, brilliantly acting upon his impatience with the poetry he criticized in his poetic manifesto, the *Defence of Poesie*, to produce a masterpiece, the first Petrarchan sequence in English. 'Poetry almost have we none', he wrote, 'but that lyrical kind of songs and sonnets', which 'if I were a mistress, would never persuade me they were in love'.[1] His poems were written to remedy this situation. Typically, none of them was published in his lifetime; along with other writings, they circulated among a small but influential coterie of family and court acquaintances during the 1580s. Sidney's vocations were those of courtier, statesman, Protestant aristocrat and patriot before that of a poet, yet his poetry was clearly a major commitment for him. Sidney's writings often served, as Hamilton argues, as the outlet for frustrated political ambition and forced inactivity.[2] *Astrophil and Stella* marks the triumphant maturity of Elizabethan poetry and the first full, belated but spectacular, adaptation of Petrarchism to English aristocratic culture. It remains today one of the most moving, delightful and provocative collections of love poems in the language, all the more powerful in its impact because of the variety of discourses that strain within it for articulation – erotic, poetic, political, religious, cultural. We may read it, as Harington did, as the articulation of thwarted, obsessive love; but it opens itself to much richer readings, and its very variety reinforces Sidney's position as the central literary and cultural figure in the English Renaissance before Shakespeare. He was also the central figure in the 'Sidney Circle', a loosely linked group of courtiers, poets, divines and educators who were dedicated, before and particularly after his death, to his ideals for the reform of literature and to an intriguing mix of political and religious ideals. They included his sister, Mary Sidney, Countess of Pembroke, and his younger brother, Robert, later Earl of Leicester; along with, at various times, such poets as Spenser, Dyer, Greville, Breton, Daniel and Fraunce.

Sidney was educated to embrace an unusual degree of political, religious, and cultural responsibility. Both the *Defence* and *Astrophil and Stella* are manifestos not only of poetic but of broader cultural and political commitments. For Sidney, poetry and its social uses were inseparable. Like Puttenham, he looked back to a figure like the Earl of Surrey for an ideal of what the poet should be, the unashamed embodiment of a noble family's ambitions, firmly committed to the glories and possibilities of the new aristocratic ideals. But like other Elizabethan court poets, Sidney's poetry is put into play within the Court in ways he could not fully know: it was both as a means of participating in the Court's power and an ambiguous articulation of its power. Where a poem like Ralegh's 'Praisd Be Dianas Faire and Harmles Light' shows the Court contemplating its own idealized image and compelling allegiance to that ideal, however, like Wyatt's, Sidney's poetry has a more uneasy relation to the Court. Although on the surface, his writing appears to embody, in Eagleton's words, a 'moment of ideological buoyancy, an achieved synthesis'[3] of courtly values, it was

Sidney's uneasy relations to court politics in the 1580s that makes his poetry an unusually revealing exposure of the ideological pretensions of the aristocratic ideals.

What we get, in fact, emerging in Sidney's poetry is precisely some of the class and gender contradictions that the Court worked to contain. More than that of any of his contemporaries before Donne and Shakespeare, Sidney's poetry evokes a felt world of bustling activity, psychosocial pressure, and cultural demand – in short, both the everyday detail of court life and, outside, the energies of a new material world pressing in upon the self-contained discourses of the court. In *Astrophil and Stella* the institutions that shaped the writing of poetry – the Court's household arrangements, its religious and political controversies – are evoked in the tournaments (41), the gossip of 'curious wits' (23), or the 'courtly nymphs' (54). But what distinguishes Sidney's poetry is the forceful way more than just the glittering surface of the Court energizes it. Despite his posthumous reputation as the perfect Renaissance courtier, Sidney's career was one of political disappointment and humiliation; he seems to have been increasingly torn between public duty and private desire, much in the way the hero of his sonnet sequence is. As McCoy has shown, all of Sidney's works are permeated with the problem of authority and submission: all his heroes (including Astrophil) are young, noble, well-educated and well-intentioned, but as they become aware of the complexities and ambiguities of the world, they become diverted or confused, and it is as if Sidney finds himself caught between compassion for and condemnation of their activities.[4] In the *Arcadia*, Sidney attempted to solve in fiction many of the tensions he was beset with in his life, and *Astrophil and Stella* similarly served as an outlet for political and social frustration. In the romance, Sidney's narrative irresolution and (in the *Old Arcadia*) the story's premature and repressive closure reveals deep and unsettling doubts in the aristocratic ethos that motivates it. In the ambivalences and hesitations, the shifting distance between poet and character, the divided responses to intellectual and emotional demands in *Astrophil and Stella*, Sidney's ambivalent roles within the Court are similarly articulated. In the *Defence*, literature is depicted as a potent ideological instrument for inculcating those virtues appropriate to the class of which he is a spokesman, but in his poetic practice (as well as in the *Arcadia* itself) inevitably it is the incomplete, uncertain, or dislocated work that is a sign that the writer is grasping to find expression for new emergent realities, dimly perceived but increasingly influential in the lived experience of his society.

What gives Sidney's life and poetry alike their particular caste is his deep Protestantism. An insistent piety continually challenges and contradicts the courtly values in Sidney's work, and also sets up contradictions in his life which helped to make him, politically at least, a failure. He never held any major court office, so in his political career, Sidney was a hot-headed Protestant aristocrat; in his poetry, in Hamilton's phrase, Sidney is 'a Protestant English Petrarch'.[5] The development of Protestant poetry seen in the gospellers and slightly more sophisticated poets like Turberville culminates in Sidney and his circle. But although the members of Sidney's Circle were, in Andrew Weiner's phrase, 'godly aristocrats',[6] actively promoting the Protestant cause in Europe and supporting the Calvinist reformers at home, none the less Sidney's Protestant poetic is rarely overtly didactic. His characteristic ideological configuration is more a *bricolage*, an assemblage of different fragments, and it is that which makes him the central poet of the whole age. For, unlike his friend Fulke Greville, for whom a radical Protestant suspicion of metaphor and writing itself constantly undermines poetry's value, Sidney tries to hold together what in the *Defence* he terms man's 'erected wit' and 'infected will'.[7] As such, his poetic can be seen as central to the poetry of the whole century: intensifying its focus on intellectual contradictions, wanting to be both militantly Protestant and courtly. Indeed, what Sidney uniquely brought to the Petrarchan lyric was a self-conscious anxiety about the dislocation of courtly celebration and Protestant inwardness, between the persuasiveness of rhetoric and the self-doubt of sinful man, between the insecurity of man's word and the absolute claims of God's Word.

The tension in Sidney's poetry between the courtly and the pious, between Calvin and Castiglione, disrupts *Astrophil and Stella* in rich and energetic ways and constitutes the basis for its varied and continuing appeal. Its contradictions open up the possibility of powerful and varied readings. Sidney's own theory sees poetry focusing on the reformation of the will, on *praxis*, and thus it is possible to read the poems as an exemplum of the perils of erotic love, in Sinfield's words, of 'the errors of ungoverned passion'.[8] Sidney, according to this reading, shows Astrophil deliberately rejecting virtue and treating Stella as a deity in an open repudiation of Christian morality. Astrophil's cleverness consists of trying to avoid or repel the claims of reason and virtue, and the outcome of the sequence is the inevitable end of self-deception – or, in a popular current reading, self-realization by Astrophil and a determination to reform. The final sonnets, 107 and 108, are a crux in such a reading, and critics have even seen one of Sidney's earlier 'Certain Sonnets' as the appropriate moralistic conclusion to the later collection:

> Leave me ô Love, which reachest but to dust,
> And thou my mind aspire to higher things:
> Grow rich in that which never taken rust:
> What ever fades, but fading pleasure brings.

But such a narrow closure emphasizes only one of the discourses which flow into *Astrophil and Stella*. The inwardness of the poems – not necessarily, it should be noted, their supposed autobiographical dimension, but their concern with Astrophil's self-conciousness, even self-centredness, as lover, poet, courtier and, through Astrophil, with the 'self' we take on when we read – is a blend of Protestant and Petrarchan self-obsession. It also points to a distinctive late sixteenth-century strain within the inherited vocabulary and rhetoric of the poet, in particular between the pragmatic demands of the Court and the demand that poetry advance the cause of Protestantism. Sidney is at the centre of this battle, determined to follow his friend Hubert Languet's advice that his talents should be at the service of 'his country, and of all good men; since you are only the steward of this gift, you will wrong Him who conferred such a great benefit on you if you prove to have abused it'.[9]

Travelling in Europe, Sidney had discovered Protestant courts where poets, scholars and musicians were encouraged more than in England. Shortly after his return, his sister Mary became the Countess of Pembroke and established at Wilton what one of her followers was to term a 'little Court',[10] dedicated, both before and after his death, to the renaissance of English courtly culture. We look back to Wilton and its earnest group of poets, theologians and philosophers and see their dedication to the Sidneian ideals, but what we can also see in the 'little Court' are the forces which, identifiable in the 1620s and 1630s, would challenge and eventually overwhelm the hegemony of the royal Court. In other words, in the very movement that was attempting to establish and glorify the domination of what were perceived as traditional courtly values lay the elements that were to challenge and shatter it. Even in Sidney's 'first and only work as a courtier-poet',[11] as Hamilton describes *The Lady of May* (1579), we can see Sidney's unease with his role as a court poet. It shows an unwillingness to be effaced in the traditional courtly manner; he asks for participation and discrimination from the Queen, but not for an authoritarian intervention. However, when at the end of the work's performance, she chooses the 'wrong' side of the argument, her decision can be read as not only a rejection of the political argument Sidney is advancing on behalf of the Leicester Circle, but also of his attempt to assert a prophetic role for the court poet rather than the residual, essentially feudal, role of entertainer and panegyrist. Sidney's career was a frustrated attempt to realize a new role for the court poet, one based upon the integrity and responsibility of values which he was unable to embody in his public life, and which more and more he poured into his writing. His remark to the Earl of Leicester during the French marriage crisis that he was kept 'from the courte since my only service is speeche and that is stopped'.[12] has wider application. It articulates a frustration towards the traditional subservience of the poet to the Court, a stubborn insistence on forging a distinctive role for the poet.

Sidney has often been characterized as balancing opposite ideological, rhetorical or vocational demands, holding together what Calvin termed a 'matching of contraries'.[13] In the *Defence* and *Astrophil and Stella* the elements of such a balance can certainly be found. Poetry is at once a fervent reaching for the sublime and yet bound to humanity's 'infected will', just as Astrophil is at once inspired by and degraded by his love for Stella. Throughout his writing, the claims of rhetoric and truth, humanism and piety, Calvin and Castiglione, make their claims on Sidney and much of the interest of his poetry is grounded in such contradictions.

Where we first see this *bricolage* of conflicting discourses in Sidney's poetry is in the versifications of the Psalms, started by him about 1579, and revised and completed by his sister the Countess of Pembroke after his death. The Sidney Psalms are the first post-Reformation religious lyrics that combine the rich emotional and spiritual life of Protestantism with the new rhetorical riches of the secular lyric. Even in Sidney's 43 Psalms (generally inferior to those of his sister), contradictions are clearly seen. There are distinctive Protestant notes – a strong stress on election in Psalm 43, echoing Beza's and Calvin's glosses rather than the original text, for instance. There are other Psalms where a strain of courtly neoplatonism is highlighted, notably in Psalm 8 which presents the human being as a privileged, glorious creation, 'attended' by God, an 'owner' of regal status and 'crowning honour'. This is hardly a typical Protestant note. Humanity emerges as free and wondrous, 'freely raunging within the zodiack of his owne wit', a phrase from the *Defence* in which Sidney typically juxtaposes, though without integrating, the great contraries of his age.[14]

At about the same time he was experimenting with the Psalms, Sidney was working over a variety of other poems – pastoral dialogues, songs, experiments in quantitative metres – which he inserted into the *Arcadia*, and a collection of miscellaneous love sonnets and songs. The 'Certain Sonnets' looks like many other collections of the 1560s and 1570s, based on the model provided by Tottel's *Miscellany* and working through the common mid-century poetic modes of blazons, songs, moralistic poems and rhetorical experiments. But as Warkentin has pointed out, through the 'Certain Sonnets' is emerging a new poetic – one based on the use of vividly dramatic voices, and one starting to exploit more fully than before in English poetry the psychology and eloquence of Petrarchism. Out of the 'Certain Sonnets' grew *Astrophil and Stella*. Sidney was tinkering with the earlier poems during 1581–82 and abandoned them the next summer to write what became the first major Petrarchan collection of the English Renaissance.[15]

This sequence of 108 sonnets and 11 songs anatomizes the love of a young, restless, self-conscious courtier, Astrophil, for a court lady, Stella. The lover's aim is set out in the opening sonnet where, he claims 'I sought fit words to paint the blackest face of woe/Studying inventions fine, her wits to entertaine.' We are taken into the familiar world of Petrarchan convention and cliché: Astrophil is the doubting, apologetically aggressive lover, Stella the golden-haired, black-eyed, chaste, (usually) distant, and (finally) unobtainable. The landscape is familiar – Hope and Absence, frustrated desire alleviated temporarily by writing, the beautiful woman with the icy heart who pitilessly resists siege and yet encourages her admirer, and the lover's final anguish at her 'absent presence' (104). Earlier Petrarchan poets like Wyatt had tried to achieve urgency or conversational informality, but read as a whole, English poetry had not, since Chaucer, been distinguished by such continual conflict and energy in a concentrated, closely knit sustained work.

Modern critics, reacting against earlier impressionistic Romantic readers of the collection, have shown how the energy and variety of Sidney's poetry rest on a thorough exploitation of the riches of Renaissance rhetoric – through use of apostrophe, dialogue, irony, shifts in decorum, modulations of voice. By his familiarity with the conventional techniques of Renaissance love verse, which he parodies in Sonnets 6, 9 or 15, Sidney uses his poems as workshops to try to improve what he saw as the inadequacy of English poetry. He tries continually to combine the demands of formal verse with an immediacy of idiom, providing a voice that will involve his reader in the often tortuous movements of his character's broodings, arguments and self-deceptions. Especially notable is the lightness and wit with which even Astrophil's most tortured self-examination is presented. Parody and the continual exaggerated use of erotic or literary clichés and puns are obvious enough, but the whole sequence is characterized by a sophisticated playfulness – for instance the outrageous puns on 'touch' in Sonnet 9 leading to the self-pity (Astrophil's, not Sidney's) of the last line:

> The windows now through which this heav'nly guest
> Looks over the world, and can find nothing such,
> Which dare claime from those lights the name of best,
> Of touch they are that without touch doth touch,
> Which *Cupid's* selfe from Beautie's myne did draw:
> Of touch they are, and poore I am their straw.

The pun is on physical and emotional touching and the glossy black of Stella's eyes: 'touch' was a shiny black stone like coal which could attract by a kind of magnetism or static. The poor lover ('poor Astrophil' we are constantly tempted to say, laughingly) is helpless, and explodes into flame, like straw before a spark. Similarly sophisticated and yet often just plain fun are the tongue-in-cheek anguish of the sonnets on Cupid, or the usually delicate uproariousness of some of the erotic sonnets, in which Sidney invites his readers to share his enjoyment at the varied follies and complexities of human love. We laugh with him; we laugh at or are sympathetic with (or perhaps disapproving of) poor Astrophil.

But what of Stella? Does she share in the fun? We should not forget how firmly *Astrophil and Stella* is encoded within a male-dominated discourse. Stella is, like other Petrarchan mistresses, reduced to a disconnected set of characteristics, acknowledged only as she is manipulated by or impinges on his consciousness. She is the product of her poet-lover's desires. Sidney's sonnets provide a theatre of desire in which the man has all the active roles, and in which the woman is silent or merely iconic, most present when she refuses him or is absent. Astrophil does not want us, although it is arguable that Sidney might, to call into question the power of his anguish or the centrality of his struggles of conscience. Yet it is legitimate to ask what Stella can reply to Astrophil's earnest self-regarding pleas for favour, just as it is more generally important to ask where the woman's voice in the Petrarchan sequence is – as Sidney's niece Mary was to do so forcefully a generation later, as I shall show in Chapter 8. Even if Stella's replies are not in most of the poems (and where they are, as in Song 8, they are, we should note, reported to us through Astrophil's words), what might she say? Is her silence the repression of the character? Or is it, more directly, that of Sidney? Or of a whole cultural blindness that fixed women as objects of gaze and analysis within a discourse they did not invent and could not control? When we consider in these ways how the dynamics of Sidney's text function, once again what is found are literary and cultural texts that are interactive, their languages rewriting each other with continual contradictions.

An older criticism faced (or avoided) these issues by focusing on the biographical origins of the sequence. In part as an outcome of the Romantic valorization of poetry as the overflow of 'sincerity' or 'genuine' experience, earlier critics sentimentalized the obvious connections between Sidney's life and the fiction of Astrophil's love for Stella into a poetic *roman-à-clef*. Yet as Warkentin has pointed out, the story in Sidney's poems is common to many mid-century sonnet collections. Sidney certainly plays with his readers' curiosity about some identification between himself and Astrophil and between Stella and Lady Penelope Rich (née Devereux) for whom Sidney was once suggested as a husband. Sidney also builds into his sequence references to his career, to his father, contemporary politics, to his friends and –

of most interest to the curious – to Lady Rich's name in two sonnets (24, 37) which were omitted from the first publication of the collection. But the relationship between Sidney and his characters and between the events of his life and those seemingly within his poems should not be simplified. Sinfield argues that 'the hints of Sidney in the poem' are made deliberately ambiguous by bringing the poet to the surface of the poems alongside and in a shifting relationship to the lover so that any desire to see Astrophil unambiguously 'as a fiction or as Sidney', or 'a stable compound' of both 'is frustrated'.[16] And just as Sidney manages simultaneously to have much in common with Astrophil, be sympathetic with him, and yet to criticize or laugh at him, so the gap between Stella and the historical Lady Rich is always shifting – at best one can regard some of the references as sly or wistful fantasies. Whether Sidney and Lady Rich were 'sexually involved, *Astrophil and Stella* gives us no firm evidence on the subject.

As we saw in Chapter 3, one of the characteristics of Petrarchism was to set the traditional debate on the nature of love in terms of what appeared to be a lover's psychology and was in fact a complex and subtle rhetoric. Part of the fascination Petrarch had for English poets in the late sixteenth century was a puzzlement about how Petrarchan conventions might fit 'real' experiences. Typically, Sidney's poems open themselves to many readings. Whether they are seen as a collection of discrete lyrics or whether we choose to read them as a sequence, thus allowing for connection, juxtaposition or qualification, the poems in *Astrophil and Stella* focus our attention on the 'thrownness' of love – on the lover finding himself within a pre-existing structuring of experience, a 'race' that 'hath neither stop nor start' (23), one which continually disrupts his sense of a stable, controlling self. But the self that is put into question is not, or not primarily, that of Sidney. We are dealing here with poems which require an unusually active involvement from their readers, and which produce meanings only within the changing encounters between poem and readers. The poet offers his poems to an audience of sympathetic listeners as a mirror less of his experiences than of theirs. Sidney's poems work on their readers, suggesting, manipulating, but never compelling, meanings. As we have seen, the Petrarchan lyric is typically inaugurating, requiring completion in its audience's experiences and responses. The continual isolation of the 'I', focused in Astrophil's obsession with the self, directs us continually to our own self-consciousness, literally so that if the poems are read aloud, and we are forced to speak all the 'I's in a sonnet like 'Because I Breathe Not Love to Everie One'. What Rudenstine calls Sidney's style, 'the outward sign of a particular style of life',[17] refers less to him than to his audiences. One such audience is other lover-poets: in Sonnet 6, for instance, where Astrophil distinguishes his own 'trembling voice' and the sincerity of his love from those of other lovers and so thereby provokes them to respond by praising their own mistress or talents. At times his suffering hero will ostensibly address another, rather special, named audience – 'I Stella's ears assayll, invade her eares', he says in 61. Or he (or Sidney) will address a friend (as in 14) or even, occasionally, himself (30). But always the most important audiences are the ones unnamed, those of us who, through the poems' history, will read them, meditate upon, and act out their drama. Such readers are addressed variously – as friends, fellow victims of love, or fellow poets. In 28, such an audience is appealed to directly: 'You that with allegorie's curious frame,/Of other's children changelings use to make . . .' Similarly the 'fooles' chided in 104 are an audience outside, though (it is hoped) sympathetic to, the conflicts the poem dramatizes.

One of the two 'Rich' sonnets, Sonnet 37, where references to Lord and Lady Rich seem to be directly made, is especially effective because of the witty complexity of its appeal to multiple audiences. It starts as a therapeutic exercise – 'My mouth doth water, and my breast doth swell', a secret disease which, since we are invited to overhear, can be cured, oddly enough, only by being talked about to others. It next seems to become a personal confession – again, we should note, private therapy publically witnessed – and then, in the final line, turns outward to an audience which knows, or now knows, or at least may have become curious about, the identification of Stella with Lady Rich. Was Penelope Devereux Rich in the original audience? Would she have been embarrassed or amused? Either would be possible – just as other listeners' and readers' reactions, and therefore their readings of the poem, could have varied from indignation to titillation, puzzlement to disapproval. We should even consider Sidney himself as part of such an audience. As with any writer, however, we invite him to our readings as a guest, not as a master of ceremonies: long before he purged himself on his death-bed of what he himself termed the 'vanity' of 'my Lady Rich' which haunted his mind, he may well have become embarrassed by or disapproved of his own poems in ways that his enthusiastic readers ever since would politely, but firmly, reject.[18]

Another place where the inevitable diversity of a specifically courtly audience's involvement is requested can be seen in the series of questions in the sestet of 31. There the lover is displayed as being overwhelmed by passion, anguish and self division, so that an audience is invited implicitly to help him in his choice:

> Then ev'n of fellowship, ô Moone, tell me
> Is constant *Love* deem'd there but want of wit?
> Are Beauties there as proud as here they be?
> Do they above love to be lov'd, and yet

> Those Lovers scorne whom that *Love* doth possesse?
> Do they call *Vertue* there ungratefulnesse?

Such questions may be seen as rhetorical only if we are, as indeed well we might be, sympathetic with Astrophil. But if we see Astrophil's self-obsessive melancholy as misguided, then we can enter into a different kind of discussion with the sonnets, responding to them as if we were in a debate on the nature of love's demands upon us. Indeed, within the courtly group among whom Sidney wrote, the poems must have variously tempted, seduced, stimulated, pleased, annoyed, even bored. The poems in *Astrophil and Stella* placed their original readers at the focal point of a network of traditionally learnt expectations and demands. They invite all their readers to bring their own experiences into the struggles and problems of Astrophil's woes, and to participate in the calculated, sophisticated poise and grace with which Sidney presents them. And whatever meanings they disclose now, they show us that they cannot be treated as texts that are complete and closed unless we ignore that they demand performance not passivity. To adapt some phrases of Barthes, Sidney's texts are not lines of words realizing a single message; they are 'multi-dimensional' spaces in which 'a variety of writings', including those of his readers, 'blend and clash'.[19]

When we look at Sidney's own delightfully self-conscious rhetoric, we can see how the stylistic strategies of *Astrophil and Stella* emphasize language that aims to open meanings in the reader's experience. One particularly successful feature is the exploitation of the gap between Astrophil's anguish and Sidney's enjoyment of his hero's fumbling enactment of 'poore Petrarch's long deceased woes' (15), 'It is most true, that eyes are form'd to serve/The inward light' (5), conveys simultaneously a brooding, self-obsessive solemnity on Astrophil's part and a sympathetic though amused delight on Sidney's – a combination seen in the lightness of movement counterpointing the solemnity of Astrophil's slightly exaggerated argument. In 10, we witness a sympathetic dramatization by Sidney of a struggle within Astrophil. As Castley notes, 'behind the straight face . . . behind the apparent self-depreciation' of such poems, 'the smile is all the time playing'.[20] The straight face is Astrophil's and in so far as we are lovers, we may sympathize or criticize; the smile is Sidney's and in so far as we respond to witty, sophisticated dramatizations of human emotional conflicts in subtle verse, we are probably delighted. In such poems, the more serious the philosophical brooding by the lover, the more it is undercut by the tone of the verse which looks out, almost with a wink, to the audience, inviting our amusement as well as our sympathy. At the end of 57, as Astrophil turns for sympathy to his audience, so Sidney turns to prompt his audience towards amusement at his hero's sufferings:

> A prety case! I hoped her to bring
>> To feele my griefes, and she with face and voice
>> So sweets my paines, that my paines me rejoyce.

'Fly, Fly My Friends' (20), is another where the sophisticated poise of the poet places him among his audience, watching, describing, and inviting discussion of (perhaps even disapproval of) his hero's antics and agonies. Such a process is encouraged even where the speaker expresses a desire for privacy. The 'trembling voice' which displays 'the Map' of Astrophil's 'state' (6) is evoked in poetry that is hardly 'trembling'. 'Because I Breathe Not Love to Everie One' (54), is an especially interesting case. The poem starts as a monologue, articulating Astrophil's humble claim that nothing matters except that 'Stella know my mind'. An even more blatant (and marvellous) contradiction is the last line. Asserting 'I breathe not love to everie one', he is heard by everyone – 'They love indeed, who quake to say they love.' Astrophil may, indeed, quake, but Sidney's brilliantly vivid rhetoric hardly quakes. Furthermore, between the quiet opening and dignified (though amusing) conclusion, monologue has turned to drama, and we overhear the argument of the 'courtly nymphs' of Astrophil's audience with him:

> . . . acquainted with the mone
>> Of them, who in their lips *Love*'s standerd beare;
>> 'What he?' say they of me, 'now I dare sweare,
>> He cannot love: no, no, let him alone.'

When the poem turns outward, directly to the 'courtly nymphs' themselves, we can imagine them as part of the original audience:

> Professe in deed I do not *Cupid*'s art;
>> But you faire maides, at length this true shall find,
>> That his right badge is but worne in the hart.

This primary audience, the 'courtly nymphs', is rebuked – and the poem turns from mocking them to a wider, more sympathetic, audience, which, of course, includes us. The result is that we become aware of a division between Sidney and his character – we sympathize with (or criticize) Astrophil in his silence, and we are delighted with Sidney in his eloquence. We become aware of ourselves as lovers of poetry and as lovers of love. Sidney's sonnets, in short, require us to respond – in complex, unpredictable ways – to the viewpoints they provoke us to produce.

Astrophil and Stella is therefore what Barthes terms a playful text, one that depends strongly on its audience.[21] It invites our participation both to reproduce the process, intellectual and emotional, by which the poem's struggles come to be verbalized; but also to go beyond them, adding our own. It has a capacity to invade us, to direct and inform our responses, but as well, to open us to an awareness that it functions only through a process of deliberate reciprocity. As readers or lovers or poets (or all three) we put ourselves at risk, inveigled as we may be into a state of sympathy and vulnerability by the text. Scholars have often pointed to the cross-fertilization at the end of the sixteenth century between the lyric poem and the drama. As Chapter 7 will suggest, Shakespeare's *Sonnets* and Donne's *Songs and Sonets* are more frequently mentioned in this way, but *Astrophil and Stella* also has some claims to be seen as dramatic. When we read Sidney's poems, we are encouraged not merely to consume them, but to enter them, as into a theatre where, in a sense, it is we who produce their meanings.

What then, of any attempt (like Harington's) to see a definitive 'story' in *Astrophil and Stella*? Surveying the history of Sidney criticism, especially in the past forty years, one discovers a curious anxiety to find a coherent, sequential organization not merely a collection of single poems. *Astrophil and Stella* is thus often read as if it were a poetic novel. Lewis cautions against treating any Petrarchan sequence as if it were 'a way of telling a story'; *Astrophil and Stella* is, he says, 'not a love story but an anatomy of love'; Putzel speaks of the poems' 'careful disorder'; but on the other hand and more typically, Hamilton argues that they are organized into a sequence or 'one larger poem' with a unifying structure, and other critics have written of what they see as careful structure and sequence.[22] In his scheme, 1–12 form an introduction, 13–30 concentrate on Astrophil's isolation, with 41–68 concerned with his moral rebellion, 71–85 with his attempt at seduction, and the final poems with his failure. The songs serve especially well to highlight the wish fulfilment of Astrophil's love – his frustration, his self-involvement, his wistful fantasies. Song 8 is especially moving in its culmination as Sidney cleverly breaks down the distance between narrator and character in the final line where he confesses that 'my' song is broken:

> Therewithall away she went,
> Leaving him so passion rent,
> With what she had done and spoken,
> That therewith my song is broken.

In the later poems, if it is read according to this narrative structure, Astrophil's fantasies seem less and less realizable. His self-pity intensifies, occasional realism breaks in, and there is acceptance of the Petrarchan stasis, vacillating between joy and pain, optimism and despair. As Hamilton points out, the mutability of human love, which haunts so many Elizabethan sonnet sequences, enters Sidney's only indirectly, but as the sequence ends, Astrophil is shown 'forever subject to love's tyranny, a victim of Chronos forever caught in time's endless linear succession'. The melancholy hopelessness of the sequence's final lines points to the stasis of despair and hope finally and frustratingly balanced between woe and joy.[23] Such a narrative sees *Astrophil and Stella* as a moral exemplar. But other divisions have been proposed – and clearly for readers who wish to find a narrative development from the initial onset of love to a final (ir)resolution rather than read the poems as exercises in love's variety, then *Astrophil and Stella* is open to such a reading. Jones has argued that it is possible (and peculiarly satisfying) to see Astrophil as undergoing a gradual disintegration and loss of control. But she also points out that Sidney's sequence does not use the linking devices of other poets, like Dante or Scève, which strongly encourage a sequential reading. It is 'dramatically disordered', she argues, and 'even at the end of his experience', Astrophil 'can predict the course of his writing no better than the course of his love', and so each sonnet becomes a new starting-place. In short, while *Astrophil and Stella* allows for a linear development, it does not force one upon a reader and encourages us just as readily to view Astrophil's experience as unpredictable and random.[24]

So far, I have taken *Astrophil and Stella* pretty much at face value – as a collection of love poems. But bearing in mind the socio-cultural context of the period's poetry, a rewarding approach is to note how Sidney's poems, though ostensibly about love, are none the less traversed by a variety of overlapping and contradictory discourses – most particularly those of court politics and Protestant theology. A recurring contradiction is between the demands of what the poems wish us to see as the 'public' world of political responsibility and the 'private' world of erotic desire. In many sonnets, Astrophil presents his love in terms of a debate between traditional abstractions like desire and reason, love and duty. Part of our enjoyment lies in our watching him, through Sidney's fond but penetrating perspective, indulging himself in false logic (52), or in seeing his dutifully constructed arguments against love undermined by the simple appearance of his beloved, (5, 10), or in 47's amusing self-contradictions:

> Vertue awake, Beautie but beautie is,
> I may, I must, I can, I will, I do
> Leave following that, which it is gaine to misse.
> Let her go. Soft, but here she comes.
> Go to, Unkind, I love you not: O me, that eye
> Doth make my heart give to my tongue the lie.

A major source of the confusion (and our enjoyment) is Sidney's placing
Astrophil's internal struggles in the context of his public responsibility.
The 'curious wits' (23) of the Court speculate on his 'dull pensiveness'
or praise him for what he attributes to Stella's inspiration (41). Astrophil
tries in vain to keep his two worlds and their discursive demands
separate. He claims that love gives him a private place, a stable sense
of self beside which the demands of courtly responsibility are shown
to be trivial but, caught between conflicting worlds of self-indulgence
and political responsibility, he ends by succeeding in neither. In some
sonnets (or one of a number of narratives) we watch him corrupting
his avowedly pure love into sensuality by the deviousness of political
rhetoric. In 23, he appears to reject the world; but in 69, he expresses
Stella's conditional encouragement of his advances in terms of the
Court's own language. Since, he argues, she has 'of her high heart
giv'n' him 'the monarchie', as king he too can take some advantage
from that power:

> . . . though she give but thus conditionally
> This realme of blisse, while vertuous course I take,
> No kings be crown'd, but they some covenants make.

The traditional formula by which the man is subjected to his lady
while at the same time the situation gives him the autonomy and
power to try to seduce her is, not coincidentally, homologous with
the relationship between the courtier and monarch. Both are built
on a structure of loyalty and subjection, frustration and rejection,
and are interlaced with devious manipulations for the favours of the
capricious, distant beloved. Thus while Astrophil speaks of the 'joy'
inspired by Stella and of his own 'noble fire', he is attempting to
manipulate Stella's vulnerability, seeking power over her in the way
the devious courtier seeks hidden but real power over the monarch.
In terms of the sexual politics of the Court, Astrophil's world is one
shared primarily by other male courtiers in relation to the monarch.
Thus we watch him indulging himself in small but subtle ways. He
continually twists Stella's words; he speaks openly of his love, but
offhandedly and half-seriously, allowing (or being unable to prevent)
the emergence of the underlying physicality of his desires in a series
of fantasies of seduction. He professes great, unselfish devotion. He
argues his love transcends any base motive; it is a private world of
high ideals. But while Astrophil claims his love is independent of and
superior to the public world, such an antithesis is self-deceiving. At the
root of Astrophil's self-deception are the contradictions of Petrarchism:
it is at once a literary convention and a serious courtly game, in
which three powerful cultural discourses interact – love, religion and

politics. Jones and Stallybrass have shown that the compliments and manipulations Astrophil performs are curiously like those 'necessary to the new courtier in relation to his prince', and further down the social system, the poet in relation to patron. They demonstrate how these homologies between lover and beloved, suitor and patron, courtier and prince, shape both 'private' and 'public' texts alike. The courtier, like the lover, waits, hopelessly, using whatever devious means he can command to shape the responses of the capricious prince. The 'game' of Petrarchan love, the dangers of which we saw coming tentatively to the surface in Dunbar and Wyatt, was late in the century, a powerful and acknowledged dimension of court life, as Ralegh's career, which we saw in Chapter 4, is a poignant reminder.[25]

If the structures of court politics dislocate the erotic titillation of *Astrophil and Stella*, so do the demands of Sidney's deep commitment to Protestantism. As Sinfield puts it, 'the protestant humanist who felt the force of protestant doctrine as well as the imaginative excitement of literature was sited at the crisis point of a sharp and persistent cultural dislocation'.[26] Throughout *Astrophil and Stella*, Protestant theology constantly judges the ebullience and self-indulgence of Sidney's hero. Yet the results are never firmly settled. In Sonnet 5, three quatrains firmly put the Protestant rejection of self-obsessive erotic love, concluding that '[It is most] true, that on earth we are but pilgrims made.' And then, in a final (dismissive or plaintive?) line comes Astrophil's rejoinder: 'True; and yet true that I must Stella love.' As Sinfield comments: 'Either truculently or regretfully, Astrophil rejects all the assumptions'[27] of Protestantism. And yet while Sidney might invite criticism of Astrophil, he does not require it. Such poems as 71, with its wonderfully poignant final line, ' "But ah", Desire still cries, "give me some food" ', is an especially interesting case – leave the reader balanced between the conflicting discourses of erotic love and Protestant theology.

It has recently become fashionable to see Sidney's poems as condemning Astrophil, even to see him by the end of the sequence learning from his moral errors. It is a reading that wishes, perhaps, to see 'Leave me o love, which reachest but to dust', from 'Certain Sonnets', as a satisfactory conclusion to the collection. Hamilton's reading of the final *Astrophil and Stella* sonnets, 107 and 108, also insists on Sidney's desire to 'resolve the whole poem'.[28] But – apart from the oddity of seeing the sonnets as a whole poem' – we might consider: why is closure so necessary? The Petrarchan situation is built precisely on the power of a lack of closure, on the perpetual deference of desire's consummation. The Protestant insistence on moral criticism and therefore on narrative closure certainly feeds into the collection but it does not dominate it, nor does it reduce it to a kind of moral tract, as some modern readers seem to want. Sidney is almost in danger of being co-opted by the Moral Majority in some recent criticism (even though such a reading of Sidney does have a precedent in Greville's). But while Greville might well have liked to have seen his friend's poems in such a light, it is obvious from *Caelica* that it was because he saw *Astrophil and Stella* as potentially highly subversive of sound Protestant doctrine. Unless a modern reader shares such religious beliefs, it is the more open reading that most will prefer.

Astrophil and Stella, then, is a quintessential site of cultural conflict where a variety of discourses, including the reader's own, struggle for mastery. We should not see Sidney, any more than any other poet, as being in 'control' of the discursive structures that speak through him. Astrophil may state that all his 'deed' is to 'copy' what in Stella 'Nature writes' (3), or assert that 'Stella' is, literally, the principle of love in the cosmos (28), or that the words he utters 'do well set forth my mind' (44), but Sidney knows, as we all do, that love and its significances and its relation to our words are far more complex matters. In love and poetry alike we are only partly in control of languages and logics we did not create and into which we find ourselves – sometimes painfully, sometimes hilariously – inserted.

Mary Sidney, Countess of Pembroke

In 1577 Mary Sidney married Henry, second Earl of Pembroke, and her home at Wilton became for some twenty years the centre of Sidney's attempt to give direction to Elizabethan high culture. Growing from informal gatherings of Sidney's friends and admirers at Wilton and elsewhere, after Sidney's death the Circle became centred on the Countess's attempt to continue her brother's ideals. In its work, its achievements and limitations alike, we can see a mixture of both residual and emergent cultural forms and practices: some look nostalgically back to medieval chivalric ideals and practices, others struggle to articulate (or repress) the emergence of a new phase of English cultural history.

Mary Sidney was not only a member of this remarkable literary family, but also a woman. One reason for the neglect was simply that seemingly neutral fact. On the surface, for her gender was not an important issue. Interpellated into the gender assignments of a daughter of a rising aristocratic family, she saw her destiny in terms of her family: in her own eyes, she was primarily a Sidney. She devoted most of her adult life to forwarding her brother's cultural ideals and, particularly, after his death, his hopes for the advancement of poetry. It was to his sister that Philip entrusted many of his manuscripts and it was she who oversaw the issuing, twelve years after his death, of an authorized edition of his works. During the last twenty years of the century, Wilton became a kind of salon to which many late Elizabethan intellectuals and poets came. Nicholas Breton spoke of it as 'a kinde of little Court' and compared it with Castiglione's Urbino, asking 'who hathe redde of the Duchesse of Urbina, may saie, the Italians wrote wel: but who knowes the Countesse of Pembroke, I think hath cause to write better', He also calls attention – as did other commentators – to one feature of Wilton that differentiated it from Urbino: it was a place of piety and theological learning. In his devotional poems, *The Countesse of Pembrookes Love* and *The Passions of the Spirit*, Mary is depicted meditating at Wilton, 'a plot of earthly paradise' and visited by a procession of courtiers, divines, and poets. What Breton's slightly sentimentalized picture of Wilton suggests is borne out by other authorities. On the other hand, Abraham Fraunce has left us a lighter, though still reverent, view of life at Wilton in *The Countesse of Pembrokes Ivychurch* where the 'peereless Pembrokiana', the damsels attending her, and the pastoral sports and hunting in Ivychurch, one of the family's properties near Wilton, are amusingly described.[29] Once again, we see the contradictions of the age brought together: courtliness and piety, Castiglione and Calvin.

The 'little Court', then, set deep in the country, became in part a retreat from the corruption and insecurities of the Court of Elizabeth, and partly, deliberately, a powerhouse for the Sidneys' attempt to manipulate the direction of literary and wider cultural change. Almost immediately it became the centre of the Countess's determination to find a wider audience for her brother's writings. Over a period of a dozen years, the Countess undertook to edit and, with some reluctance, publish her brother's works. She argued with Greville over the nature and intentions of the *Arcadia*. She approved a corrected version of *Astrophil and Stella* after Thomas Newman had published, with a preface by Thomas Nashe, an extremely corrupt, pirated edition in 1591. She added an approved edition of the *Defence* (first published separately in 1595) to the 1598 edition of Sidney's *Works*. It is this edition of 1598 which represents one part of the culmination of her supervision of her brother's writings.

Another part is her own poetry. There are four categories of the Countess's writings: three original poems directly associated with her brother, an elegy and two poems dedicating the completed versification of the Psalms to the Queen and to the memory of Philip; the Psalms themselves; three translations from French and Italian, including the magnificent version of Petrarch's poem *Trionfo della Morte* in English *terza rima*; and a small handful of other poems. The Petrarch will be considered in Chapter 8; here I will consider those poems associated directly with her brother.

Probably the earliest of the three poems Mary Sidney wrote to her brother's memory is the so-called 'Doleful Lay of Clorinda', published with Spenser's 'Astrophel' in 'The Ruines of Time', but probably written by her.[30] The 'Lay', with its mixture of personal intensity, solid metrical competence, much flat padding, and tangled syntax, reads like the work of a competent amateur. Two others, written to Philip's memory, are a dedicatory poem addressed to the Queen, and another signed 'By the Sister of that incomparable Sidney', and entitled 'To the Angell Spirit of the most excellent Sir Philip Sidney'. The latter poem is interesting for the way the conventional encomium is interrupted by stanzas of private grief and dedication. Other poems written about the same time include a verse translation of Robert Garnier's *Antonie* and a pastoral dialogue 'between two shepherds, Thenot and Piers, in praise of Astrea', which was published in Francis Davison's court miscellany, *A Poetical Rhapsody*.

The most substantial expression of Mary Sidney's dedication to her brother is found in the Psalms, which were well known to contemporaries and which kept her reputation alive during the 30 or 40 years after her brother's death. The 'Sidnean Psalmes', as John Donne called these poems,[31] were in fact mainly composed by the Countess. Sidney had translated Psalms 1–43; she revised his versions and then finished the remainder herself. She was, however, not merely content with a mere literal versification. From the manuscripts we can see the Countess feeling her way into the demands of tone and texture. In taking upon herself the task of completing his versions, she also took up the problem of learning the sweat and grind of actual composition, the search for apt metaphor, flexible versification and appropriate tone. She had her models – of positive and negative kinds – in other metrical versions. Her most important precedent was nevertheless the fertility of rhetorical and formal inventiveness and the grasp of appropriate tone shown in her brother's poetry. The metrical, stanzaic and tonal variety of her Psalms is more a tribute to the inspiration of *Astrophil and Stella* than to earlier versified Psalters. By the late 1580s she had her own group of poetic protégés with whom she shared her problems: Daniel was with her between 1585 and 1587, and actively encouraged by her; Fraunce was experimenting with some of the Psalms himself by 1588; and Breton's religious lyrics also date from the late 1580s and early 1590s .

But we should not overemphasize the group nature of her poetical experiments. Evidence for that is scanty and partly based on the remarks of writers anxious to be associated with her. So far as her poetry is concerned, the real work came in her own mulling over her

brother's manuscript, altering his text from a constant desire to practise
the rudiments of verse construction and, eventually, to bring what was
obviously an unfinished manuscript entrusted to her to a fuller stage
of completion. She was dissatisfied with Sidney's awkward phrasing
at certain points; she removed irregular stanzas, smoothed rhymes and
metres. She is especially adept at evoking a tone of joy or celebration (as
in the opening of 81), and at changing moods by dramatically breaking
up the syntax. She seems, in Rathmell's words, 'to have meditated on
the text before her, and the force of her version derives from her sense of
personal involvement . . . it is her capacity to appreciate the underlying
meaning that vivifies her poems'.[32] Usually, if not exclusively, it is the
'underlying meaning' that she is concerned to evoke. She has an especial
preference for the sharply ironical or paradoxical, and on occasions her
verse can resemble that of Greville or Ralegh in its terseness of tone
or sparseness of illusion. In other Psalms, her rhetoric can be elaborate
and rich. To Psalm 148, 8–12, she adds a picture, typical of the most
serene of Elizabethan cosmological thought, of the universe moving
mysteriously at God's command in a complex, courtly dance:

> O praise him Sunne, the sea of light,
> O praise him Moone, the light of sea:
> You preaty starrs in robe of night,
> As spangles twinckling do as they.
> Thou spheare within whose bosom play
> The rest that earth emball:
> You waters banck'd with starry bay,
> O praise, O praise him all.

A particularly delightful 'courtly' addition to the religious original is
45, where a marriage ceremony is alive with the swirl of robes and
dancing:

> This Queene that can a king her father call,
> Doth only shee in upper garment shine?
> Naie under clothes, and what she weareth all,
> Golde is the stuffe, the fasshion Arte divine;
> Brought to the king in robe imbrodied fine. . . .

In these lines the religious allegory which Protestant commentators
brought out in the Psalm combines with a sensual description of courtly
fashion: courtliness and Protestantism, Castiglione and Calvin.

Although, as with most lengthy collections of poems, the quality of
the *Psalms* varies greatly, at their best the Countess's, even more than
Sidney's, display a remarkable intensity of poetic evocation, formal

inventiveness and intellectual subtlety. They constitute a landmark in the development of the religious lyric: 'when recognition is accorded to the Sidney Psalter the history of the metaphysical revival of our time will have to be rewritten'.[33] They are as important a part of the Elizabethan literary revolution as *The Shepheardes Calender* and *Astrophil and Stella*.

In looking at *Astrophil and Stella* I noted how its poems became the site of conflicting religious and political discourses. The Sidney Psalms are religious verse, but they are no less striated by contradictions. In general, the Countess's translations stay close to the Calvinist Geneva Bible, and there are even Psalms where her version intensifies the Protestant emphasis, sometimes taking up a suggestion from Calvin or Beza. But there are also examples where the intention of Protestant orthodoxy is undermined by a contrary position – where Castiglione, to return to my earlier distinction, contradicts Calvin. In many cases, these intellectual contraries reflect contrasting intellectual drives in the originals that more dogmatic translations smooth out; but as well, they often bring out the recurring intellectual dislocations of the Countess and the whole Sidney Circle. Most interesting are those Psalms where Sidney imported not only the rhetorical vigour and flexibility of the court lyric, but also some of the sophisticated courtly philosophy that the secular lyric served to express. One example I have already noted is Sidney's version of Psalm 8, a paean to the glorious creation of Man which worried the Geneva Bible translators so much that it notes that God had no need to come 'so low as to man, which is but dust'. It is especially uneasy on the psalm's stress on the 'crowning' of man which is glossed as only 'touching his first creation'. Calvin is in even more difficulties. First of all, he disapproves of the Psalm's rhetorical extravagance – God, he comments on Psalm 8. 3, has no great need of great rhetoricians, but merely of distinct speech. He then argues that the Psalm stresses the miseries of man, 'this miserable and vyle creature', and comments 'it is a wonder that the creator of Heaven submitteth himselfe so lowe, as to vowtsafe too take uppon him the care of mankind'. Such a conjunction of divine grace and what Calvin sees as the depravity of man evidently worries him; he describes it tellingly, once again, as 'this matching of contraries'.

The Sidneys' version, certainly, has the appropriate Protestant wonder that man, a fallen creature, should be thus elevated by God, but at the same time there is a note of glorification that obviously reflects the sophisticated courtliness of the Elizabethan aristocrat:

> Then thinck I: Ah, what is this man
>   Whom that greate God remember can?
>   And what the race, of him descended,

> It should be ought of God attended?
> For though in lesse than Angells state
> Thou planted hast this earthly mate;
> Yet hast thou made ev'n hym an owner
> Of glorious crown, and crowning honor.

Courtly philosophy here is juxtaposed with Calvinist theology. With the celebration of man's creative autonomy, the Calvinist view of man as a sinful and limited being is contradicted. As so often seems to be the case with all the Sidneys' poetry, the great intellectual contraries of the age interact and rewrite one another in the tissue of the Psalms.

Robert Sidney

I will return to Mary Sidney in Chapter 8 to consider the poems, mainly verse translations, that she wrote relatively independent of her brother – as a woman and a poet, as it were, not simply as a Sidney. The third of the Sidney poets is the younger brother, Robert. Unlike his more famous brother and sister, Robert's career as a poet was probably confined to a few years, possibly as few as two. But the rediscovery of the manuscript of his poems only twenty years ago added an important voice to the court poets of the age. In his manuscript's ninety pages of nervous, often corrected, handwriting are the works of a poet of outstanding interest for our understanding of the dynamics of the century's poetry.

The place of poetry in Robert's career is typical of most Elizabethan courtiers. Although references to the literary interests of all the Sidneys are found in many dedications, letters and prefaces of the period, there are few if any references to him, specifically, as a poet. In 'To Penshurst' Jonson speaks of how Sidney's children

> . . . may, every day,
> Reade, in their vertuous parents noble parts,
> The mysteries of manners, armes, and arts

– which, at the very least, is ambiguous. In 1609, Chapman wrote of him as 'the most Learned and Noble Concluder of the Warres Art, and the Muses'. There is a tradition that he wrote the lyrics for his godson Robert Dowland's *Musicall Banquet*, and he may have written verses in honour of his daughter's marriage.[34] Certainly, like the rest of his family, Robert was widely praised as a generous patron of literature, and it is significant that the distinctive note of the other Sidneys' encouragement of poets was that they were poets themselves.

During his life and after, Robert was overshadowed by the brilliance of his elder brother. In his early life, Robert had none of Philip's prestige or flamboyance. He dutifully went on a tour of Europe, pursued by letters of advice from his brother as to his reading, chivalric bearing, friends and finances. In 1585 he accompanied Philip, who had been appointed governor of Flushing, to the Low Countries, and was present at the Battle of Zutphen where Philip was mortally wounded. In short, Robert underwent the usual initiation of the Elizabethan courtier – with the additional burden of being the younger brother of the mercurial Protestant knight so admired by European Protestants, statesmen, courtiers and men of letters. In 1584, he married Barbara Gamage, a young Welsh heiress, after some rather sordid negotiations. Their letters later show them to have grown into a most loving couple: he constantly addresses her as 'sweet heart' or 'dear heart' and the letters are full of sadness of his absence from her. In 1594 he wrote 'there is no desyre in me so dear as the love I bear you and our children . . . you are married, my dear Barbara, to a husband that is now drawn so into the world and the actions of yt as there is no way to retire myself without trying fortune further'.[35]

The intense strain of being an honest courtier during the 1590s is evident throughout his letters. Indeed, we might say with a little (obvious) exaggeration that Philip had the good fortune to die in 1586; Robert had to live on. In 1587, Robert was his brother's chief mourner and like his sister Mary, may have turned to poetry as a similar, though less public, attempt to continue his brother's intentions for poetry. He may have decided that Mary, more permanently settled at Wilton in the 1580s with the increasing comings and goings of Greville, Spenser, Daniel, and other poets, was better placed to forward the Sidneian literary revolution. It is to her that he sent the one extant copy of his manuscript, possibly in one of his much anticipated but infrequent visits to England.

Like his brother's, Robert's poems take the form of a Petrarchan miscellany of sonnets and songs, although they show a greater variety of metrical and stanzaic patterns than the normal sonnet sequence of the 1580s and 1590s – and this is a characteristic he shared with Mary, whose Psalms involve the most impressive formal experimentation in English verse before Hopkins. Robert's are technically less ambitious, but they certainly reflect a similar interest in working with a variety of complex patterns of verse – as evidenced by the three unusual thirteen-line stanzas of 'Upon a Wretch That Wastes Away'. Here the complex rhyme scheme (aaab cccb ddeeb) and the varying line length (8886888633666 syllables) are reminiscent of the Countess's experiments, although none of Robert's patterns exactly matches any of hers, and his diction is naturally closer to the typical love poetry of the era (such as in *England's Helicon*) than to her psalms. But they are born out of the same fascination with formal experimentation: just as in Mary's psalms only once is the stanzaic pattern repeated, so in Robert's twenty-four songs he never repeats a pattern, and within particular poems, too, there is displayed a technical virtuosity comparable with his brother's and sister's: Song 1, 'O Eyes, O Lights Divine', for instance, skilfully mixes lines of varied length, with a predominantly iambic beat. Like both Philip and Mary, Robert uses feminine rhyme effectively in the songs (as in Song 10, 'You Who Favour Do Enjoy'), and his technical skill is seen in such sophisticated mixtures as the blending of rhyming anapaests with the regular iambics in Song 4 ('My soul in purest fire/Doth not aspire'). Like Mary, Robert shows an excellent control of movement and balance within single lines, as for instance in the final lines of Sonnet 21:

> Or if on me from my fair heaven are seen
> Some scattered beams – know such heat gives their light
> As frosty morning's sun, as moonshine night.[36]

If Robert shares something of Mary's technical daring, nevertheless the most important influence is that of his brother. The sequence is clearly modelled on *Astrophil and Stella*: it mingles sonnets with longer, more emotionally diffuse songs, and like Philip's, Robert's sequence contains occasional transformations of biographical reference into devious fictions. The whole sequence is characterized by an opaque melancholy, a mood of disturbance and brooding which, while endemic to Petrarchan sonnets in general, nevertheless takes as its subject Robert's reading of his own political and personal career, not least as a Sidney. But while the collection is a typical Petrarchan miscellany, it is even less united than *Astrophil and Stella* by narrative or characters.

When we set Robert's poems alongside Philip's, what do we discover? He does not possess Philip's dazzling control of changing dramatic mood within a poem: the emotions of his verse express themselves in broader sweeps, concentrating on generalized feelings about pain, disillusion, absence and death. But his ear is highly sensitive, and his poems often reverberate with deep, sensuous moods. Perhaps the closest parallel is with a poet whose work I looked at in Chapter 4, one who often (literally) just dropped his poems into ladies' pockets and who also never collected his verse, Ralegh. For both, poetry made up a small part of their lives, though their commitment to its craft and insight was intense. Like Ralegh's too, the strengths of Robert Sidney's poems lie in the ways their broodings on the great commonplaces of Elizabethan life – time, absence, grief, deprivation – reveal much of the pressures upon poetry by its place in the ideology of the Court. The comparison is perhaps particularly apt because one of the most powerful poems of each poet was based upon the old Walsingham ballad (a version of which Ophelia sings in *Hamlet*) and while Ralegh's is tighter and more evocative in its rich, almost indefinable melancholy, Robert's is more personal, the emotions more diffuse yet no less keenly communicated. Both are poems by men who brooded intensely over the experiences with which their poems attempted to deal; both, perhaps, turned to poetry occasionally as an escape from the world's pressures; both found in it a commitment that went beyond mere emotional solace. Most interesting of all, both collections of poems reveal far more than their authors recognized of the ideological power of the Elizabethan Court upon those who struggled within its frantic centre or (in Robert's case) on its anxious margins.

Having looked at the affinities between Robert's poetry and that of his better-known brother and sister, let us look at it, then, in the context of the sixteenth century and, especially, the late Elizabethan Court. His poetry, like Ralegh's, is in a sense spoken by rather than just for or (occasionally) in the Court. Most of Robert's poetry was probably written during his long, frustrating tour of duty in the Low Countries, perhaps started (like Mary's) in the late 1580s, but (at least in the only manuscript copy extant) copied probably at some time between 1596 and 1598. Perhaps turning to poetry was a reaction not only to his depressing exile from England, but to the melancholy duty of following in his brother's old post. It is possible that having used verse as an emotional relief, it lost its importance for him once he had hopes of returning, and eventually did actually return, to England. Much of Robert's verse could therefore be read as a moving expression of a frustrated politician's escape-world, yearning for his wife and children back home at Penshurst.

But in placing the 'poetical text' within the 'social text', giving a biographical explanation of these poems would be to oversimplify them. Sidney's life is relevant as one typical of the late Elizabethan courtiers and courtly poets. With any newly discovered poet, it is perhaps inevitable that we will at first want to set the texts of life and poetry alongside each other. Criticism of Robert's work to date (which, after all dates only from the mid-1970s) has been predominantly of this biographical kind. But as we have seen with other poets, his verse is haunted by many pre-texts, subtexts and post-texts which call into question any naïve biographical reading. Like Ralegh's or his brother's, Robert Sidney's poems are sites of struggle where the 'self' of the poems is a cultural creation not to be simply identified with the historical figure who held the pen and wrote them. They were the means by which he tried to write himself into the world. But there is a sense in which we should speak of 'Sidney' and 'his' poems as texts that need to be read against what they seem, or would like, to articulate, that speak as much in their silences as in their insistences.

So there are clearly poems where details from Sidney's life are certainly used, where 'the hardy captain, unused to retire', speaks directly of his turning from the Low Countries where he feels exiled 'to the West' where 'love fast holds his heart' (Sonnet 7; Song 6). The sixth song of the collection is an especially revealing piece – as well as being perhaps the most impressive poetically. Like Ralegh's famous and haunting 'As You Came from the Holy Land', it is based upon the traditional lost ballad of a pilgrim travelling to Walsingham. Robert Sidney's version is an evocative 136–line dialogue between a pilgrim and a lady who presumably represents Robert's wife, while 'the knight that loves me best', and whose 'griefs livery wears', and who 'to the West . . . turns his eyes' is Robert's wistful projection of his own exiled self, held by duty to the Low Countries away from 'the lady that doth rest near Medwayes sandy bed'. Penshurst Place, the Sidney home, stands on the Medway River just outside Tonbridge and almost due west of Flushing (Robert actually revised this particular line to read 'near ritch Tons sandy bed', which of course refers to Tonbridge).

The sixth song is the most clearly autobiographical poem in the sequence, projecting the partly calculated, partly wistful view of a frustrated personal and political career. The bulk of the collection, in traditional Petrarchan fashion, is ostensibly concerned with love, and is similar to a host of sequences written in the 1590s such as Daniel's *Delia* and Drayton's *Idea*, although no poem mentions any identifiable or even coherently fictional mistress. The diction is typical of the English *petrarchisti*. The lover's 'soul' exists in 'purest fyre' (Song 4); he accepts both the joys and griefs of love, in his 'bonds of service without ende' (13) This is the altogether familiar Petrarchan world of plaint and paradox: on the one hand, the high idealism of the lover who affirms the beauty of 'those fair eyes' which 'shine in their clear former light' (12); on the other hand, the 'pains which I uncessantly sustain' (2). The beloved's beauties are 'born of the heavens, my sowles delight' (3), while the lover's passions are 'purest flames kindled by beauties rare' (4) As he contemplates in pleasurable agony how she takes 'pleasure' in his 'cruelty' (25), he asks why she 'nourishes' poisonous weeds of cold despair in love's garden instead of the plants and trees of love's faith and zeal (Song 22).

This basic Petrarchan situation of frustration, contradiction and paradox is decked out in familiar neoplatonic garb. The world is a dark cave where love's lights never shine except through the beloved's eyes, the 'purest stars, whose never dying fires' (1) constantly burn a path between the heavens and the lover's soul. Sexual desire is rarely explicitly mentioned: the dominant mood is that of melancholy; of the lover's self-torturing helplessness; and to an unusual degree, of torture, disease and violence. The lover is a continually lashed slave, flung from rocks, a leper, racked by gangrene and always in violent wars. In Chapter 4, I noted the underlying psychological patterns embodied in such metaphors.

Robert's poems are less versatile metrically and metaphorically than Philip's, with no double sestinas or quantitative verse, and little of Philip's sly humour. What distinguishes his poems from the mass of second-rate verse at the time is the remarkable and usually consistent control of form, tone and frequent use of a cryptic and direct address, not unlike the aphoristic tone of some of Greville's poems. Typical is the brief, pessimistic Song 17, which on one level, at any rate, seems to reflect upon a deeply tragic event in the poet's experience. The first stanza sets the note of brooding melancholy:

> The sun is set, and maskèd night
> Veils heaven's fair eyes:
> Ah what trust is there to a light
> That so swift flies.

In the second stanza of this superb, cryptic little poem, the speaker perhaps a woman (unusual, for Sidney), expresses a helpless, brooding bitterness:

> A new world doth his flames enjoy,
> New hearts rejoice:
> In other eyes is now his joy,
> In other choice.

Like Philip and Mary's, Robert's poetry shows a deep commitment to the craft of poetry as well as to its consolations for erotic or political loss of favour. The poems show a highly sensitive ear, and a range of tone which, while not broad, is deeply resonant, and especially receptive to the way emotions may he attached to metaphors. Intellectually, however, his poems rarely get beyond the conventional. In *Caelica*, as we have seen, Greville demystifies the common Petrarchan assertion that, when apart, true lovers are paradoxically closer because of the spiritual nature of their love, by placing it in a grimly realistic context and acknowledging that 'absence is pain'. Robert Sidney's brooding over absence, delay and loneliness have a far more conventional tenor: the lover suffers incessantly from 'griefs sent from her whom in my soul I bless' (Song 23); continually he feels that 'delays are death' (Song 18), as he waits 'on unknown shore, with weather hard distressed' (Sonnet 22). He presents himself repeatedly as an exiled and neglected knight who has beseeched the pilgrim of the Walsingham poem to be able to give his abandoned lady his undying devotion. Such common Petrarchan motifs are often made peculiarly effective by the grave, deliberate, melancholic movement of the lines, which convey the passion, the hopelessness, and yet the continuing devotion of the lover. We are reading poetry of an exceptionally high level of craftsmanship, written by a poet skilled as much in the details of the poetic craft as in the range of poetic forms, from the courtly blazon of the lady's beauties in Sonnet 32 to the ballad form of the Walsingham poem. But intellectually, Robert's verse is not as rich a revelation of the peculiar strains and repressions of the Elizabethan period as that of Philip or Mary. An aspiring and anxious courtier, directing his poems at particular (rarely, of course, directly stated) political ends, intellectually they remain the stock-in-trade of the Petrarchan poet. Nor, indeed, do the religious references suggest that he shared the intensity of theological interest of his brother, sister or Greville. Where religious references do occur in the poems, they are used to darken the established mood or to glance at a necessarily understated political aim rather than to transform a conventional motif into a profound religious speculation.

The particular feature of Robert Sidney's poetry which makes his poems of interest to us is the way the struggles of the Elizabethan Court invade them. The exile of which Song 6 speaks is couched in language seemingly depoliticized, yet represents the political insecurity all Elizabethan courtiers felt within (or especially, as in Sidney's case, on the margins of) the Court. Most of his poems use the frustrated sexual passion of a lover as a metaphor for political powerlessness and aspiration. The 'lights divine' from which the lover is 'exiled' – 'the only cause for which I care to see', 'these purest flames kindled by beauties rare' – all may be read as conventional neoplatonic compliments of a beloved only if the realities of Elizabethan politics and the Court's control of the discursive structures of both politics and poetry are ignored. The shepherd, with 'weights of change oppressed', and 'the hardy captain' who is 'scorned, repulsed, heartbroken', who is 'summoned by so great truth' while he remains in exile 'on unknown shore', and jealous of those 'who favour do enjoy/And spend and keep love's treasure', evoke not merely the bereft lover but the anxious courtier, thwarted yet ambitious, powerless yet continually plotting for power – in Sidney's case, he was literally in exile, afraid precisely of being 'scorned' and 'unknown'. He was in the Low Countries and unable to participate in the political manoeuvring of the Court except by proxy. No less than Ralegh's Scynthia poems, Robert Sidney's articulate the ideological dominance of the Elizabethan Court; unlike Ralegh's –

except in their intense anxiousness and their over-insistent protest of absolute devotion they do not articulate any opposition to the Court.

Though, as *Astrophil and Stella* so triumphantly shows, one of the distinctive features of Petrarchan poetry is its encouragement to readers to decode it in a variety of ways – as erotic self-evaluation, philosophical meditation, or moral debate – Robert's poems acquire an urgency and become rooted in the material life of late Elizabethan society. But they are compensations for the political powerlessness not simply of their author but of a particular class of men. The political world in which Robert Sidney had, between 1586 and 1598, a marginal part, can be read from his poetical text: the poetical text (the poems in his slim notebook) and the social text (the events and broader social changes in which he wrote) are finally indistinguishable.

The Sidney Circle and the Sidney family romance: the second generation of Sidney poets

Sir Philip Sidney's death, wrote Greville, 'is a death that I think Death is sorry for'.[37] Both Mary's and Robert's poems were written with their brother's example and aspirations in mind, and the relationships among them, which were not simply literary, are complex and intriguing. The presence of Philip Sidney in English literary and broader culture was continued by what is loosely referred to as the Sidney Circle which continued the family's interest in poetry into the next generation, especially in the writings and patronage of Mary Wroth, Robert's eldest daughter, and William, third earl of Pembroke, Mary's eldest son. To complicate matters further, these two first cousins were not only poets (and in Wroth's case, a highly accomplished writer of prose romance and verse drama) but lovers who had two (illegitimate) children together. Wroth's poetry will be given some attention in Chapter 8, since she is the period's major woman poet; Pembroke's falls outside the period limits of this book, but is mentioned briefly here since it helps complete our consideration of the Sidneys.[38]

But despite their continuing interest in, and practice of, poetry, the Sidneys and their circle were already, in the 1580s, being bypassed by a variety of cultural challenges far beyond their sympathy or understanding. Even Greville whose increasing pessimism, as we have seen, is an articulation of some awareness of the new cultural and political forms of Jacobean society, saw as the only viable alternatives the abandonment of the values underlying Sidneian poetry and a quietist renunciation of the new politics. Literary tastes changed; along with the radical new developments in the public theatre, lyric and satiric poetry, picaresque prose, fiction, and the new sparseness in expository prose a new social conjunction was emerging. Neoclassical drama, like the Countess of Pembroke's *Antonie*, polyphonic romance like the *Arcadia*, and the Petrarchan love lyric were not, as the next decades came through, the really significant developments in literature. The Sidney Psalms did help to initiate one of the new age's significant literary movements, but the tradition of religious lyric that links Mary Sidney, Greville, Herbert, Vaughan and Traherne is significant as much for its representing a reaction against the dominant literary fashions and social patterns of the age as for its merits as moving devotional verse. The kinds of poetry that dominated the sixteenth century were to become increasingly marginalized over the next sixty years or so.

To call the values and attitudes of the Sidney Circle reactionary, however correct, would however short-circuit an illuminating investigation of the forces that were in fact becoming dominant in late sixteenth-century poetry and the wider culture. The transition in English culture marked by the Civil War, the Commonwealth and the Restoration is part of a fundamental change in the cultural life of England. As Perez Zagorin puts it, it 'belongs to the handful of the "great revolutions" of Europe and the West – cataclysms which appear to mark the turning of times and to signify some fundamental change in the condition of humanity'.[39] It is not surprising that few writers in the 1590s and early 1600s were able to pick out and articulate the direction in which their world was moving. Shakespeare was certainly one who did; Donne, Webster, perhaps Jonson, were others. As well, a variety of lesser writers felt and fitfully expressed something of the transition and it is often the writers and artists who are not fully aware of what they are articulating who reveal most markedly the disruptive forces within a society making for important change. In a period when new experiences and values are disturbing, one understandable reaction is to take refuge in the past or in a belief in the degeneracy of the present. Sidney represented such a refuge for a significant number of courtiers, poets and public figures in the Jacobean Court. In his poetry, in his life and ideals, and increasingly in the myth that was built around him, many in the reigns of James and Charles saw an ideal from which their times had degenerated. As certain aspects of the Stuart Court became increasingly unpalatable to those English courtiers who recalled, or thought they recalled, a more dignified age, the Spirit of Sidney as the epitome of that age was almost superstitiously invoked. Ben Jonson often praised Sidney, his brother, and indeed the whole family as embodying a virtue of which his contemporaries were losing sight. Greville spoke for the new age: 'it delights me', he wrote, 'to keepe companie with him even after esteeming his actions, words, and conversation the daintiest treasure my mynde could then lay up, or can at this daye impart with our posteritie'.[40] His works went into numerous editions; poems or references to his memory abound, even as late as Ann Bradstreet's elegy on him, written in New England in 1638, and expressing pride in her Dudley ancestry and so being related to Sidney.

If the perpetuation of the myth of Sidney as a reminder of the lost virtue and glory of the Elizabethan age is an example of the nostalgia and retrospective values of the Sidney Circle, can one find any points of emergence within the Sidneys' poetry? To answer that, we should perhaps return to Breton's description of Wilton as a 'little Court'. The myth of virtue and wholeness which Breton saw at Wilton was passing from the centralized Court of the high Renaissance to the great country houses like Wilton, Great Tew or Penshurst. The culture of the early seventeenth century likewise shows a tendency towards decentralization, paralleling such literary changes as the development of more introspective literary forms, such as the meditative devotional lyric. One central symbol of much seventeenth-century literature is the *hortus conclusus*, the enclosed garden of retirement of the mind: Herbert's rectory in Bemerton, Vaughan's retreat into the Welsh hills, Milton's retirement from the public world and his return to his epic ambitions. Another symbolic focus is the attributed virtue of the country gentry and the values of what Zagorin and others have depicted as the 'country party' of the early seventeenth century. Flattering courtiers or preachers like John Reynolds could continue to assert to the then Prince Charles that 'your Highnesse Court is a true and conspicuous Academie of Generositie and Honour', but men increasingly were experiencing the opposite. To quote Clarendon, 'by . . . the passion, insolence, and ambition of particular persons, the Court measured the temper and affection of the country, and by the same standard the people considered the honour, justice and piety of the Court'.[41]

Sidney's retirement to Wilton in the late 1570s, then, is not only a retreat from the Court, from the cultural centre of the high Elizabethan age. The establishment of the 'little Court' at Wilton in the late 1570s is an anticipation of an important cultural development in the next seventy years. The conflict between King and Parliament, 'Court' and 'Country', was not just fought out between members of the Commons and the King, but in minds, in the conscious and dimly perceived structures of thought and feeling experienced by men and women. In the movement from the Court to the Country, from public responsibility to private virtue, we can see new material practices and structures struggling to emerge. The Sidneys' intellectual tensions, the conflicting languages of Philip's and Robert's love sonnets, the great-house literature of the *Arcadia*, the combination of courtly sophistication and piety in the Sidney *Psalms*, and the neoclassical movement were, on the conscious level, the result of an attempt to hold back the forces of change, but paradoxically they contributed to the breakdown of the cultural hegemony of the Court and of aristocratic culture. The idealization of the feudal values of the Sidneys in Ben Jonson's 'To Penshurst', for instance, shows us how a new ideology is slowly forming, as the pastoral moves from the Court to the country house. The Court is ceasing to be the dominant and respected centre of social existence and no longer monopolizes the allegiance of society at large. The result is a new society and with it, a new poetry. In the beliefs and the tensions of the Sidney Circle, we can see, better than they knew, the seeds of that new world and new poetry.

Notes

1. Sir John Harington, quoted in A.C. Hamilton, *Sir Philip Sidney* (Cambridge, 1977), p. 86; Sidney, *Astrophil and Stella*, 15; *A Defence of Poesie*, in *Miscellaneous Prose of Sir Philip Sidney*, edited by Katherine Duncan-Jones and Jan Van Dorsten (Oxford, 1973), pp. 116–17. Quotations from Sidney's poems are taken from *The Poems of Sir Philip Sidney*, edited by William A. Ringler Jr (Oxford, 1962).

2. Hamilton, *Sidney*, pp. 34–35.

3. Terry Eagleton, *Criticism and Ideology* (London, 1976), p. 19.

4. Richard C. *McCoy, Sir Philip Sidney: Rebellion in Arcadia* (New Brunswick, 1978).

5. Hamilton, *Sidney*, p. 86.

6. Andrew D. Weiner, *Sir Philip Sidney and the Poetics of Protestantism* (Minneapolis, 1978), p.70.

7. Sidney, *Miscellaneous Prose*, p. 79.

8. Alan Sinfield, *Literature in Protestant England* (Brighton, 1983), pp. 56, 57.

9. *The Correspondence of Sir Philip Sidney and Hubert Languet*, translated by Stewart A. Pears (London, 1845), p. 2.

10. Nicholas Breton, *Wits Trenchmour* (1593), p. 18; *The Pilgrimage to Paradise* (1592), sig. 12ʳ.

11. Hamilton, *Sidney*, p. 20.

12. Sidney, *Works*, III, 129.

13. *The Psalms of David with M. Calvins Commentaries*, translated by Arthur Golding (London, 1571), Psalm 8.

14. Sidney, *Defence*, p. 78.

15. Germaine Warkentin, 'Sidney's Certain Sonnets: Speculations on the Evolution of the Text', *The Library*, 6.2 (1980), pp. 430–44 (p.442); Ringler, p. lxiv.

16. Alan Sinfield, 'Sidney and Astrophil', *SEL*, 20 (1980), 25–41 (p. 35).

17. Neil E. Rudenstine, *Sir Philip Sidney's Poetic Development* (Cambridge, Mass., 1967), p. 50.

18. Sidney, *Miscellaneous Prose*, p. 50.

19. Roland Barthes, *S/Z*, translated by Richard Miller (New York, 1974), pp. 5–6; *Image, Music, Text*, translated by Stephen Heath (New York, 1977), p. 146.

20. J . P. Castley, SJ, 'Astrophil and Stella – High "Sidneian Love" or Courtly Compliment?', *Melbourne Critical Review*, 5 (1962), 54–65 (pp. 57–58).

21. Barthes, 'Theory of the Text', in *Untying the Text*, edited by Robert Young (London, 1981), pp. 31–47 (p. 42); Jacques Derrida, 'Signature Event Context', *Glyph*, 1(1977), 172–97 (p. 174).

22. Lewis, *English Literature of the Sixteenth Century*, p. 327; *Astrophil and Stella*, edited by Max Putzel (Garden City, 1967), p. xviii; Hamilton, *Sidney*, p. 86.

23. A. C. Hamilton, ' "The Mine of Time": Time and Love in Sidney's *Astrophil and Stella*', *Mosaic*, 13, no. 1(1979), 81–91.

24. Ann Rosalind Jones, 'The Lyric Sequence: Poetic Performance as Plot' (unpublished doctoral dissertation, Cornell University, 1976), p. 144.

25. Ann Rosalind Jones and Peter Stallybrass, 'The Politics of Astrophil and Stella', *SEL*, 24 (1984), 53–69.

26. Sinfield, *Literature in Protestant England*, p. 23.

27. Sinfield, *Literature in Protestant England*, p. 57.

28. See Gary Waller, 'Sidney and the New New Criticism', *SNew*, 4, no. 2 (1984), 3–6.

29. Breton, *Wits Trenchmour*, p. 18; *Pilgrimage to Paradise*, Dedication, sig. 12r; Abraham Fraunce, *The Third Part of the Countesse of Pembrokes Ivychurch* (London, 1592), sig. A2r; *The Countess of Pembrokes Ivychurch* (London, 1591), sigs. B2v, Elv, E2v.

30. For a discussion of the authorship question, see Gary Waller, *Mary Sidney, Countess of Pembroke: A Critical Study of her Writings and Literary Milieu* (Salzburg, 1979), pp. 90–5.

31. John Donne, *The Divine Poems*, edited by Helen Gardner (Oxford, 1952), pp. 34, 35. For an account of the Psalms MSS, see Waller, *Triumph of Death*, pp. 18–28, 222–25.

32. *The Psalms of Sir Philip Sidney and the Countess of Pembroke*, edited by J. C. A. Rathmell (New York, 1963), p. xx.

33. Rathmell, *Psalms*, pp. xi, xv; J. C. A. Rathmell, 'Hopkins, Ruskin, and the Sidney Psalter', *Lon. Mag.*, 6, no. 9 (1959), 51–66 (p. 51).

34. Ben Jonson, 'To Penshurst', *Poems*, p. 79; Thomas Thorpe, *Catalogue of Manuscripts* (London, 1833), p. 96; Thomas Nashe, *Pierce Pennilesse*, in *Works*, edited by E. D. McKerrow, revised by F. P. Wilson and W. W. Gill (London, 1958), 1, 159.

35. HMC, *De Lisle and Dudley*, II, 145; see also II, 160, 164.

36. Quotations from the poems are taken from *The Poems of Robert Sidney*, edited by P. J. Croft (Oxford, 1984).

37. HMC, *Salisbury*, 111, 189.

38. For William Herbert, see Andreas Gebauer, *Von Macht und Mäzenatentum: Leben und Werk William Herberts, der dritten Earl von Pembroke* (Heidelberg, 1987) and Gary Waller, *The Sidney Family Romance* (Detroit, 1993).

39. Perez Zagorin, *The Court and the Country* (Toronto, 1970), p. 5.

40. Greville, *Life*, p. 105.

41. John Reynolds, *Treatise of the Court*, sig. A1r-v; Clarendon, *History*, 1, 5.

Chapter 6
Spenser and *The Faerie Queene*

Introduction

In 1590 were published the first three books of the one poetic work that, more than any other, epitomizes the glory and contradictions of the Elizabethan Court and its poetry. In 1596 the poem was reissued, with some revisions and with three further books. The reorganization, revisions and additions brought out what the early books, in retrospect, can be seen to have largely, though not entirely, repressed – that *The Faerie Queene*, the most ambitious poetic glorification of the Elizabethan regime, could not celebrate the power which permitted it to exist without revealing the strains and contradictions that were already radically dislocating that power. Spenser's whole career, indeed, epitomizes the strengths and limitations by which power was exerted over all literary and social discourse by the Court. Spenser's epic manifests both the powerlessness of poetry and yet its relative autonomy – how it may offer, despite its intentions, a radical critique of the power that brings it into being. We have seen how this dual process worked in Ralegh's and Greville's poems; part of the distinctive interest of Spenser's epic rests also on its capacity to bring such contradiction into play – perhaps, except for Shakespeare's plays, more extensively than in any writings of the period.

C. S. Lewis once asserted that everything that Spenser wrote outside *The Faerie Queene* was 'something of a diversion'. However much of an exaggeration that may be, none the less *The Faerie Queene* remains by far his most important work. Spenser's early work, written in the late 1560s, first flowered spectacularly in the *Shepherdes Calender* (1579) which was praised by Sidney in the *Defence*, although Lewis notes that Spenser 'was soon to write and perhaps had already written poetry which deprives the *Calender* of all importance'.[1] He was working on the epic during the 1580s; during that decade he also produced a tribute to Sidney, 'Astrophel' (1586), *Colin Clouts Come Home Again* (1589–90), and, about the same time, *Daphnaida, The Ruines of Time*, and

Muiopotmos. Spenser's other minor poems include the four *Hymns* (the first two perhaps written in the late 1570s, the latter two fifteen years later) and *Amoretti*, an unusually (given the dominant English emphasis) Christianized Petrarchan sonnet sequence.

Much of Spenser's early work, including *Virgil's Gnat, Mother Hubbard's Tale*, and *The Teares of the Muses* (much of which was revised for publication twenty or more years later) is closely related to the typical poetical preoccupations of the mid-century: it includes political allegory, heavy didacticism, with some stanzaic and metrical experimentation. These poems are still in the world of Turberville and Googe. With such poems, Spenser was establishing himself as a serious Protestant poet. The publication of the *Calender* in 1579 is often seen as marking a turning-point in the age's poetry. But unlike *Astrophil and Stella*, the poem is not a courtly work – it continues rather in the tradition of the militant Protestant poets of mid-century. It is serious, moralistic and satiric, its elements incorporated into a firm Protestant didacticism. Spenser, in fact, seemed relatively indifferent to the Petrarchan fashions of his more courtly contemporaries. In part this was because he saw epic poetry as his vocation, and the lyric as a diversion from his aims. As Helgerson points out, he was unique in his generation for presenting himself not as a courtly amateur but 'as a Poet, as a man who considered writing a duty rather than a distraction'.[2] Above all, he is self-consciously the regime's servant in his poetry as much as he was in his political career, as a loyal Protestant, civil servant and planter in occupied Ireland. As such he seemingly naturally turned to the most serious, most traditionally approved, poetic kinds in which to celebrate the regime and to the religious principles that he saw as his duty, as Protestant and patriot, to uphold. The *Calender* announces the compatibility of all these goals. Over the next two decades, as Spenser saw his ideals ignored, marginalized or defeated, that optimism waned, and *The Faerie Queene* is a very complex register of that disillusion – which was not Spenser's alone, but part of the growing strains of the end of the century.

Amoretti, written in the early 1590s, is his only venture into the lyric, and it too is characteristically moralistic – in Sinfield's words, an 'unprecedented puritan humanist adaptation of the sonnet sequence to a relationship which ends in marriage'. The sequence is usually read as a fictionalization of Spenser's courtship of his second wife, Elizabeth Boyle. It sets out, occasionally amusingly but in serious terms, a pattern of desire that leads not to frustration and defeat but to marriage and mutual submission to God's will. Setting *Amoretti* in the context of the discussion of Petrarchism in Chapter 3 is to realize the vast difference between Spenser and Sidney. Although the lover occasionally takes up the subservient role familiar from the Petrarchan scheme, the sequence is firmly articulated as a moral narrative: the mistress is even at times lovingly criticized. As Marotti notes, 'Spenser's speaker acts as his beloved's intellectual and ethical superior, a position from which he can comically, but affectionately, condescend to her at various points in the sequence'.[3] Nor does Spenser wish to see the self as fluctuating and always in process. He turns in effect to the second half of Petrarch's *Canzoniere* – the poems written after Laura's death – and sees the unchangeableness of the beloved within the love of God as a model for the unchangeableness of a Christian love. *Amoretti* provides a Protestant critique of the persuasiveness of Petrachan modes of thought and expression. The pattern of dominance and passivity, the sadistic/masochistic games in which the two partners may take up quite different roles are sternly rejected. The Protestant, ever mindful of God's will and public duty, must subordinate sexual desire to higher goals. Although the early poems of the collection (those before 67) are often light, even occasionally titillating, at the point at which the praise and gentle admonition of the beloved give way to a celebration of Christian marriage, the tone changes. Petrarchan praise is forced into the service of Christian duty: the beloved may often be a distraction from higher commitments, not only God but also the Queen and the poet's own vocation to write the great poem in which he will 'enlarge' the Queen's 'living prayses', which is a 'sufficient worke for one mans simple head' (33). So in the latter part of the collection, notably in 80 (where he defends the pleasure of the lyric) the primacy of the Queen, Christian commitments, and dedication to public duty are never wavered from. The primary role of his poems is that of the dutiful Protestant laureate. Of course, Spenser was treading on slightly difficult ground in that Queen Elizabeth surrounded herself with the trappings of Petrarchism. His emphasis on marriage as the holy end of desire is a call to his fellow courtiers, poets and even (though at a distance) to the Queen herself to turn to a rediscretion of desire into pretty and national loyalty. *Amoretti* is thus more than a critique of the Petrarchan love poem: it is a demand that England should stop 'seeing itself as [an] imitation of Renaissance Italy' and rather 'see itself as a Protestant opponent to Catholic Italy'.[4]

Sixteenth-century poetry, I have argued, is characterized by fascinating fissures, contradictions, and repressions. Of all the age's poetry, *The Faerie Queene* is at once the most grandiose in its claims for wholeness of vision and the most dislocated and disrupted. To speak of 'fissures', 'flaws', 'contradictions' or 'dislocations' is not to play down a poem's importance or, to use the traditional term, its 'greatness'. Spenser's epic is the most important single poem of the century precisely because it brings so compellingly to our attention the conflicting voices by and against which it was written; it allows us more richly than any other poem of the age to construct those voices which spoke so powerfully to create the hegemony of the Elizabethan regime. *The Faerie Queene* emerges in a cultural space radically crossed by impulses and structures which it vainly tries to discipline, and which over and over at key moments in its unfolding, articulate the ideological struggles of late Elizabethan society.

The last decade of Spenser's life, following Sidney's death, was when his epic reached its eventual, though probably not its intended, final shape. It coincides with an increasing restlessness in the Elizabethan Court, with many obvious and many underlying strains upon the economy and the broader social practices of the country – failing harvests, rural discontent, rising unemployment, increasing inflation, religious intolerance and outbursts of unusually strong xenophobia directed against Spaniards, Catholics and (as the plays of both Marlowe and Shakespeare witness) Jews. But the poem's history started much earlier. Spenser was working on what became *The Faerie Queene* at least as early as the time Sidney was experimenting with *Astrophil and Stella* and the *Defence*. By the mid-1580s, parts of the poem had been circulating in England; in 1589 Spenser journeyed from his plantation in an increasingly rebellious and oppressed Ireland to be presented at Court by his friend Ralegh. In 1590 the first three books were published, and the following year Spenser was rewarded for his devotion to the Queen with a lifetime pension of fifty pounds a year. Evidently disquieted by what he saw at Court, Spenser returned to Ireland. By 1592 Ralegh was in prison and something of his high-risk (and in Spenser's highly partial view, misunderstood) career is reflected upon in Books IV and VI which, along with a fifth book closely based on Spenser's interpretation of the Irish occupation, were published in 1596. In the last years of his life he started but probably did not complete another. That, as well as the changes between the two parts, gives us a clue to the ways even such a loyal upholder of the regime was dislocated by the world he perceived – though as the ensuing discussion will show, his perceptions are revealing far beyond what he himself knew. He continued to serve in Ireland until 1598 when, driven from his house in Kilcolman by an upsurge in the Irish resistance, he once again journeyed to England. He died early the next year, leaving behind a fragment of a seventh book.

In this survey of Spenser's career, it is important to stress the dislocations in the writing and revisions of *The Faerie Queene*, not least because of the strange way it has been read by modern scholars if not as complete, at least as united, and in an almost mystical sense, whole. Even most modern commentators, from the *Variorum Spenser* in the 1930s to *The Spenser Encyclopedia* (1990), have largely taken for granted the ideological world foregrounded by the poem, and, have depicted the poet as a master of intentional control and the poem as massively and complexly (even if often, it seems, inexplicably) unified.

The authority of the Great Author and the unity of the Great Work have seemingly been unchallengeable – and the result has been that our own time's dominant reading is close to what would have been that of the Elizabethan regime itself. Only since the late 1970s, initially in the work of Goldberg, Greenblatt and Montrose, and latterly in a variety of postmodern or Marxist readings, by Miller or Shepherd, have we seen the development of any symptomatic reading of the poem that did not try to explain away its dislocated nature. In part this is attributable to the success of an impressive Spenser industry fascinated with detailed annotations and even more with the assumption of the work's 'unity'. It is a fascinating instance of how an archaic political power maintains its hold over one of its cultural products even after 400 years. As a side-note, however, one early reader of the poem whose perspective, eight years after his mother's execution and seven years before his own accession to the English throne she had (possibly) sought, was notably antagonistic and not at all in accord with the dominant reading. That reader was James VI of Scotland, whose remarks on Book V will be touched upon later.[5]

The Faerie Queene

The Faerie Queene, then – and most especially its last books, particularly the sixth, in which Spenser deals directly with the Court and courtesy – is the most significant poetic document of its age. It is especially crucial to our understanding of the transition in English cultural life, and not only in poetry, between the death of Sidney in 1586 and the outbreak of the Civil War over fifty years later. Deliberately (and as it grew, increasingly) nostalgic, retrogressive and disillusioned, *The Faerie Queene* opens for us, in the way the poetry of any transitional period does, the forces which were eventually to shatter the world it celebrates and from which it traced its origins and inspiration. Spenser criticism has rarely confronted this contradiction, preferring to explain away the poem's dislocations by searching, probably as desperately as Spenser did, for principles of unity and harmony. Traditional readings have for the most part been what Goldberg, following Barthes, terms 'theological', assuming that the poem 'in some way . . . gains stability and order from replicating the assumed harmony of the universe' it works to valorize.[6]

Even hostile critics have rarely challenged this view, preferring rather to find the poem's sense of order archaic and dull. Traversi, in the *Pelican Guide to English Literature*, wrote that the poem was the dead end of a medieval tradition and an 'undeniable failure'. In the revised edition of the *Guide*, Spenser is transferred from *The Age of Chaucer* to *The Age of Shakespeare* volume, but Robson's assessment is no less astringent: 'modern readers, even those who still read poetry, simply find (Spenser) tedious'; his poems are 'the preserve of lovers of crossword puzzles and esoteric scholarship'.[7] Such dismissive scepticism remains tied to notions of organic form, and the authority of the great poet as the tradition it pillories – it is just that Spenser is seen to fail the test. We do not read him (to return, as Robson does, to Leavis's test for poetry) as we read the living. Where contradictions or a falling off in poetic power are acknowledged, traditional Spenser criticism has usually had recourse to the admission that every long poem has some weaknesses, or has put them down to Spenser's growing (but inevitably conscious) disillusion with the corruption of his age. The ending of Book II, especially the destruction of the Bower of Bliss, the (sometimes) disturbing ferocity of Book V, the ambiguous allegiances to public duty of Book VI or the seeming renunciation of the world, even of his own poem, in the Mutability Cantos, have been diversely read, but rarely has Spenser's awareness of whatever he was doing been put into question. It is only recently that quite different readings have been occasionally risked or even seen as possible.

First, what vision does Spenser himself want – at least when he first planned and wrote the poem and probably throughout its writing – a reader to gain? I use the archaic word 'vision' advisedly, since the poem is designed to exemplify a poetic and a metaphysic of stasis; ultimately the poem reproduces the ideological universe of which it is a constituent part. Throughout, Spenser's militant Protestant humanism is insistently foregrounded. Book I, the Book of Holiness, embodies a theologically cautious but firm outline of the Reformed doctrine of justification by faith, the division of mankind into elect and reprobate, and the quest to find true salvation. While Spenser does not write as a systematic theologian, the theological implications are solidly in accord with those of the moderate left wing of the Elizabethan Church on such doctrines as Providence, Predestination, the Fall, Grace, Free Will and Election. All history is set under the judgment of the Word of God, and the allegory directed to demonstrating God's purposes through His chosen people. Later books play down such explicit theologizing, but when Book I was written, Spenser's intentions seem clear enough.

Similarly clear is the intention, often announced quite explicitly, of building a magniloquent pageant-like celebration of the ordered universe's manifestation of harmony. The poem is built upon the traditional belief that reality is indivisible, that it embraces the whole of creation. Thus in Book VI, courtly behaviour – obligation, respect, obedience, magnanimity – is the social manipulation of an order expressed in the whole creation. The different facets of an indivisible reality, often presented as a dance, circle or pageant, or in emblems of reciprocity, symmetry and harmony, are expressed in the structure of the whole poem – in the parallel and symmetrical quests of the knights with their 'like' races 'to run', the graceful and continuous replenishment of the world from the Garden of Adonis (Book III), the pageant of Mutability (Book VII), or the dance of the Graces on Mount Acidale (Book VI). With such recurring metaphors, *The Faerie Queene* – like Sidney's *Arcadia*, the only work of the age to rival it in scope and sophistication – attempts to stop the all too obvious flux and unpredictability of history by the assertion of timeless myths of origin, explanation and cosmic destiny.

The poem uses the trappings of chivalry – knights, ladies, tournaments, dragons, talking trees – with which modern children are familiar in comic books or television programmes. In the Elizabethan Age, chivalry was obviously taken more seriously, but taken lightly, it may not be a real barrier for the modern reader. Before dismissing it as archaic (and interestingly, there were a few Elizabethans who did just that), we should acknowledge that chivalry, as I noted in Chapter 2, contained some very powerful contradictions – it had a reassuringly traditional emphasis on hierarchy along with the intense competitiveness of struggle; it insisted on a deference to the Queen's untouchable supremacy and yet encouraged her subject's individual prowess and ambitions. With its heraldic pageantry, it could define both the idealized history of the regime and its nervous competitiveness. Similarly, such rituals, progresses and tournaments occupy a key role in both Spenser's poems and the Court. In the Court, they were cultural mechanisms designed at once to encourage and contain criticism and opposition – as we can see in Sidney's *Lady of May* or the pageant staged by Sidney, Greville and other courtiers in 1581, *The Four Foster Children of Desire*, where antagonistic political positions were articulated and then reconciled. In *The Faerie Queene*, chivalry likewise tries to provide a mechanism for establishing an apparent reconciliation of contention to which all can give allegiance. By presenting harmony as something achieved by the reconciliation of all disharmony, the poem seeks to affirm a belief that the values it celebrates are beyond challenge, and that its own order both reflects and is valorized by the whole cosmic order. To read the poem in accord with such belief would be, in Spenser's view, to read it correctly. Hence, the poem thrusts at its readers a formidable repertoire of strategies designed to produce such a reading.

So far, I have tied discussion of *The Faerie Queene* closely to Spenser's career in, or in relation to, the Elizabethan Court. However, his life enters the poem in other ways, and much more than he knew. Williams notes about Sidney's *Arcadia* that the work 'which gives a continuing title to English neopastoral was written in a park which had been made by enclosing a whole village and evicting the tenants. The elegant game was then only at arm's length – a rough arm's length – from the visible reality of country life'.[8] *The Faerie Queene* was planned and partly written at a greater distance from the Elizabethan Court than *Arcadia* and part of its intense idealization of the Court arises from Spenser's position as an outsider. His visit to the Court in 1589–90 must have forced him to see something analogous to the 'visible reality' of which Williams speaks. *Colin Clouts Come Home Again* is Spenser's pastoral re-creation of his visit, written as he contemplated both his reception at the Court of Gloriana and his continuing celebration of it. One senses from the poem, in Bennett's words, that 'Ireland had never been "home" to him until he had been part of the court',[9] but Spenser still tries to insist on setting the all too evident corruption of the Court in the context of a redeeming ideal. As he contemplates the Court's sophisticated barbarism from what had seemed his exile among rude barbarians, he is still confident in his devotion to the Queen (who had, after all, rewarded him with fifty pounds a year). The poem includes some devastating criticism of 'courtiers as bladders blowen up with wynd' and of 'faire dissembling curtesie', but it is emphatic in its praise of the Queen and the ' ring' of those faithful courtiers who like the dead Sidney and his sister, truly reflect their Queen's glory.

This dual role of celebrating the ideal while warning against breaches of it and harking back to traditional verities, is one that, as we have seen, characterizes court poetry throughout the century; it is also one that Spenser had adopted early in his career, when he similarly juxtaposed his criticism of corrupt courtiers with a radiant vision of Elizabeth in the April eclogue of the *Calender*. It is the expected role of the court poet to conceal or reconcile ideological antagonisms and to replace the possibility of debating real alternatives by an assertion of their ultimate harmony. It is the role Spenser confidently continues in the first three books and which also informs Book IV and most of Book V, one able to countenance and even give voice to attacks on the Elizabethan Court while celebrating unambiguously its glory and place in the cosmic order. Thus Spenser combines the role of Protestant humanist moral critic with what he perceives as the Virgilian role of the poet's moral power in a society he at once loyally celebrates and judiciously criticizes. In the early books, his confidence in his role is seen as analogous to the plenitude with which the Queen herself embodies those same ideals. As he asserts at the start of Book II:

> And thou, O fairest Princesse under sky,
> In this faire mirrhour maist behold thy face,

And thine owne realmes in lond of Faery,
And in this antique Image thy great auncestry.

(II, proem 4, 6–9)[10]

In her allegorical role of Belphoebe, the Queen attacks and defeats
challenges to her power with the same confidence that Spenser himself is
attacking them in the poem as a whole. When in Book II Braggadocchio
flatters Belphoebe (II. 3. 39) she sternly rejects Braggadocchio's view of
the court as a place of frivolity, just as Spenser himself did in *Mother
Hubbard's Tale*, in *Colin Clouts Come Home Again*, and throughout the
early books of *The Faerie Queene* itself. In such passages are not only
the absolute distinctions made between the dedicated, active life and the
frivolous life of pleasure, but the poem's confidence in moral absolutes,
in the transcendent ideals that permit and even demand such absolutes,
and in the power of the poet to articulate them. This is the confidence
that shows how Spenser was claiming a central place for poetry in
the late Elizabethan regime and which attempts to sustain it (and,
presumably, Spenser himself) through the complexities, moral as well
as poetical, of his treatment in Books IV to VI of chastity, friendship,
and justice.

Such attitudes are central to the confidence of the early books of the
poem. Spenser appropriates the Virgilian role of celebrating the nation:
he is both the prophet justifying a providential reading of history, and
the Protestant nationalist assuming the public good can be served in
the order, harmony and wonder of the most serious kind of poetry,
the epic. Classical epic and Italian romance are combined to justify
Christian heroism in an assimilation of the same elements of the past
used throughout the century by educators, propagandists and poets to
create and uphold the Protestant Tudor regime. In his letter to Ralegh,
Spenser claims to be following Homer, Virgil, Ariosto and Tasso; he
echoes the *Aeneid* in the poem's opening, he alludes to Italian romance
epic throughout; he speaks of 'magnificence' as the ethical basis of the
poem, and he directs his reader continuously to Christian theology. He
wants, too, to root his ideals in the Court. As he put it to Ralegh, the
poem was designed 'to fashion a gentleman or noble person in vertuous
and gentle discipline'.

His letter to Ralegh is useful as a revelation of some of Spenser's
intentions, at least at the time he wrote it. But the outline he gives
there is just not reflected in the poem as we have it. He does not
confine himself to 'Aristotles twelve morall virtues'; the relationships
between individual knights and their particular virtues vary greatly;
and Arthur never acquires the central place Spenser may have once
intended. In short, the letter to Ralegh cannot, except in the most general
terms, account for the poem's growth or suggest how it could be read

satisfactorily. For today's readers, the letter is useful as a reminder that the poem calls into question any imposition of unity, even its author's. The poem is, in fact, a rambling, open-ended, disrupted work. It starts plot strands it cannot finish; its characters metamorphose continually; instead of the reassuring pleasures of a finished text which would reflect a stable world of universal values, *The Faerie Queene* is the quintessential example of copia in the period, a flow of textuality which undergoes what Goldberg terms 'continuous reconstitution'. Its continuities are those of repeated frustration and absence, a continual undermining of any 'possibility of fixed character and fixed meaning'.[11]

In the letter to Ralegh, too, Spenser writes of his poem as a 'continued Allegory or darke conceit'. Once again, it is important not to treat allegory simply as a 'literary' device, but to root it in the material practices of the day, the 'social' text of late sixteenth-century England and Ireland. Allegory was becoming increasingly archaic, however strong the interest in it at the Elizabethan Court was. A century later it was to be laughed at: 'it was the vice of those Times to affect superstitiously the Allegory', whereby 'nothing would then be current without a mystical meaning', wrote Rymer in 1674, in an age that was operating with quite different assumptions about the relation of signifier to meaning. But for Spenser, allegory still seemed to grow naturally from an order of discourse whereby individual parts of the material world were given significance as parts of an interconnected universe of meanings. It looked back to increasingly archaic modes of thought – to *Piers Plowman*, Lydgate, or to *A Mirror for Magistrates* – and, interestingly, it was Spenser's fellow Protestants who were most scornful of it. They might have considered the point that Puttenham makes when he writes that both poet and courtier use allegory when 'we speake one thing and think another' and when 'our wordes and our meanings meete not'.[12] Indeed, it is strange that given the Protestant suspicion of it, allegory did not strike the Protestant Spenser as odd for a Reformed poet to use. Yet he showed himself more shrewd than his fellow Protestants, at least in his poetic practices if not in his own comments and glosses on his poem. The choice to write an allegory meant that the poem came to focus on the central poetic issue of the age, the relationship of meaning to language. Allegory is characterized by a deliberate and radical subordination of the signifier to the apparently signified; typically, it incorporates comments upon the process by which language works, by the relation between icon and metaphor, and thus raises the fundamental question, in MacCaffery's phrase, of 'how far we may trust the basic medium, language'.[13]

Coupled with the need to establish an extraverbal authority is the need to repress aberrant readings of the text. Cheney speaks of the 'strong universal compulsion of readers . . . to master books and every-day experience by imposing order and coherence where mere random circumstance is felt to be intolerable and threatening'.[14] How ironical it is, therefore, that the seeming endlessness of modern interpretations of Spenserian allegory does precisely the opposite of what Spenser consciously intended – multiplying in a promiscuity of signification the signs, whereas 'rightly' read, the poem should point to permanent, ahistorical truths. But Cheney's point is a crucial one. Allegory represents an absolute desire to bring writing, and in one sense history, to an end. It tries rigorously to exclude anything that might disturb and challenge the monolithic readings the poet (as distinct, as we shall see, from the poem) intended. Allegory tries to create and position a reader who, educated correctly, will read not necessarily simple or single but certainly consistent and unified meanings, and repress undesirable ones: for instance thinking 'incorrectly' that in Book I, 'Errour' might stand for Protestant (rather than Catholic) heresy or that (in James VI's 'erroneous' reading) Mercilla in Book V, as a 'type' of Mary Queen of Scots, is mistreated, in both the text of the poem and the text of history. Spenser's formidable control of rhetoric, structure and above all of the poem's atmosphere tries to pressure the reader into accepting the poet's terms on such interpretations. As readers, we are continually called to insert ourselves into a discourse where exploration and enjoyment are real but none the less carefully controlled.

Yet any reading of *The Faerie Queene* is determined not by Spenser's intention but by its status as powerful language. And, paradoxically, the language-density of the poem itself continually expands and so subverts the author's attempt to control meaning. As Goldberg argues, the endless quality of the poem as text 'denies hermeneutic closure'. Continually, the text invites us, lures us, to desire meaning, 'and then obliterates the possibility' of it. *The Faerie Queene* encourages what it deliberately tries to avoid; despite its terms being selected with what Eagleton calls 'fetishistic' force, the promiscuity of its language 'spreads infinitely'. One means by which Spenser tries to limit meaning is an insistence that allegory is a 'darke' conceit, that a correct reading is accessible only by arduous study, by the subordination of textuality to authorial intention, and by the insistence that the hidden 'true' meaning is available only to an elite. As Murrin has argued, the Renaissance allegorist wanted his text at once to open the truth to the properly subordinate reader, but remain inaccessible to the undisciplined one. Thus Spenser works hard to direct his reader by prefacing each canto with quaintly archaic quatrains, as if to underline the required meanings and thereby limit allegorical reading. As Quilligan notes, however, the quatrains only prove 'that Spenser, however great an allegorical poet, was not the best reader of his own poem when he had to resort to being an allegorical critic of it'.[15] But it is there, in the quatrains, where Spenser's affinities with the Protestant anxieties over the promiscuity of language become very clear. His is the dilemma not only of the allegorist, but specifically of the Protestant allegorist, anxious about how fallen man's words might embody God's truths.

If the moralizing quatrains (like some of the glosses appended to the *Calender*) try to be signposts to a 'right' reading, the body of the poem is rich with more subtle structural and stylistic directions. To read the poem is to enter not a geographical landscape which provides a background to action, but a moral landscape – a world of moral choices. The poem speaks of Faeryland as a 'mirror', an 'antique image': it is designed to let us see and explore the significance of the material world in the way dreams momentarily explore the displaced or repressed significances of our waking world. Spenser wants to create the impression of an atemporal, mythic world where quests, conquests, fears and tensions are occurring all the time – and, where we are always (it is assumed) like Red Cross, engaged in a quest for perfection; like Guyon, in a quest for the appropriate and rational action; in our sexual relations, we are always faced with choices among different demands on our emotional and moral allegiances, like the lovers in Books III and IV. In short, the world of Faeryland is meant to be a world of complex psychological and cultural discoveries. We are not given insights into the 'characters' of Belphoebe or Britomart or Florimel; rather, they are parts of an attempt to create and educate the poem's readers as subjects within its seductive discourse. In one sense, *we* are its characters.

The dominant narrative form of our culture since the early eighteenth century has been the novel, in which characters and their actions become part of an effaced illusion of realism, suppressing the contradictions of how those realistic effects are, in fact, constructed.[16] In particular, realism attempts to exclude any shifting in this involvement of reader, writer and textual surface; we are asked to judge character and action by consistency and fidelity to a socially dominant norm. No such constraints are demanded by *The Faerie Queene*: what is foregrounded is rather a desire for rigorous ideological, not narrative or character, consistency. Character, landscape and setting, action and motive are all manipulated without regard for verisimilitude or consistency. It makes no sense (we are meant to assume, though of course we may resist) to ask: 'where in the forest is Belphoebe's pavilion?' Or the House of Mammon? Or to ask whether Amoret 'really' loved Scudamour? Nor is narrative consistency especially important. The poem simultaneously sets a goal before us and continually postpones achieving it by multiplying situations, characters and complications into seemingly infinite variations. Instead of having the pleasures of classic realism and, especially, the consistency of the novel, we are thrust into a paradoxical, even contradictory experience. The poem asks us to think and respond in terms of universals, and believe that the moral, intellectual and emotional confrontations it displays are somehow part of a permanent battle between good and evil. But we may experience it rather as a text populated with figures continually 'moving in flux, constantly resituated, momentarily lodged in relationships from which they are as quickly dislodged, inevitably undone', a world of textuality where the focus is always on the reader caught 'in the middest', manipulated, teased and faced with what Lewis called 'states of the heart', with challenges to learn our own possibilities.[17] The ever-present threat is what Spenser would have seen as the fallen nature of the will, which he embodies in the dangerous, labyrinthine forest, and which is paradoxically embodied in the equally labyrinthine nature of the text.

In the space available to me, it would be foolish to attempt a detailed reading of all of *The Faerie Queene*. For stimulating accounts from a variety of critical viewpoints, readers are directed to such critics as Hamilton on the first two books, Roche or Hieatt on Book III, Goldberg on Book IV, Cheney or O'Connor on Book V, and Tonkin on Book VI. Spenserian scholarship is perhaps best summed up in the *Spenser Encyclopedia* (1990), which has attempted to bring together the best of modern and contemporary work on Spenser; the very multifariousness of its contributors' perspectives is a tribute to a multifaceted postmodern Spenser just as the Variorum edition nearly fifty years earlier was to a Victorian and modernist Spenser.

What follows are necessarily brief outlines of Books I to V, followed by a detailed consideration of Book VI, where Spenser comes closest to and yet is most at odds with the Queen and her Court. The Cantos of Mutability, the fragment of an unfinished Book VII, will then be considered in the final section where I give a symptomatic overview of the place of the poem in Elizabethan poetry and culture.

Book I, of Holiness, takes its reader into the adventures of a young, inexperienced quester, the Red Cross Knight, whose Christian significance is made clear from the start. In an opening symbolic montage, details are deliberately chosen to try to direct a reader's allegiances – the ideological exclusiveness of Red Cross's badge, the Protestant emphasis on struggle and alienation as value tests of faith, the direct characterization of Catholicism as Error ('Errour') and the threat and unpredictability of the forest. Yet the deeper we go into the moral landscape of Book I, the more problematic become the moral dilemmas. The narrative unravels as undecidable choices. The first and easiest battle, with Error, seems clear cut; thereafter, the issues are less easily decided. The high points in Spenser's overall plan are clear however; Red Cross's temptations to suicide (Canto 9); and (an even more interesting temptation, especially given Spenser's later disillusion with the world of Elizabeth's Court) that to abandon the quest and flee from Cleopolis, the Earthly City, the city of man, to the Heavenly City; and finally, after the temptation to abandon the quest has been rejected, the magnificent emblematic stage-piece of Red Cross's battle with the dragon.

Spenser's didactic Christian epic commences, then, with holiness, to emphasize man's dependence on God's grace. He bases his Christian allegory upon the patriotic legend of St George, and mixes history and theology with some vivid melodrama to persuade his readers to consider the issue of how to achieve a right relationship with God. Book II comes down to earth, and focuses on Sir Guyon, the Knight of Temperance, a virtue presented in Protestant humanist terms as the means by which human actions may be aligned to virtuous ends by self-control. Guyon is the only leading knight of the poem who is not in love, and one of the whole poem's most important episodes is the destruction of the Bower of Bliss (Canto 12) which focuses, in superlative and richly ambiguous detail, on the place of erotic attraction in human affairs. It marks the culmination of Guyon's task to overcome the witch Acrasia, depicted in 46 extraordinarily evocative stanzas in which Guyon enters the Bower and lays violent waste to it and its inhabitants. The Bower has the alluring sensuality of a striptease, and Spenser's text varies tantalisingly between strong moral condemnation and seductiveness. He tells us that Guyon is unaffected:

> Much wondred Guyon at the faire aspect
> Of that sweet place, yet suffred no delight
> to sinke into his sence, nor mind affect . . .

Yet not only may a reader recognize the traditional seductive power of teasing, flirtation, withholding, display, gazing and promised abandonment, but the richness of Spenser's poetry suggests that the strong moral condemnation of such pleasures represents an over-reaction on the poet's, and his culture's, part as violent as Guyon's destruction of the Bower. We are in sight of what makes Spenser's poem still so compelling: in such vivid scenes, he articulates, without being able to fully control, some of the recurring aspects of western, masculinist ideology. Civilization, Freud argued, is built upon the displacement of desire: Spenser reveals himself on the side of 'civilization' just as surely in the destruction of the Bower as he was in advocating a scorched earth policy in Ireland to further English 'civilization'. In both cases, the cries of the human body, disciplined, tortured, or destroyed, cry out against the distortions it is forced to make.[18]

Book III continues to explore, often in ways that reveal more than its author saw, some of the same contradictions. It is perhaps the most accessible to a modern reader despite its virtue – chastity. Spenser mounts a critique of what he saw as the idolatry (what I earlier termed the 'perversity') of Petrarchism. The poem is packed with what Freud termed the 'overvaluation' of desire. Despite (some readers would say because) of the strong disapproval of the Bower of Bliss, Spenser in some ways is very positive about sexuality – witness the richly suggestive celebration of the female genitals as the centre of human experience, placed as it is right at the centre of the first version of the poem – and Book III can be seen, as Paglia has rather floridly claimed, 'an encyclopedic catalog' of sexual 'perversions' akin to 'Krafft-Ebing's *Psychopathia Sexualis*: not only rape and homosexuality but priapism, nymphomania, exhibitionism, incest, bestiality, necrophilia, fetishism, transvestism and transsexualism'.[19] Book III, in fact, gives a surprisingly Lawrentian reading of the quest for integrity in love. It is full of the violence and contradictions of love – obsession, domination, invasion, the violent imposition of the ways we express desire.

The book's knight is a woman, Britomart; her name combines 'Britain' with 'martial', suggesting her patriotic significance within Spenser's allegory – and also the quite unselfconscious way chivalric metaphors can appropriate gender. In her adventures, we are taken through a complex process of discovery about the interconnection of desire and civilization, to return to Freud's terms, marked variously by naivety, over-reaction, and some chastened learning on the part of the heroine. What marks a major difference in the book is Spenser's allegorical technique; where Books I and II tend to focus on the adventures of a single knight, Book III is more polyphonic, a complex opening of mirrors-within-mirrors. Britomart disappears from the main action and is replaced by other heroines – Florimell, Amoret, Belphoebe – who take us into different, more complex, challenges to our experience of desire. The book's major set piece, too, does not directly concern its ostensible heroine: it is a richly evocative description of the Garden of Adonis, the birthplace of the twins Amoret and Belphoebe, and the seedplace of all the fecundity of the universe – including (an aspect to which we will return when we look at the remnant of Book VII) the great enemy of humankind, time. The book culminates in four of the most impressive cantos of the whole poem, and indeed one of the highest points of the whole age's poetry, the narrative of Amoret's capture by the magician Busirane, her subsequent rescue by Britomart, and (in the first (1590) version) her reconciliation with her lover Scudamour – who, as a male and thus the embodiment of so many of the destructive myths of sexual desire by which Spenser's age apprehended love, has been unable to rescue her. In the 1590 edition, Canto 12, stanzas 43–47, brought the first published part of *The Faerie*

Queene to its conclusion. In their celebration of unity through struggle and reconciliation they constitute an appropriate conclusion – confident, rapturous, serious – to the harmonious reflection in human desire and marriage of the order and fecundity of the universe. But its optimism embodied a finality that the poem would, as it grew, no longer be able to uphold. As it stands, the conclusion of Book III is a replete and dignified ending in which Spenser turned to his lovers and his audience to exhort them: 'Now cease your worke, and at your pleasure play;/Now cease your worke, tomorrow is an holy day.' But it was a moment that did not last. Indeed, it is not even sustained in Book III itself: the very division of the heroine into different women figures suggests the dislocative nature of desire, and also opens more unfinished narrative strands than was characteristic of the first two books.

Book IV, of Friendship, which was the first of the Books added in 1596, but which was probably in part written around the same time as some of Book III, is the most disparate. Spenser continues many of the polyphonic strands of Book III, and in some ways Book IV should be seen as a continued outfolding of the previous book. But it is more disturbing, not so much in its ostensible content as in its technique of continually moving among multiple narrative threads, which continually undermines, in Goldberg's terms, 'the possibility of fixed character and fixed meaning'[20] in order to focus on the contradictory shapes of desire. Florimell is the most powerful example. An extraordinary combination of male myths and fears about women are embodied in her adventures. Her stories span Books III to V, and includes an escape from multiple attempted rapes, her loss of her girdle, symbolizing the chastity that protects beauty, the creation of a 'false' Florimell when the real one proves elusive, the culminating confrontation between the pretenders to her 'real' nature, and her final marriage to Marinell in the third canto of Book V. Book IV multiplies the complications of her story, and of the poem's treatment of desire though such figures as Lust or Corflambo (flaming heart, the infectious nature of desire), and (as the poem seems to move increasingly and uncomfortably closer to the world of Elizabethan politics) the love between Belphoebe and Timias, fictional projections of the Queen and Ralegh. In the story of Timias, which starts in Books III and is resumed in IV and VI, we can see Spenser dealing delicately with the controversial figure of Ralegh. It is, of course, too simple to say that Timias 'stands for' Ralegh: the poem is too multiple in its focus to allow for such reductive identification. But in Timias, Spenser seems to provide a very partial interpretation of his friend's relations with the Queen. Ralegh, after all, was perhaps the most blatantly manipulative of all Elizabeth's courtiers. Something of his flamboyant role-playing can be sensed in Timias's relationship with

Belphoebe, where he takes the role Ralegh enacted to perfection in
the English Court of the 1580s, that of the devoted yet unrewarded
servant, 'captived in endlesse durance/Of sorrow and despaire without
aleggeaunce' (III. 5. 42). But at some point in the second half of the
poem, as (most probably) Spenser finished and revised his earlier draft
of the Book of Friendship, contemporary events increasingly disturbed
him into taking up the questions of courtly values in ways the first
three books had not anticipated. There are signs that as he considered
Ralegh's fall from favour in 1592 Spenser found himself caught between
conflicting allegiances to the Queen and to what he perceived as the
injustice of his patron's treatment. The delicate ambiguity of Spenser's
treatment of Timias's guilt at being taken with Amoret, 'handling soft
the hurts, which she did get' (IV. 7. 35), becomes a delightful comedy.
Mistakes and overreactions occur on both sides and Spenser balances
the seductive sensuality of Amoret with the fierce exclusiveness of
Belphoebe who

> . . . in her wrath she thought them both have thrild,
> With that selfe arrow, which the Carle had kild.
> Yet held her wrathfull hand from vengeance sore,
> But drawing nigh, ere he her well beheld;
> Is this the faith, she said, and said no more,
> But turnd her face, and fled away for evermore.
>
> (IV. 7. 36)

This is a particularly balanced moment; more typical of the poem,
the treatment of desire operates primarily on the level of firm moral
analysis – for Spenser, as for most of his contemporaries, the rational
ought to control the irruptions of desire in the human psyche –
but that very approach, stressing control and duty, serve finally to
stress the disruptiveness of human emotions as decentred in its own
way as the unpredictability and dislocation of the 'self' of Petrarchan
poetry on which I commented in Chapter 3. It is perhaps the very
uncontrollability of human desire that underlies Spenser's inabilty
to end stories, to provide the closure for which his moral scheme
calls.

   When he came to England at the end of the 1580s, Spenser had
certainly conceived and possibly finished Book IV. 'It belongs in spirit,
design, and even execution, to the 1580s', Sale notes, and parts of
Book V also were written before Spenser's visit, at a time when he
was anxious to defend the principles of Elizabethan power embodied in
Grey's ruthless dealings with what the English saw as the Irish rebels.[21]
He can certainly be critical of his own government, even though it is
in high philosophical terms. He looks back to the Golden Age and the
note of criticism is unusually sweeping:

> For that which all men then did vertue call,
> Is now cald vice; and that which vice was hight,
> Is now hight vertue, and so us'd of all
>
> (V. Proem, 4)

But, when it comes down to particulars, his loyalty never wavers. From both Book V and his tract, *A View of the Present State of Ireland* (written 1596, although not published until 1633), we see how Spenser could be, as he was in his poem, critical of government policy. Yet he was fiercely, even brutally, loyal to its underlying principles, criticizing Elizabeth's government for pusillanimity not cruelty, and concluding in his treatise that Ireland should be immediately devastated by a massive application of English military force and replacement by English settlers. In Book V, the pressure of history upon the poem becomes most obvious, and strikingly destructive of the poem's intentions. In Lewis's strong words, 'Spenser was the instrument of a detestable policy in Ireland, and in his fifth book the wickedness he had shared begins to corrupt his imagination.'[22] The book deals fairly summarily with the execution of Mary Queen of Scots, the Armada, and then, in great detail, produces an allegorical justification of the English occupation of Ireland in which Spenser 'had both an ideological and material stake'. Spenser's defence is both racist and universalizing, depicting the English brutalizing of Ireland as an eternal battle between good and evil. It is perhaps significant that in the 1970s some American critics began to read Book V for an analogous 'underlying' moral allegory rather than deal with the blatant political issues. Such readings were patently ideological, largely the product of the contemporary cold war, and interestingly attuned to attempts (like Spenser's, not totally deliberate) to cover and mystify awkward political realities. The fifth book undoubtedly expresses Spenser's unease before the strains of the last decades of the century just as these recent readings register a helplessness before the seeming inexorability of contemporary politics. We should remember too, that the first three books of the poem had been written before Spenser's visit to England where, for the first time in a decade, he saw something of the realities of court life. The 1580s had seen the death of Sidney and the rise of a new generation of such ambitious and ruthless courtiers as Ralegh and Essex. For Spenser himself, it had brought the responsibility of his duties in Ireland, first under Lord Grey whom he fictionalized in part as the Knight of Justice in Book V, and then under Grey's successors as Lord Deputy of Ireland.

Spenser's personal and literary careers, until some time in the mid 1590s, therefore, both show similar patterns. But when we turn to Book VI, we start to see, more obviously than before the ideological contradictions from which the poem was born and to which, despite itself, it increasingly alludes. A note of disquiet starts to emerge that does more than simply call into question the cruder and more obviously reprehensible kinds of policies of the Elizabethan Court. In Book V, Spenser posed the problem of finding himself, as he must have done often in Ireland, surrounded by acute contradictions between his ideals and what he saw as social realities. The gloomy, unresolved ending of Book V testifies to Spenser's realization that the gap between the actual Court of Gloriana and his celebration of it was uncomfortably, perhaps unbridgeably, wide. In Book VI, he turns directly to the virtue that did, or should, uphold the life of the Court he served and by which, during both his visit to England and in his faithful service in Ireland, he felt so disturbed – courtesy.

The Book of Courtesy

Book VI seems to invite us to relax with a delightfully leisured, pastoral interlude, and enjoy calmness and gentility as well as exciting battles; it promises a civilized contrast with the gloomy brutality of Book V. Spenser presents courtesy as the manifestation in social relations of those higher virtues he has already treated. Among all the virtues, the poem serenely asserts in its opening, there

> . . . growes not a fayrer flowre,
> Then is the bloosme of comely courtesie,
> Which though it on a lowly stalke doe bowre,
> Yet brancheth forth in brave nobilitie,
> And spreds it selfe through all civilitie.
>
> (VI. Proem, 4)

But a poem by a poet whose disquiet at the Court had been expressed in *Colin Clouts Come Home Again* could not rest easy with that bland assertion, and throughout Book VI there emerges a deep anxiety about the reality of courtly life. In the 'present age', the Proem continues, courtesy may seem to abound, 'yet being matcht with plaine Antiquitie,/Ye will them all but fayned showes esteeme,/Which carry colours faire, that feeble eies misdeeme'. The mode of criticism in *Colin Clout* had been that of the servant of the Court appalled by the Court's irresponsibility and superficiality. Here the criticism goes much deeper:

> But in the triall of true curtesie,
> Its now so farre from that, which then it was,

That it indeed is nought but forgerie,
Fashion'd to please the eies of them, that pas.

(VI. Proem, 4, 5)

The central (if usually absent) figure of *The Faerie Queene* had been, to this point, the Queen: and, just as in *Colin Clout* the Lady Cynthia was excluded from the general criticism of the Court, so here too Spenser still highlights Elizabeth as the fairest pattern of courtesy, superior to all those of both Antiquity and the present. It is from her that the Court derives its being and also what reminders of grace and integrity it retains. Like the virtuous courtiers singled out in *Colin Clout*, the Queen is praised as the fountain, the ocean, the source, of all the 'goodly vertues' which 'well/Into the rest, which round about you ring, Faire Lords and Ladies, which about you dwell,/And doe adorne your Court, where courtesies excell'. (VI. Proem, 7) But if, as the poem had sadly stated, all contemporary courtesy is 'but fayned showes', 'nought but forgerie', then the apparently excelling courtesy of the present age is mere surface. Similarly, while it is argued that 'vertues seat is deepe within the mynd,/And not in outward shows' and false courtesy is 'a glas so gay, that it can blynd/The wisest sight, to thinke gold that is bras', only eight lines later, the Queen herself, the source of the true courtesy, is also described as 'a mirrour sheene', her brightness also serving to 'inflame/The eyes of all, which thereon fixed beene' (VI. Proem, 5, 6). Spenser's choice of metaphor and the contradictions of his argument would seem to be produced by his repressed antagonism towards the political oppression of which he was part. Even though such confusions are marginalized, they point to fierce ideological tensions entering into the poem of which Spenser was perhaps not entirely conscious and yet which, by the end of the book, are radically undermining the ideals he is celebrating.

Social text and literary text, then, forcefully flow into each other. The England which Spenser saw on his visit impinges more directly on the gentle, pastoral landscape of Book VI than might have first been imagined. But there is one characteristic of Book VI which opens up Spenser's disaffection with his world particularly revealingly. It is the near absence of the original inspiration for the poem: Book VI is the only one in which there is no allegorical representation of the Queen within the narrative. Everything that seems to be undermining the order Spenser had celebrated in earlier books is here embodied in the figure of the Blatant Beast – protean, indiscriminate and, finally, impossible to enchain. Whether we see the Blatant Beast as detraction, slander, backbiting or something more general, it stands for a distinctively courtly perversion and one that Spenser saw attacking the Court of Elizabeth so successfully that the chosen champion of courtesy, Sir

Calidore, pursues but cannot finally defeat it. Presumably, it would have been possible for Spenser to have put an allegorical embodiment in the book finally to defeat or at least counterbalance the Beast. That would have been an assertion of the continuing power of the Queen's inspiration. Instead he restricts her presence solely to the Proem and to brief references in later cantos. Even these references are uneasy or obligatory, and show Spenser coming closer than he knew to calling the ideals on which the Court was built radically into question.

There are other parts of Book VI where the realities of the 1590s provide a subtext which significantly swerves the poem from its intention. But when Timias reappears in Book VI, the ambiguity is no longer quite so comic or delicate. In VI. 3, Spenser attempts to deal, as Ralegh himself was attempting to do, with the Queen's anger at his marriage with Elizabeth Throckmorton. Spenser comes down firmly on his friend's side, and blames both the Blatant Beast, the slanderous enemy of courtesy, who 'in his wide great mouth' has seized Serena (VI. 3. 24), and the three Knights of Discourtesy, Despetto, Decetto, and Defetto, who have attacked and wounded the gallant squire. Like Ralegh himself, Spenser could not face the possibility that his commitment to the Court had proved so futile and unrewarding that the Court itself was corrupt and destructive; like Ralegh, he could only blame misunderstanding and malice which had, somehow, deceived even the Queen.

The world of the late Elizabethan Court, then, comes uneasily close to the surface of Book VI, despite the significant absence of the Queen herself within its narrative structure. Even more disturbing to the apparent serenity of this 'delightfull land of Faery', however, is a pessimism that contrasts radically with the tone of earlier books. It is prefigured in the Proem to Book V, where Spenser broods over the 'state of present time' comparing it with 'the image of the antique world', and able to find evidence only for degeneration: 'Me seemes the world is runne quite out of square,/From the first point of his appointed sourse,/And being once amisse growes daily wourse and wourse' (V. Proem, 1). All around is the dissolution of human history; only the chosen instruments of justice, like Artegall, stand between mankind and chaos. Implied here is a view of history startlingly different from that of earlier books, where degeneration was seen as only a temporary phase in a pattern of natural replenishment and regeneration. An optimistic, cyclical view of history has been replaced by a view of history as entropic, a view that is stressed even more strongly at the start of Book VI. There too the antique world's true virtue has been abandoned for 'fayned showes', 'forgerie' and deception, and Sir Calidore's quest, unlike that of any previous hero, has taken him further and further from fulfilment. At the end of the book, the Blatant

Beast escapes and 'raungeth through the world againe' (VI. 12. 41). The poem's pessimism has become not merely that of a disillusioned, ageing courtier or public servant disturbed by the evident surface corruption of the late Elizabethan Court. The end of *The Faerie Queeene* records a deeper disillusion, one that links the poem more closely than Spenser (and many of his modern admirers would like) to the generation of cynically quietist, deeply disillusioned, radicals of the 1590s – with the tortured, dislocated writings of Donne, Marston, Greville and Webster, and with the deeply pessimistic Shakespeare of *Troilus and Cressida*. All of these younger men lived into the Jacobean period; each had his conscious or suppressed ways of reacting to the pressure of that disillusion. Spenser was to die shortly before the peculiar Jacobean schizophrenia could claim him. What he must have started to sense is poignantly recorded in Book VI.

At the start of the book, the poem turns to define courtesy and thus to set the expected quest in motion. We are told, in a conventional enough starting-point, that 'Courtesie' is derived from 'Court'. But the terms in which this commonplace is expressed are curiously contradictory: 'Of Court it seemes, men Courtesie doe call,/For that it there most useth to abound.' 'Seemes' and 'most useth' are more tentative than a wholehearted assertion of the virtue of courtesy might demand. 'Useth' suggests habitual or accustomed expectation as well as a hint of nostalgia; 'seemes' recalls the 'fayned showes' which the Proem has mentioned. Furthermore, Spenser goes on: 'Right so in Faery court it did redound,/Where curteous Knights and Ladies most did won/Of all on earth, and made a matchlesse paragon' (VI. 1. 1). The switch to the past tense reinforces the tentativeness of Spenser's discussion of courtesy. Next we encounter a description of his Knight of courtesy, and the same ambiguity continues. While Calidore is depicted as 'none more courteous', it is difficult to take the Greek origin of his name (Beautiful Gift) seriously without simultaneously admitting that either Spenser is verging on satire or is interestingly unaware of the contradictions. Calidore, we are told, has 'gentlenesse of spright', 'manners milde', 'gracious speech', 'faire usage and conditions sound', and is shown to be restrained, disciplined, and ceremonious. Yet the emphasis on such characteristics is qualified by Spenser's habitual use of 'seemes' (e.g. VI. 1. 2) and by the distinctive choice of terms to describe Calidore. To his natural graces, he 'add's 'comely guize'. While he is 'well approv'd in batteilous affray', yet his 'faire usage' 'purchast' him 'place' and reputation. It is difficult to argue that these terms do not undercut any affirmation of courtesy as the triumphant harmonization of opposites.

While Spenser sets up a contrast in the Proem between calculated externalized 'showes' of courtesy and the hidden virtues within, as he moves through Faeryland in Book VI, refining and testing his initial definition of courtesy, some revealing contradictions emerge. At the start of the third canto, the poem qualifies the earlier insistence upon true courtesy lying deep within the mind by asserting that outward manners can, in fact, be taken as a reliable guide to inward virtue. But now courtesy is said to be bound up with externals, behaving with decorum and bearing oneself 'aright/To all of each degree, as doth behove'. In the fifth canto, we are assured further that there is always a firm connection between gentle behaviour and noble birth, between external grace and internal virtue, even if it may not be easily discernible. Spenser asserts that Calidore 'loathd leasing and base flattery,/And loved simple truth and stedfast honesty' (VI. 1. 3), but the difference between these admirable characteristics and the 'comely guize' and the 'greatest grace' that Calidore 'with the greatest purchast' is not made clear. At one with his age's most conservative moralists, Spenser asserts that a noble, trotting stallion rarely begets an awkward, ambling colt. He seems to be deeply concerned to hold social change at bay and to preserve the traditional standards he clearly saw being eroded in the Court of the 1590s. Such contradictions show how the beginning of Book VI simply cannot maintain the moral distinctions on which his exploration of the Court and courtesy needed to be based. Even Spenser himself was increasingly unable to make such distinctions with his earlier certainty. The world he creates, instead of testing and refining his chosen virtue, comes increasingly to call it radically into question.

In accordance with the expected pattern of the whole poem, then, Calidore goes off on his quest. It is striking that, embodying a virtue which 'useth' to be found at Court, Calidore will eventually find it best manifest in the country. It is also noteworthy that as a knight representing or searching for a distinctively social virtue, courtesy, he goes off alone. His world in fact becomes an increasingly lonely one, dominated by the unpredictability of fortune and the ambiguity of moral choice. 'All flesh is frayle, and full of ficklenesse', he learns, 'subject to fortunes chance, still chaunging new' (VI. 1. 41). The dichotomy between good and evil which is traditionally a central part of the chivalric quest is also missing. Calidore's foe, the Blatant Beast – the savage vilifier of Timias, the adversary who has escaped Artegall's savage hand in Book V – emerges as a savage parody of courtesy, 'fostred long in Stygian fen,/Till he to perfect ripeness grew, and then,/Into this wicked world he forth was sent'. Such terms recall the nurturing of Amoret and Belphoebe, and the 'infinite shapes of creatures' bred in the Garden of Adonis (III. 6. 35). Indeed, part of the Beast's threat seems to lie in its being uncannily close to the virtue it seeks to oppose: the enemy of courtesy is not an alien force, but a variant of courtesy itself.

The impression that Calidore and his adversaries share a world
of common values is brought out in Calidore's confrontation with
Maleffort and Briana. Both sides in the battle use the language and art
of courtesy: she accuses Calidore of scorning and shaming the decorum
of chivalry by murdering her servants and sends word to her champion
Crudor to

> . . . desire that he would
> Vouchsafe to reskue her against a Knight,
> Who through strong powre had now her self in hould,
> Having late slaine her Seneschall in fight,
> And all her people murdred with outragious might.
>
> (VI.1.29)

In similar terms Crudor vows to 'succour her' and in appropriate
chivalric manner sends 'to her his basenet, as a faithfull band' (31).
In order to stress their shared values, Spenser does not, as he does
so often in earlier books, give moral asides to direct his readers.
Instead, he stresses Calidore's precipitate violence. He sees a knight
approaching, and

> Well weend he streight, that he should be the same,
> Which tooke in hand her quarrell to maintaine;
> Ne stayd to aske if it were he by name,
> But couch his speare, and ran at him amaine.
>
> (VI. 1. 33)

The two combatants are almost indistinguishable as they fight, and
when Calidore is finally victorious, he comments upon the dubious
outcome in a revealing line, confessing to his vanquished enemy that
'What haps to day to me, to morrow may to you' (41). It is as if they are
struggling not in a world of moral absolutes, but for alternate versions
of courtesy. Such relativism is a strange departure for *The Faerie Queene*
and one that seems contradictory to Spenser's announced intentions.

The episode following, with the squire Tristram, also brings out the
ways in which conservatism and moral relativism contradict each other.
Calidore's initial hostility to Tristram's 'hand too bold...embrewed/in
blood of knight' (VI. 2. 7) is tempered when he learns of the discourtesy
of Tristram's victim, and instead of seeing Tristram's behaviour as
discourteous, he accommodates the youngster's behaviour to necessity
– 'what he did, he did him selfe to save'. He then enunciates a principle
which would seem, logically, to justify the behaviour not only of
Tristram but of Crudor in the previous episode: that 'knights and
all men this by nature have,/Towards all womenkind them kindly

to behave' (VI. 2. 14). Spenser later tries to smooth out the moral contradictions: Tristram turns out to be of noble birth, the son of 'good king Meliogras' of Cornwall, and so his behaviour is legitimized.

These and the other early episodes in Book VI unravel, then, as nodes of contradiction. Spenser's difficulty in reconciling his conservative moral absolutism with an increasingly relativistic world comes out particularly in Calidore's need, most intriguing in a knight representing a supposedly inner virtue, to rely on the 'fayned showes' and the values of reputation and appearance which have been indignantly repudiated at the book's start. Calidore (and, in Canto 5, Arthur) are perfectly entitled, it seems, to use deceit, subterfuge, and cunning to achieve their ends. What seems to differentiate their true from others' false courtesy is simply success. Perhaps we are just meant to assume that Calidore and Arthur are by definition right, but if so, an important moral ambiguity surfaces: his methods are difficult or impossible to distinguish from those of his or Calidore's enemies. We are meant to take his virtue for granted even though his actions seem indistinguishable from those of his enemies.

It may be that Spenser was partly aware of the contradictions he was building into his poem. But they undoubtedly articulate a more widespread unease and confusion than his 'intention' knew. We can recognize how such an earnest, committed servant of the Elizabethan Court would react to what he saw as the crumbling away of the ideals on which the Court was built. But what language did he have to articulate his distress? In what ways could he have articulated the dislocation of the emerging modern subject? What he inevitably falls back on is the residual language of religious renunciation. Yet he did so only as the poem came to what was to be its premature end. In Book I the Red Cross Knight was given a vision of the Heavenly City, and, overwhelmed by its transcendence even of the Earthly City, Cleopolis, had prayed to be allowed to abandon his quest and enter into the world of eternity. He was sent firmly back into the world to complete his quest, just as Spenser applied himself faithfully to his duties in Ireland. But when, in the middle of Book VI, a similar situation arises in the Blatant Beast's attack on Timias and Serena the temptation of withdrawal from the world arises again. Timias and Serena take refuge with a Hermit, and for once, Spenser creates a character who, although unquestionably embodying what he wants us to see as a signpost towards truth, seems at odds with the ostensible virtue of the poem. He has, he tells them, renounced the Court:

> . . . he had bene a man of mickle name,
> Renowmed much in armes and derring doe:
> But being aged now and weary to

Of warres delight, and worlds contentious toyle,
  The name of knighthood he did disavow,
  And hanging up his armes and warlike spoyle,
From all this worlds incombraunce did himselfe assoyle.

                                                    (VI. 5. 37)

The terms in which the Hermit is described suggest a restful reward for
many years of devotion to the 'worlds contentious toyle', yet the cure
he prescribes for Timias and Serena – who are still 'young' (VI. 5. 11)
and 'faire' (VI. 5. 39) – is also renunciation of the toil of courtly strife.
He entertains them. His counsel is to 'avoide the occasion' of their pain,
to 'abstaine from pleasure', and 'subdue desire' (VI. 6. 14) – to give
over, in other words, the delights of the courtly life. Obviously, the
Hermit's advice is perfectly in accord with Spenser's earlier emphasis
that true virtue lies deep within the mind, yet it does lie uncomfortably
beside the active life of courtesy the book has so far celebrated.

   The second half of Book VI brings these contradictions more into
the open. What I have so far highlighted might be described as no
more perhaps than a sense of unease on Spenser's part, most probably
produced by his own experiences in the Court, his reaction to Ralegh's
fall from favour, and, simply, his own increasing age and weariness.
From Canto 7 onwards, this unease brings Spenser to focus on the one
commitment to which, it seems, he held even more strongly than to his
political duties – his poetry. As Book VI draws to its conclusion, the
belief in national destiny that lay at the root of his original choice of the
epic written to celebrate England and the Court of Elizabeth seems to
falter, and we can see emerging an even greater contradiction. Unable
to celebrate the Court and its virtues as unambiguously as he once did,
his poem starts to evaluate even its author's role as the celebrant of the
Queen and her Court. The Blatant Beast attacks not only virtuous and
unwary courtiers, but the basis of the very art that has brought him
into being:

     Ne spareth he most learned wits to rate,
     Ne spareth he the gentle Poets rime,
   But rends without regard of person or of time.

   Ne may this homely verse, of many meanest
     Hope to escape his venemous despite . . .

                                                    (VI. 12. 40–41)

In this melancholy and somewhat waspish tone, Spenser in fact goes
on to conclude Book VI: the forces which threaten society and civility
are also attacking the poet and poetry itself, seemingly without restraint.
How does a poet, therefore, whose life was dedicated to celebrating the

Court, deal with its rejection not only of the ideals of courtesy on which
it is itself founded, but of the poet who would draw them back to
those ideals? In the second half of the book, the power and value of
poetry in the Court becomes a central subject, and what emerges is
a deep unease about the reciprocity of Court and poet on which *The
Faerie Queene* had been built. While the final six cantos of the book
are ostensibly centred on Calidore, they have as an urgent underlying
concern Spenser's commitment to the very poem to which he had
devoted so much of his life. We can see perhaps Calidore and Colin
Clout, who appears in Canto 9 as an embodiment of the figure of the
troubled poet, as two aspects of Spenser himself, or more generally, of
the court poet (a Sidney, a Wyatt, Ralegh or Sidney, all of whom, as
we have seen, committed themselves so strongly to the importance of
poetry in the Court). In the writing of *The Faerie Queene*, it may be
that Spenser himself, however partially, became uneasily aware of an
incompatibility between the courtier's life and the courtly poem. The
poem itself starts to educate if not its writer at least its readers in ways
its writer had not anticipated.

Let us trace something of this gradually opening fissure in the poem.
The affinities between the Knight of courtesy and his opponents become
much more explicit when Calidore abandons his quest to live with the
shepherds in the pastoral world. His quest has taken him throughout
the world:

> Him first from court he to the citties coursed,
> And from the citties to the townes him prest,
> And from the townes into the countrie forsed,
> And from the country back to private farmes he scorsed.
>
> (VI. 9. 3)

When he finds a group of shepherds who have never seen such a
creature as the Blatant Beast, he stays with them, and proceeds to woo
a country girl, Pastorella. Calidore's addresses to her uncomfortably
recall the 'outward showes' rejected at the book's start. He adopts
shepherd's clothes and crook in the hope of making an appropriate
impression. Once he sees that she had never 'such knightly service
seene' and 'did little whit regard his courteous guize' he

> . . . thought it best
> To chaunge the manner of his loftie looke;
> And doffing his bright armes, himselfe addrest
> In shepheards weed, and in his hand he tooke,
> In stead of steelehead speare, a shepheards hooke.
>
> (VI. 9. 35, 36)

He defies Coridon, his rival, in terms strongly reminiscent of his earlier encounter with Briana and Maleffort, and then uses his superior courtly graces to win Pastorella from the angry shepherd. We are told by Spenser that all commended him 'for courtesie amongst the rudest breeds/Good will and favour' (VI. 9. 45), but the terms by which his victory is achieved are all too reminiscent of the patronizing, manipulative skills of the devious courtier. When he launches into a conventional praise of the pastoral life, and Pastorella's father replies that all men must accept their places in the universe since 'it is the mynd that maketh wretch or happie, rich or poore', Calidore does not see the irony of the comment, and moreover, immediately manipulates the discussion to further his desire for Pastorella.

When we are shown Calidore as the spectator of the stately vision on Mount Acidale, we are aware that, as with other doctrinal nodes of the poem, Spenser is focusing with as much intensity as he can on the issues underlying his poem. In this superbly evocative episode, there is inserted a mysterious and striking figure. Besides the ring of dancers on the Mount is the figure of the poet named as Colin Clout. It is striking that Spenser should introduce what amounts to a charmingly deprecative self-portrait at a moment in the poem when the courtly vision seems closest to faltering. It is one of the high points of the whole poem – dignified, passionate, redolent with suggestiveness, and an episode into which Spenser put most explicitly his anxieties about his courtly vocation. It starts by recalling the book's opening, the terms of which have, as we have seen, become increasingly ambivalent as the adventures have proceeded. The pastoral world, we are told, far transcends the world of courtly vanity, 'Save onely Glorianaes heavenly hew/To which what can compare?' (VI. 10. 4). Perhaps Spenser's unease at where his poem is now turning makes him draw attention to this obligatory exception to courtly degeneration. Certainly, the vision Calidore is given on the Mount seems to call into question the value and power of the Court. In the centre of the Grace's dance is not the Queen, not virtuous courtiers, not an abstract, untested virtue, but Colin Clout's own shepherd lass who 'another grace . . . well deserves to be' (VI. 10. 27). There is a brief, though charming, apology for seeming to replace the Queen – and yet the transposition has been made. But of course, it is not Colin but Calidore who is the book's central figure and so it is he who breaks into the dance and makes the vision disappear. Interestingly, while Colin may instruct Calidore (and us) on its significance, there is no sense that (unlike the allegorical set pieces in earlier books) the Knight will benefit from the vision he has been given. Instead, he turns back to his devious pursuits. Returning to Pastorella, he discovers the fact of her noble parentage and then that she has been captured by brigands.

How do we read this division in the book's culminating scene? It is as if we must choose between Calidore and Colin at this point. Book VI seems to have increasingly revealed contradictions in Spenser's celebration of the Court. We might argue that he seems aware of these contradictions to the extent that he can, with some unease, but without apology, project contradictory aspects of his vision into Calidore and Colin Clout. But it is the incompatibility which comes most strongly through in the poem in ways the poet could not have anticipated. The Beast has infected all estates of society, has been temporarily captured, and in the short-lived triumph of its capture what the knight and his enemy have in common becomes quite explicit. All question of moral superiority is gone; instead, we have the spectacle of public adulation in which all 'much admyr'd the Beast, but more admyr'd the Knight' (VI. 12. 37). The Beast then breaks his bonds and rages through the world again.

The Faerie Queene's place in Elizabethan culture

The Faerie Queene is the ultimate test case in Elizabethan poetry for the ways in which power seeks to control language. It is a poem expressly dedicated to the praise of the Queen, her Court, and the cultural practices by which the Elizabethan regime established and maintained its power. Spenser accepts his role as that of the Orphic bard, praising, warning and celebrating the society that not only rewarded but in a real sense created him. Thus his poem's central figure is the Queen – as head of the Church as well as the State, triumphing over heresy on the one hand and political dissent on the other, and as the inspiration of the poem itself. The Queen's response to the poem, at least to the first part published, was to reward Spenser with a pension, and in 1598 an appointment (ironically after he had fled his home after a rising of the Irish) as Sheriff of Cork. To have even a self-styled laureate praising her regime so fulsomely was to acknowledge poetry's use as part of its ideological underpinning. More consciously than any other poem in the last two decades of the century, *The Faerie Queene* is 'Art become a work of State', asserting that despite the material word's unpredictabilities, the ideals of the regime are without contradiction and that when its norms are transgressed, chaos will result. The poem is offered as a microcosm of this truth.

To speak of *The Faerie Queene* as the most magnificent articulation of the Elizabethan Court's dominant ideology is, however, a claim that is contradicted by the poem itself. The poem raises the question of how a deeply conservative poet can be surpassed by his own poem so that his readers see the ideological contradictions, not just the ideological mystifications, of his society. As Shepherd comments ironically, 'in a sense it's an old story: distressed conservatives produce fascinating radical analyses that they themselves can't tolerate'.[23] A symptomatic reading of the poem allows us to see the contradictions struggling to emerge. The very length of time Spenser spent on his poem, perhaps twenty years, helps us open up the poem to such a symptomatic reading. The poem may have started as a celebration, and even with some plan like that which Spenser outlined in a letter to Ralegh, where he spoke of twelve books, each with its own virtue and a culminating feast in the court of Gloriana. But by 1596, the original design had been abandoned. Lewis suggests we speak not of a 'whole' poem, but rather of fragments: A (1590, Books I–III), B (1596 IV–VI), and C (Mutability).[24] Certainly, between the image of mutuality and confidence in the reconciliation of Amoret and Scudamour in the cancelled final stanzas of the 1590 edition and the darker late books there are too many contradictions to ignore. The poem encodes many of the real historical conflicts and tensions of its time, dealing with them not (as Shakespeare was already starting to do in the mid-1590s) by juxtaposing and so exploring their rival claims to truth and allegiance, but by trying arbitrarily to displace and condense them to maintain the power of the dominant ideology. The poet's desire is clear: to justify the cultural and ideological practices of the Elizabethan regime. And yet his poem is fragmented by potent ideological breaks and contradictions. Book V is particularly revealing: in the opening canto, for instance, Artegall dismisses chivalric reconciliation as ineffective in deciding the conflict between Sanglier and his opponent, asserting that 'doubtfull causes' can be decided only by force. Conflict is settled not by knights acknowledging their places in a hierarchy but by brutal militarism. Ultimately, ideological domination is dependent not on self-evident truth, but on force.

What the poem attempts – in the early books buoyantly, in the later ones desperately – is a denial of historical change. *The Faerie Queene* yearns for stasis, to project truth as unalterable in the face of unpredictability and, in its manifestation in Elizabeth and her Court, as natural, given, and unassailable. It is built therefore on a poetic that tries to avoid debate, to efface all contradiction, and to reconcile all partial truths into a higher harmony or ruthlessly to exclude them as heretical or unnatural. It tries likewise to create a reader who is active but subservient – a loyal participant in the decipherment of emblem, hieroglyph and allegory. He or she is interpellated as part of a great celebration of ideological plenitude, just as the Elizabethan courtier was

enculturated and socialized by accepting his or her proper place in the
Court. But just as there was in the Court, so in Spenser's poem there
is an anxiety that emerges as continual contradiction. As we have seen,
Sidney's independence of mind, Ralegh's devious rebellion (and earlier,
Wyatt's bursts of moral scepticism) could be dealt with by various state
apparatuses – by exclusion, imprisonment, silence or threat. But in
Spenser's poem the pressures and contradictions of the history which it
tries to exclude continually seep back into it. Despite its claim to speak
for the Elizabethan regime, thoughts and actions that challenged it none
the less enter the poem.

Even sympathetic readers note this unease in the poem, although they
might put it down to failures of poetic style instead of symptomatic,
culturally produced, characteristics. I suggest that it is one important
role of the reader not to accede to the poet's demands, but rather to
reconstruct the ways by which the text was produced. It is important
to look for the signs of contradiction, uneasiness and incompletion in
The Faerie Queene – because of the continuing power of the dominant
reading. Such a reading strategy is not looking for 'faults' in any
'aesthetic' sense, but rather perhaps in something like the geological
sense – as signs of the eruption of history into the production of the
text. Two further, brief, examples may be given from the later books.
As was noted earlier, Spenser's unease before the Queen's treatment of
Ralegh surfaces in Books IV and VI. These are episodes the poet himself
foregrounds, no doubt because Ralegh was one of his sponsors; but
Spenser is also controlled and limited by Elizabeth's own reading of the
situation. In IV, Belphoebe's absence limits the claims of mistreatment
Timias can make; in VI, the poem is further paralysed by Ralegh's fate.
We note the powerlessness of the court poet: all his poem can seemingly
do is acknowledge the power that was, outside it, imprisoning and
condemning Spenser's patron. We can even construct Ralegh's own
reading of the Timias episode, perhaps, in his own poetry, especially
in 'Ocean to Scinthia' where he grimly complains of the seeming waste
of his twelve years in the Queen's service.

A second example comes from Book V. Goldberg has pointed out
how one particular reader of the poem whose misreading, however
creative or 'strong' in the sense I suggested modern readings should
be, is deliberately rejected by Spenser's allegory and would be not only
considered 'wrong' but heretical by Spenser. James VI of Scotland read
Book V as an insult to his mother, Mary Queen of Scots, executed
in 1588, and demanded (in vain) that the poet be punished. In the
poem, in fact, the very same demand that Duessa (Mary's allegorical
surrogate) receive fair treatment is rigorously 'raced out' (V. 9. 26),
and her poet Bonfont is renamed Malfont and has his tongue nailed
to a post. As Goldberg notes, 'public dismemberment – including the

beheading of Mary Queen of Scots – is congruent with numerous actions' that occur in Book V: it 'was one way in which the power of the monarch displayed itself, inscribing itself on the body of the condemned'.[25] What James's objection assumed was that the power of the Elizabethan regime stood behind Spenser's poem – after all, it was Spenser himself who insists that *The Faerie Queene* is indeed Elizabeth's, that Artegall is her, not his, knight (V. Proem) and that he is merely the articulator and not the originator of the unchanging principles, beyond argument or opposition, of law and justice. Artegall's imposition of justice is a confirmation not of eternal principles but of force. Book V enacts the ways the Queen's power operates over poetry; it displays *The Faerie Queene*'s origins in Elizabethan ideology, and we can see James's reading of the poem as perhaps the earliest unveiling of those origins. James, who did not object to being flattered, might not have been quite so pleased with being described as an early demystifier of ideological repression, but his reading is a model for the kind I am suggesting modern readers produce – where a body of powerful questions are asked of the poem, especially ones the poem does not want to answer.

Further, observing such explicit ways ideology marks the seemingly innocent literary text allows us to look at other places in the poem where similar struggles occur and where they have been, perhaps, more successfully effaced. Anderson has observed how even in Book III, the portrait of Belphoebe distances her 'as a mythic ideal' from 'any living referent' – precisely the process which we can observe in the way the Queen operated within the social text of Elizabethan culture. In IV, the same process is at work in the reconciliation of Belphoebe and Timias, which can be read as a desirable fantasy, but what in the dangerous world of late Elizabethan politics was becoming increasingly impossible, and before which poetry was increasingly helpless.[26]

It seems that the closer we probe the textual practices of *The Faerie Queene*, the more we must ask whether it makes sense to speak of its 'unity' at all. It is a different question from: to what extent would Spenser have wanted to have his readers find unity in it? The dislocations are obvious in later books but even in the early books, ideology and textuality seem to pull in different directions. Kaske has pointed to the unsettling relativistic universe the poem creates – as distinct from its assertions of absolute principles – by its unfinished quests, the increasing heterogeneity of its virtues, the uneasy slippage between Christian and classical principles. Even in the poem's opening canto, there is a real sense in which the first adversary, the monster Error, embodies a fundamental principle of its writerly quality. As Parker notes, 'Spenser's own book is like the monster "Error" in that it, too, has swallowed a multitude of books and recognizing them is part of the devious process of "reading"'.[27]

Spenser's loss of his original epic vision is taken a further step in Lewis's fragment C, the Cantos of Mutability, where one of the recurring enemies of the poem's vision is at last faced. The Garden of Adonis (III. 6) had been an earlier attempt to turn history to myth by showing how the universal changes of nature had an underlying principle of stability. The Garden is the source 'of all things, that are borne to live and die'. And yet it is dominated by the figure that recurs so powerfully in Elizabethan mythology – Time. Time is the arbiter of human life, the destroyer of youth, beauty, and the rude challenger to the order of human society. Time, we are told

> . . . with his scyth addrest,
> Does mow the flowring herbes and goodly things,
> And all their glory to the ground downe flings . . .
> All things decay in time, and to their end do draw.
>
> (III. 6. 39–40)

But, in the vision Spenser wishes to assert, Time's power over each creature can be only a partial truth. Without change and death, Nature could not fulfil its regenerative purposes. What matters is not that individual creatures are inevitably subject to transience, but that through all change, the universal and God-given natural principles of procreation and fertility continue. The principles of the universe are 'eterne in mutabilitie'. In the Mutability Cantos, Time reappears as the demigoddess, Mutability, who challenges the power of the gods and claims to be the single universal principle. Occasionally, modern scholars have pointed out Spenser's affinities with avant-garde philosophers, such as Bruno, in this book. But if any ideas from Bruno are referred to here, they are invoked only to be rejected. The Lucretian law that all things are powerless to resist time is firmly set in the contexts of the natural creative order and the explicitly Christian perspective of God's eternity. In one of Bruno's dialogues, *The Expulsion of the Triumphant Beast*, Fortune (like Spenser's Mutability) argues for the gods' recognition of change as an autonomous principle of the universe. For Bruno, mutability is a discovery of liberation and creativity. For Spenser, however seductive Mutability appears, she is the enemy and must be rejected. Mutability's claim is that both heaven and earth are subject to change:

> For, who sees not, that *Time* on all doth pray?
> But *Times* do change and move continually.
> So nothing here long standeth in one stay:
> Wherefore, this lower world who can deny
> But to be subject still to *Mutabilitie*?
>
> (VII. 7. 47)

Once again, Time and its power are placed in the context of a larger purpose: the more Mutability demonstrates the facts of change, the more it is obvious that Nature includes Mutability in itself, that change and death are part of a universal order – just as the Elizabethan regime itself must be seen as unchanging and constant, centred, in Ralegh's words, on the 'Lady whom Time hath forgot'.

In the final stanzas of this fragment of two cantos and two disconnected stanzas, Spenser explicitly invokes the orthodox Christian framework, in which time is transcended by an eternal realm which

> . . . is contrayr to *Mutabilitie*:
> For, all that moveth, doth in *Change* delight:
> But thence-forth all shall rest eternally
> With Him that is the God of Sabbaoth hight:
> O that great Sabbaoth God, graunt me that Sabaoths sight.
>
> (VII. 8. 2)

So, at least, is the argument of the Mutability Cantos. Its fragmentary nature makes it difficult to see it unambiguously as a coherent whole or as a continuation of the rest of the poem. Many aspects of the cantos continue the concerns of earlier books but there are many which do not fit. As Campbell notes, 'for all their affinities with the rest of the poem, what the Mutability Cantos offer us is not so much a recapitulation as a reversal, or at least a dislocation of our experience of the world of *The Faerie Queene*'. The stance of the narrator is one such dislocation: he is 'clearly shaken by the tale he tells and he finds himself unable to proceed with his customary confidence and objectivity'.[28] Even more telling is the apocalyptic note in the final cantos in which the poet turns back to his poem and, in effect, rejects the poem itself.

There is an irony in the poem's final fragments that may turn a reader back to that point in Book I where the Red Cross Knight was enjoined not to turn his back on the world but to pursue his quest to the end. There, he did so in part to enforce the reader also to pursue a quest for the principles of holiness, temperance, love, friendship, justice and courtesy upon which the poem's vision would be built. Yet, as the poem proceeded and we read on, those virtues became increasingly blurred. The Mutability Cantos likewise show an uneasiness before the terms they propose. The two great adversaries, Cynthia (representing the status quo) and Mutability, both appeal to the same 'sterne' principles (VII. 6. 12,13) and even when they turn to Jove for judgement, he has no firm means of distinguishing between them. As Jove and Mutability face each other, it is difficult to distinguish their speeches as if, in Miller's words, by the end of these two encounters there is no hierarchy remaining except by the force of assertion. As we saw in VI, the poet has to step in himself to show the truth. But here he does so in such terms that the poem itself is rejected. Throughout, part of *The Faerie Queene*'s energy has been built upon its author's firm intentions, and the clash between those intentions and the multiplicity and deferrals of the poem itself. As Neuse puts it, '*The Faerie Queene* opens up what Elizabeth and her regime tried to prevent, a public space for debate'.[29] Now, in the Cantos of Mutability, the despair of the poem to affirm a final truth finally surfaces explicitly. Just as Sidney, at his death, was to ask for his 'toys' and 'vanities' to be destroyed, so Spenser is, in effect, rejecting his whole poem. The final stanzas concede the failure of his undertaking: they look back and see that as the poem has developed, there are secretly proliferated contradictions which break the poem apart. Spenser might have attributed it to mutability or the fall, but in the final stanzas of the poem as we have it, Nature vanishes, the world is dismissed, and so is poetry. What remains is an absence that undermines what Spenser has devoted his whole life to make present in his poem.

Set in the context of sixteenth-century poetry (and even if we look ahead and acknowledge the presence of early modern England's other great epic, *Paradise Lost*), *The Faerie Queene* can be seen as the last attempt to decipher the world by affirming as natural, given and eternal the secret resemblances and hierarchy behind its plethora of signs. It attempts to create a reading of nature, society, man and poetry as an interconnected network of harmony and hierarchy, the whole recognized and valorized by each individual part – only to find that each part breaks into its separate world. At the poem's end, left with only his words, he discovers that they too have lost their divine resemblance. It is as if Spenser sensed how language could no longer function as marks of a divine order.

If, as I asserted at the start of this chapter, *The Faerie Queene* is unquestionably the 'greatest' poem of the century, what do I mean? Clearly not that it is united, or finished; or that its vision is noble, coherent, let alone 'true'. Spenser's poem is one of the most fascinating in all our poetry, at once one of the richest and the emptiest poems, one to which readers can return endlessly because it is an encyclopedia of the ways ideology and textuality interact, and of the processes by which languages intersect and rewrite one another. There is a deep longing for meaning and stasis in *The Faerie Queene* which is contradicted at the deepest level by its own being. It attempts to transform history into culture, culture into nature, and to fix that which inevitably changes in some kind of stasis. As such it epitomizes all that the Elizabethan Court itself likewise tried and failed to do. Spenser's poem may be described as 'great' on two main counts. First, like the society which produced it, it could not remain faithful to the desires which motivated it, and the more those were asserted to be natural and true, the more their falsity and the naked power on which they rested is revealed. *The Faerie Queene* is thus a rich and fascinating articulation of a complex and fascinating cultural formation. Second, as a text (as, to be precise, textuality, as the stimulus to seductive and multiple readings), it remains intriguing, perplexing, rich, unmistakably a great work of poetry.

Notes

1. C. S. Lewis, *English Literature in the Sixteenth Century Excluding Drama* (Oxford, 1954), pp. 358–64.

2. Richard Helgerson, 'The New Poet Presents Himself: Spenser and the Idea of a Literary Career', *PMLA*, 93 (1978), 893–911 (p. 893).

3. Alan Sinfield, *Literature in Protestant England* (Brighton, 1983), p. 66; Arthur F. Marotti, ' "Love is not Love": Elizabethan Sonnet Sequences and the Social Order', *ELH* 49 (1982), 396–428 (p. 417).

4. Reed Way Dasenbrook, *Imitating the Italians: Wyatt, Spenser, Synge, Pound, Joyce* (Baltimore, 1991), p. 83.

5. Jonathan Goldberg, 'The Poet's Authority: Spenser, Jonson and James VI and I', *Genre*, 15 (1982), 81–121.

6. Jonathan Goldberg, *Endlesse Worke* (Baltimore, 1981), p. 27.

7. Derek Traversi, 'Spenser's Faerie Queene', in *The Age of Chaucer*, edited by Boris Ford (Harmondsworth, 1959), pp. 211–20 (p. 217); W. W. Robson, 'Spenser and The Faerie Queene', in *The Age of Shakespeare*, edited by Boris Ford, revised edition (Harmondsworth, 1982), pp. 119–36 (p. 120).

8. Raymond Williams, *The Country and the City* (London, 1973), p. 33.

9. Josephine Bennett, *The Evolution of 'The Faerie Queene'* (Chicago, 1942), p. 157.

10. Quotations from *The Faerie Queene* and the 'Letter to Ralegh' are taken from *The Faerie Queene*, edited by A. C. Hamilton (London 1977); from other poems, from *The Yale Edition of the Shorter Poems of Edmund Spenser*, edited by William A. Oram *et al.* (New Haven, 1989).

11. Goldberg, *Endlesse Worke*, pp. 9, 21, 77.

12. Thomas Rhymer, quoted by Rosemary Freeman, *Elizabethan Emblem Books* (London, 1948), p. 2; George Puttenham, *The Arte of English Poesie*, edited by Gladys Doidge Willcock and Alice Walker (Cambridge, 1936), pp. 186–8.

13. Isabel MacCaffery, *Spenser's Allegory: The Anatomy of Imagination* (Princeton, 1976), p. 9.

14. Donald Cheney, review of Jonathan Goldberg, *Endlesse Worke*, in SpN, 13, no. 2 (1982), 34–37 (p. 35).

15. Goldberg, *Endlesse Worke*, p. 76, n. 1; Maureen Quilligan, *The Language of Allegory: Defining the Genre* (Ithaca, 1979), pp. 35, 29, 31; Terry Eagleton, *Walter Benjamin or Towards a Revolutionary Criticism* (London, 1981), pp. 10, 22; Michael Murrin, *The Veil of Allegory* (Chicago, 1969), p. 168.

16. Catherine Belsey, *Critical Practice* (London, 1980), pp. 74, 82.

17. Lewis, p. 380.

18. Stephen Greenblatt, *Renaissance Self-Fashioning* (Chicago, 1980), pp. 157–92.

19. Paglia, *Sexual Personae*, p. 189.

20. Goldberg, *Endlesse Worke*, p. 77.

21. Roger Sale, *Reading Spenser: An Introduction to The Faerie Queene* (New York, 1968), p.162.

22. Lewis, p. 349.

23. Simon Shepherd, *Spenser* (1989), p. 119.

24. Lewis, pp. 378–79.

25. Jonathan Goldberg, *James I and the Politics of Literature* (Baltimore, 1983), p. 5.

26. Judith H. Anderson, ' "In Living Colours and Right Hew": The Queen of Spenser's Central Books', in *Poetic Traditions of the English Renaissance*, edited by Maynard Mack and George de Forest Lord (New Haven, 1982), pp. 17–66 (pp. 49–50).

27. Goldberg, *Endlesse Worke*, p. 88; Carol V. Kaske, 'Spenser's Pluralistic Universe: The View from the Mount of Contemplation (FQ.1.x)', in *Contemporary Thought on Edmund Spenser*, edited by Richard C. Frushell and Bernard J. Vondersmith (London, 1975), pp. 121–49; Patricia A. Parker, *Inescapable Romance* (Princeton, 1980), p.14.

28. Marion Campbell, 'Spenser's Mutabilitie Cantos and the End of The Faerie Queene', *Southern Review* (Adelaide), 15 (1982), 46–59 (p. 53).

29. Miller, 'Authority', p. 111; Richard Neuse, in *SpN*, 14, no. 2 (1983), 49.

Chapter 7
The Poetry of Shakespeare and the Early Donne

Shakespeare

In the 1590s and early 1600s it was, in retrospect, the theatre that was able to embody emergent cultural forces more easily than any other literary form, in part because it grew up outside (though it was still subject to the control of) the Court. The Court's preferred theatrical form, the masque, was devised to inculcate the ideology of order and hierarchy, but the plays of the public theatre were embracing the social forces that were gradually challenging the Court's hegemony, such as the centralizing of state power, political corruption, the restriction of ancient liberties, and the subordination of personal values to the State.[1] A frequent attender of the public theatre in the 1590s was a law student, an ex-Catholic, an aspiring courtier, and an increasingly fashionable poet (at least among his friends). He was John Donne – and it is his poetry which, along with Shakespeare's, marks the culmination of sixteenth-century poetry and points beyond it. Their poetry will be the subject of this chapter.

In considering Shakespeare at all, of course, we are face to face with the epitome of the idealization of the Elizabethan age I discussed in Chapter 1. With Shakespeare, we are dealing less with a body of writing than with an institution – or rather a concept mediated through a series of institutions, educational, cultural and political. Shakespeare seems, even in our own time, safe from both his own history and ours, a transcendent figure, somehow a guarantor of the national culture. But like all texts, Shakespeare's poems (and plays) have a history, even if in this case, that history is largely one of successive mystifications into a symbol of whatever high culture, civilization and educational standards are taken to be. Nor is Shakespeare simply a British phenomenon: the success of transatlantic Shakespeare festivals, Shakespeare societies, lecture series, celebrations, not to mention university courses, textbooks and libraries, have turned 'him' into an international guarantor of Western civilization. The approach here to Shakespeare's poems – themselves a marginal part of his activities and therefore in some ways easier to consider with a fresh perspective – will place the life of Shakespeare's texts in their history and ours, asking some of our questions of them as well as consider the questions their original readers might have posed.

Although we consider him the greatest dramatist of our language, we should not forget that Shakespeare also served an apprenticeship in some other literary forms more directly controlled by the Court. Paradoxically, although the theatre was closely regulated and at times censored by court officials, the very nature of public performance provided, in practice if not in law, a relative autonomy alongside the more obviously court-dominated arts of music, lyric poetry, romance fiction and masque. But early in his career, Shakespeare did turn briefly to the fashionable courtly forms of verse romance, probably when the theatres were closed or under severe financial pressure. His short erotic verse narratives, *Venus and Adonis* (*c.*1592) and *The Rape of Lucrece* (1594), are typical examples of a fashionable literary genre, and show his versatility in a poetic mode that was clearly a sideline for him. Other incidental verse he wrote in the 1590s included contributions to the miscellany, *The Passionate Pilgrim* (1599), and *The Phoenix and the Turtle*, a cryptic allegorical poem written for a collection of poems appended to *Love's Martyr* (1601), an allegorical prose treatment of love by Robert Chester. At some time, probably in the last five years of the century, he, too, wrote a collection of sonnets.

For his initial venture into non-dramatic poetry, Shakespeare chose to work in the popular Ovidian verse romance. The presence of Ovid in Elizabethan verse is a particularly pervasive one. *The Metamorphoses* in particular not only provided intriguing and spicy narrative, but also moral insights and a lush melancholy. It also appealed to the Elizabethans' fascination for copiousness. Ovid is also intriguing because rather than asserting an unchanging reality 'behind' the world which words exist to 'express', his writing suggests that change and variety are the primary realities of experience, and that poetry should express that. Where the Middle Ages (and, indeed, some Elizabethans like Sidney's friend William Golding) moralized Ovid, finding sound philosophical truths in the *Metamorphoses*, increasingly he was admired and imitated for less rigid qualities. From the 1590s fashion for Ovidian romance, Marlowe's *Hero and Leander* and Shakespeare's *Venus and Adonis* are the most readable today. *Venus and Adonis* is a narrative poem in six-line stanzas, mixing classical mythology and surprisingly (and often incongruously) detailed descriptions of country life designed to illustrate the story of the seduction of the beautiful youth Adonis by the comically desperate ageing goddess, Venus. Alongside Marlowe's luxuriant, fluid masterpiece, Shakespeare's is rather static, with too much argument and insufficient sensuality to make it pleasurable reading. Its treatment of love relies too heavily upon neoplatonic and Ovidian commonplaces, and (unlike *Hero and Leander*) upon heavy moralizing allegory, with Venus representing the flesh and Adonis something like spiritual longing. Its articulation of the nature of the love that separates them is abstract and often unintentionally comic, although Shakespeare's characterization of Venus as a garrulous plump matron does bring something of his theatrical powers into the poem. *Venus and Adonis* was certainly popular, going through ten editions in as many years, possibly because its early readers thought it fashionably sensual.

The *Rape of Lucrece* is the 'graver labor' which Shakespeare promised to his patron Southampton in the preface to *Venus and Adonis*. Again, he takes up a current poetical fashion, the melancholy verse complaint, and in effect writes a miniature drama in verse, a melodrama celebrating the prototypical example of matronly chastity, the Roman lady Lucrece's suicide after she was raped. The central moral issue – that of honour – at times almost becomes a serious treatment of the psychology of self-revulsion, but the moralistic conventions of the complaint form certainly do not afford the scope of a stage play. There are some fine local atmospheric effects, which in their declamatory power occasionally bring the directness and power of the stage into the verse. But overall it is less impressive than might be expected from Shakespeare. Likewise, *The Phoenix and the Turtle*, an allegorical celebration of an ideal love union, is a rather static piece. It consists of a description of a funeral procession of mourners, a funeral anthem and a final lament. It is dignified, abstract and solemn but never achieves much life.

As this survey shows, Shakespeare's incidental poems clearly grew out of fashions of the 1590s. Like other ambitious writers and intellectuals on the fringe of the Court, he was attempting fashionable kinds of poems, and they are interesting primarily because it was Shakespeare who wrote them. His *Sonnets*, on the other hand, to which detailed attention will be given, constitute perhaps the language's greatest collection of lyrics. They clearly grow from the social, erotic and literary contexts of his age: on the simple level of verbal echoes and borrowing, they are criss-crossed by the ubiquitous language of Petrarchan and neoplatonic praise, the conventional motifs of worship, fear, betrayal, temporality, dedication, sacrifice and disillusion. Most of the conventional topoi of traditional Petrarchan poetry are here – the unity in diversity of lovers (36, 40), the power of poetry to immortalize the beloved (18, 19, 55), contests between eye and heart, beauty and virtue (46, 141), the contrast of shadow and substance (53, 98, 101). As with Petrarch's or Sidney's poems, it would be easy to create a schematic account of love from them. But to do so would be to nullify the extraordinary impact they have had, especially in the past two centuries.

Since the early nineteenth century, probably more critical ingenuity has been exercised on Shakespeare's sonnets than on any other work of our literature, even perhaps including *Hamlet*. In five and a half pages, Booth briefly summarizes facts that, however few, have led (or led away) to a plethora of speculation on such matters as text, authenticity, date, arrangement and biographical implications. The *Sonnets* were published in 1609, although 138 and 144 had appeared in the miscellany *The Passionate Pilgrim* a decade before. Some were composed before 1598 and they are usually dated in the late 1590s. It is conventional to divide them into two groups – 1 to 126, purportedly addressed to or related to a young man, the so-called 'Fair Youth' who is often presented as a patron for whom some sonnets are 'the barren tender of a poet's debt' (83); and 127 to 152, addressed to the so-called 'Dark Lady'. Such a division is arbitrary at best: within each major group there are detachable sub-groups, and without the weight of the conventional arrangement, many sonnets would not seem to have a natural place in either. 1–17 (or perhaps 18) are concerned with a plea for a young man to marry, but even in this, what may seem to be the most unified (and conventional) group, there are disruptive suggestions that challenge such a conventional arrangement. The 1609 order, in Booth's words, feels throughout 'both urgent and wanting', purposeful and yet 'to have just barely failed of its purpose'. Their order has provoked many attempts at reordering, usually to create a story of dedication, rivalry and betrayal among the 'Poet', the 'Rival Poet', the 'Dark Lady', and other 'characters'. Many of the suggested rearrangements construct very ingenious narratives. Booth remarks that the *Sonnets* give us the latitude to arrange and select so that, he concludes, 'all the rearrangers are right', but none represents the 'correct' order. Perhaps (as we saw with attempts to construct narratives from *Astrophil and Stella*), they largely fulfil an understandable anxiety on the part of some readers to see narrative continuity rather than variations and repetition. The story behind them, as Booth puts it, has 'evoked some notoriously creative scholarship': speculation on the identity of the 'Fair Youth', of Mr W. H., to whom the sequence is dedicated by the printer (and who may be the same young man), of the 'Dark Lady', and of the rival poet or poets mentioned in some sonnets. Likewise, there is the question whether Shakespeare had any (for his age) deviant sexual preferences. On this latter subject, Booth majestically concludes, Shakespeare 'was almost certainly homosexual, bisexual or heterosexual. The sonnets provide no evidence on the matter.' His view somewhat overstates the matter; regardless of his own sexual orientation, the *Sonnets* do put into discourse the period's strong fascination with homoeroticism. The classical educators so beloved by humanists helped naturalize emotional interactions that clearly challenged sexual orthodoxies: as Norbrook and Woudhuysen comment, 'reading the classics from the perspective of compulsory heterosexuality was always an act of bowdlerization'. Richard Barnfield and Christopher Marlowe both wrote poems that speak frankly about homosexual passion, and many of the *Sonnets*, 20 in particular, brood compellingly over the intermingling of heterosexual and homosexual attraction.[2] I return to this topic in Chapter 8.

The biographical speculations – which reached their peak in critics and readers wedded to the sentimental Romantic insistence on an intimate tie between literary and historical events – are in one sense a tribute to the power of the *Sonnets*. They illuminate not only Shakespeare's life, but the lives of his readers. In that sense, they are as dramatic as any of his plays. Better than any other lyrics of the age, they illustrate how meanings can be concretized only in the different lives of readers: as we read Shakespeare's sonnets, we may easily find ourselves as we all struggle for self-understanding. Each is like a little script. Each certainly contains (often powerful) directions on reading and enactment, but finally each is built on an awareness that textual meanings are not given but made anew by every new reader within his or her own individual and social life. What Sonnet 87 terms 'misprision' stands for the necessary process by which the sonnet is produced within each reading through its history.

Like most Petrarchan collections, Shakespeare's *Sonnets* see the nature of desire as intimately bound up with the sense of being a 'self'. But rarely are the extremes of erotic revelation offered in such rawness and complexity or with such obsessive anguish over the glorious failure of language to constitute or reassure the vulnerable self. They are a unique imaginative proving-ground where the feelings about love and the language traditionally used to capture them intermingle with and contradict each other. But what may strike contemporary readers, and not merely after an initial acquaintance with them, is the apparently unjustified level of idealization of the beloved. There is a tone of adulation, an idealization of love, that to a post-Freudian world may seem comforting but rather archaic, just too idealistic, too absolute. They seem to lack insights into the contradictions that we take as central to our experience of love – and of which indeed, the Renaissance was certainly not unaware. The early sonnets are saturated in the clichés of Petrarchan and neoplatonic praise; in 105–108, the language verges on the sacramental. While the lover protests that his love cannot be called idolatrous, the beloved is the culmination of centuries of 'antique' praise (106), such that the rest of history is seen as waste. The continual self-effacement of the anguished lover, the worship of the 'god in love, to whom I am confined' (110), the poet's claim to be immortalizing 'his beautie . . . in these black lines' (63), helpless idealizations of absolute commitment – are what we come across in the lyrics of second-rate pop songs or remember from the losses of our first loves at seventeen. Indeed, an interesting exercise is to compile a list of the metaphors of idealization in today's popular songs – not to show how degenerate they are (or the whole modern world has become), but to point up the difficulty of seeing the idealization of the beloved in Shakespeare's lyrics as fresh and untouched by history. Of course, students of sixteenth-century poetry (including readers of this book) will then further point out just how conventional they were even then – we are, they might say, always already in such conventionality.

But today we may respond more easily to the darkness and pain. The most celebrated sonnets of idealism, Like 'Shall I Compare Thee to a Summer's Day?' (18) or 'Let Me Not the Marriage of True Minds' (116) may even seem cloyingly sweet, their texts seemingly rejecting (or is it repressing?) any subtextual challenges to their idealism. 18 is the classic case. It seemingly requires to be read in a solemn murmur, almost as if one were in church. It seems totally serene, as if taking into consideration all possibilities in order to affirm the uniqueness and irreplaceability of the beloved:

> But thy eternal summer shall not fade,
> Nor lose possession of that fair thou ow'st,
> Nor shall death brag thou wand'rest in his shade,
> When in eternal lines to time thou grow'st.

So powerful a part of our literary and erotic heritage are such sentiments that we may feel guilty if we choose to query such confidence and read such sonnets against the grain, trying to make them give us insights into love as we know it today.

Yet part of the greatness of the *Sonnets* is, perhaps, the way they invite and try to absorb such scepticism. As the sonnet had developed since Petrarch, it had become, as we have seen, a potent rhetorical instrument for evoking a reader's or a listener's participation in the making or the concrete particularization of meanings. Shakespeare uses a curiously large number of deliberately generalized epithets, indeterminate signifiers and floating referents which provoke meaning from their readers rather than provide it. Each line contains echoes, suggestions and contradictions which require an extraordinary degree of emotional activity by the reader. The so-called Shakespearian sonnet, with its three quatrains and concluding couplet allows especially for the concentration of a single, usually meditative mood. It is held together less by the apparent logic (for instance, the recurring 'when . . . then' pattern) than by its atmosphere of invitation to the reader to enter into and become part of the dramatization of a brooding, devoted, self-obsessed mind. The focus is on emotional richness rather than logical coherence; on evoking the immediacy of felt rather than rationalized experience. The concluding couplets also frequently offer a reader powerfully indeterminate statements. Even in reading they seem to break down any attempt at limiting meaning, as in the conclusion to 33: 'Yet him for this my love no whit disdaineth;/Suns of the world may stain when heav'n's sun staineth.' The weighty generality of 'him', 'this', 'love', and, especially of 'stain' and 'staineth' attempts to set up an undecidability of meaning, that can only be resolved by particular and changing applications in Shakespeare's readers' own lives. In particular lines, too, these poems achieve amazing power by their lack of logical specificity and their emotional openness. 'So long lives this and this gives life to thee' concludes 18, each word having suggestions that are at once definable and extendable.

As Booth points out, many lines show 'a constructive vagueness' by which a word or phrase is made to do multiple duty – by placing it 'in a context to which it pertains but which it does not quite fit idiomatically' or by using phrases which are both illogical and charged with meaning. He instances 'separable spite' in 36 as a phrase rich with suggestion which can be vitiated by scholarly teasing out of a limited if coherent sense.[3] Another example would be the bewilderingly ordinary yet suggestive epithets in the opening of 64:

> When I have seen by time's hand defaced
> The rich proud cost of outborn buried age,
> When sometime lofty towers I see down razed,
> And brass eternal slave to mortal rage . . .

The greatest of the *sonnets* – 60, 64, 129 and many others – have this extraordinary combination of general, even abstract, words and unspecified emotional power that we may take it as a major rhetorical characteristic of the collection. An intense and concentrated reading can be caught up in a seemingly endless and indeterminate flow as the words bump against one another, setting up multiple and never fully identifiable suggestions of power, determinism and helplessness by the undecidability of their connections. It is extraordinarily difficult, probably impossible, to paraphrase such lines without nullifying their power. Often this process occurs by a syntactical movement which is modified or contradicted by associations set up by words and phrases. Booth argues that such constructions are usually made meaningful 'because of clear intent implied by context, or because of a syntactical momentum that carries a reader into clarity and thereby dispels puzzlement'. Yet when he wants to see the 'capacity to communicate' as the 'most important' effect of a Shakespeare sonnet, he misses the point. Often, the reader is simply forced on, into the void of the insecure and journeying self the poem brings into existence. There is, indeed, usually a syntactical or logical framework in the sonnet but if we read slowly and carefully, so powerful can be the contradictory, random and disruptive effects occurring incidentally as the syntax unfolds that to reduce any sonnet to its seemingly logical framework is to miss its potential effects.[4]

To discuss these poems adequately, we need an adequate vocabulary. Perhaps that is why readers in the late twentieth century are unusually well equipped to understand what Knights pointed out many years ago that one of the most urgent subjects of the *Sonnets* we usually notice today is not the commonplaces of Renaissance thinking about love, nor the powerful concern with the power of art, but rather what Sonnet 16 calls our 'war upon this bloody tyrant Time'.[5] It is no accident that the 'discovery' of the *Sonnets*' concern with time and mutability dates from the 1940s when the impact of Kierkegaard, Nietzsche, Heidegger and Existentialism was starting to be widely felt in Britain and America. It is from such sources that we have gained what now seems to be a 'natural' vocabulary in which to discuss the *Sonnets*. They invite us to see our temporality not merely as an abstract problem but as part of what Heidegger terms our 'thrownness', our sense of being thrown into the world. Such perceptions, it now seems commonplace to say, are there, 'in' the *Sonnets*. It is perhaps the best example in the period of what in Chapter 1 I termed a powerful reading meeting a powerful text. Even so, even with what seems an adequate vocabulary, we are still in the paradoxical situation of finding a language adequate only to point up language's inadequacy. Unpredictability and change are at the heart of the *Sonnets*. But it is a continually shifting heart, one that conceives of human love as definable only in terms of such change, finitude and final silence. The *Sonnets*' anxiety about time shifts under our gaze. Time does not provide a stable centre. The cry of protest the *Sonnets* direct us towards deliberately avoids (except in the strangely detached Sonnet 146 with its apparent medieval Christian emphasis) the transcendentalism of Chaucer's beseeching his young lovers to turn from the world, or Spenser's rejection of change for the reassurance of God's eternity and His providential guidance of time to His own mysterious ends. Like the speculations of Heidegger or Nietzsche, Shakespeare's sonnets overwhelm us with questions and contradictions, with the perplexity of our own contingency. They involve us less in abstract solutions to the problem of time than in the experience of it upon our pulses:

> Like as the waves make towards the pebbled shore,
> So do our minutes hasten to their end,
> Each changing place with that which goes before,
> In sequent toil all forwards do contend.

(60)

In such lines, it is not an abstraction like 'time' but we ourselves who are the problem – decentred, swept along in the very movement of the lines, defined by the change the poem purports to deal with. Time is not thrust at us as an impartial or abstract background. Even where it is glanced at as a pattern observable in nature or man, it is evoked as a disruptive experience which cannot be dealt with as a philosophical problem or by the assertion that our experiences are held together by a vulnerable yet none the less central self. Some sonnets face us with time as a sinister impersonal determinism; others thrust time at us instead as unforeseeable chances and changes, what 115 calls our 'millioned accidents'. We are taken straight into a moment of insight that immediately, and as we read, dislocates us – 'When I consider everything that grows/Holds in perfection but a little moment . . .' (15) – until we are faced with what we fear most, that our most cherished ideals, our most defended integrity, our sense of the presence and irreducibility of our inner selves, are always already disintegrated: 'Ruin hath taught me thus to ruminate,/That time will come and take my love away' (64).

With such awareness, what affirmations (the sonnets ask, over and over) are possible? Whether time is felt as determinism or chance, each reader may find that the very formal characteristics of the sonnet sit uneasily with such insights. How could, we might say, Shakespeare write in this artificial form when he saw, with such clarity, the darkness within? To read Sonnet 15, for instance, tempts us to articulate an understandable protest against time inevitably destroying its own creations (a commonplace enough Renaissance sentiment), and accede, in abstract, to a sense of helplessness before a malignant force greater than the individual. But as we read, the sonnet tries, through its carefully structured argument, to create in us a consciousness that seeks to understand and so control this awareness. It thrusts at us lines, or single words, that uncannily undermine that temporary satisfaction of the sonnet form. Such, for instance, is the force of 15's 'everything that grows/Holds in perfection but a little moment'. If we pause over the words, what is the application of 'everything'? Or the emotional effect of the way the line builds to a seemingly replete climax in 'perfection' and then tumbles into chaos in 'but a little moment'? The sonnet does not and need not answer such questions – and, in a real sense, cannot answer them, for we all, in so far as we are attentive to what the poem opens up in us, can only acknowledge its power in our own contingent lives. It is we who must answer, or run from, them. Similarly, what is shocking is not merely the commonplace that 'never-resting time leads summer on/To hideous winter and confounds him there' (5), but that each reader fights against and so disrupts the logical and aesthetic coherence offered by the sonnet and with it his or her own personal sense of change and betrayal. There is, in short, not merely a thematic concern with time, but the appallingly relentless process of reading ourselves into an awareness of our own fragility. As we read, each of us (like the young man of 16) is being exhorted to realize the difficult truth that 'to give away yourself' paradoxically 'keeps your self still'. What can that mean? Perhaps we apprehend it as a challenge to open ourselves at our points of greatest vulnerability. Yet we may pause over 'still'. Do we gloss it as 'nevertheless', 'continually', 'forever'? To attempt to place the *Sonnets* within our personal histories is, therefore, to an unusual degree to be challenged to expose ourselves to a kind of creative therapy. In this way, the *Sonnets* are the culmination of sixteenth-century poetry's attempt to involve its audience in the making and remaking of the poem. They try to manipulate their readers into areas of vulnerability, and the result is a creation of a shifting, vulnerable self which reads, ponders, and returns to the suggestive futility of the words.

But, like every 'I' in a Petrarchan sequence, the 'I' of Shakespeare's sonnets is a shattered, decentred voice that searches in vain for stability. In these poems, the radical break with the collective 'I' of the medieval lyric and the dominant transcendental ideology has been finally made. Instead, we have a montage of the subject caught up into language, undertaking to speak his or her desire, reaching to relate to another 'I' and finding there is no such thing and that fragmentation is the only universal characteristic of the human condition. The 'I' of the *Sonnets* can be constituted as a stable subject only because it continually experiences itself as changing. The 'I' is aware only of a lack, which has set desire in motion; it articulates this lack by inserting itself in language, which serves only as a further decentring, as it moves along an endless chain of signification, unable to capture the derived plenitude of significance it attributes to the object of desire. As Eagleton comments, 'to speak is to lack: and it's in this lack that the movement of desire is set up, the movement whereby I move restlessly from sign to sign without ever being able to close my fist over some primordial plenitude of sense, a movement which will be satisfied only in death'.[6] The Cartesian ego, fifty years later, would try desperately to pin down some unassailable centre to the experience of 'I'. Shakespeare's sonnets, like Donne's, show the futility of the attempt. The 'I' strives to constitute itself a basis for identity, a coherent source of order and control, and finds itself always already within an endlessly frustrating plethora of differences while producing the illusion of autonomy.

A further example of the way in which vulnerability is both a key thematic obsession and a stratagem of the readers' involvement in the *Sonnets* is the recurring dwelling upon the lover's age. The most pressing concern with the Fair Youth's vulnerability to time is found in the recurring motif of growing old. It starts, usually, as protest or defiance and ends in fear:

> My glass shall not persuade me I am old
> So long as youth and thou are of one date,
> But when in thee time's furrows I behold,
> Then look I death my days should expiate.
>
> (22)

More brutally, the relationship with the Dark Lady is also one where the lover is '. . . vainly thinking that she thinks me young,/Although she knows my days are past the best' (138). In the same poem's question, 'wherefore say not I that I am old?' Why this insistence on old age? The simplistic answer is that the speaker is older. But even if we concede there are biographical origins for many of the sonnets, there is no evidence that Shakespeare was in fact old: if we can make the too-easy equation between poet and speaker, he was probably thirty to thirty-five when he wrote the *Sonnets*. Of course he may have felt old. But put it in the context of a possible biographical situation for a moment: when one falls in love with a much younger woman or man, does one not inevitably feel the insecurity of a generation gap? Grey hair, middle-age spread on the one side; inexperience on the other? Clearly that is something of what is alluded to. But what is insisted upon more strongly is that age or youthfulness are not important in themselves: it is that the insistence itself is important, not the mere fact of age – just as it is the anxiety with which a man or woman watches the wrinkles beneath the eyes that is important, not the wrinkles themselves. The note of insistence is not attached merely to the speaker's age: it stands for some wider psychological revelation, a desire to face (or not face) the vulnerability which we all encounter opening up in ourselves in any relationship that is real and growing, and therefore unpredictable and risky. Such a revelation usually starts with a confident boast:

> To me, fair friend, you never can be old,
> For as you were when first your eye I eyed,
> Such seems your beauty still.

Here the pun on 'I' – a play that occurs throughout – concentrates, as Booth notes, in a 'showy combination of pun (eye, I), polyptoton (eye, eyed) and epizeuxis',[7] focusing our attention on the interrelation of the self and ageing. But then, characteristically, boasting inevitably succumbs to shock:

> Ah yet doth beauty, like a dial hand,
> Steal from his figure, and no pace perceived;
> So your sweet hue, which methinks still doth stand,
> Hath motion, and mine eye may be deceived.
>
> (104)

The delusion that the 'I' stands still is harshly undermined.

And yet without vulnerability and contingency, without the decentred-ness of the 'I' – there can be no growth. Hence the poet invites us ruefully to accept what the fact of his greater age evokes – an openness to ridicule or rejection. The insistence on our being open to the insecurity represented by age hints not merely to a contrast between the speaker and his two lovers but to a radical self-division. This is so especially in the so-called 'Dark Lady' sonnets, where we are invited to witness and participate in some of the most savage self-laceration ever evoked in poetry, particularly in the fearful exhaustion of 129, where vulnerability is evoked not as potential or growth, but as paralysis. At once logically relentless and emotionally centrifugal, 129 has the power, as we read it, to draw our own memories, fears, or vulnerability into its compulsive ejaculations of self-disgust. Nothing is specified: the strategies of the poem work to make a reader recognize his or her own compulsions and revulsions:

> Th'expense of spirit in a waste of shame
> Is lust in action, and till action lust
> Is perjured, murd'rous, bloody, full of blame,
> Savage, extreme, rude, cruel, not to trust . . .

The physical, psychological, and cultural basis of such lines are all too easily recognizable to 'all men'; we are invited to face our most vulnerable experiences which are never quite specified by the poem's words but, as we read, are difficult not to acknowledge. The sonnet does not give us words for the details of the experiences, or incidents, that come to mind as we read them. That may make us aware of our desires to repress them because they are potentially so embarrassing or so destructive.

This strain of insecurity and uncertainty, to which we are asked to contribute repeatedly, is not only found within the explicit lacerations of the Dark Lady sonnets. Even those sonnets celebrating the Fair Youth are frequently undermined by contradictions, weak logic, and helpless self-torturing before the unacceptable. 'That thou are blamed shall not be thy defect' (70), or 'I in your sweet thoughts would be forgot,/If thinking on me then should make you woe' (71), are typical protests of willing self-immolation that echo throughout. The absolute self-denial of love is of course an emphasis familiar in both Christian and courtly Petrarchan codes: 'You are my all the world, and I must strive/To know my shames and praises from your tongue' (112) is merely self-denying and not particularly threatening to us. We may indeed admire such devotion. But do we respond more uneasily, perhaps, to the masochism of 'That god forbid, that made me first your slave,/I should in thought control your times of pleasure' (58) or of 'the injuries that to myself I do,/Doing thee vantage, double vantage me' (88), coupled with the obsession of 113 where whatever is seen, 'sweet favor or deformed'st creature', is shaped to the beloved's taste and feature? Do we find the invitation to participate in such painful self-immolation as growth or maturity? At what point does devotion become self-destructive?

We habitually use words like 'maturity' or 'fulfilment' about love experiences which are mutual, awakening in the partners some authentic and creative springs. Yet even in the seemingly most serene sonnets in the collection that affirm such experiences, there are inevitably dark shadows of insecurity and anxiety. Absence and loss were always the primary subjects of the Petrarchan sonnet, as the lover seeks to recover what he imagines into being precisely as loss and, on the level of the signifier, as the poem strives to materialize an object which always escapes. 116 is perhaps the best-known and loved example of a poem seemingly triumphant over such anxieties. As Booth notes, it is 'the most universally admired of Shakespeare's sonnets'. It is, he asserts, a 'grand, noble, absolute, convincing and moving gesture', a 'single-minded presentation of constancy as the only matter worth considering'. Its argument is that a love which alters with time and circumstances is not a true, but a self-regarding, love, and the heterogeneous effects of the world's impermanence do nothing to diminish or intrude upon such single-mindedness:

> Let me not to the marriage of true minds
> Admit impediments. Love is not love
> Which alters when it alteration finds . . .

Booth's argument is the one to which many, perhaps most, readers would accede: the poem is so strongly yet serenely assertive that, he asserts, no challenges to its power enter a reader's mind – 'the poem's assertions sound as if they took cognizance of all viewpoints on all things related to love and were derived from and informative about every aspect of love'.[8] But what if a reader were to resist the pressure of the poem's syntactical sweep? In what interesting ways might we read it against its own seeming intentions, and thus make it answer our questions, not only its own? Once again consider the way the courtly lyric characteristically invites its reader's participation. Where

Sidney's poems encourage us, tantalize us, even with the pleasure of participation, exhibiting and delighting in the varied experiences of love, Shakespeare's exposure of the decentring of the self is much less comforting. 116 looks as if it is a triumphant rejection of such painful insecurity. Its pressure is enormous, its confidence seemingly replete. Yet, as with a dream, even if the struggles beneath are not revealed, the marks of the erasure of those struggles can be seen. What has been repressed, crowded out of the passageway to consciousness, in the making of 116? What, to use Derrida's metaphor, is there that 'remains in the drawing, covered over in the palimpsest'?[9] The sonnet purports to define true love by negatives; 'Let me not . . .' If we deliberately negate those negatives, what emerges is a shadow beneath the poem's apparently unassailable affirmation of a mature, self-giving, other-directed love. The poem asserts that we should not admit impediments; if we do admit them, if we assert, against what (apparently) the poem wants, and play with the idea that love is indeed love which 'alters when it alteration finds', that love is a never-'fixed' mark and, most especially, that love is indeed 'time's fool', we can connect the poem to the powerful strain of insecurity about the nature of change in human love which echoes throughout the whole age and also strikes an intiguingly modern note.

There are, by contrast, sonnets which, although less assertive, do show a willingness to be vulnerable, to re-evaluate constantly, to swear permanence within, not despite, transience – to be, in the words of St Paul, deceivers yet true. The kind of creative fragility 116, at least in intention, tries to ignore is evoked more positively in the conclusion to 49 when the poet admits his vulnerability: 'To leave poor me thou hast the strength of laws,/Since why to love I can allege no cause.' This is an affirmation of a different order – or rather an acknowledgement that love must not be defined by confidence but by vulnerability. We can affirm the authenticity of the erotic only if the possibility that it is not absolute is also admitted. Love, that is, has no absolute legal, moral or casual claims to make upon us; nor in the final analysis, can love acknowledge the bonds of law or family or State – or if, finally, they are acknowledged, it is because they grow from love itself. Love moves by its own internal dynamic; it is not motivated by a series of external compulsions. Ultimately it asks from the lover the *nolo contendere* of commitment: do with me what you will. A real, that is to say, an altering, bending, never fixed and unpredictable love is always surrounded by, and at times seems to live by, battle, plots, subterfuges, quarrels and irony. And at the root of such experiences is the acknowledgement that any affirmation is made because of, not despite, time and human mortality. As 12 puts it, having surveyed the fearful unpredictability of all life, finally we must realize that it is even 'thy beauty', the beauty of the beloved, that the lover must question. This thought may be 'as a death' (64), a 'fearful meditation' (65). Even the most precious of all human creations will age, wrinkle, fade – and we should extend the list since, subtle Petrarchan that he is, Shakespeare makes us feed in our own fearful meditations – get fat, bald, impotent and die. Just how can one affirm in the face of that degree of reality?

Under the pressure of such questioning, the apparent affirmation of 116 might be seen as a kind of bad faith, a false dread – false, because it freezes us in inactivity when we should, on the contrary, accept our finitude as possibility. The very fragility of beauty, love, poetry, Fair Youth and Dark Lady alike, enhances their desirability: it is just because they are indeed among the wastes of time that they are beautiful; they are desirable not because they are immortal but precisely because they are irrevocably time-bound. One of the most disturbing truths that we know is expressed in arguably the greatest (certainly among the simplest) lines:

> Ruin hath taught me thus to ruminate,
> That time will come and take my love away.
> This thought is as a death, which cannot choose
> But weep to have that which it fears to lose.
>
> (64)

The power of such lines goes far beyond the serenity of 116. At our most courageous, we do not merely affirm love as some of the sonnets try to insist, despite the forces of change and unpredictability which provide the ever-shifting centres of our lives. On the contrary, we discover our greatest strengths not despite, but because of our own contingency. Shakespeare does often dramatize the familiar, and comforting, posture of hyperbolic defiance despite, as in the conclusion to 19: 'Yet do thy worst, old Time: despite thy woes,/My love shall in my verse ever live young'. There is the 'despite'. But elsewhere, we realize that it is rather because there is no fixed centre in love, that it is precisely because of time – because 'your' beauty, wit, virtue or youth are subject to time – that they are so valuable. To accept rather than deny time is to prove that our deepest life ultimately does not recognize stasis but always craves growth, that fulfilment is built not upon the need for finality, 'ever fixed', but the need to exceed our apparent limits, to push forward or die.

So, unlike 116, many of the *Sonnets* depict love not as a serene affirmation of an irreducible core of commitment. Rather they challenge us radically to reorientate our understanding of ourselves even while time passes and continues to change us. We are asked not to dismiss our fears, but to affirm that while, as 29 puts it, 'I all alone beweep my outcast state', I may discover that:

> . . . in these thoughts myself almost despising,
> Haply I think on thee, and then my state,
> Like to the lark at break of day arising
> From sullen earth, sings hymns at heaven's gate.

It is in the midst of contingency, when our meditations are overwhelmed by the betrayals of the past, while 'I sigh the lack of many a thing I sought,/And with old woes new wail my dear time's waste' (30), that love may open up the future as possibility, not as completion – so long as we accept that it is time itself that offers us such possibility, not any attempt to escape from time.

At this point in my construction of what may seem to be an exclusively 'contemporary' reading of the *Sonnets*, a historical comparison is useful to get some additional perspective. The typical Renaissance attitude to time and mutability is one of fear or resignation unless, as in Spenser, the traditional Christian context can be evoked as compensation. But for Shakespeare – Bruno is the only contemporary who comes close to him here – the enormous energies released by the Renaissance are wasted in trying to escape the burden of temporality. The drive to find some stasis is a desire to escape the burden of realizing that there are some transformations which love cannot effect. Ultimately we cannot get inside our lover's soul, even under his or her skin, however much we tear and sieze and penetrate. The drive to possess and so to annihilate is a desire derived from the old Platonic ideal of original oneness, which only Shakespeare and Donne among the sixteenth-century poets seem to have seen as a clear and fearful perversion. It certainly haunts the lover of the Dark Lady sonnets and we are invited to stand and shudder at the poet-lover's neo-Augustinian self-lacerations. In 144 the two loves he has 'of comfort and despair/which like two spirits do suggest me still', are not just a 'man right fair' and a 'woman colour'd ill': they are the contradictory aspects of the lover's self, and the two loves between which we may be paralysed unless we realize that the self is not whole, but multiple and changing.

Throughout this discussion of the *Sonnets*, what has been stressed is that their power rests on the seemingly fragile basis not of Shakespeare's but their readers' shifting and unpredictable experiences. In this they stand not as certain affirmations but, as 60 puts it, 'to times in hope'. They insist that, at their most authentic, our affirmations are often made through pain – pain faced and not vanquished but accepted as the dark visceral element in which we all must live and struggle. Many of the Dark Lady sonnets are grim precisely because the lover can see no way to break through such pain. What they lack, fundamentally is that open-endedness of hope. 124 is particularly suggestive here – perhaps it is one of the key sonnets of the collection precisely because it is so radically undecidable at crucial points. The sonnet categorizes love as 'dear' (costly) not only because it is 'fond' (beloved), but because it is affirmed in the knowledge of the world. Moreover, while it 'fears not policy' it is none the less 'hugely politic'. How do we explain the strange equivocation here? Love must be adaptable, cunning, even deceptive, aware of the untrustworthiness of the world from which it can never be abstracted: 'it nor grows with heat, nor drowns with showers'. Finally the poet affirms with a strong and yet (when we recall 116) ironic twist: 'To this I witness call the fools of Time,/Which die for goodness, we have lived for crime.' As Booth notes, 124 'is the most extreme example of Shakespeare's constructive vagueness'; its key word is 'it' which, 'like all pronouns, is specific, hard, concrete, and yet imprecise and general – able to include anything or nothing'. 'It' occurs five times. Each time it becomes more indeterminate, surrounded by negatives, 'precisely evocative words in apparently communicative syntaxes which come to nothing'. By contrast, 'the word it stands sure, constant, forthright, simple and blank'.[10]

The 'blank'ness to which Booth points has been filled very specifically by many puzzled readers to yield up a reading consistent with the dominant reading of 116. For instance, the key phrase, 'the fools of time', is usually glossed as an example of political or religious time servers. But less anxiously pursued for exact meaning, the phrase suggests rather that we are all fools of time, without more specific reference. When 116 affirms that 'Love's not time's fool' it betrays, it might be argued, a deliberate and fearful repression, an unwillingness to acknowledge that Love is not able to overcome Time as something that can be fulfilled only as it presents opportunity and possibility to us. In 124, we are challenged to become fools – jesters, dancers in attendance to Time, holy fools before the creative challenge of our finitude – and we 'die', are fulfilled sexually, existentially, only if we submit ourselves, 'hugely politic', to the inevitable compromises, violence and disruption which is life. We 'die for goodness' because we have all 'lived for crime'. We are deceivers yet true; the truest acts, like the truest poetry, may be the most feigning.

The sonnet conventionally regarded as the conclusion of the first part of the sequence, the twelve-line 126, provides an interesting gloss here. It is a serene poem, yet it acknowledges that, even if the Fair Youth is indeed Nature's 'minion', even he eventually must be 'rendered'. This realism does not detract from the Youth's beauty or desirability – in fact, it constitutes its power. Because we must 'render' (give back as well as destroy) our deepest experiences and richest language, they are the more valuable to us.

I have looked at Shakespeare's sonnets as part of the – perhaps, indeed, *the* – culmination of the Petrarchan obsession with the vulnerability of the 'I' or 'self' in the discourse of love. And undoubtedly, through their history, the *Sonnets* have been primarily read as documents of erotic desire and unfortunately too often as documentation of the author's love life. But there is always a wider socio-cultural dimension to consider. The *Sonnets'* concern with sexual desire and its language coexists with a concern with other, especially political, desires and contradictions. Shakespeare's presentation of the self of the poems as the socially insecure petitioner searching for an influential patron is obvious enough, but less obvious are the ways in which the public roles of the actors in the drama force greater insecurity upon the 'I' of the poems. As Marotti has argued, even the serene affirmation of 29, with its assertion of love's 'power to compensate wonderfully for social losses and defeats' has a manic quality which 'suggests the degree to which the self-consolation is forced and inadequate'. 'When, in disgrace with fortune and men's eyes/I all alone beweep my outcast state' is succeeded by, as compensation, 'Yet in these thoughts myself almost despising/Haply I think on thee . . .' However desirable it would be, the private world cannot be isolated from the public; both are traversed and constituted by the same languages.[11]

Within the history of the poetry of the sixteenth century, Shakespeare's sonnets occupy a pivotal place. They are both the culmination and the destruction of a long and richly contradictory tradition; they anticipate the intensification and the demise of the lyric in its characteristic form. They draw on the Petrarchan lyric and yet anxiously anticipate the fragile ego of Cartesianism that was to dominate Europe for the next 300 years. They are also an enigma within our cultural history. Whether we try to identify the Fair Youth or the Dark Lady sonnets, whether we attempt to see a 'hidden' order to them all, or even if we wish to see a story of even some kind of biographical origin 'within' them, their greatness rests on their refusal to offer even the possibility of solutions to the problems they make us raise. They disturb, provoke and raise more than merely 'aesthetic' values or questions; read singly or together, they make us face (or hide from) and raise questions about the most fundamental ways we live. Poetry, love, time, death, values – all are put into question. More than most literary works, they raise questions about our whole, not merely our scholarly or literary, lives.

The early Donne

For a century – from the time of Grierson's 1912 edition and Eliot's influential essays in the 1920s – our age has valued Donne over any other sixteenth-century poet except Shakespeare. Why should this be? One answer is that we discovered, at last, that he was a 'better', more lifelike, poet than the others. Literary gossip undoubtedly helped. Donne's reputation as a reformed rake, a handsome roué, who married unwisely but passionately, and ended as Dean of St Paul's, all added to his appeal. His poems also lent themselves to those crucial confining strategies of close formalist reading, the explicationary class or seminar. Donne's poetry was thus at once difficult poetry for a difficult age and yet conquerable within a fifty-minute class period. But there were deep-seated ideological reasons for this modern – more accurately, modernist – revaluation of Donne's poetry. For many twentieth-century liberals his poetry perhaps articulated some of their own aspirations: Donne was born into a persecuted minority, was a bold experimenter, a man who dared to face the emotional consequences of the 'new philosophy', and who explored in his poetry a refreshingly direct sexuality and then gradually found a way of integrating his youthful radicalism into a mature and ordered framework which he accepted with no less energy but a more ordered perspective. A few revisionists criticized the neatness of this narrative, what Empson termed Donne's 'slow capitulation to orthodoxy'.[12] Some recent commentators have written more of Donne's vacillations and contradictions, but the consensus has been that we can observe the emergence of a wiser, chastened Donne, whose writing is no less rich in his sermons than in his lyrics, a man who continued to speak with the voice of the living not only of the disturbing new discoveries of his time but also of the reassuring wisdom of European scholasticism and humanism. Would it were true, so this narrative suggests, of our own time.

To read Donne anew now, at the end of the twentieth century, and set him again in the history of sixteenth-century poetry from his own time to ours is therefore to have to take notice of what our recent history has made of him. It is also to have to examine the other conventional context into which his work is put. Donne has often been seen not as a sixteenth-century poet at all, but as initiating a new school, sometimes termed the 'Metaphysicals' or 'the School of Donne' and vaguely located in the early seventeenth century. 'From Donne to Marvell' is both the title of an influential study of the period and a typical title of a university course. The poems with which this chapter is concerned are necessarily those written before or around the end of the century – mainly the *Satires*, and most of the *Songs and Sonets*.

Thus they are more or less contemporary with Spenser's late work, Shakespeare's sonnets, and Jonson's early plays. The dominant cultural trends of the 1580s and the 1590s – those centred in particular on the Sidneian ideals of the Wilton Circle and on the Court of Elizabeth – were being transformed by a variety of deep-seated changes. It is not surprising that few writers at the end of the century were able to articulate explicitly the direction in which their world was moving. We have often valorized Shakespeare as one who, to an unusual extent, could do so; Donne is often looked to as another. Of all the new poets of the 1590s, Donne presents us with an especially interesting case – not only because his poetry has been used to define the transition to the next century, but because his career articulates so compellingly the peculiar pressures under which poetry came in the later part of our period.

Since the presence of Petrarch is so ubiquitous in sixteenth-century poetry, let us glance briefly at Donne's relations with Petrarchism. Like any poet, Donne had to work against the pressures of his predecessors, and among the voices which speak through his lines, one of the most insistent is probably, naturally enough, Petrarch's. Donne wrestles to rewrite Petrarchan motifs and tropes as emphatically as he can. 'The Blossom' uses the broken, unwanted heart motif, and throughout the poems the tyrannical, sudden nature of love, its violence and surprise, are 'givens' with which the poems struggle. Like the poems of the other English *petrarchisti*, too, Donne's are obsessed with their own failure as language. In the face of the beloved's absence, the Petrarchan poem broods over its own status as discourse, asking questions about the adequacy, even the impossibility, of constructing words for desire. Donne's approach is typically one of bravado: 'I am two fooles, I know,/For loving, and for saying so/In whining Poetry' ('The triple Foole'). The helpless inevitability of bringing 'grief' to 'numbers' is matched only by the impossibility of doing so.[13]

The randomness and unpredictability of love is the note of Petrarchism to which Donne most responded. Overall, and frequently within a single poem or line, his poetry presents such a variety of tones and moods that it is often difficult to pin down any centre of serious commitment that purports to lie behind it. It is unnecessary (though for some people clearly tempting and reassuring) to construct a systematic metaphysic of love out of Donne's poems. Each poem grows out of or evokes a different, often isolated, mood in the vast and contradictory range of human experience. What is impressive about the variety of moods of the poems is Donne's attempt to be faithful to individual moments of experience and to the importance of crucial points of time, each of which overwhelms us with the sudden awareness of limitless significance. This is not merely a repeated and effective trope. Donne's poetry not only brings into play many conflicting voices, but voices that are demonstrably culturally produced. Like the plays he supposedly liked to frequent, his lyrics let us witness intimate scenes of conflict and contradiction. Furthermore, unlike Sidney's or Spenser's, Donne's lyrics are notoriously indifferent to consistency and closure. Vibrant in all the lyrics – expressed in the diverse poses of advocacy, negative argument, positions momentarily held, rhetorical extravagance, or dramatic peripeteia – is a continually decentred subject that tests, and is tested by, the infinite (and often fearful) multiplicity of human experience to which his words try to cling. The opening of 'The Canonization', 'For Godsake hold your tongue and let me love', opens up innumerable contexts in readers' minds – personal and dramatic, erotic, social and intellectual. Not only is there anger, anxiety, over-reaction, as we read that line; there are, as well, the pressures, social as well as personal, that produce their sharp urgency. It is a characteristic summed up by a line in one of Donne's verse letters where he asserts that things 'as they are circumstanced, they be'. Experiences struggle with words not to produce an ideal unity of signifier and signified but only as things are 'circumstanced'. The voices of the poems continually shift, cancelling the seemingly confident conclusions elsewhere in the same poem, and if we look at the *Songs and Sonets* as a whole, there is no pretence at narrative order or consistency. Any meanings which we may confidently take from a particular reading disintegrate as we leap from one poem to the next. It may even be, as Rajan speculates, that Donne 'deliberately randomised the arrangement of his poems in order to challenge the conventional assumption of the reading-process as a linear movement in which a "truth" is progressively explored and consolidated as the reader moves forward'. The fulfilment, even the presence, of love is never possessed and never final. In Donne's own words, mankind 'hath raised up nothing . . . if these things could fill us, yet they could not satisfie us, because they cannot stay with us, or we with them'.[14]

How do we account for this peculiarly dislocative poetic mode? It is like something that Wyatt's or Sidney's poetry acknowledges as disturbance but that must (if possible) be dealt with; it is akin to what Spenser views with anxiety and, finally, renunciation; it is what Shakespeare's *Sonnets* articulate as part of the melancholy and ambiguity of love. Donne characteristically refuses to look for a philosophical absolute beyond the way the self is 'circumstanced'. What we get is his fascination with the problematic nature of the self. Moreover he 'circumstances' that self in a recognizable and appropriate setting for such dislocation. Donne is our earliest, and still one of the best, articulators of the characteristically anxious, overstimulated, dislocated urban sensibility. Everett has depicted him as the typical East Ender, looking anxiously westward to Westminster – the son of a city merchant who aspired to and eventually reached the Court, on the fringes of which he spent most of his youthful adult life.[15] His *Satires* in particular take us directly into the restless confusion of the aspiring intellectuals living in London, and in particular into the peculiarly brittle and artificial self which, in a mixture of longing and antagonism, wishes to locate itself in that world. Donne's satires create an impression of tactile, optic shock, conveying the restless movements that walking through a city involves us in – the shocks, collisions, contradictions.

But Donne brought to his early poetry more than just the culturally created sensibility of the urbanite aspiring to enter the seemingly more secure world of the Court. With a recusant background, he had a special need for tact, caution and loyalty. Carey has presented a view of Donne as a man writing under intense, even paranoid, alienation in the growing religious intolerance of late Elizabethan England. In this view, Donne grows up in apostasy – he feels himself superior to the ordinary Englishman because of his religion, his European education, and his temperament, and his love poems raise questions 'affected by his betrayal of Catholicism and the anxieties it bred'. What Donne does, argues Carey, is to use his love poems as 'a veil for religious perturbation', as a 'private theatre in which unresolvable oppositions could be entertained as they could not in the decisive business of life'. Treachery and betrayal, experiences which must have loomed large to the young recusant Donne, could be removed from the dangerous sphere of religion 'where in real life it belonged', and transferred 'to the relatively innocuous department of sexual ethics'.[16]

But Donne's situation as an alienated intellectual is not to be discussed totally in terms of his religion. His situation was not unique: the families of most Englishmen in the sixteenth century were, at some time, at least nominally Catholic. During the last twenty years of the century there was a growing number of intellectuals without secure or continuous attachment to the centres of the country's political power. They constituted insoluble groups of either Catholic or (increasingly) Puritan intellectuals who became alienated in a period of growing restlessness and could find employment spasmodically or only on the fringes of the Court.[17] Donne is typical of this class of dislocated intellectuals and his career may be read as an attempt to integrate himself into the establishment. His satires all display the witty irreverence and gusto of a typical 1590s Inns of Court man, but they are careful to articulate very clearly a sense of moral dedication to the appropriate public concerns of the ambitious public servant. They take us into the cynicism of that group, especially into its desire to occupy a place within power. Their rhetorical pose is that of surveying the more bizarre or corrupt aspects of society in the light of the traditional sources of humanist wisdom. They stress the evils of ambition, affirm the contemplative life over (without scorning) the active, and above all express allegiance to the traditional ideals of justice, harmony, piety and truth which have seemingly been lost by the 'age of rusty iron' (Satire 5) – except, needless to say, by those like Donne who serve the 'greatest and fairest Empresse', and his employer Egerton.

Donne's *Satires*, then, like Marston's or Hall's, are radical only in their self-conscious choice of a modish rhetoric. Accents are deliberately harsh, lines dislocated, the structure of argument developed by rapid shifts rather than smoothness, details are piled up seemingly at random, and the whole held together, seemingly, only by the indignant voice of the speaker. But the rhetorical fireworks are belied by the cannily, even cynically, conservative values. Only Satire 3 stands slightly aside; it is valuable because it seems to use satiric means to non-satiric ends, and provides a valuable commentary on both the fashion for verse satire and on some of the contradictions of the age upon which Donne was brooding, yet trying to accommodate. The satires are playing a habitual game: they are competitive, aggressive, and rhetorically self-conscious because of fashion; they are episodic in the way that Marston's *Scourge of Villanie* and Guilpin's *Skialetheia* are, crowding together seemingly random and scattered experiences of the city and Court and yet asserting that the satirist knows how he can surmount and control them. Helgerson has described the typical Elizabethan amateur poet of this period as one who sets himself in opposition to literary fashions in order precisely to demonstrate his 'fitness for the sort of service against which he was rebelling', in particular rejecting the 'self-as-poet in order to reveal the dutiful and employable self-as-civil-servant'.[18]

In the *Satires*, then, Donne's poetry brings into play some of the age's most crucial cultural contradictions. They are not merely the product of a personal crisis, even though they are insistently articulated as confusing and wounding the self. The *Satires* record a fascination with being thrown into experience and finding no way of examining its meaning except from within: even when the observer feels cut off from the world of politics, he still wants desperately to be a participant. In Satire 1, we meet two characters, a long-winded philosopher who is 'consorted' with his books and a giddy, unpredictable and ambitious courtier who is at once fascinated and repulsed by the world. The poem gives us the conventional rejection of the Court as corrupt and trivial; but there is as well a clear fascination with it as a place of experience and employment. The Court is the emblem of the world at large; although the traditional humanist commonplaces, by which the self's seeming stability is valorized, reject the Court as corrupt and immoral, the self is in fact defined by it. The Court may be a 'bladder' where the 'puffed nobility' are all 'players' of various seemingly pointless games (4), but we also realize that tedium, impatience, role-playing (including playing that of the apparently uninvolved spectator) are unavoidable if one is to prosper. Satires 4 and 5 grapple with this realization. In one manuscript, 4 is subtitled 'A Satire against the Court'. The poem opens with an ejaculation of relief for surviving an unwanted visit to the Court and is followed by a re-creation, with grim hilarity, of the pressures upon an especially sensitive observer of the fashions, viciousness and unpredictability of the Court, of which 'there be few/Better pictures of vice'. We perceive the Court not merely through commonplace description but through the reactions of the speaker. He tries to set himself apart as a discriminating observer who prefers to be 'at home in wholesome solitariness' rather than among the 'gay painted things' of the Court. And yet, despite the disclaimers, there is a relishing at the sheer detail and outrageousness of the Court's habits. We may sense the gusto with which the observations are rendered as he notes 'who wasts in meat, in clothes, in horse . . . who loves whores, who boyes, and who goats'. The outrageousness undermines the condemnations – after all, Donne's primary audience shared his amused tolerance of the Court as a given, even while they sensed its moral offensiveness. So they would not simply condemn it for its apparent indifference to traditional values. While they would be aware of the Court as immoral – why, we are asked in Satire 4, with mock naïvety, is the 'great chamber' hung 'with the seaven deadly sinnes?' – they recognize that in its variety, colour and stimulation, it is both autonomous and inescapable, indifferent to any effective moral categories they might attempt to impose upon it yet (no little matter) alluringly attractive. So it is with the narrator. Whatever peace is restored by his leaving it, something fascinating has gone out of his life. He can moralize over what he sees, but morality seems irrelevant to the way the world is 'circumstanc'd'. The Court is a play, the would-be courtier an actor. The picture of the Court at the poem's end is not morally indignant, but conveys the superiority of the witty and sophisticated courtier enjoying himself and looking to an audience with similar responses.

Satire 5 starts with a similarly dislocative *jeu d'ésprit* – it may be possible to have rules to 'make good Courtiers, but who Courtiers good?' It seems to be addressed indirectly to the Queen, 'greatest and fairest Empresse', and to Donne's employer, Sir Thomas Egerton – 'You Sir, whose righteousness she loves, whom I/By having leave to serve, am most richly/For service paid . . .' The basis of its observations is, however, the contingent practicality of administration rather than humanist moral principles. Here is a further decentring. Donne's employer, Egerton, was a member of Elizabeth's civil service. He had by hard work and graft become Lord Keeper of the Great Seal in 1596, and was later Lord Chamberlain under James I. Like him, Donne was a Lincoln's Inn man and when in 1597 he became Egerton's secretary, his security seemed assured. In 1599, he was a sword-bearer at the funeral of one of Egerton's sons, and by 1601, under Egerton's patronage, had become Member of Parliament for Brackley. The tone of Satire 5 is therefore not that of the angry outsider but rather of a talented junior associate of a high cabinet official, a man who had access to the details of Elizabethan policy and who thought with seriousness and practicality about its principles and application.

Donne's letters written about this time (c. 1599–1600) show him, in fact, to be on the edge of the Essex Circle: he had participated in Essex's attack on Cadiz in 1596 and may well have admired the flamboyance of the Earl, another brilliant young man challenging the dominance of a staid establishment. After the fall of Essex in 1601, Donne wrote the bitter and cryptic poetic fragment, 'The Progress of the Soule', which seems to reflect on the fall of Essex and his own change in fortune. But in 1599 or 1600, the probable date of Satire 5, Donne's disappointments lay in the future. The poem is, therefore, written with the restrained vehemence of a concerned insider, and both its rhetorical fireworks and its moral platitudes are subordinate to practical policy. Bald comments that Donne's writings at this time are 'so full of contempt for the ways of the Court and of a sense of the depravity of the age that one is inclined to wonder how Donne could have been satisfied with the way of life he had chosen'.[19] But the moral stance of the satire is very much attuned to the Court's dominance. Donne's closest friends of the time were men of similar ambitions and they provided him with the primary audience for his satires and verse letters: Christopher Brooke, Rowland Woodward, Henry Wotton and Thomas Goodyere were all lawyers, courtiers, diplomats or clergymen, perhaps without Donne's flamboyance or poetical talents, but certainly sharing similar ambitions. They had read their Castiglione and their Machiavelli as well as their Livy and Cicero. They were members of the ambitious, cynical, post-Sidneian generation, determined to make their way in a competitive and at times ugly world. Their favourite art forms were the public theatres, Ovidian verse and this new satiric poetry. They were politically or socially radical only to the extent of, perhaps, looking to a charismatic figure like Essex to provide a sense of excitement in a time that seemed to be, at its gloomiest, what Donne called an 'age of rusty iron', but one in which they were determined to be successful.

Donne's satires, then, grow from a distinctive class and cultural atmosphere. In their aggressiveness, too, they are often blatantly masculinist, written for and addressed to self-consciously fashionable and ambitious young men. There is, argues Puttenham, 'another kind of Poet, who intended to taxe the common abuses and vice of the people in rough and bitter speaches, and their invectives were called Satyres, and them selves Satyricques.' Associating 'satire' with base, rough reprovers, the 'gods of the woods, whom they called Satyres', accounts for the peculiar etymology of the term and led the English satirists of the 1590s to adopt a rough and aggressive manner. Sidney suggests a milder alternative, that the satirist's attacks 'sportingly' are directed 'at folly, and . . . to laugh at himselfe'.[20] But the fashion for epigram and satire in the last decade of the century is peculiar for its virulence, its focus on social scandal and moral corruption: Davies, Guilpin, Hall, Marston, Wither, Rowlands all work variations on the equivalence of 'satire' and 'satyre'. Of the three major satirists, Hall's are more literary exercises – six books, divided into 'Toothlesse Satyrs' and 'byting Satyres', including many literary references and pastiche and some vicious pen-portraits. Marston's are more obscure, violent, sexually obsessed and pessimistic. Donne's stand aside but for their intensity of dramatization and the underlying fragility and waywardness of the self in a powerful public world.

Satire 3 is the exception. John Carey terms it 'the great, crucial poem of Donne's early manhood',[21] and sees its contradictions and insecurities pointing back to his religious anxieties as he moved away from Catholicism. The anxiety of Donne's need to seek 'true religion' is clear; but so too is a helplessness before ambition and worldly success. 'Wee are not sent into this world to Suffer but to Doe', he writes, and the first decade of his life in London exemplifies a brilliant attempt to insert himself into public life. As with Shakespeare's sonnets, the 'self' of Donne's satire is, then, a brittle one. Personal value follows from social value, 'an aspect', as Aers and Kress put it, 'of market transactions';[22] it includes an awareness that to be outside the public world is not to 'be' at all.

By the turn of the century, then, Donne was a member of parliament and private secretary to Egerton, a rising young man confidently waiting on the fringes of the Court, his satirical poetry and verse letters those of a fashionably cynical young man on the make. By 1602, he was in prison, married but out of a job, his career at Court in ruins. Much has been written of the social disaster and private fulfilment of his marriage. Reading Donne's first letters to his new, somewhat reluctant father-in-law, we might be struck not only by the appropriately desperate sincerity of his professions of love, but by his superficially confident insistence that his private affairs should not affect his public career. He insists on the reciprocity of love – 'we adventured equally' – and on the public priority and social decorum of his actions, assuring Sir George More that he deliberately avoided involving 'any such person who . . . might violate any trust or duty' towards him. But that was not the way More saw the matter; nor did Egerton who dismissed him. From prison and after, Donne petitioned Egerton for reinstatement, but he was not reinstated. Egerton remained firm: it was 'inconsistent with his place and credit to discharge and re-admit servants at the request of passionate petitioners'.[23] A young man, however promising, was obviously expendable.

So far I have hardly mentioned Donne's most celebrated poetry. How can we set the *Songs and Sonets* in this context? Modern commentators on the poems have tended to concentrate on seemingly literary considerations: their relation to Elizabethan rhetoric, Petrarchism, their striking conceits and dramatic voice, or Donne's biography. Yet even on a cursory reading they are not simply love poems. His women are even more shadowy figures than those of most Petrarchan poets; even more than *Astrophil and Stella*, they tease us with their dislocated 'I'. Their status as *rime sparse* is extreme. We can, of course, radically simplify them into an almost infinitely adaptable handbook of seduction, compliment, frustration and anger, but the interest of these poems is not their focus on the psychology or physiology of love, but on the fragmentation of the speaking self.

Most of Donne's lyrics simulate the dramatic voice. They ask to be read with the immediacy of a stage performance, with the urgency and authority of the speaking voice and a sense of a multiplicity of an audience which is required to validate and assess their demands. Readers are invariably asked to imagine a pre-existent situation that the speaking voice is attempting to control. The poems are willing to abuse logic, shift ground, make magniloquent or devious gestures, reply to unspoken objections, and even end by denying the premises of the original situation. The reader's stated role is usually that of witness and admirer. The 'I' of the *Songs and Sonets*, seems even more wildly dislocated than most Petrarchan poetry. There is no pretence even at continuity or sequence. The site of meaning is wherever the 'I' is thrown; the drama of the poem is the gestures and struggles whereby the 'I' tries to carve out an area of significance in situations that insist on continuous decentring. In an age where, as we have seen, the self is simultaneously reified and dispersed, Donne's poems, probably better than any others in the century, exemplify the decentring process. Thirty years later Descartes would attempt to hypostasize the stable ego, and for two centuries the individual or 'mankind' would be the stable object upon which the human sciences would be built up. Donne's poems register the enormous insecurity that underlies that reification.

Two contradictory obsessions with temporality haunt those poems. One is a preoccupation with the residual philosophical concern with stasis, moments of permanent significance, within time. Harding has argued that Donne indulges in 'fantasies of permanence', attempts to escape the pressures of mutability on human life by anticipation or artificial prolongation of an event.[24] We might question whether 'fantasy' is too dismissive for the kind of imaginative elaboration of the experienced moment Donne seeks to evoke in a poem like 'The good-morrow'. Unlike the wish-fulfilment poems of the Cavaliers, there is little *carpe diem* melancholy in Donne: the awareness of time and death may be important in, say, 'The Anniversarie', but there is no hint of a melancholy seizing of fleeting joys; only the joyous affirmation of the moment that fulfils time while time's passing is admitted and faced. For a man so imbued with religious and philosophical traditions which affirmed man as an irreducible self created by an eternal God, it is fascinating to note how many of the *Songs and Sonets* acknowledge that time and mutability are categories bound up with man's deepest nature. The lover of 'A Feaver' asserts that he 'had rather owner bee/Of thee one houre, then all else ever'. The strength of such a claim is found not in the irreducible selves of the individual lovers themselves, but in their explored and growing relationships. 'Aire and Angels' is particularly powerful for the way it rejects the error of anchoring the reality of love in anything but the indefinable, changing, love of a relationship. 'The Anniversarie' similarly depicts a mutual love that is at once limited and yet fulfilled by time's power. Indeed, it is precisely because of time's passing that love exists and grows. The real fears that transitoriness, loss, and death can bring are faced clearly and then calmly set aside. There is no sense of escapism in the poem's conclusion:

> Let us love nobly, and live, and adde againe
> Yeares and yeares unto yeares, till we attaine
> To write threescore: this is the second of our raigne.

As with Shakespeare's sonnets, often it seems that it is only because of time's passing that love can exist and grow. The lovers' seemingly self-sufficient world can be complete only by accepting the need to move beyond it. Just as 'Love must not be, but take a body too', ('Aire and Angels') so love's growth can occur only through time. 'Love's growth' suggests that the fullest experience of life involves the acceptance of change: 'Me thinkes I lyed all winter, when I swore,/My love was infinite, if spring make'it more'. Love is 'elemented' and must 'endure/Vicissitude, and season, as the grasse'. Each poem articulates both different and incomplete stances. Read either collectively or at random, Donne's *Songs and Sonets* are the most powerful articulation of dislocation and self-contradiction in the period. In Rajan's words, the poems 'mutually qualify each other within a larger structure which cannot be grasped in its entirety from the standpoint of any one poem'.[25]

Gardner has argued persuasively that we can identify a group of the lyrics written around the turn of the century, including 'The Canonization', all of which are centred on an opposition between the values of love and the values of the Court. These are crucial poems for our understanding of Donne, especially for the way they articulate a conflict that was not a purely personal one, but one rooted in his whole age. The Court was for Donne both a place of fascination and a set of demands upon him which both excited and drew him into activity. In 'The Canonization', however it is reviled, the power of the Court is never questioned. What is at issue is how, while acknowledging its overwhelming pressure, the individual can affirm a commitment to experiences and values which the Court denies. What place does love occupy in its economy? What place does language? Gardner describes 'The Canonization' as *contemptus mundi* poetry,[26] but this is too crude; the opposition between the Court and love seems total, but neither is unambiguously affirmed or abandoned. With its marvellous combination of anger, petulance, flippancy and solemnity, the poem dramatizes an attempt to assert private commitments which are contradicted by public demands that seem unavoidable. The initial outburst of anger sets up an absolute opposition between the ambitious, responsible courtier and the indignant lover, but the anger is all the stronger because of the overwhelming commonsense of the unspoken argument. We might want to read the outspoken lover and the sensible courtier alike as two manifestations of the same dislocated self angrily torn by the contradictory claims of incompatible sets of values. The power of the poem's defiance, its urgent search for justification, and its triumphant or irresponsible abandonment of the glories of the public world – war, glory, fame, chronicle – for the more fragile fulfilment of love, are dependent upon the acknowledgement that the argument can be defeated only by being ignored. Even where the Court is most vehemently rejected and triumphantly transcended, its power and demands are irresistible. In other poems of the same group (if we accept Gardner's linking of them) it is noticeable that even when the logic of the poem demands otherwise, the integrity and importance of love are acknowledged to be always under pressure from the Court and its values. Even when the autonomy of the lovers' world is asserted, in 'The good-morrow', for instance, their love's maturity is likened not to pastoral innocence but to the sophistication of the Court or city: 'I wonder by my troth, what Thou, and I/Did, till we lov'd? were we not wean'd till then?/But suck'd on countrey pleasures, childishly?' Like the Court itself, love is distinguished by refinement and complexity, not by innocence. Even a poem like 'The Sun Rising', which asserts so confidently the autonomy of love's fulfilment, does so only by acknowledging and trying to match the power of the Court from which it asserts its independence. It expresses a view of the lovers as distinctive from the claims of the public world, 'the rage of time', and yet describable only in the terms of the world they reject. Some of Donne's poems may attempt to reject the world, to assert as in 'The good-morrow', that 'each hath one, and is one', but the self that the poems try to create is called into being by that alien world. 'The Sunne Rising' tries to situate its lovers in an intense, fixed moment, but its very power is based on its context. By denial we are made aware of what it tries to exclude. 'I wonder by my troth, what thou, and I/Did, till we lov'd . . .' has its corollary: and what will we do after? What do we do this afternoon? Tomorrow? The very intensity of the setting – the bedroom and bed – is a performative site which draws in as an unwanted but inevitable pressure the world outside, and with it the darkness that frantic activity has (momentarily) kept out.

If we turn outside the *Songs and Sonets* to Donne's other writings at the time, especially his letters, in both prose and verse, we can see something of the fascination and, in more private moments, of bitter frustration at his lack of activity in the wider world from which he had been excluded. Many of his letters express what was clearly anguished frustration at his inactivity in the decade following his marriage. He was forced to exist, in relative penury, on the edge of the Court, in what, like Ralegh and Greville, he experienced as exile. He confessed to Goodyere that he still retained 'the same desires' as 'when I went with the tyde, and enjoyed fairer hopes than now', and in a verse letter to Wotton, he similarly bewailed the 'tediousness of my life'. Continually, his correspondence begs for news of the Court. He complains to John Harington of being 'far removed from court and knowledge of foreign passages' and of his 'emptiness'. While his letters show that he can wittily caricature the court, nevertheless he yearns relentlessly to be in it.[27]

It is interesting to contrast two of his verse letters to Wotton, one written before his marriage (probably about 1598), the other after (in 1604). The first is witty, familiar, rejecting the temptations of 'Countries, Courts, Towns' with the assurance of one totally at ease in all three. Donne can afford to depict himself as 'Parch'd in the Court' and of the Court as a 'Theatre' just because of his own total security within its roles and acts. The tone is of a young man generalizing suavely about the world with the easy dismissiveness of one for whom everything, seemingly, lies open. The later letter has an entirely different tone. It is entitled 'To Sir H[enry] W[otton], at his going Ambassador to Venice', and contains lines which are immensely revealing of Donne's exile from court life:

> 'Tis therefore well your spirits now are plac'd
>   In their last Furnace, in activity;
> Which fits them (Schooles and Courts and Warres o'rpast)
>   To touch and test in any best degree.

'Activity' is the crucial term here: the self must be tested, not merely find its own self-satisfaction. Love, of course, may be an activity – it may 'sometime contemplate, sometime do' – but exiled from the dangerous, artificial, but always alluring Court, Donne seems to have lost his most exciting challenge to discover meaning in life's (and love's) variety. The result is a restlessness which is expressed as a calling into question of his whole self:

> For mee, (if there be such a thing as I)
>   Fortune (if there be such a thing as shee)
> Spies that I beare so well her tyranny,
>   That she thinks nothing else so fit for mee.

'Fortune' here is not a general malevolent force; it is the felt absence of the 'chances and changes' of life that still made the Court so alluring for Donne. It has been replaced by a paralysing inactivity which he interprets as 'tyranny'. It is interesting that Donne was so clearly incapable of taking his own advice to Wotton, to 'be then thine own home, and in thyself dwell'. Such noble neo-Stoicism was all very well when one is actually in the world; in exile, what struck home was his restlessness and insecurity. Another later letter, to Goodyere, reinforces this point. In 1608, he wrote:

> Every Tuesday I make account that I turn a great hour-glass, and consider that a week's life is run out since I writ. But if I ask myself what I have done in the last watch, or would do in the next, I can say nothing; if I say that I have passed it without hurting any, so may the spider in my window . . . I would fain do something, but that I cannot tell what is no wonder . . .to be no part of anybody is to be nothing. . . . At most, the greatest persons are but great warts and excrescences; men of wit and delight conversation but as moles for ornament, except they be so incorporated into the body of the world that they contribute something to the sustenation of the whole.[28]

The world of activity, of great persons, wit and public service – the world in which Donne could see Wotton acting – is for him the ultimate 'furnace', where he could be fired and purified. That is how life is 'circumstanced'.

To continue this account would be to take us well beyond the confines of the sixteenth century. There seems little to challenge Empson's judgement that the first decade of the new age shows, for Donne, a 'slow capitulation to orthodoxy' – except to say that 'orthodoxy' had always been the centre of Donne's world. In 1614 he took orders in the Church of England, and his ordination gave him, however unexpectedly, what his struggle in the 1590s had aimed at: a place in the Court which he had first, confidently, then despairingly and at times even tastelessly sought. He willingly became one of the clergy who were increasingly crucial to the Stuart regime as the Civil War came closer, and who were responsible for articulating government policy to the faithful, just as the homilies had been promulgated by the clergy of Elizabeth's reign. Despite our century's romanticizing of him Donne was a court poet, whose self and texts alike speak of the vast power of the institutions he inhabited and which (in a real sense) inhabited him.

Notes

1. See Alvin Kernan, 'The Plays and the Playwrights', in *The Revels History of Drama in English*, edited by J. Leeds Barroll *et al.* (London, 1975), pp. 251–94; Robert P. Adams, 'Transformation in the Late Elizabethan Tragic Sense of Life: New Critical Approaches', *MLQ*, 35 (1974), 352–63 (p. 356).

2. *Shakespeare's Sonnets*, edited by Stephen Booth (New Haven, 1978), p. 545, 546–8; Stephen Booth, *An Essay on Shakespeare's Sonnets* (New Haven, 1969), p. 116; Norbrook and Woudhuysen, *Renaissance Verse*, pp. 41–2.

3. Booth (ed.), p. 366.

4. Booth (ed.), p. 367.

5. L. C. Knights, *Explorations* (Harmondsworth, 1946).

6. Terry Eagleton, 'Marx, Freud and Morality', *New Blackfriars*, 58 (January 1977), 22–29 (p. 27).

7. Booth (ed.), p. 333.

8. Booth (ed.), pp. 387–89.

9. Jacques Derrida, 'White Mythology: Metaphor in the Text of Philosophy', *NLH*, 6 (1976), 5–74 (p. II).

10. Booth (ed.), p. 419.

11. Arthur F. Marotti, ' "Love is not Love": Elizabethan Sonnet Sequences and the Social Order', *ELH*, 49 (1982), 396–428 (p. 411).

12. William Empson, 'Donne in the New Edition', *CQ*, 8 (1966), 255–80 (p. 274).

13. Quotations from Donne's poems are taken from *The Poems of John Donne*, edited by H. J. C. Grierson, 2 vols. (London, 1912).

14. Tilottama Rajan, ' "Nothing Sooner Broke": Donne's Songs and Sonnets as Self-Consuming Artifact', *ELH*, 49 (1982), 805–28 (pp. 822, 823).

15. Barbara Everett, *Donne as a London Poet* (London 1972), p. 13.

16. John Carey, *John Donne: Life, Mind and Art* (London, 1981), pp. 37–8, 46.

17. David Aers and Gunther Kress, ' "Darke Texts Need Notes": Versions of Self in Donne's Verse Epistles', *Literature and History*, no. 8 (Autumn 1978), 138–58 (p. 147); Michael Walzer, *The Revolution of the Saints* (New York, 1965).

18. Richard Helgerson, 'The Elizabethan Laureate: Self-Preservation and the Literary System', *ELH*, 46 (1979),193–200 (p. 200).

19. R. C. Bald, *John Donne: A Life* (London, 1970), p. 122.

20. George Puttenham, *The Arte of English Poesie*, edited by Gladys Doidge Willcock and Alice Walker (Cambridge, 1936), p. 26; Sir Philip Sidney, *A Defence of Poetry*, in *Miscellaneous Prose of Sir Philip Sidney*, edited by Katherine Duncan-Jones and Jan van Dorsten (Oxford, 1973), p. 95.

21. Carey, p. 26.

22. Aers and Kress, p. 138.

23. Life and *Letters of John Donne*, edited by Edmund Gosse (Gloucester, Mass., 1959), II, 113.

24. D. W. Harding, *Experience into Words* (London, 1963), pp. 11–13.

25. Rajan, p. 822.

26. *The Elegies and the Songs and Sonnets*, edited by Helen Gardner (Oxford, 1965), pp. lviii–lx.

27. *Life and Letters*, 1, 168.

28. *Life and Letters*, 1, 190.

Chapter 8

Gendering the Muse: Women's Poetry, Gay Voices

'By a woman writt'

Most sixteenth-century poetry was written by, and for, men. Much of it was about women. Yet women were not expected to initiate discussion of this fact. The courtesy writer Robert Cleaver voiced his culture's subjection of women's language: 'as the echo answereth but one word for many, which are spoken to her; so a woman's answer should be in a word'.[1] The ideal woman was one who exemplifies what Donne expressed in 'A Valediction Forbidding Mourning,' giving enthusiastic, unselfconscious voice to a great sexist commonplace: 'Thy firmness makes my Circle just/And makes me end where I begun'. There are relatively few women poets from our period, and those whose writings have come down to us are fixed in such still centres: like Astrophil's Stella, they exist, largely silent, within discourses they did not invent and could not control. When permitted to write, they were largely confined to religious writing or translation, and acknowledged their boldness in the unusual intensity with which they use the traditional humility *topoi* to apologize for entering a male domain. For those who did, a condition of their permission to write was often the acceptance of constraints which denied them authentic speech. Repression, that is to say, is not only located within social systems, but very specifically in language, which, in the early modern period, provided women poets only gaps, silences, the role of the other, within male discourse. 'The relations of power are perhaps among the most hidden things in the social body', writes Foucault, and it is in language, or more revealingly, the gaps and silences in language, that the operations of power can be seen most clearly.[2] What books (and not just poetry) that were written by sixteenth-century women are full of a revealing contradiction – on the one hand, many contain apologies for intervening in an activity forbidden to or at least unsuitable for women; on the other, they often express satisfaction that women were making their marks in an activity supposedly more natural to men.

It is still conventional to speak of the Renaissance (which includes the sixteenth century) as a period of expansion, discovery and progress in which 'the full, whole nature of man' came to triumphant fruition. Such a view of the period has been attacked from too many sides to be of much use, but (like the myth of the 'golden age' of Elizabeth or the 'discovery' of North America by Columbus) it remains a powerful residual myth in our time. Years ago, Joan Kelly-Gadol queried whether this model of Renaissance history we have inherited from Burckhardt actually fits women's (as opposed to men's) history, arguing that there was certainly no renaissance for women at the time.[3] Yet in the sixteenth century, and (since strict chronological divisions are always artificial) if we look a little beyond, we can see vigorous signs of women starting to move, as both readers and writers of poetry, out of Donne's still centre. Indeed, if we extend the scope of the sixteenth century just by a decade or so, we discover three or four women who wrote sufficient poetry to have constituted careers as poets no less than a Philip or Robert Sidney; and there were many who, like their male counterparts, wrote occasional poems. If we look further forward into the seventeenth century, there were many women poets, even if they have rarely been acknowledged in standard histories of the poetry of that period: there were, as a substantial modern anthology of women's poetry of the seventeenth century, running to almost 500 pages, puts it, many 'guerrilleras, untrained, ill-equipped, isolated, and vulnerable . . . who tried to storm the citadel of "sacred poetry" '.[4]

Without anticipating such later developments, between the beginning of our period and 1621, the date of publication (though they were in part written earlier) of two substantial collections of poems by women, the poetry written by women that has survived includes occasional verse by the Protestants Anne Askew and Anne Dowriche, the learned daughters of a number of members of the aristocracy, including Anne, Margaret and Jane Seymour, whose father was Lord Protector under Edward VI, the Cooke Sisters (including Lady Elizabeth Hoby, the wife of the translator of Castiglione's *Il Cortegiano*), Queen Elizabeth I, the Scottish aristocrat Elizabeth Melville, and a number of anonymous women poets, including at least one unidentified member of the Sidney family. Of the women who not only wrote but published substantial amounts of poetry, Isabella Whitney was the author of *The copy of a letter, lately written in meeter by a yonge Gentilwoman: to her unconstant Lover* (1567), and *A sweet nosegay* (1573), both heavily didactic, the former advocating women's chastity and constancy, the latter a three-part collection of moral advice. Aemilia Lanyer, a court lady who has been claimed, on highly dubious grounds, to be Shakespeare's 'Dark Lady', published a collection of religious, dedicatory and topographical verse, *Salve Deus Rex Judaeorum*, in 1611. In 1621, Rachel Speght's *Mortalities*

Memorandum was published; it is a religious allegory of a quest for true knowledge, culminating in an affirmation of the resurrection and personal immortality.[5] The two most important women poets of the period are, not surprisingly, members of the Sidney family. I have already glanced at Sidney's sister as a poet, while the period's most important woman poet, and the most significant woman writer in English before Aphra Behn (who may have been her granddaughter) was the Countess of Pembroke's niece, Mary Sidney Wroth (1586?-1653?).[6] In this chapter, I will review those aspects of the Countess of Pembroke's poetical career not discussed in Chapter 5, and then provide a more substantial discussion of the 'other' Mary Sidney, Lady Mary Wroth, the subject of much recent comment. Finally, I glance at some more disturbing, 'deviant' voices.

Mary Sidney, Countess of Pembroke

As I noted in Chapter 5, one reason for the relative neglect, until recently, of Mary Sidney was simply that she was Philip Sidney's sister. She was a distinguished patron, a fine poet, but above all, in her own eyes, she was a Sidney. She devoted most of her adult life to forwarding her brother's cultural ideals and after his death, his hopes for the advancement of poetry. There are four categories of the Countess's writings: three original poems directly associated with her brother, an elegy and two poems dedicating the completed versification of her Psalms to the Queen and the memory of Philip; the Psalms themselves; three translations from French and Italian, including the magnificent version of Petrarch's poem *Trionfo della Morte* in English *terza rima*; and a small handful of other poems. I have commented on the poems related to Philip; the *Triumph of Death* deserves more attention here.

Translating a (male-authored) original was assumed to be more appropriate for a woman than original composition, and Petrarch's original has been termed 'the most triumphant poem of the early Renaissance'.[7] For more than a century the reputation of the work outshone both that of the *Divine Comedy* and Petrarch's own lyrics, and in the mid sixteenth century, it was so popular that Ascham bewailed that Englishmen revered the poem above *Genesis*. The separate poems that make up the work were written during Petrarch's period of exile in the 1340s and 1350, and were first published in 1470. Building upon the precedents of Dante's *Purgatorio*, XXIX (the meeting with Beatrice) and Boccaccio's *Amora Visione*, Petrarch's work is a series of dream visions portraying the successive triumphs of Love, Chastity, Death,

Fame, Time and Eternity. It is a solemn, learned, and at times moving work especially in the *Trionfo della Morte* itself. In particular, there is a deeply poignant evocation of Laura who at last admits her long and faithful love for her poet. The combination of high romantic love and the *ubi sunt* theme probably appealed strongly to the Countess. It reflects, one might speculate, her own deeply idealized love for her brother, the impossibility of consummation, and the realization that his poetic inspiration for her is the only real and lasting fruit of her love.[8]

Earlier translations (by Thomas Morley and William Fowler) are clumsy and wordy; Mary Sidney's is undoubtedly the finest rendition into English of any part of the work before Ernest Hatch Wilkin's modern version. The most outstanding technical feature is the Countess's reproduction of Petrarch's original stanzaic pattern: his poem is written in *terza rima*, where the middle line of one stanza rhymes with the outer lines of the next tercet – aba, bcb, cdc, etc. In the Countess's version, each of Petrarch's terzine is, almost without exception, rendered by an equivalent in English, yet as Rees remarks, 'in spite of this close adherence to her originals she succeeds in maintaining that fluency and naturalness which verse translations often lack'.[9] It is a remarkable performance. She shows constant ingenuity in changing the original eleven-syllable line into English iambic decasyllables and her determined practice to adhere closely to the original is remarkably successful, demonstrating that she had both an acute ear for the movement and tone of both the English poetical line and that of her original, and a consistent grasp of the high emotional level required. Her version is also remarkably succinct and there are few errors of translation. At the poem's great moments of idealized passion and elevated suffering, the Countess's version is especially impressive. The opening, with its delicate vowels and stately movement, is typical of her reading of the poem as a courtly pageant, an allegory of passion confronting death:

> That gallant Ladie, gloriouslie bright,
> The statelie piller once of worthinesse,
> And now a little dust, a naked spright:
>
> Turn'd from hir warres a joyefull Conqueresse.
> Hir warres, where she had foyl'd the mightie foe,
> whose wylie stratagems the world distresse,
>
> And foyl'd him, not with sword, with speare or bowe,
> But with chaste heart, faire visage, upright thought,
> wise speache, which did with honor linked goe.[10]

(I, 1–9)

The grim description of Death, 'stealing on with unexpected wound', the praise of Laura, her voice 'repleate with Angell-lyke delight' (I, 44, 150), and the formal sombreness of the poem's conclusion all stand out as superbly evoked in image and tone, the more remarkable because of the tightness of form. Where the Countess does expand images or phrases, she consistently makes her original more concrete. 'In Petrarch's original', it has been suggested, in perhaps something of an overstatement, 'despite its eloquence and nobility, one feels at times that the language is a little vague, a little stylised. The poetic tool seems to have become a shade worn and blunted. Lady Pembroke seems to refurbish it and give it a new edge'.[11] She certainly uses vigorously active verbs and ringing epithets. Some of Sidney's favourite devices occur: a liking for double epithets – 'never-numbred summe' (I. 74), 'devoutlie-fixed' (II. 40), 'sadlie-uttered' (II. 54), the frequent employment of simple and emotionally direct questions or statements. The emotions evoked in the *Triumph* are strong and passionate, and the poem's style is appropriately elevated and energetic. It is a triumph of tightly controlled, evocative verse, mixing passionate sorrow and celebratory affirmation, rising to the final culmination of Laura's farewell to the poet – and perhaps expressive of Mary's own farewell to her brother:

> Ladie (quoth I) your words most sweetlie kinde
> Have easie made, what ever erst I bare,
> But what is left of yow to live behinde.
>
> Therfore to know this, my onelie care,
> If sloe or swift shall com our meeting-daye.
> She parting saide, As my conjectures are,
> Thow without me long time on earth shalt staie.
>
> (II, 184–90)

Mary Sidney, Lady Wroth

When, in 1621 Mary Wroth's *Urania*, a prose romance in the manner of her uncle Philip's *Arcadia*, was published, appended was a collection of sonnets and songs purportedly written by the romance's heroine, Pamphilia. The poems scattered through *Urania* and the appended collection of poems, *Pamphilia to Amphilanthus*, together are cultural documents of primary importance for our understanding of the nature of women's poetry in the period. Following the publication of the work,

Lord Denny admonished Wroth for not following the lead of her aunt; if a woman must write at all, she should dedicate herself to pious writing, not scandalous romance. His hostility is a response not merely to what he felt were satires on his family, but to something much deeper. Wroth's writings were, as Denny sensed, an act of sexual and social defiance; she was asserting a woman's right and ability to write, publish and deal with the most intense of concerns in writing. Add to this the fact that Wroth had a long-standing affair with her first cousin, William Herbert, third earl of Pembroke, and had two illegitimate children by him, then her life too was an act of defiance against the conventions of the time.

The date in which *Pamphilia to Amphilanthus* was published is important; it calls into question the usefulness of conventional periodization when women's poetry is concerned. 1621 is some thirty years after the main vogue of sonneteering in England (and twelve years after even Shakespeare's also belated and probably pirated, collection appeared). For more than a decade, Wroth had been mentioned by family members, friends and dependents in a predictably adulatory manner as an inheritor of the Sidney poetic genius, but nothing was published until *Urania* appeared, and then it was probably without the author's permission. Despite its date, then, *Pamphilia to Amphilanthus* can be usefully seen as the last major sixteenth-century Petrarchan collection, a major document at the end of the dominant tradition of Renaissance love poetry. It is also a prime source for our attempting to read, today, what it was to be gendered as a woman in early modern England, and to try to write poetry within and against the structures of desire determined by that gender assignment.

Wroth was a Sidney. So was her lover and fellow (very minor) poet William Herbert, third earl of Pembroke. As I suggested in Chapter 5, this fascinating family romance had literary as well as personal and family dimensions: she was the daughter of Robert Sidney, he the son of Mary, Countess of Pembroke; they were the niece and nephew of Philip. In writing in the Petrarchan mode, Mary Wroth was following paths that were (to put it mildly) heavily trodden, but they are doubly 'belated,' to use Harold Bloom's term, in relation to her own family. Roberts, Miller and others have pointed to the echoes and evident borrowings from both her father's and uncle's poems.[12] The commitment to the poetic vocation and to the details of craft that all three of the first generation Sidney poets – Philip, Mary, and Robert – showed is also evident in her work. The family influences include not only verbal echoes and verse forms, but no doubt also the encouragement, or the provocation, to write – the assumption, that because she was a Sidney, writing poetry was an appropriate means of self-assertion even for a woman. What difference did growing

up within such a family make to Wroth's possibility of becoming a
poet? How did writing poetry bind her to or liberate her from her
family? What psychological and ideological dynamics were involved in
being a writing woman? Was it emulation? Rivalry? The conscious or
unconscious rejection of the mother in favour of the power of the father?
As well, what did it mean to a woman to be interpellated into the fantasy
world of late chivalry that was so central to the Sidney family, with its
gender ideology of masculine heroism and male ostentation, centred
upon the authority of the warrior-prince, the courtier, the patriarch?
Aristocratic women occupied essential parts in the rituals of chivalry – if
not as homebodies, let us say, at least as 'great house' bodies. They were
required to be decorative, inspiring, constant – moving but unmoved,
in multiple senses. In *Urania*, the men are, like Philip and Robert
Sidney and Pembroke in their political careers, in continual movement,
pursuing adventure in an expansive, half real, half fantastic, landscape;
the women are mostly either expected to wait at home, however restless
or trapped they appear, or – should they rebel against their restrictions –
be put at risk for their boldness or their outspokenness. Even Pamphilia,
although a queen, is made unhappy by her responsibilities, and when
her husband dies, she returns home to her father. How did such a
repressive situation allow Mary Wroth to become a poet?

We get fascinating answers to those questions when we turn to the
poems. On the surface, we are back in the 1580s and 90s, in the familiar
Petrarchan world of plaint and paradox, sophisticated but generalized
emotion and rhetorical smoothness occasionally counterpointed by the
mild disruption of question, ejaculation, despair, or joy. Wroth's poems
often read like the collections that had been fashionable twenty and
more years before, in which, over and over, 'Feare and Desire . . .
inwardly contend'. It is easy to construct from her poems a miscellany
of such Petrarchan clichés, almost three hundred years old by the time
she is writing. Love is 'truth, and doth delight', and yet makes the
lover 'true slave to Fortune's spite'; it is at once the 'hottest beames
of zeale' and shows a 'coldenesse' which 'can but my despaires descry'.
The lover's spirit is 'cloyd with griefe and paine', captive and yet free;
the joys of love are rapturous and yet 'heape disdaine' on the lover;
the spring which the lovers see around them reflects back on the 'sad
sowrs/Which from mine eyes doe flow' inside the lover's minds, which
exist in the delicious agony of frustration and indecision: 'Restlese I
live, consulting what to doe,/And, more I study, more I still undoe'.[13]
Such conventional paradoxes and complaints are frequently dressed
in familiar neoplatonic garb; her verse can sound like the drabbest
of poets thirty years earlier, at others like that of a Jacobean court
wit. Around 1610, perhaps about the same time as she was starting
to write what became *Pamphilia to Amphilanthus*, Lord Dudley North

dedicated a treatise on poetry to her, which contains a strong attack on what was to become known as 'Metaphysical' poetry and a defence of the plain style. Predictably setting his argument in terms of the prestige of the Sidney family, he claims that 'the admirable inventions and matter of your unimitable Uncles extant works flourish in applause of all', and praises such features as 'the well wrought and exquisite harmony of their Cadence', their 'round, cogent cleare and gracefull delivery', and asserts that 'the best eloquence is to make our selves clearly understood'. It may well be that Wroth herself was starting to write with such notions in mind about the time that North was writing. Her poetry can therefore be placed in a transitional position between Elizabethan 'drab' verse and the Jonsonian style which grew from it.[14]

But the most significant aspect of her writing, and one that is not just historically intriguing, arises from the contradictions between the predominantly masculinist rhetoric of the Petrarchan tradition and her sense of her own gendered position as a woman. We need to ask what difference does the author's gender make to her sequence? Or is she rendered so controlled a subject that we hear the dominant discourse, speaking without interruption, through her? Wroth is, after all, writing within a genre entirely structured by male categories: by the distancing of the erotic by logic, by the fixing of the female as a body which is the subject of power, requiring her passivity as the object of anguish or manipulation. Do we see any signs at all of what is increasingly seen today as the psychic distortion and alienation that occurs when a woman writer represses her gender-specific desires to write?

As I noted in Chapter 3, the Petrarchan poem centres on its 'I'. It is a device, at once rhetorical and psychological, that functions to provide an impression of stability and continuity to the experience the poem tries to encode. Within this exposure of the dislocations of desire and the self, desire and language, the place of gender raises special problems. Petrarchism involves the encoding of a set of recurrent, perhaps even inherent, male strategies for dealing with desire. I say 'even inherent': a more optimistic reading suggests that they are typical of a society that rigidly hierarchizes gender differences along the lines of domination and submission, and since they are historically constructed, are not inherent. But they have clearly been an overwhelming part of our history. So, what variations and distortions occur when a woman, traditionally occupying the place of the ostensible object of the poet's devotion, the focus of the 'I''s gaze, takes up the subject position itself? Necessarily caught up in the enormously powerful discourses of an authoritarian patriarchy that went far beyond poetry, what opportunities did a woman poet at this time have to discover a voice that she herself owned, if not 'individually', at least as a woman voicing the shared subjectivity of other women? In a society where male formulations of desire were so dominant, could she settle for (or even envisage) anything more than fragmentation? Would it be the 'same' fragmentation as that articulated on behalf of the male subject position? While these questions are fundamental to our understanding of Wroth and will recur in my discussion, rather than categorizing her as a 'woman poet', as if that were a self-explanatory category determined by a fixed gender role, I want to ask how her options and possibilities as a writer were affected by her gender assignment within her society and (clearly not irrelevant) her family.

Writing is an act shared by Pamphilia with her creator. So far as Wroth's writing is concerned, we should not underemphasize its importance as an act of self-affirmation, even of defiance, despite the encouragement afforded by being a member of the Sidney family. Hazard has noted that, typically, a Petrarchan poet fashions, within the poems, a fictive role (which may at times be close to that claimed by the poet outside the poems).[15] The one constructed in *Pamphilia to Amphilanthus* for both writer and character includes both a degree of passivity, what the poems term 'constancy', but also includes a measure of defiance and self-assertion against the passive role assigned to a woman, and which undoubtedly echoes something of the desires of the author herself. Even though her family probably encouraged her to see herself as a writer, Wroth took that permission far more daringly than her aunt had. To write a prose romance, a pastoral play and perhaps above all, a collection of Petrarchan love poems, was to go well beyond what the family might have seen fit – and it is significant that it was in part because she exceeded what were felt to be the decorous precedence of translation and devotional works set by her pious aunt that Wroth was bitterly attacked by Denny upon the publication of *Urania*. Even the seemingly mundane acts of arrangement, revision and circulation of her poems – or, not to be underestimated as an act of choice, the refusal to circulate them – were acts of assertion.[16] Within the poems, too, writing is depicted as a way of giving a woman not merely reactive roles to male desires but multiple and changing voices. Like the male Petrarchan lover, Pamphilia determines to 'seeke for some small ease by lines,' only to realize that 'greife is nott cur'd by art'. Poetry 'tires' her mind, yet the 'debate' it produces in her makes her realize that it is her thinking, brooding mind that is carving out an area of autonomy – even through her pain – that affords her not only comfort but power.[17] While others, men in particular, may be subject to the whims of the king, or to some 'pleasing past time' required by their roles at Court, she claims only a small but autonomous space to explore:

> When every one to pleasing pastime hies
> Some hunt, some hauke, some play, while some delight
> In sweet discourse, and musique showes joys might
> Yett I my thoughts doe farr above thes prise.[18]

The psychological space necessary for women's sense of autonomy, and not least, their creative imaginations to develop, is reflected in recurring scenes in *Urania* and *Pamphilia to Amphilanthus* of inner spaces, like private chambers and gardens, as places of self-contemplation and self-assertion without an audience. Bassin suggests that the recurring metaphor of a woman's inner space should be regarded as equivalent to – though, historically it has never attained the dominant position of – male phallic activity and its representations. Pamphilia frequently describes herself as desiring isolation and silence – desiring, that is, to have her organs of self-assertion, her mouth (for speech), her genitals (for sexual pleasure) and the door or gate of her room, house, or garden closed or locked.[19] She knows that by voicing her miseries, or by pursuing love, or by going abroad, she could overcome her victimization, but instead she accepts her assignment of silence, isolation and frigidity. Her posture is frequently described as sleeping, or near sleep, or lying down in a small space, and addressing the shadows around her as comforting, even if confusing. In one poem she broods:

> How oft in you I have laine heere opprest,
>   And have my miseries in woefull cries
>   Deliver'd forth, mounting up to the skies
> Yett helples back returnd to wound my brest.

In the next sonnet, she states that '[I]lay'd down to ease my paine'; again, she feels trapped and is enabled to rise only by 'Fortune', who is described as a fellow woman lover who 'in her bless'd arms did me inchaine'. As she rises, she acknowledges that even with another woman, she is responding rather than initiating : 'I, her obay'd, and rising felt that love/Indeed was best, when I did least itt move'.[20] Discussing what he believed to be the inherently masochistic situation of being a woman, Freud claimed that it consisted of neurotic passivity, whether shown in ordinary timidity or the 'extreme instance' of sexual satisfaction being 'conditional upon suffering physical or mental pain at the hands of the sexual object'. Either way he saw it as an individual aberration, and one inherent in being a woman. But the construction of female (or for that matter, male) masochism in our cultural history is far more complex than Freud's account. The unconscious is not a given, biological 'place'; it is rather a metaphor for those assumptions and practices whereby the contradictions of a society's ideology are repressed, transferred and reproduced. The passivity that Pamphilia sometimes displays – and I choose that exhibitionist term deliberately – is more a cultural construct that the 'individual' neurosis of which Freud speaks. 'Female masochism' is not, as Freud thought, biological: even though biological factors enter into its being woman's most characteristic perversion; it is predominantly the result of women's socialization and gender assignments in patriarchal society.[21] In the Petrarchan scheme, the lover typically asserts that he becomes the victim of the power of the beloved. From such a systematization of the dynamics of desire, it seems that only two possible gender positions are possible, 'one of rapacious domination, the other of docile submission'.[22] Yet though the (male) lover may assert that he is trapped or paralysed by the power of the beloved, he is inevitably the active participant: he pursues, is called to public duties as courtier or soldier; he speaks out, and he writes. A man has the independence to move, to be restless, unfaithful or simply assume the freedom to move through the world; a woman remains at home, constant, reassuring, mothering. Wroth's emphasis on Pamphilia's constancy never removes her from this male world in which a man may move, travel, or choose, and a woman stays at home. The woman's role is to be the focus for his self-division and both his physical and emotional restlessness. Moreover, her absence or coldness, while a matter for complaint, and the cause of his insecurity, is often the necessary stimulus for his being able to feel that self-division and to write about it. If she were present, which he desires, he would not write, which he also desires. She is therefore required to be absent so he can desire her presence, a paradox that Greville grimly deconstructs in *Caelica* 45 when he insists that absence, far from being the ideal state of love, the 'glorious bright' of absence is in fact, 'pain'. Greville's is a rare unqualified demystification of the Petrarchan pose by a male poet. Wroth's critique is more detailed and more interesting because it is written by and on behalf of a woman.

The role of Petrarchan mistress which Pamphilia is given is primarily, then, a passive one. Her desire is defined and licensed by (a constant pun on Pembroke's name) a man's 'will'. She is positioned by forces, reified as 'love,' that are, she assumes, outside her control and the range of feelings she is permitted include the largely negative ones of entrapment, loss and bondage. Unlike her male lover, she has no recourse to other activities. She must wait upon his initiative: the female 'complement to the male refusal to recognize the other is woman's own acceptance of her lack of subjectivity, her willingness to offer recognition without expecting it in return'.[23] She makes herself available to her lover when he chooses to visit her. Moreover, she feels, in part, that she is a willing accomplice, as if the 'molestation' she experiences is not merely a tragic consequence of her being a woman but in some sense her fault. A woman is more helpless than a man before love's deceptiveness since she does not have the male assumption of agency in love – the ability to change and revel in unpredictability. She cannot claim any autonomy, it seems, without submitting to further pain and disillusion.

The dominant code by which women have historically been made available for male pleasure rather than their own, or even for mutual pleasure, is based on this reification of a woman's constancy. Beilin has argued that 'constancy', which is particularly intensely apostrophized in the final sonnet of *Pamphilia to Amphilanthus*, has a 'fundamental importance' in Wroth's scheme, and that 'fully separated from Amphilanthus . . . Pamphilia is wholly dedicated to the love of virtue'.[24] But repeatedly, constancy seems to be a role forced upon a woman in a dangerous or determined environment, a defensive posture at best, an assigned and unavoidable role within an aggressively patriarchal situation at worst. In her constancy, Pamphilia has internalized the residual female role of possessing a 'faith untouch'd, pure thoughts . . . where constancy bears sway', and even the resignation of traditional religion. In one of the later sonnets of the collection, she acknowledges that 'no time, noe roome, no thought, or writing' can give her 'loving heart' quiet, and yet she is powerless to give up her love:

> Yett would I nott (deere love) thou shouldst depart
>   Butt lett my passions as they first began
>   Rule, wounde, and please, itt is thy choysest art
> To give disquiett which seemes ease to man.

The erotic Cupid can give only 'disquiett'; by contrast, the divine offers 'glory,' presented as a relief from the perpetual disease of erotic desire:

> When all alone, I think upon thy paine
>   How thou doest traveile owr best selves to gaine;
>   Then howerly thy lessons I doe learne,
>
> Think on thy glory which shall still assend
>   Untill the world come to a finall end,
>   And then shall wee thy lasting powre deserne.[25]

Constancy, then, is hardly the positive virtue it seems when it is asserted by a male poet like Sidney or Donne. Indeed, in a remarkable demystification of it as, in effect, a device of patriarchy to keep women under control and available whenever the needs of their struggles for individuation become unbearable, to be in a state of unchanging constancy to relieve men of some anxieties, not as act of women's agency; Amphilanthus's own sister Urania points out to Pamphilia that 'tis pittie . . . that ever that fruitlesse thing Constancy was taught you as a vertue'. Men are not required to be constant. Why then should women? Whereas a courtier, like Amphilanthus, has a sense of assigned agency, the autonomy of continual adventure and innumerable mistresses, Pamphilia must wait, resigned and insecure, threatened by her love and by her own faithfulness:

> Love grown proud with victory,
>   Seekes by sleights to conquer me,
>   Painted showes he thinkes can bind
>   His commands in womens mind,
> Love but glories in fond loving,
> I most joy in not removing.[26]

The 'painted showes' of the Court – such as the masques and celebrations that had won Wroth herself some momentary 'glories' – are here taken as a metonymy for the seductive attractions by which the court lady is assigned her passive, decorative role. Love, like the Court, is characterized by superficiality and insecurity. And the speaker? Do we read the last line as 'most' or 'must'? If as 'most,' then the passive, masochistic, self-punishing role has been accepted; if 'must,' then the reluctance to accept such a role is inevitable but still resented. Either way, 'constancy', with its idealized tone of willing devotion and dedication, is proved to be deceiving, a construct designed by men to keep women in subjection.

Perhaps the idealization of constancy throughout the collection is a clear, and depressing, indication of how a dominant masculinist ideology has been internalized. Seen in that light, it acts to cover over the contradictions of Pamphilia's assigned roles. The ninth sonnet records a protracted degree of bitterness at such an assignment, as it bitterly describes the lover married only to sorrow in a socially constructed world where faithfulness, although imposed as a duty and a sign of belonging to a male lover, seems nonetheless an imposition:

> Bee you all pleas'd? your pleasures grieve nott mee:
>   Do you delight? I envy not your joy:
>   Have you content? contentment with you bee:
>   Hope you for bliss? hope still and still injoye:
>
> Lett sad misfortune, haples me destroy,
>   Leave crosses to rule mee, and still rule free,
>   While all delights theyr contraries imploy
>   To keepe good backe, and I butt torments see.
>
> Joyes are beereav'd, harmes doe only tarry,
>   Despaire takes place, disdaine hath gott the hand:

> Yett firme love holds my sences in such band
> As since despis'ed, I with sorrow marry;
> Then if with griefe I now must coupled bee
> Sorrow I'le wed: Dispaire thus governs mee.[27]

The poem is racked by a deep and helpless bitterness. Demands are made upon the speaker that are seemingly irresistible; petulant defiance seems the most positive alternative to helpless acquiescence. Although one of the more extreme of the sonnets, it is typical in that love is presented not only as deceptive and disruptive, as it is so often to a male Petrarchan lover, but as enforcing helplessness and passivity. A woman is a 'stage of woe' on which others' desires, not her own, are acted out. Her constancy, the virtue with which she is most praised and thereby imprisoned, may be opening her to further victimization. Writing on 'mourning and melancholia', Freud speaks of the melancholic's sense of loss involving 'painful dejection, cessation of the interest in the outside world, loss of the capacity to love, inhibition of all activity and a lowering of the self-regarding feelings to a degree that finds utterance in self-reproaches and self-revilings'.[28] Many sonnets show Pamphilia withdrawn to her bed, both night and day, brooding over her misery and her lover's absence. But where Freud insisted that narcissistic melancholia was an 'individual' neurosis, Wroth's poems show how thoroughly it is socially constructed. It is as if the need for secrecy, the sense of nonfulfilment and above all the awareness that the beloved is an active agent elsewhere – hunting, travelling, moving through more complex social worlds – provides a contrast that is at once humiliating and yet inescapable. Pamphilia's withdrawal attempts to restore some sense of an acceptable self-representation. She needs the sense of her own loss and pain to buttress what feelings she retains of having any coherent sense of self.

One of the recurring metaphors of male Petrarchism is the controlling power of the male gaze. It is built upon an assumption so deeply rooted in the age's dominant ideologies of perception and knowledge production that it must have seemed unassailably true as well as harmless. Men gaze at women; women are gazed at, and as Stoller puts it, 'the man's excited responses to her body reassure the woman that she actually exists'.[29] What response could a female protagonist have to such a situation? Was it possible to construct an alternative to the dominance of the gaze? Part of Pamphilia's enforced (or chosen) passivity, her acknowledgement that love 'indeed was best, when I did least it move', is the awareness that she is being watched by others for signs of her love and in a sense given an identity by their gazes. Within recent feminist theory, the psychosocial dynamics of the gaze have been much debated. A standard viewpoint, represented by the work of Modleski and Mulvey, has focused on the male gaze as the normal subject position for the viewer of classic cinema, and on the need to construct a political alternative, especially for women viewers. More recently, Studlar has argued that many films interpellate a male viewer based on a masochistic fear/desire of being dominated and absorbed by women. Neither explanation, however at times each seems to fit what we ourselves may have experienced intensely and therefore want to claim as 'universal' experiences, accounts for the historical preponderance of the behaviour and assumptions that have been built upon the dominance of the male gaze. It is only recently that it has seemed important to discuss the confounding of such situations by the woman's active participation in the gaze. As Penley puts it, if the gaze in traditional art is 'an inscription of the look on the body of the mother, we must now begin to consider the possibilities of the mother returning the look'.[30] What happens if 'she' looks back? Or actively watches herself being watched and instead of feeling positioned as an object, assumes it as a subject position? If vision means aggression and control, can a woman – even while she knows she is the object of the gaze – appropriate its power? Wroth's poems explore a number of these subject positions. At times Pamphilia is 'molested' by her role as an object of the desiring gaze; at others she tries to escape the gaze of lover and others, in loneliness, isolation, or sleep. Such reactions are attempts to avoid the repetitive constructing of sexual relations by patterns of male domination and female submission. In such relationships, the values of the patriarchal male predominate: they emerge as the urge to overwhelm, penetrate, defeat and triumph over.

As I suggested in Chapter 3, an analysis of the gender politics of Petrarchism suggests that this, one of the dominant discourses of love in the western world, has been overwhelmingly destructive for at least half of those human subjects caught up in it: the traditional Petrarchan situation against which *Pamphilia to Amphilanthus* is written is part of a historical pattern of 'normal' sexuality as defined by western society, in which, as Stoller puts it, 'an essential purpose is for one to be superior to, harmful to, triumphant over another'.[31] The seeming neutrality of 'one' in Stoller's remark covers the preponderant historical identification of the gaze and its wider cultural associations with the male. Beneath the language of sexual dependence, idealized admiration, even of sexual reciprocity that Petrarchism lays claim to, there is a one-sided emphasis on domination and submission, underlain by the destructive dynamics of hostility, revenge and destruction. One of the poems in Wroth's opening sequence in *Pamphilia to Amphilanthus* is a remarkable critique of this whole tradition. It attempts to subvert the dominant male subject position by appropriating the gaze and its pleasure:

Take heed mine eyes, how you your lookes do cast
  Least they beetray my harts most secrett thought;
  Bee true unto your selves for nothings bought
  More deere then doubt which brings a lovers fast.

Or Catch you all waching eyes, ere they bee past
  take yours fixt wher your best love hath sought
  The pride of your desires; lett them be taught
  Theyr faults for shame, they could noe truer last;

Then looke, and looke for joye for conquest wunn
  Of those that search't your hurt in double kinde;
  Soe you kept safe, lett them themselves looke blinde
  Watch, gaze, and marke till they to madnes runn,

While you, mine eyes injoye full sight of love
Contented that such happinesses move.[32]

The poem opens with a warning against indiscretion, but the tone is unusually paranoid, as if guarding not just against betrayal of a secret to which she has been entrusted, but of the multiple 'selves' in which she lives. The tactics of the poem, indeed, become not the passive slipping into a role of secret love or that of the modest object of a forbidden desire, but the more aggressive one of 'catching', or trapping and defeating 'all watching eyes'. Given that identity consists in being assigned a multiplicity of roles, that very multiplicity and its contradictory assigned positions will become her basis for action. Her fantasy of female agency becomes based on her returning the gaze, on reminding herself to 'looke with joye for conquest wunn', and acknowledging that it is her own active desire, accepting her construction by the contradictory gazes and returning them, that affords her power. Stoller remarks – as so often, irritatingly essentializing but nonetheless pointing to a seemingly fixed aspect of western patriarchy – on the little boy's assumed 'right to sexual looking and a little girl's training that she is not to permit that looking'. Placed within the history of gender assignment, Wroth's Pamphilia marks an attempt, spasmodic and isolated, to break with such a pattern. She is not merely fixed by the gaze, but turns it to an active and defiant exhibitionism. She has started to reappropriate herself as a subject, distancing herself from the narcissism of self-involvement, and starting to see herself as a man might see her. But because she sees with both the eyes of a woman and the gaze of a man, by involvement and reflection, she acquires a secret authority unknown to the men who gaze on her and think they control her. It is the clearest expression of the fantasy of emulation, what Kaplan terms 'a retribution scenario, a vengeance on those who have been assigned to abandon and mutilation'.[33] Or, more optimistically, she has asserted her right to gaze back, just as her poems assert the right to talk back.

This poem also reflects upon another part of the Petrarchan situation, the interpellation of the reader (him)self as a voyeur. The gaze of the (male) reader is a part of the male display built into Petrarchism: Sidney's poems, for instance, typically look out to their audiences, often with a wink or an invitation to laugh, inviting his reader's amusement as well as disapproval or sympathy to his dilemmas. *Astrophil and Stella* is typical of the mode: it is what Barthes terms a playful text, one that depends strongly on an audience, inviting its participation, asking us to watch, identify, judge, laugh, learn. But it assumes a 'universal' gaze that in fact is that of the dominant male and the sympathy it asks for is for the suffering male, wanting separation from and yet desiring the presence of, the woman. What we are asked to watch, is 'naturally' the textual/sexual spectacle of another human displaying him or herself according to gender-specific stereotypes – or refusing to, which in its effect on the viewer amounts to the same thing. Women display for men; men display for themselves, and then are authorized to display, in writing, their accounts of the experience. What happens when such a situation is complicated by a woman protagonist/poet? By a woman who displays herself, not merely sexually but textually as well, in her act of writing? The reader's trajectory of desire makes his (or her) complicity more complex; in particular, it raises the issue of gender roles very explicitly. Where the male reader/spectator sees his own gendered roles in harmony with those valorized by the poems, the gaze can appear neutral. When the gaze is complicated by gender, either by a woman reader or, as here, by a woman writer, then the male power over objects in the Petrarchan scheme is called into question.

Wroth's poems, foregrounding the gender of both their author and protagonist, catches us in a reading situation where the shifts in subject position call into question any 'natural' order of gender. In Wroth's poem, we are not simply observing the woman's acceptance of the conventional role of cruel beauty and perpetual tease, produced by male desire to both generate desire and to overcome his own fears of that desire. However fitfully, we are looking at the slow and contradictory emergence of alternative subject positions. As Belsey, Barker and others have argued, women were afforded places within the period's dominant ideology only by being incorporated into structures and discourses which assigned them subsidiary roles, as objects of others' desires, not as subjects of their own. There is, in the early modern period – in *Hamlet*, most forcefully – the emergence of a new sense of subjectivity, a claim for a unique and 'essential interiority', which even if it is never fully articulated, and is therefore historically 'premature', nonetheless anticipates the emergent claims of a bourgeois subjectivity that will emerge in the next century or more. Wroth's poems record the stirrings – against enormous odds, it needs to be stressed – to establish an equivalent female subject position. Her poems' struggle to find an authentic voice for a woman are related to the frustrations of gender assignment. The dominant gendered subject positions of early modern England did not permit such autonomy to a woman writer or protagonist – any more than they did, as I will briefly note, to gays. But we can note, across the range of constructed gender roles, points of strain and contradiction where alternatives are struggling to emerge.[34]

When a woman does emerge into the world, including the world of writing, what does she encounter? In psychoanalytic terms, to turn to writing is to turn from the mother to the father, to choose assertion, activity, possession of the phallus over passivity, castration and masochism. Yet the choice is never easy, and its difficulty is registered in the tensions and contradictions of Wroth's poems. The poems present a fantasy of autonomy by a woman struggling in what they repeatedly term a 'labyrinth'. The recurring use of the word 'molestation', too, is a sign of this tension. Behind the term are both physical realities and myths. Sexual assault and domination may well have been part of Wroth's own experience of love but, as well, she is evoking part of the cultural unconscious, the fears built into being a woman in a masculinist society. It may be too that a woman who expresses any degree of sexual autonomy or demand falls victim to one of patriarchy's recurring myths about sexual molestation: that if they stray from their assigned places women may suffer rape. Molestation is thus what Anna Clark terms an 'extension of the social construction of male sexuality as active, dominant and aggressive'.[35]

If writing is an act – or at least an enacted fantasy – of agency for a woman, what of desire itself? If, as Marx put it, praxis – meaning sensuous human activity, the practices of the body – is the basis of real power, what space is *Pamphilia to Amphilanthus* trying to carve out not only for its protagonist but also for its author, and for the language and praxis of women's desire? Wroth overwhelmingly offers us a distinctively privileged perspective on the negative eros produced by male domination and female masochism. It allows us to see the relative paucity of love 'objects' to which a woman had access in the early modern period. Freud noted frequently that repressed objects of desire are represented by a series of unsatisfying substitutes: Pamphilia's growing self-awareness, her 'waking' as a lover, brings her the realization of the distinctive kind of cruelty Cupid affords women. He is responsible for the blame of 'cruelty disgrace', the producer of displays, for male delectation, of 'sad Disasters' upon 'this Stage of woe,' ending in self-immolation, even death, 'a Tombe for sad misfortunes spright'. Repeatedly, the love is 'in chaines' or trapped in a labyrinth.[36]

The 'labyrinth' is the nightmare underside of a woman's private space. The extremely popular mazes in Elizabethan and Jacobean gardens reflect an obsessive concern with what Wotton termed a 'very wilde Regularitie', a special place designed to transgress the restrictions of the house and its regime of harmony and control. But such a view is from the point of view of the proprietor of the house or the architect. For someone lost in the labyrinth, the point of view may be very different. The private chamber is an area of orderliness and control, however compromised by its surroundings; the labyrinth consists of potentially infinite attempts to find an escape: it constructs a series of 'tense' blind spaces that produce incessant, frustrated, 'restless' movements to escape. Petrarch used the labyrinth as an image of the emotional confusion of love and there were a number of commonplace analogies between the labyrinth and the sonnet itself.[37]

The 'crowne of Sonetts dedicated to Love,' which are grouped together towards the end of *Pamphilia to Amphilanthus* explore some of these difficulties from the viewpoint of the woman lover trapped within (and certainly not a designer or owner of) labyrinths. The 'crowne' consists of fourteen sonnets, the last lines of each constituting the first line of the next. Roberts speaks of the 'universalized concept of love' in the Crowne and Beilin of its 'catalogues of love's divinity', but it is more distinctive in its demarcation of contradictions than in its acceptance of some kind of transcendent resignation. The labyrinth is, despite its emphasis on puzzlement and entrapment, a metaphor of action: one enters a labyrinth and tries to find one's way out, or to its heart, or both. Pamphilia, surrounded by alternatives, nonetheless insists that it is contradiction and difficulty that offer her choices:

> In this strang labourinth how shall I turne?
>> Wayes are on all sids while the way I misse:
>> If to the right hand, ther, in love I burne;
>> Lett mee goe forward, therin danger is.

Her determination is to 'take the thread of love,' to be constant to her love, to 'feele the weight of true desire', to produce a mutual, united love. Such agency within contradiction allows each lover to open him (or her) self to previously unsensed possibilities: 'Itt doth inrich the witts, and make you see/That in your self, which you knew nott before'. Even in such a fantasy of love, stasis – what she terms 'constancy' – is never the end. The final poem points to the self-exploration that love has opened, not to achieve a goal so much as to open a never-ending search: 'Soe though in Love I fervently doe burne,/In this strange labourinth how shall I turne?'[38]

So far, I have read Wroth's poems as if they struggle, fitfully and almost accidentally, to assert any sustained agency for women. They give voice to one of the dominant fantasies of early modern women, that of achieving the agency that has been promised, as he emerges from childhood, to a boy. Becoming a man, he will, like his father, assume independence, autonomy, power over others, especially over women. There are, however, signs in *Pamphilia to Amphilanthus* of another, more active, counter-discourse taking shape. Lamb has pointed out how thoroughly in the early modern period women were sexualized as writers and readers: conventionally, 'the sexualization of women's words – in their reading, their speech, their writing – represented a formidable obstacle to authorship which, while it did not prevent a woman's writing, affected what they could write'. She suggests that in her writing, Wroth capitalizes upon this assignment, acknowledging 'the sexuality permeating her writing to defend it, even to heroize it'.[39] Her argument deserves to be extended from writing to more general sexual practices. *Urania* has many women characters who dare to make sexual choices, often – indeed, almost inevitably – suffering from doing so, but nonetheless repeatedly insisting on making them. There is, as well, the acknowledgment that the victimization of women is not Pamphilia's alone: other women share her helplessness or anger. The poems frequently address other women, sometimes an unnamed friend and sometimes, as Miller points out, those women who have been described in the lines of men's poems. In the sonnet just quoted, for instance, Fortune is described as Pamphilia's supporter. Fortune is, conventionally, female and a consoler of the suffering male; but because the poem is spoken and written by a woman, Fortune takes on a less conventional role. She becomes a fellow female sufferer, helping Pamphilia face the anguish of being a mistress whose desires are controlled by her lover. The community of 'oprest' women lovers in the poems includes Night, Reclining and other personifications of the assigned female passive role providing, as Miller puts it, a 'litany of parallels' with Pamphilia's grief, which in some of the poems often deepens into anger at being pressured by overwhelming social forces into accepting the roles society thrusts upon them because they are women. As Lamb notes in her splendid analysis of anger in *Urania*, 'the Renaissance offered women few healthy models for encouraging the expression of justified rage or for acknowledging the heroism of their ordinary lives'.[40] It offered even fewer models for an alternative fantasy of genuinely mutual constancy.

Master-mistress: gay voices in poetry

Sexual and gender differences were, like class, a means of securing social order. The eruption of women's voices was a challenge to that order, threatening what nature and God had created. Another was to call into question the universality of heterosexuality. This, too, plays itself out in poetry. Patterns of sexual preference that we label 'homosexual' were proscribed, but passion, supposedly non-sexual, between men and even women were idealized. A man's preferred 'other' was, by nature, a man, not as an object of sexual feelings but of equality and admiration, yet 'sodomy' (which covered a multitude of practices) was a capital offence. As with other politically deviant behaviour, the public drama (e.g. Marlowe's *Edward II* and *Dido Queen of Carthage*) explored sexual deviance: in Rosalind/Ganymede in Shakespeare's *As You Like It*, or in the titillating and, to some members of the audience, disturbing fantasies of cross-dressing and the play of gender identity in the boy actors taking on female parts. Cross-dressing made the theatre a place where transgressive or Utopian gender identities might be contemplated.

Poems may also be such play-spaces. The period's poetry is saturated with a contradiction: abomination of 'unnatural' practices; idealizations of male friendship. Spenser's *Scudamour* refers to men 'lincked to true harts consent' who 'on chast venture grounded their desire', and achieve 'endlesse happinesse' (*Faerie Queene* IV. 10. 26, 28). Many of Shakespeare's sonnets explore desire across traditional gender/sex distinctions: some, notably twenty, have been depicted as exploring a 'natural' heterosexual's 'unnatural' attraction to another man. Less conflicted are the sonnets in Barnfield's *Cynthia*, which has a homo-sexual protagonist: 'Sometimes I wish that I his pillow were,/So might I steale a kisse, and yet not seene'. Such references could be allegorized, but put into play a host of transgressive fantasies that would eventually emerge in less proscribed discourses. Donne's joke in *Satire IV* about noting 'who loves whome, who boyes, and who goats' probably betrayed more than fashionable cynicism. But there is no acceptable discourse of homosexuality. As with women's poetry, however, the obscurities of our history of our culture's attempts to recognize and explore difference and multiplicity do not excuse us from trying to explore that spasmodic history. 'Guerrilla voices' they may have been, but they may also now be recognized as freedom fighters.[41]

Notes

1. Robert Cleaver, *A Godly Form of Household Government* (London, 1630), p. 3.

2. Michel Foucault, 'The History of Sexuality: Interview', *Oxford Literary Review*, 4, no. 2 (1980), 3–14 (pp. 10–11).

3. Joan [Kelly-] Gadol, 'Notes on Women in the Renaissance and Renaissance Historiography', in *Conceptual Frameworks for Studying Women's History*, edited by Marylin Arthur *et al.* (Lawrence, 1975), pp. 6–7.

4. *Kissing the Rod*, edited by Germaine Greer *et al.* (New York, 1988), p. 1.

5. A detailed bibliography of the poets mentioned here may be found in Elaine V. Beilin, 'Current Bibliography of English Women Writers, 1500–1640', in *The Renaissance Englishwoman in Print*, edited by Anne M. Haselkorn and Betty S. Travitsky (Amherst, 1990), pp. 347–60.

6. For the connection with Behn, see *Reading Mary Wroth*, edited by Naomi J. Miller and Gary Waller (Knoxville, 1991), p. 10. Quotations from Wroth's poetry are taken from *The Poems of Lady Mary Wroth*, edited by Josephine A. Roberts (Baton Rouge, 1983).

7. Robert Coogan, 'Petrarch's Trionfi and the Renaissance', *SRen*, 67 (1970), 306–27 (p. 311).

8. For another, more conservative view of the Countess's relationship with her brother, see Margaret Hannay, *Philip's Phoenix* (Oxford, 1990).

9. D. G. Rees, 'Petrarch's "Trionfi della Morte" in English', *Ital. Stud.*, 7 (1952), 82–96 (p. 83).

10. Quotations from the poem are taken from *The Triumph of Death and other Unpublished and Uncollected Poems by Mary Sidney Countess of Pembroke*, edited by Gary Waller (Salzburg, 1977).

11. Rees, pp. 86–87.

12. Harold Bloom, *The Anxiety of Influence: A Theory of Poetry* (New York, 1973), p. 94.

13. *Poems*, p. 151.

14 See Lester Beaurline, 'Dudley North's Criticism of Metaphysical Poetry', *Huntington Library Quarterly*, 35 (1935), 299–313 (p.304).

15. Mary E. Hazard, 'Absent Presence and Present Absence: Cross-Couple Convention in Elizabethan Culture', *Texas Studies in Language and Literature*, 29 (1987), 4.

16. Jeff Masten,' "Shall I turne Blabb?": Circulation, Gender, and Subjectivity in Mary Wroth's Sonnets', in *Reading Mary Wroth*, pp. 82–85.

17. *Poems*, pp. 90, 91, 92.

18. *Poems*, pp. 99–100.

19. Donna Bassin, 'Woman's Images of Inner Space: Data Towards Expanded Interpretive Categories', *International Review of Psychoanalysis*, 9 (1982), pp. 191–203; Peter Stallybrass, 'Patriarchal Territories: The Body Enclosed', in *Rewriting the Renaissance: the Discourses of Sexual Difference in Early Modern Europe*, edited by Margaret W. Ferguson, Maureen Quilligan, and Nancy J. Vickers (Chicago, 1986), p. 129.

20. *Poems*, pp. 104, 105.

21. Freud, 'Three Essays on Sexuality', *Standard Edition*, Vol 7, p.159; Juliet Mitchell, *Psychoanalysis and Feminism* (London, 1974), p. 413; Kaplan, *Female Perversions*, p. 518.

22. Kaplan, *Female Perversions*, p. 238.

23. Benjamin, *Bonds of Love*, p. 78.

24. Elaine Beilin, *Redeeming Eve: Women Writers of the English Renaissance* (Princeton, 1987), p. 241.

25. *Poems*, pp. 134, 141.

26. Mary Wroth, *The Countess of Mountgomeries Urania* (1621), pp. 351, 549.

27. *Poems*, p. 91.

28. *Poems*, p. 111; Freud, 'Mourning and Melancholia', *Standard Edition*, 14, p. 244; 'Three Essays on Sexuality', *Standard Edition*, 7, p.157; Kaplan, *Female Perversions*, pp. 105, 258.

29. Stoller, *Perversion*, p. 90.

30. Stephen Heath, 'Difference', *Screen*, 19 (1978), 97. See also *Laura Mulvey, Visual and Other Pleasures* (Bloomington, 1988), pp. 361–73; Gaylyn Studlar, *In the Realm of Pleasure: Von Sternberg, Dietrich, and the Masochistic Aesthetic* (Urbana, 1988).

31. Stoller, *Perversion*, p. 90.

32. *Poems*, p. 106.

33. Kaplan, *Female Perversions*, p. 257.

34. Francis Barker, *The Tremulous Private Body: Essays on Subjection* (London, 1984), pp. 31, 36; Catherine Belsey, *The Subject of Tragedy: Identity and Difference in Renaissance Drama* (London, 1985).

35. Anna Clark, *Women's Silence Men's Violence: Sexual Assault in England 1770–1845* (London, 1987), p. 6.

36. See e. g. Freud, 'A Special Type of Object Choice made by Men. (Contributions to the Psychology of Love I)', *Standard Edition*, 11, p. 140; Poems, pp. 85, 92, 111, 123.

37. Scott Wilson, 'Sir Philip Sidney and the Extraordinary Forms of Desire', *Assays*, 7 (1993).

38. *Poems*, pp. 45, 127, 130, 134; Beilin, *Redeeming Eve*, pp. 238–40.

39. Mary Ellen Lamb, *Gender and Authorship in the Sidney Circle* (Madison, 1990), pp. 140–1.

40. Naomi J. Miller, 'Ancient Fictions and True Forms: the Role of the Lady in Lady Mary Wroth's Pamphilia to Amphilanthus', unpub. paper, 8; Lamb, *Gender and Authorship*, p.141.

41. See Alan Bray, *Homosexuality in Renaissance England* (London, 1982); Jonathan Dollimore, *Sexual Dissidence* (Oxford, 1991).

Chapter 9

Conclusion – Reopening the Canon

Beyond the sixteenth century

As I noted in Chapter 1, we have long looked back to the sixteenth century, as Arnold or Palgrave saw it, as one of the glorious periods of high English culture. It is an evaluation that would have pleased most of the original readers of the period's poetry, at least that written in or in relation to the Court. While today we see the plays of the public theatre, especially that of Shakespeare, as the central cultural texts of the age, in ways that would have puzzled those who held cultural sway at the time, the poetry of Wyatt, Sidney, Spenser, Donne and Shakespeare has been revered in ways their writers and first audiences would have wished, as glorious manifestations of a noble and ordered culture.

This study has been written in part to rewrite such an account of sixteenth-century poetry. We live in a quite different world and the uses to which we put sixteenth-century poetry are acts of cultural selectivity and appropriation no less partial than Palgrave's or Eliot's or the New Critics'. No history is innocent; no use of any cultural product is ever pure – and that includes, needless to say, the original uses. To study our history is to study, from within, a discontinuous struggle to appropriate and control the production of the history and the languages that have in a sense written us and in which we struggle to speak. We write and rewrite our history – and that includes the history of our literature – not to create a 'true' picture, or (let us hope) to construct an antiquarian's dream of a lost glorious past, but to realize what struggles, what achievements and exclusions alike, have made us what we are in the present. Major revaluations of history occur when especially strong rewritings of the past are acknowledged and, in its turn, appropriated. In all cases, we battle with the dominant, residual readings of that past in order to make our own readings plausible and, perhaps, to let them be heard at all. This study is therefore, an essay – *un essai* in Montaigne's sense – an attempt to pose and suggest possible answers to the question Marx asked about ancient Greek tragedy over a century ago: how is it we can still admire works when their original occasions, social structure, cultural assumptions and socio-economic system have all long disappeared? Not because the poetry of this period embodies some inherent 'essence' of literary excellence, some universal or transcendent meaning. As Barthes noted, in a remark which should give reassurance to the beleaguered humanist and avid postmodernist alike, if we were unfortunate enough to lose all the human sciences, the one we must keep above all else is the study of literature and the ways its languages have formed and speak through us. This is why, finally, we might (relatively) privilege literature, including poetry – not to 'preserve' it (with all the revealing smell of formaldehyde or pickle jars in that metaphor) but to use it for a perspective on the present and the languages which speak through us. It is in its capacity to surprise, in the potential, or unrealized, power of the texts we read, that we find the ways to get a perspective on our own place in history, to extend our possession of the pasts which have made us and therefore which are making our possible futures.

In this concluding chapter, I wish to look briefly beyond the period, and then at the received canon of sixteenth-century poetry with which (except for the mention of women's and gay poetry in Chapter 8) I have been concerned and raise also the matter of how it is that such canons are in fact created. First, to glance ahead, beyond sixteenth-century poetry to what eventually came through into the next century – and to raise the question of what did not come through. In particular, we should look at the increasing power of what was to become the dominant mode of literary discourse less than a century later – the rise of neoclassicism, where, in Francis Barker's words, it seems 'we emerge at last into a clear, known world of facts'.[1] There was, of course, a developing classical movement long before Jonson's poems, plays, and prefaces started to appear in the 1590s. One of the residual clichés about the Renaissance is that it involved a rediscovery and appropriation of ancient literature. That view, promulgated especially by Burckhardt in the nineteenth century, is today heavily qualified, but it was certainly a view advocated by humanist propagandists like Erasmus, More or Ascham, and it was in turn appropriated by the later Tudor propaganda machine. An idealized classical past was ruthlessly made to stand as a reminder of a stability and clarity which the barbarous, dark, papist Middle Ages had lost. On the level of language what evolved into a systematic set of principles concentrated not merely on revising, Christianizing, and then propagating Greek and Roman authors, but on the control of the signifier, on simplifying the message-transferring function of language. The instrumentalizing of language is given its first full literary articulation in Jonson's theory and poetical practices around 1600. Poetry was to serve as the vehicle of permanent truth, of 'matter'; and to achieve an unhindered transference between author(ity) and reader. Metaphor is suspect; substance is stressed over the deceptive promiscuity of rhetoric; Sidney's 'moving' is made strictly subordinate to 'teaching'. When we think of revolutionary movements in the 1590s, we usually think of Donne or the theatre. But it is Ben Jonson who is the real radical. If we look ahead, to the time of Milton – the founding of the Royal Society in the 1660s is often pointed to as a landmark – a new view of language, and with it, a whole new order of things, to use Foucault's phrase, has emerged. We can find traces of opposition – in Milton, the sectarian writers, and in the last trickle of the lyric before it goes underground into the Methodist hymns or folksong – but the dominant voice of the eighteenth century (or that view of it that has come down to us) is one in which Jonson's principles have triumphed.

Jonson's literary career starts to take shape in the 1590s and it is in that turbulent decade (perhaps it should be extended to the whole period 1586–1603, between the symbolic deaths of Sir Philip Sidney and the Queen, the lady of whom Ralegh, characteristically pious in his hypocrisy, once remarked that time had forgot) that we may perceive many changes and disruptions symptomatic of wider cultural change. Conventional literary histories have rightly pointed to the upsurge and popularity of many new or revived literary genres, most especially in the drama. But in the poetry of the time, too, some significant dislocations and new directions can be sensed – and not only the new poetical kinds which were becoming fashionable, but in a distinctive confusion of kinds. Polonius's disdainful recitation of the mixture offered by the players visiting Elsinore – 'pastoral-comical, historical-pastoral, tragical-historical, tragical-comical-historical-pastoral' (*Hamlet* II. 2. 397) points to a wider cultural dislocation. In poetry something similar can be sensed – for instance in the epyllion, the short, versified Ovidian narrative (variously serious, comic, erotic, serious- or comic-erotic like *Venus and Adonis* or the richly sensual *Hero and Leander*, by Marlowe and (completed and thereby dislocated in a more serious vein) Chapman. It is in the erotic-comic mixture that the generic unease can be seen most easily to connect with wider social dislocation. The writers of such poems were working within the tradition of Ovid *moralisé* and inevitably undermine it – by irony, by lengthy passages of sensuality, and especially by bringing in their hostility to the dominant courtly modes of idealized lyricism and traditional civic and Christian moralization. The romanticized comments of virtuous lovers are invariably undermined by ironic narrators and by cleverly involving their readers in acknowledging their own sensuality – a wonderfully subversive parody of Sidneian 'delight' and 'moving'. It is the poetry of a generation increasingly unsure of its cultural allegiances. The dialogic nature of textuality is foregrounded, the conflicting discourses clash and rub against one another. It is typical of all avant-garde literature: the languages that can be teased out of these texts are tentative and self-dislocating. The poets were facing, as it were, several ways at once, maintaining an ironic distance from a culture from which they were breaking and yet to which still were irresistibly tied.

In the same way the much commented upon fashion for verse satire in the 1590s shows its ambivalent, uneasily transitional, nature. Typical of the decade, it is vigorous and iconoclastic. Hall, for instance, in his *Virgidemiae*, attacks courtly romance as extravagant and incredulous. He rejects romantic Petrarchan sonnets as conventional, idolatrous and insincere:

> The love-sicke Poet, whose importune prayer
> Repulsed is with resolute dispayre
> Hopeth to conquer his disdainfull dame,
> With publique plaints of his conceived flame.
> Then poures he forth in patched *Sonettings*
> His love, his lust, and loathsome flatterings.

Yet Hall exempts Spenser and Sidney from his criticism, and underneath the iconoclasm is the Puritanism of the man who would end as Bishop of Norfolk. We have seen the same phenomenon with Donne's satires. The combination of iconoclasm and conservatism energizes Hall's; the same point can be made for Marston or Guilpin. The satirist is a 'satyr', abusive, rough but self-conscious in his rhetorical skills; yet he has half an eye on accommodating the institutions he rejects. In short, the contradictions of the satires of the 1590s have socio-cultural and not simply rhetorical origins. The satirist argues that his aim is to speak the truth and yet he continually draws attention to his own prowess and superiority:

> The Satyre onely and Epigramatist
> (Concise Epigrame, and sharpe Satyrist)
> Keepe diet from this surfet of excesse,
> Tempring themselves from such licenciousness.
> The bitter censures of their Critticke spleenes,
> Are Antidotes to penitentiall sinnes.[2]

The satirist is rhetorician and moralist, at once self-effacing and egocentric. The verse satires of Hall, Marston, Donne, Guilpin and others represent the taste of highly educated, ambitious yet cynical young men-on-the-make, eager to become part of what they are excluded from – an increasingly narrow and paranoid ruling class. Theirs is the same virulence and intellectual wavering that Shakespeare so brilliantly exploits in *Hamlet* and *Troilus and Cressida*, where a tired but still powerful public discourse is at once called into question by new and disturbing experiences and yet remains residually strong enough to overcome any challenge to its authority. Shakespeare's so-called 'problem' plays have often been linked to personal crises, as have Marston's, Donne's and Hall's satires. But such crises, however real and powerful, are not merely personal. They are simultaneously private and public, as if in the powerful collective representation of order – or the continuing desire for what was represented as 'order' as opposed to 'disorder' – and in the growing uneasiness between real and apparent power, as well as in the increasingly intensely experienced pressures of different social relationships, the old languages, and with them the old poetry, were no longer adequate. It is in the crises – the discontinuities, the silences, and repressions – of such a period that we can sense, better than the men and women of the time, the growing points of history. Williams writes of the way, in what we call avant-garde literature, the cultural practices which are reaching beyond the residual are never fully realized in textual form, in language, because while they might be apprehended in practice, they cannot be put into words – for there are as yet no words for them.

Our reading of the poetry of the late sixteenth century is therefore inevitably affected by our knowledge of what occurred in subsequent history. The shadow of the Civil War, the failed Revolution of the mid-seventeenth century, and the Restoration of the monarchy cast their shadows not only forward, but backward. To write history is to realize how the future in a real sense determines the past. 'Determines' is perhaps too strong a word, unless we use it in the same sense Williams argues for, as the application of pressures or the recognition of limits. Perhaps 'opens up' is more appropriate, since a vital part of writing an account of a period of our cultural history is to question the seemingly most assuredly given aspects of that history – the cultural artefacts themselves. Here I approach a probably controversial part of this final chapter. Surely, it might be argued, regardless of how interpretations may differ, we know what poetry the poets between Dunbar and Wroth produced; we may change our ways of reading it, and occasionally discover in manuscript new poems or even, rarely, a whole new poet's work, but the masterpieces – the poetry of Wyatt, Sidney, Donne, Shakespeare – are known and unassailable. Perhaps it is so, although the history of taste and criticism does not bear such confidence out. In Palgrave's *Golden Treasury*, where is the place of Greville? Or Donne? It took twentieth-century critics and readers, with their changing questions and interests, to read their poetry back into the accepted account of the period. But even if such matters can be shown to be determined by taste or (more accurately) ideological appropriation, none the less there has in recent years been developing an awareness that the whole notion of a received canon of poetry from our past is suspect, that the received, seemingly stable, monuments of our literary history are present for us only because of a ruthless and continuing struggle to make them present. It is not a question of saying, to adapt a phrase of Stanley Fish, there is 'no text in this class', but rather an assertion that what we call the canon of texts has been historically constructed.

The historical production of the poetry we have considered in this study is material, complex, yet if not objectively explicable, certainly able to be discussed and theorized. But the significance of any text is not inherent only in its original production: it is generated by criticism, by use in educational institutions, by appropriation into courses and literary histories and by being made to serve different ideological and political purposes. As Eagleton puts it, the 'unquestioned "great tradition" . . . has to be recognized as . . . fashioned by particular people for particular reasons at a certain time'. And it is always a highly selective process. Behind the writings of the canon lie the repressed or vanished remains of other writings. If all writing is the product of socio-cultural struggle, where are the adversaries that were rejected and defeated? Some, it is true, have survived; others lie buried by the triumphant texts of the dominant canon. As Jameson argues,

> since by definition the cultural monuments that have survived tend necessarily to perpetuate only a single voice . . . the voice of a hegemonic class, they cannot properly be assigned their relational place in a dialogical system without the restoration or artificial reconstruction of the voice to which they were initially opposed, a voice for the most part stifled and reduced to silence, marginalised, its own utterances scattered to the winds, or reappropriated in their turn by the hegemonic culture.[3]

And so how do we discover such voices? Where is the underground counter-culture, the Elizabethan *samizdat*? Women's and gay poetry, as I argued before, is one such area. The other is what we might loosely call 'popular culture', specifically the poetry written or, in most cases handed down, by oral transmission outside the dominant court culture and assimilated in large part by it in the form of ballads, songs, low-life characters in drama, jokes, bawdy or low-life stories. Some can be found in the drama: the interaction of theatre and social rituals has been carefully assembled by the work of such critics as Barber and Weimann, and by the discussion of the gradual suppression of carnivalesque elements of the Middle Ages.[4] The success of the Renaissance authorities' repression of popular opposition to the dominant court culture, whether in scatological 'flytings' or as expressed in folk customs and rituals, can occasionally be seen in the poetry. The bulk of such oppositional poetry is lost; some was collected and somewhat gentrified in the eighteenth century by Bishop Percy and others, and on occasion, incorporated and assimilated into the canon. As Scott comments on the popular poetry of late medieval Scotland, where much of the most powerful of this material flourished most vigorously, 'behind, under, around and through the art-poetry of court and cloister'.[5] It lurked on the cultural margins, and was passed down, usually orally, among clans and families, embodying the repressed or puzzled inarticulate emotions and yearnings of the dispossessed, and serving (as Falstaff does in Shakespeare's *Henry IV* plays) to remind us of the energies that were lost and destroyed in the ruthless struggles of the period. It turns up, less in the poetry than in the drama, that most polylogic of all Elizabethan forms, to disrupt and challenge the apparently unquestioned dominance of other culturally hegemonous forms of discourse – as the world of Falstaff challenges that of the Royal Court, Autolycus the Court of Sicily, or Caliban the power of Prospero. It is usually neutralized and tamed, and resides as a reminder of how energetic counter-dominant cultural modes can be both appropriated and yet remain dormant, waiting for later readers and social formations to tease them into new life.

We can see something of how the canon was established by glancing back once again at Puttenham's disapproval of Skelton's metrics and political sympathies. As Edwards notes, Skelton 'was the first English writer whose works excited interest across a wide social spectrum during his own lifetime', but by the end of the century, Skelton was being scorned for his condescending to write in the common style instead of the golden, harmonious concord of the courtly maker.[6] The low popular culture with which Skelton was identified is closely associated with the oral tradition of folk wisdom and anti-aristocratic complaint and with the anarchic melancholy of the ballad. At least in the written records, it becomes less and less central to the dominant culture of the sixteenth century as the Court gradually exercises its hegemony. We often (as in the case of the Walsingham ballad, mentioned or used by such poets as Robert Sidney, Ralegh and Shakespeare) have to reconstruct this increasingly marginalized folk-poetry by means of collections put together between the late seventeenth to nineteenth centuries in England or, slightly earlier, from the collections of work from Scotland where the popular tradition resisted assimilation more strongly largely because, as we have seen, of the virtual disappearance of the Court from Scotland after 1603. Ballads, broadsides, versified Robin Hood tales and folk-poetry are permitted to become the material of comedy, anti-masque, or incidental effects in the public theatre, but they are largely excluded from the canon of polite verse. Significantly, such material rarely appears in the pastoral where, one might have thought, the Court's taste should be closest to the material practices of the society. But the pastoral in the sixteenth century is primarily the preserve of the urban, sophisticated courtly aspirant, 'the product', Montrose notes, 'of a handful of ambitious young men who came to social and political maturity in the later 1570s and 1580s'.[7]

In short, to trace the disappearance, marginalization or assimilation of popular poetry through the sixteenth century is another means by which we can see the development of the Court's hegemony. A process of active struggle is going on behind and through the establishing of a poetic canon by marginalization, incorporation and repression. Such a process shows how a culture attempts to impose its dominance and marginalize the texts of any potential counter-culture. In the drama of the time something similar happens, in the form of state control, through censorship and bureaucracy, increasing first over the traditional religious drama, and then over the closely regulated secular plays, which were strongly encouraged to reflect the Tudor regime's view of cosmic and centralized national order. Like the poetry, the period's drama became not the glorious manifestation of a whole national culture but part of an institutionalized plan to use the apparatuses of society to, once again, make 'art a work of state'. The Puritans' abolition of the public theatre in 1642 cannot be totally explained in terms of religious iconoclasm; rather, it represents the calculated assertion of counter-dominant political and cultural forces. Like poetry, the drama had become an instrument of state policy.

Conclusions

The final chapter in a study like this should properly not just sum up but point forward to the work being done on bringing the poetry of the sixteenth century alive for us. The poetry of Shakespeare, Donne Spenser, Sidney, Wroth, Marlowe, and others is so central to what is conceived of as our cultural heritage that to insist (as I have) on the disruptive nature of textuality, the gaps of discourse as well as its plenitude, to demystify and deconstruct, to look more closely at fragmentation and silence than what has appeared to us as replete presence, may all suggest a monstrous perversion of the historian's role and the critic's responsibility. What supports me in the task is the inherently collaborative nature of reading and writing history. I refer not only to the many scholars and critics who are carrying on the same work today, but to the critical community which has made up this poetry's history, its common readers: Sidney's friends, Dryden and Johnson, Coleridge, Browning, Eliot, all the well-remembered and forgotten common readers, the self-consciously differently gendered readers of Wyatt's 'They Flee from Me', Shakespeare's 'Let Me Not to the Marriage of True Minds', or Donne's 'For God's Sake, Hold your Tongue and Let Me Love'. All of us have reinscribed the poems of the sixteenth century in our own lives and our own languages; throughout their history, their words have struggled to be heard through our appropriations of them. Literary history is not the careful preservation of a fixed canon, nor the humble prostration before the fixed stars of an unalterable past. It is the perpetual struggle to write ourselves into our own history, and to do so in the company of as many of those who have struggled before us.

This study is offered therefore as one such re-enactment of a most fascinating and demanding part of our cultural past. Our history is, as Sinfield has insisted, paradoxically both alien to us, and yet inescapably ours.[8] Every aspect of the past that has made us exists as a judgement upon what we have made of it. Sixteenth-century poetry is not, or should not, be seen as, an arcane or antiquarian world of 'treasures' into which we can escape: to read and study poetry, to 'delight' in it, in Sidney's terms, is to become aware of how 'worldly' it is. At the end of Shakespeare's *The Tempest*, Prospero, the poet-magician-scientist-politician, steps out of the play and addresses the audience, asking them (in a moving version of an old trope) for applause. But he also asks for something more difficult. He acknowledges that the play the audience has just witnessed will be 'confined', trapped, nullified, unless its impact is taken out of the theatre, into the lives as well as the words, of its audience. How they will do that is not up to the actor who speaks; nor is it up to the dramatist who wrote his lines. It is up to the members of the audience themselves, to break the confines of the theatre, of art, of literature, and go into the world and to become themselves, in Edward Said's use of the term, 'worldly'. We must learn that literature, and in particular poetry, are not separate from the rest of the world around and within us. We are spoken by, given language by, our past as well as our present, and that language is at its most powerful in poets like those studied in this book. That is why we read and reread the poetry of the sixteenth century – that we may know, and use, its power.

Notes

1. Francis Barker, 'The Tremulous Private Body', in *1642: Literature and Power in the Seventeenth Century* (Colchester, 1981), pp. 1–10 (p. 2).

2. Joseph Hall, *Collected Poems*, edited by Arnold Davenport (Liverpool, 1969), p. 18.

3. Terry Eagleton, *Literary Theory: An Introduction* (Oxford, 1983), p. 11. Fredric Jameson, *The Political Unconscious* (Princeton, 1980), p. 85.

4. See Mikhail Bachtin, *Rabelais and his World*, translated by Helen Iswolsky (Cambridge, Mass., 1968); C. L. Barber, *Shakespeare's Festive Comedy* (Princeton, 1959); Robert Weimann, *Shakespeare and the Popular Tradition in the Theatre* (Baltimore, 1978); Michael Bristol, *Carnival and Theatre: Plebeian Culture and the Structure of Authority in Early Modern England* (London, 1985).

5. *Late Medieval Scots Poetry*, edited by Tom Scott (London, 1967), p. 32.

6. *Skelton: The Critical Heritage*, edited by Anthony S. G. Edwards (London, 1981), p. 59.

7. Louis A. Montrose, 'Of Gentlemen and Shepherds: The Politics of Elizabethan Pastoral Form', *ELH*, 50 (1983), 415–60 (p. 433).

8. Alan Sinfield, 'Against Appropriation', *Essays in Criticism*, 31, no. 3 (July 1981), 181–95 (p. 182).

Chronology

Note: One problem of establishing a chronology for poetry of this period is that most of the poetry written was not published, or often not for many years. Dating of poems and poets' work is often, therefore, very difficult. Dates in this chronology are necessarily more approximate when they refer to writing (w.) than the date of publication (p.).

DATE	WORKS OF POETRY	OTHER WORKS	HISTORICAL/CULTURAL EVENTS
1460			James II of Scotland killed at Roxburgh; accession of James III
1461			Henry VI of England deposed; Edward IV ascends throne
1462	Henryson *Fables* (w.) *Testiment of Cresseid* about now		
1470		Malory *Morte D'Arthur* (w.)	Henry VI (deposed 1461) restored as King of England (–1471); Edward IV deposed
1471			Henry VI murdered in Tower; Edward IV becomes King of England again (reigned previously 1461–70)
1474		Caxton *Recuyelle of the Histories of Troye* (w.) – first book printed in English	

DATE	WORKS OF POETRY	OTHER WORKS	HISTORICAL/CULTURAL EVENTS
1475	*Cockelbie's Sow* (w.) (appears in Bannatyne Manuscript, 1568)		
1476			Establishment of printing press in England by Caxton
1477	Dunbar writing about now	*Dictes and Sayings of the Philosophers* (p.) – first dated book printed in England	
1478	Chaucer *The Canterbury Tales* (p.)		
1481		Caxton *Godeffroy of Boloyne* (tr.) *Mirror of the World* (tr.)	
1483		Caxton *The Golden Legend* (tr.)	Edward IV dies; his 12-year-old son succeeds as Edward V; Richard Duke of Gloucester seizes power, becomes Richard III Herald's College founded
1484		Caxton *Book of the Knight of La Tour-Landry* (tr.)	
1485		Malory *Morte D'Arthur* (p.)	Battle of Bosworth Field; end of the War of the Roses; Henry Tudor marries Elizabeth (daughter of Edward IV of York) and so unites houses of Lancaster and York; ascends throne as Henry VII

DATE	WORKS OF POETRY	OTHER WORKS	HISTORICAL/CULTURAL EVENTS
1486		Medwall *Fulgens and Lucrece* (p.)	Diaz circumnavigates the Cape
1488		Caxton *The Royal Book* (tr.)	James III of Scotland murdered; accession of James IV
1490			The Oxford Humanist Reformers (Linacre, Grocyn, Colet, Erasmus, More) active (–1520)
1492			Columbus, commissioned by Isabella of Castile, voyages to the New World
1494	Lydgate *Fall of Princes* (w.) (p. with and as an addition to the suppressed first edition of *A Mirror for Magistrates*, 1555)		
1496	Douglas writing		
1497			Cabot reaches America
1498	Skelton *The Bowge of Court* (w.)		
1500		Erasmus *Adages* (p.) *Everyman*	
1501	Douglas *Pallace of Honour* (w.) (p. London c.1553, Edinburgh 1579)	Sannazaro *Arcadia* (p.)	

DATE	WORKS OF POETRY	OTHER WORKS	HISTORICAL/CULTURAL EVENTS
1503	Dunbar *Thistle and the Rose* (w.)	Erasmus *Enchiridion* (p.)	Michelangelo active
1504	Skelton *Philip Sparrow* (w.) Hawes *Exemple of Vertu* (w.) (p. 1509)		Colet Dean of St Paul's Raphael active
1505			Christ's College, Cambridge founded

1506	Dunbar
	*Lament for the
	  Makaris* (w.)
			Ariosto begins writing
			  Orlando Furioso

1509	Barclay
	Ship of Fools (p.)
	
	Hawes
	*The Pastyme of
	  Pleasure* (p.)
		Erasmus
		Moriae Encomium (w.)
			Accession of Henry
			  VIII and his marriage
			  to Catherine of
			  Aragon
			Brasenose College,
			  Oxford founded

1510			Colet founds St Paul's School

1511			Henry joins the Holy
			  League
			Erasmus becomes
			  Reader in Greek at
			  Cambridge

1512	Douglas *Eneados* (w.) – translation of *Aeneid* (p. 1553)		

1513		Machiavelli
		Il Principe (w., p. 1532;
		  English tr. 1640)
			James IV of Scotland
			  killed; accession of
			  James V

1514	Barclay *Eclogues,* I–III (w.)		

DATE	WORKS OF POETRY	OTHER WORKS	HISTORICAL/CULTURAL EVENTS
1515			Wolsey becomes cardinal
1516	Ariosto *Orlando Furioso* (p.), 2nd edition 1521, final edition 1532	More *Utopia* (p.)	Mary, later Queen of England, daughter of Henry VIII and Catherine of Aragon, born Titian active
1517			Luther's Wittenberg Theses
1519			Cortés invades Mexico Magellan begins voyage around the world
1520			Field of the Cloth of Gold
1521	Skelton *Speake Parot* *Colin Clout* (w.)	Henry VIII *A Defence of the Seven Sacraments* (p.)	Diet of Worms
1522	Skelton *Why Come Ye Not to Court* (w.)		
1523	Barclay *The Mirror of Good Manners* (p.)		Pope Clement VII accedes
1525		Tyndale *New Testament* printed at Worms – first English translation of any part of the Bible	

DATE	WORKS OF POETRY	OTHER WORKS	HISTORICAL/CULTURAL EVENTS
1528	Lindsay *The Dreme* (p.)	Castiglione *Il Libro del Cortegiano* (p.); 1st English tr. by Hoby, 1561	
1529	Lindsay *Complaint* (w.)		The Reformation Parliament
1531		Elyot *Book of the Governor* (p.)	
1532		Rabelais *Pantagruel* (p.)	Henry divorces Catherine of Aragon
1533	Wyatt writing first satires about now		Cranmer becomes Archbishop of Canterbury; Henry excommunicated; marries Anne Boleyn; Elizabeth born; separation of English Church from Rome
1534		Rabelais *Gargantua* (p.)	Act of Supremacy; Henry VIII Head of Church of England
1535		Coverdale, first complete English Bible	More and Fisher executed
1536		Calvin *Institutes of the Christian Religion* (p.); 1st English tr. by Norton, 1561	Anne Boleyn's miscarriage and execution; Henry VIII marries Jane Seymour
1537		Cranmer *Institution of a Christian Man* (p.)	Jane Seymour dies giving birth to Edward (later King)

DATE	WORKS OF POETRY	OTHER WORKS	HISTORICAL/CULTURAL EVENTS
1538		Elyot *Dictionaire* (p.)	James V of Scotland marries Marie de Guise
1539		The Great Bible (p.)	Greater Abbeys suppressed
1540	Wyatt *Defence* (w.)	Lindsay *Satire of the Three Estates* performed (p. 1602)	Fall and execution of Cromwell Henry marries Anne of Cleves; marriage annulled; marries Catherine Howard
1542		Hall *Chronicle* (p.)	Catherine Howard executed
1543		Copernicus *De Revolutionibus* (p.)	Mary Queen of Scots betrothed to the Dauphin; goes to France Henry marries Catherine Parr
1545		Henry VIII *Primer* (p.)	Council of Trent opens
1546			Christ Church, Oxford founded; Trinity College, Cambridge, founded
1547			Henry VIII dies; Edward VI succeeds Execution of Surrey
1548	Sternhold *Certain Psalms* (p.)	*The Book of Common Prayer* (largely work of Cranmer) Hall *Union of . . . York and Lancaster* (p.)	

DATE	WORKS OF POETRY	OTHER WORKS	HISTORICAL/CULTURAL EVENTS
1549	Wyatt *Certain Psalms drawn into English Meter* (p.)	Du Bellay *Défence et Illustration de la langue française* (p.)	
1552		Second English Prayer *Book:* considerable doctrinal changes	
1553	Lindsay *A Dialogue between Experience and a Courtier of the Miserable Estate of the World* (p.)	Wilson *The Art of Rhetoric* (p.)	Edward VI dies; Mary accedes
1554	Lindsay *The Monarchie* (p.)		Execution of Lady Jane Grey Marriage of Mary to Philip of Spain; England reconciled with Rome but Mary retains title of Supreme Head
1555	Abortive first attempt to print *A Mirror for Magistrates;* two variant title pages and one leaf of text extant	Heywood *Two Hundred Epigrams* (p.)	Persecution of Protestants in England: Latimer and Ridley burnt at the stake; Cranmer burnt
1557	Tottel's *Miscellany* (p.)		Stationers' Company incorporated
1558		Marguerite De Navarre *Heptameron* (p.)	Loss of Calais to France; Mary dies, Elizabeth I accedes
1559	Baldwin *A Mirror for Magistrates* (full edition) (p.)	Foxe *Actes and Monuments* (p. in Latin; 1st edition tr. 1563)	Pope Pius IV succeeds; Matthew Parker Archbishop of Canterbury Acts of Uniformity

DATE	WORKS OF POETRY	OTHER WORKS	HISTORICAL/CULTURAL EVENTS
1560		Geneva Bible (tr.)	
1561	Robinson, tr. of More *Utopia* (p.) Stowe edition of Chaucer (p.)	Googe, tr. of Palingenius *Zodiake of Life* Hoby *The Courtier* (p.); tr. of Castiglione	
1562	Sternold, Hopkins, Norton, and others *The Whole Book of Metrical Psalms* (p.)	Jewel *Apologia pro Ecclesia Anglicana* (p.)	
1563	Googe *Eclogues, Epitaphs and Sonnets* (p.) Sackville *Induction* to portion of 1563 edition of *A Mirror for Magistrates*		
1565	Golding, tr. of Ovid *Metamorphoses*, I–IV (p.)		
1566	Painter *Palace of Pleasure* (p.)		
1567	Drant, tr. of Horace *Art of Poetry, Epistles, Satires* (p.) Turberville *Epitaphs, Epigrams, Songs and Sonnets* (p.)		Revolt of the Netherlands
1568	Bannatyne Manuscript compiled		English College at Douai founded

DATE	WORKS OF POETRY	OTHER WORKS	HISTORICAL/CULTURAL EVENTS
1569	Spenser *The Visions of Bellay* *The Visions of Petrarch* (p.)		
1570		Ascham *Scholemaster* (p.) Foxe *Ecclesiastical History* (p.)	Pope Pius V excommunicates and announces deposition of Elizabeth I
1571	Third edition of *A Mirror for Magistrates* (p.)		
1572			Pope Gregory XIII accedes Massacre of St Bartholomew
1573	Du Bartas *Judith* (p.) Gascoigne *A Hundred Sundry Flowers* *The Adventures of Master F.J.* (p.) (prose romance, includes poetry) Tasso *Aminta* (p.)	Cartwright *Reply to an Answer* (p.)	
1575	Breton *A Small Handful of Fragrant Flowers* (p.) Churchyard *The First Part of Churchyard's Chippes* (p.) Gascoigne *The Poesies of Gascoigne* (p.) Ronsard *Sonnets Pour Hélène* (p.) Tasso *Gerusalemme Liberata* (p.)	Laneham *A Letter* (p.)	

DATE	WORKS OF POETRY	OTHER WORKS	HISTORICAL/CULTURAL EVENTS
1576	Edwards (ed.) *Paradise of Dainty Devices* (p.) Gascoigne *Princely Pleasure of . . . Kenilworth* *The Steele Glas* (p.)		The Theatre in London built
1577		Peacham *Garden of Eloquence* (p.) Gascoigne *Glass of Government* (p.)	Drake begins voyage around the world
1578	Du Bartas *Sepmaines* (p.)	Lyly *Euphues, the Anatomy of Wit* (p.)	Mary Sidney marries William Herbert, Earl of Pembroke
1579	Churchyard *General Rehearsal of Wars* (p.) Spenser *Shepheardes Calender* (p.)	Gosson *School of Abuse* North, tr. of Plutarch *Lives of the Noble Grecians* and *Romans*	Pope Gregory XIII sets up Jesuit College in Rome; sends missions to England
1580	Sidney *Astrophil and Stella* (w.; p. 1591)	Harvey *Three Proper Letters* *Two other Letters* (p.) Lyly *Euphues and his England* (p.) Sidney *Defence of Poesie* (w.; p. 1595) *Arcadia* begun (p. 1590)	
1581	Howell *Howell his Devices* (p.)	Mulcaster *Positions* (p.) Pettie, tr. of Guazzo *Civil Conversation*	French marriage crisis

DATE	WORKS OF POETRY	OTHER WORKS	HISTORICAL/CULTURAL EVENTS
1582	Ralegh's poems written (–1592) and circulated at Court Watson *Hecatompathia* (p.) Whitestone *Heptameron of Civil Discorses (Aurelia)* (p.)		Bruno in England
1583			Whitgift Archbishop of Canterbury
1584		Bruno *Cena delle Cinere* *De La Causa* *De L'infinito* (p.) Peele *Arraignment of Paris* acted (p.) Scott *Discovery of Witchcraft* (p.)	Ralegh founds first English colony in Virginia; failure of the colony Cambridge University press founded
1585	Bruno *Eroici Furori* (p.)		
1586	Warner *Albion's England*, I–IV (p.)	Knox *The History of Reformation of Religion Within the Realm of Scotland* (p.) Kyd *Spanish Tragedy* acted? Pettie, tr. of Guazzo *Civil Conversation* (p.) Webbe *Discourse of English Poetry* (p.) Whetstone *English Mirror* (p.)	Sir Philip Sidney dies of wounds in Battle of Zutphen; Robert Sidney becomes Governor of Flushing Trial of Mary, Queen of Scots James VI signs Treaty of Berwick with Elizabeth I

DATE	WORKS OF POETRY	OTHER WORKS	HISTORICAL/CULTURAL EVENTS
1587	Fraunce, tr. of Watson *Amyntas* (p.) Monteverdi first book of madrigals	Day, tr. of Longus *Daphnis and Chloe* (p.) Golding and Sidney, tr. of Du Plessis Mornay *Of the Trueness of the Christian Religion* (p.) Marlowe *Tamburlaine*, Pts I and II acted	The Pope proclaims a crusade against England Execution of Mary, Queen of Scots
1588	Byrd *Psalms, Sonnets and Songs* (p.)	Fraunce *Arcadian Rhetoric* (p.)	The Spanish Armada defeated
1589		Nashe *Anatomy of Absurdity* (p.) Puttenham *The Arte of English Poesie* (p.) *The Marprelate Tracts* (p.)	
1590	Spenser *The Faerie Queene*, I–III (p.) Watson *First Set of Madrigals Englished* (p.) Monteverdi second book of madrigals (p.)	Guarini *Pastor Fido* (p.) Lodge *Rosalynde* (p.) Marlowe *Tamburlaine the Great* (w.) Shakespeare *The Comedy of Errors* (w.) Sidney *Arcadia*, revised edition (p.)	

DATE	WORKS OF POETRY	OTHER WORKS	HISTORICAL/CULTURAL EVENTS
1591	Breton *Briton's Bower of Delights* (p.) Fraunce *Countess of Pembroke's Emanuel* (p.) Harington, tr. of Ariosto *Orlando Furioso* (w. 1506–16) Sidney, Sir Philip *Astrophil and Stella* (p.) Southwell *Mary Magdelene's Tears* (p.) Spenser *Complaints Daphnaida* (p.)	Greene *Notable Discovery of Couzenage* Ralegh *A Report about the Flight of the Isles of Azores*	Trinity College, Dublin, founded Ralegh imprisoned and released
1592	Breton *Pilgrimage to Paradise* *The Countess of Pembrokes Passion* (p.) Constable *Diana* (p.) Daniel *Delia . . . with the Complaint of Rosamund* (p.) Harvey *Four Letters and Certain Sonnets* (p.) Sylvester, 1st instalment of tr. of Du Bartas *Sepmaines* Warner *Albion's England,* I–VIII (p.)	Marlowe *Edward II* acted? Nashe *Pierce Penniless* (p.) Shakespeare *Richard III* (w.)	Essex recalled to Court by Elizabeth Rose Theatre opened

DATE	WORKS OF POETRY	OTHER WORKS	HISTORICAL/CULTURAL EVENTS
1593	Barnes *Parthenophil and Parthenophe* Drayton *Idea* *The Shepherds' Garland* (p.) Marlowe *Hero and Leander* (entered in Stationer's Register) Shakespeare *Venus and Adonis* *Phoenix Nest* (w.)	Harvey *Pierce's Supererogation* (p.) Nashe *Christ's Tears Over Jerusalem* (p.)	Theatres closed by the plague
1594	Barnfield *The Affectionate Shepherd* (p.) Constable *Diana Augmented* (p.) Daniel *Delia* *Rosamond augmented* *Cleopatra* (p.) Davies *Orchestra* (w.) Drayton *Idea's Mirror* (p.) Shakespeare *The Rape of Lucrece* (p.)	Hooker *Ecclesiastical Polity*, I–IV (p.) Kyd *Spanish Tragedy* (p.) Shakespeare *Titus Andronicus* *The Taming of the Shrew* *Two Gentlemen of Verona* *Love's Labour's Lost* (w.) Tasso *Discorsi del Poema Eroica* (p.)	Beginning of a period of bad harvests in England Swan Theatre built (–1596)

DATE	WORKS OF POETRY	OTHER WORKS	HISTORICAL/CULTURAL EVENTS
1595	Barnes *A Divine Century of Spiritual Sonnets* (p.) Barnfield *Cynthia with Certain Sonnets* (p.) Breton *Mary Magdalen's Love* (p.) Campion *Poemata* (p.) Chapman *Ovid's Banquet of Sense* (p.) Donne's early poetry circulating in MS Drayton *Endimion and Phoebe* (p.) Shakespeare's sonnets (w. ?–1599) Southwell *Saint Peter's Complaint* (w.) Spenser *Amoretti* *Epithalamion* *Colin Clouts Come Home Again* (p.)	Ford *Ornatus and Artesia* (p.) Montaigne *Essais* (final ed. p.) Shakespeare *A Mid-Summer Night's Dream* (w.) Sidney *Apology for Poetry (Defence of Poesie* p.; w. 1580)	Execution of Southwell Unsuccessful voyage of Drake and Hawkins to the West Indies and deaths of both
1596	Davies, Sir John *Orchestra* (p.) Harington *Metamorphosis of Ajax* (p.) Smith *Chloris* (p.) Spenser *The Faerie Queene*, IV–VI, and new edition of I–III (p.)	Deloney *John Winchcomb (Jack of Newbury*, entered in Stationer's Register) Nashe *Have With You To Saffron Walden* (p.) Ralegh *Discovery of Guiana* (p.) Shakespeare *Romeo and Juliet* *The Merchant of Venice* (w.)	Essex storms Cadiz

DATE	WORKS OF POETRY	OTHER WORKS	HISTORICAL/CULTURAL EVENTS
1597	Dowland *First Book of Songs* (p.) Drayton *England's Heroical Epistles* (p.) Montgomerie *The Cherrie and the Slaye* (p.)	Chapman *Humorous Day's Mirth* acted? James I *Demonology* (p.) Shakespeare *Henry IV*, 1, 2 *Henry V* *Merry Wives of Windsor* (–1600) (w.)	Philip's second Armada dispersed by bad weather
1598	Chapman-Marlowe *Hero and Leander* (p.) Hall *Virgidemiarum* IV–VI (p.) Marston *Scourge of Villainy* (p.)	Jonson *Every Man in his Humour* (p.) Shakespeare *Much Ado about Nothing* (w.) Young, tr. of Montemayo *Diana* (p.) Meres *Palladis Tamia Wit's Treasury* (p.)	
1599	Daniel *Poetical Essays* (including *Civil Wars*, I–V) *Musophilus* (p.) Marston *Scourge of Villainy Corrected with New Satires* (p.) *The Passionate Pilgrim* (p.)	James I *Basilikon Doron* (p.) Shakespeare *As You Like it Julius Caesar* (w.)	Essex rebellion Globe Theatre built for Shakespeare's company
1600	Bodenham (ed.) *England's Helicon* (p.) Dowland *Second Book of Songs* (p.) Davies *All Ovids Elegies: Three Books* (p.)	Jonson *Cynthia's Revels* acted Fairfax, tr. of Tasso *Godfrey of Bouloigne* Gilbert *De Magnete* (p.) Shakespeare *Hamlet* (w.)	Bruno burnt at Rome Fortune Theatre opened

DATE	WORKS OF POETRY	OTHER WORKS	HISTORICAL/CULTURAL EVENTS
1601	Campion *A Book of Airs* (p.) Shakespeare *The Phoenix and the Turtle* (p.)	Shakespeare *Twelfth Night* *Troilus and Cressida* (w.)	East India Company founded
1602	*A Poetical Rhapsody* (p.)	Campion *Observations on the Art of English Poesie* (p.) Shakespeare *All's Well That Ends Well* (w.)	Bodleian Library, Oxford founded
1603	John Davies of Hereford *Microcosmos* (p.)	Daniel *Defence of Ryme* (p.) James I *The True Law of Free Monarchies* (p.)	Elizabeth I dies; James I (James VI of Scotland) accedes

General Bibliographies

(i)   Approach and methodology
(ii) General background studies (historical and cultural)
(iii) General studies of literature
(iv) Studies and anthologies of poetry

Note: Place of publication is London unless otherwise stated.

(i) Approach and methodology

Sixteenth-century poetry and Renaissance and early modern literature generally have been well served by some energetic scholarship from the late 1970s onward, and especially by exciting developments in literary theory. In particular, we have seen the development of 'new' or 'revisionist' literary studies of the period, sometimes lumped together as New Historicism. But there are many New Historicisms, and it is useful to single out Cultural Materialism and feminism as equally important strands in the contestation over the period. There is a succinct description of the new movements' British and American manifestations, with some fine distinctions between the two, in Jonathan Dollimore's review of Jonathan Goldberg's *James I and the Politics of Literature*, in *Criticism*, 26 (1984), 83–86; see also Goldberg's 'The Politics of Renaissance Literature: A Review Essay', *ELH*, 49 (1982). Stephen Greenblatt's *Renaissance Self-Fashioning: From More to Shakespeare* (Chicago, 1980), is often seen as an early manifesto of New Historicism, just as *Political Shakespeare*, ed. Alan Sinfield and Jonathan Dollimore (Manchester, 1984) may be regarded as a masthead for Cultural Materialism. Greenblatt's *Shakespearean Negotiations: the Circulation of Social Energy in Renaissance England* (Berkeley, 1988) is another important New Historicist collection. Louis Montrose's 'Shaping Fantasies: Figurations of Gender and Power in Elizabethan Culture', *Representations* 1 (1983) is a representative essay of one of the most suggestive New Historicist critics. Raymond Williams's writings lie behind much Cultural Materialist criticism. See especially *Marxism and Literature* (Oxford, 1977) and *Problems in Materialism and Culture* (1982); and a fascinating account of two great keywords in our cultural history, *The Country and the City* (1973). The last named is especially relevant for this period in its treatment of Sidney and country-house poems. Terry Eagleton's *Walter Benjamin or Towards a Revolutionary Criticism* (1981) is very useful for its 'little history of Rhetoric'. Behind many of these studies is the ubiquitous figure of Louis Althusser. The essay on 'Ideological State Apparatuses' in *Lenin and Philosophy and other Essays*, translated by Ben Brewster (New York, 1972) is particularly important. Francis Barker's *The Tremulous Private Body: Essays on Subjection* (1984) is an important attack on humanist criticism in the Althusserian vein.

Feminism and psychoanalysis have also made major contributions to the rewriting of the period. Carol Thomas Neely's article, 'Constructing the Subject: Feminist

Practice and the new Renaissance Discourses', *English Literary Renaissance*, 18 (1988) attacks the gender blindness of both New Historicism and Cultural Materialism. Gary Waller's *The Sidney Family Romance: Gender Construction in Early Modern England* (Detroit, 1993) combines psychoanalytical and gender analysis within a predominantly cultural materialist perspective. For psychoanalytical studies of the period relevant to the poetry, see Barbara Freedman, *Staging the Gaze: Psychoanalysis, Postmodernism, and Shakespearean Comedy* (Ithaca, 1990) and Coppélia Kahn, *Man's Estate: Masculine Identity in Shakespeare* (Berkeley, 1981). More general studies linking history to psychoanalysis, include the overstated but intriguing book by Camille Paglia, *Sexual Personae: Art and Decadence from Nefertiti to Emily Dickinson* (New York, 1991), Klaus Theweleit's complex and important *Male Fantasies* (Minneapolis, 1987), Jessica Benjamin's *The Bonds of Love: Psychoanalysis, Feminism, and the Problem of Domination* (New York; 1988), and Louise Kaplan's *Female Perversions* (New York, 1991).

(ii) General background studies (historical and cultural)

Coming directly to the sixteenth century and the Renaissance period generally, the classic study against which all subsequent scholarship has argued, usually in admiration, has been Jacob Burckhardt's *The Civilization of the Renaissance in Italy*, translated by S. G. C. Middlemore, 2 vols (New York, 1958). Of the older historicist accounts of this century, E. M. W. Tillyard's *The Elizabethan World Picture* (1943) is outdated and simplistic. It is mentioned only because it resides on the bookshelves (and book lists) of many university teachers. Much more useful older studies are L. C. Knights's *Drama and Society in the Age of Jonson* (1937) and John Buxton's attractive, if idealizing, picture of the period in *Elizabethan Taste* (1963). A corrective to Tillyard and to the dominant aristocratic view of the period is the important work of social history, Carlo Ginzburg's *The Cheese and the Worms*, translated by John and Anne Tedeschi (Baltimore, 1980), which provides a startling account of the 'world-view' of an ordinary Renaissance man. Oversimplified but amusing reading are A. L. Rowse's *The Elizabethan Renaissance: The Life of Society* (1971) and *The Cultural Achievement* (1972). Substantial historical studies are Lawrence Stone's classic and much debated *The Crisis of the Aristocracy 1558–1640* (Oxford, 1965), and Perez Zagorin's *The Court and the Country* (1970). *Patronage in the Renaissance*, edited by Guy Fitch Lytle and Stephen Orgel (Princeton, 1981) contains a number of essays on a topic long dominated by unexamined commonplaces. The Pembroke family's patronage is surveyed by Michael Brennan, *Literary Patronage in the English Renaissance: The Pembroke Family* (1987). Annabel Patterson's *Censorship and Interpretation: The Conditions of Writing and Reading in Early Modern England* (1984) is an important study of how writers avoided much direct control over their activities.

Of the general studies of the poetry, Maurice Evans's *English Poetry in the Sixteenth Century* (1955) is still a useful, compact summary. Fred Inglis's *The Elizabethan Poets* (1970) is stimulating, and like Douglas L. Peterson's *The English Lyric from Wyatt to Donne* (Princeton, 1967) concentrates on the so-called 'plain style' tradition. J. W. Lever's *The Elizabethan Love Sonnet* (second edn, 1968) argues for a distinctive moralization of Petrarch by the Elizabethan poets. Petrarchism itself is excellently treated in Leonard Forster's *The Icy Fire* (Cambridge, 1969). An important book dealing with the adaptation of Petrarchan and other courtly modes in the English Court is John Stevens's rich and suggestive *Music and Poetry in the Early Tudor Court* (1961). Stevens's later views on Elizabethan poetry were briefly but highly suggestively put in *The Old Sound and the New* (Cambridge, 1982) which deals with the century's metrical revolution.

(iii) General studies of literature

It is often difficult to distinguish purely 'literary' accounts from those discussed under section (ii) above. One of the marks of the most important recent work on the period is a stress on the indissolubility of the codes of literary and other cultural texts. But works that focus on the literature rather than the politics or philosophy are listed here, including anthologies and collections of criticism. A useful collection of primary sources in the criticism of the period is J. W. H. Atkins's *English Literary Criticism: The Renaissance* (1962). The standard collection, *Elizabethan Critical Essays*, edited by G. Gregory Smith, 2 vols (Oxford, 1904) is still useful. Of the many surveys of the period's literature in general, readers might consult (with care) the revised edition of the Pelican *The Age of Shakespeare*, edited by Boris Ford (Harmondsworth, 1955; revised edition 1982). The emphasis remains astringently Leavisite but includes new essays, on Sidney and Spenser, by J. C. A. Rathmell and W. W. Robson respectively, which (in the former case at least) change the direction very slightly. C. S. Lewis's magisterial, lively, prejudiced (depending on one's taste) *English Literature in the Sixteenth Century Excluding Drama* (Oxford, 1954) is still remarkably provocative as well as thorough. Gregory Krantzmann's *Anglo-Scottish Literary Relations 1430–1550* (Cambridge, 1980), is an indispensable survey of a neglected subject. Social and political contexts are discussed well by David Norbrook, *Poetry and Politics in the English Renaissance* (1984) and Alan Sinfield *Literature in Protestant England 1588–1660* (Brighton, 1983). Sinfield's study is both methodologically rich and provocative, and so far is the best and most lively account of the impact of religious ideas on the period's literature. It might be read alongside another suggestive and rigorous study, *Radical Tragedy*, by Jonathan Dollimore (1983) which deals primarily with the period's drama. Sinfield and Dollimore represent the recent Cultural Materialist criticism in the period; their work connects (and in some respects can be interestingly contrasted) with some recent American New Historicism, notably by Goldberg, Whigham, already noted, and by Louis A. Montrose, who has produced an important series of essays on the interaction of literary forms and socio-cultural production. See for instance 'Celebration and Insinuation: Sir Philip Sidney and the Motives of Elizabethan Courtship', *Ren. Drama*, n.s. 8 (1977), 3–35; or 'Of Gentlemen and Shepherds: The Politics of Elizabethan Pastoral Form', *ELH*, 50 (1983), 415–20.

Secondary studies of the period's criticism include Robert L. Montgomery's *The Reader's Eye: Studies in Didactic Literary Theory from Dante to Tasso* (Berkeley, 1979). Marion Trousdale's *Shakespeare and the Rhetoricians* (1982) is a careful application of recent theories of language to a topic long dominated by antiquarianism, while Frank Whigham's article in *PMLA*, 76 (1980), 864–82, 'The Rhetoric of Elizabethan Suitor's Letters', is similarly ground breaking. Brian Vickers's *In Defence of Rhetoric* (Oxford, 1988) includes an important section on the Renaissance. Howard C. Cole's *A Quest of Inquirie: Some Contexts of Tudor Literature* (Indianapolis, 1973) discusses literary theory along with much else that is relevant in a rambling, chatty and very suggestive study. Perhaps the best brief introduction to Elizabethan poetic theory is

Earl Miner's 'Assaying the Golden World of English Renaissance Poetics', *Centrum*, 4 (1976), 5–20.

(iv) Studies and anthologies of poetry

When we turn specifically to poetry, there are many useful anthologies for readers to browse in, in addition to scholarly editions or selections of particular poets. The most useful currently are *The New Oxford Book of Sixteenth Century Verse*, ed. Emrys Jones (Oxford, 1991), which is organized chronologicaly, and *The Penguin Book of Renaissance Verse*, ed. David Norbrook and H.R. Woudhuysen (1992), which usefully extends the canon to include women's and some regional poetry and relates the poetry to current critical issues. Among older selections, Nigel Alexander's *Elizabethan Narrative Verse* (1968), is useful, as is Elizabeth S. Donno's *Elizabethan Minor Epics* (1963). More specialized is H. E. Rollins's edition of *Tottel's Miscellany* (1557–67), 2 vols (Cambridge, Mass., 1965). Scottish verse is conveniently found in Joan Hughes and W. S. Ramson, eds, *The Poetry of the Stewart Court* (Canberra, 1983), a valuable collection of poetry from the Bannatyne Manuscript covers up to the mid-sixteenth century, while R.D.S. Jack's *A Choice of Scottish Verse 1560–1660* (1978) covers the next hundred years. John MacQueen's *Ballatis of Luve* (Edinburgh, 1979) is a brief collection of love songs.

Specialized studies of poetry worth pursuing include Richard Helgerson's two studies, *The Elizabethan Prodigals* (Berkeley, 1976) on the 'new generation' of late Elizabethan writers, and *Self-Crowned Laureates: Spenser, Jonson, Milton and the Literary System* (Berkeley, 1983) which discusses the vocationalism of late Elizabethan poetry. E. W. Pomeroy studies *The Elizabethan Miscellanies: Their Development and Conventions* in a useful if rather superficial survey (Berkeley, 1973). Patricia Fumerton draws suggestive parallels with portraiture in ' "Secret Arts" Elizabethan Miniatures and Sonnets', *Representations* 15 (1986), 57–97. Roger Kuin's suggestive articles on Petrarchan poetry include 'Feint/Frenzy: Madness and the Elizabethan Love Sonnet', *Criticism* 31 (1989), 1–20. A major study of poetry in the Court is David Javitch's *Poetry and Courtliness in Renaissance England* (Princeton, 1978). Javitch was the first to show in detail the overlap between the courtly life and its poetic. See also his 'The Impure Motives of Elizabethan Poetry', *Genre*, 15 (1982), 225–38. The political dimension of the sonnets is dealt with in an important article by Arthur F. Marotti, 'Love is not Love: Elizabethan Sonnet Sequence and the Social Order', *ELH*, 49 (1982), 396–428. Charles Altieri's 'Rhetoric, Rhetoricity and the Sonnet as Performance', *Tennessee Studies in Literature*, 25 (1980), 1–23, is an intriguing reading of the sonnet's concern with its audience, and Steven W. May's *The Elizabethan Courtier Poets* (Columbia, 1991) surveys the canon and circulation of the courtier poets. *Soliciting Interpretation: Literary Theory and Seventeenth-Century English Poetry*, edited by Elizabeth D. Harvey and Katherine Eisaman Maus (Chicago, 1990) contains stimulating essays relevant to the early period, especially those by David Norbrook and Annabel Patterson on Donne, Arthur Marotti on Shakespeare, and Maureen Quilligan on Wroth.

While Sinfield's study of Protestantism and literature (noted above) is more stimulating, John N. King's *English Reformation Literature: The Tudor Origins of the Protestant Tradition* (Princeton, 1982) is a solidly researched compilation of material from the neglected Protestant poets of the mid-century period. Recent work on women poets includes Margaret Hannay, ed., *Silent But for the Word* (Kent, 1984), Elaine Beilin, *Redeeming Eve: Women Writers of the English Renaissance* (Princeton,

1987), Betty Travitsky and Ann Haselkorn, eds, *The Renaissance Englishwoman in Print: Counterbalancing the Canon* (Amherst, 1990), and Mary Ellen Lamb's especially stimulating *Gender and Authorship in the Sidney Circle* (Madison, 1990). Derek Attridge's *Well-Weighed Syllables: Elizabethan Verse in Classical Metres* (Cambridge, 1974) is likely long to be the standard work on an obscure topic. Susanne Woods's elegant study, *Natural Emphasis: English Versification from Chaucer to Dryden* (San Marino, 1984) is careful and valuable; a more general study by Antony Easthope, *Poetry as Discourse* (1983), is important as an account of the pentameter as an hegemonous cultural form with deep implications for this period.

Individual Authors

Notes on biography, major works and criticism

ALEXANDER, Sir William, Earl of Stirling (1567–1640), Scottish poet and statesman who came to England in 1603 with James I and VI after a distinguished career as a poet and courtier in the Scottish Court. Author of four verse tragedies written 1603–07, the *Monarchicke Tragedies*, and poems including sonnets published in *Aurora* (1604). He had been one of King James's poetical proteges in the Scottish Court, and although his literary career went well beyond the sixteenth century (he lived, indeed, nearly until the start of the Civil War), his poetical style in the new century remained Elizabethan rather than Jacobean. His work was influenced by his contacts with the later phase of the Sidney Circle, and his *Aurora* is a rather feeble late manifestation of the Sidneian mode. The verse tragedies attracted the attention of the admirers of the Countess of Pembroke's attempts to encourage Senecan verse tragedy.

> Kastner, L. E. and Charlton, H. B., eds, *The Poetical Works* (Edinburgh, 1921–29). (The standard edition).

See: Waller, G. F., 'Sir William Alexander and Renaissance Court Culture', *Aevum*, 51 (1977), 505–15. (Widens the discussion to consider the disintegration of Scottish court culture.)

BARCLAY, Alexander (1457?–1552), courtier, monk, poet. Probably born in Scotland, educated in England, France, and Italy, and became a religious. His best-known work is a moralistic adaptation of a German original, *The Ship of Fools* (1509).

> *Certayne Ecloges* (reprinted New York, 1967).

BARNES, Barnabe (c.1569–1609), poet, educated at Oxford, though left without a degree. Volunteer in the expedition led by the Earl of Essex to Dieppe to assist Henry IV of France, 1591. His poetry drew heavily on French originals, mediating the Petrarchan tradition from continental rather than English models. He also dabbled in religious sonnets. See *Divine Century of Spiritual Sonnets* (1595). Frequently ridiculed for the preciousness of his conceits, notably by Nashe and Campion.

> Doyno, Victor A., ed., *Parthenophil and Parthenophe, 1593* (1971). (A critical edition of Barnes's main Petrarchan collection.)

See: Blank, Philip E. Jr, *Lyric Forms in the Sonnet Sequences of Barnabe Barnes* (The Hague, 1974).

BARNFIELD, Richard (1574–1626), country gentleman and poet. He was educated at Oxford, taking his B.A. in 1592, and went to London to seek court preferment. Before he was twenty-five, he had published three collections of sonnets, *The Affectionate Shepherd* (1594) which was dedicated to Lady Penelope Rich; *Cynthia* (1595); and *The Encomion of Lady Pecunia* (1598). He sought the friendship and patronage of other authors and noblemen, including the Sidneys. *Cynthia* is the first Petrarchan sequence in English with an overtly homosexual speaker.

> Klawitter, George, ed., *The Complete Poems* (Selinsgrove, 1991).

> See: Morris, Harry, *Richard Barnfield, Colin's Child* (Tampa, 1963).

BRETON, Nicholas (1545?–1627?), an enormously prolific and popular poet. He was the son of a prosperous London trader, and (after his father's death) stepson of the poet George Gascoigne. Probably educated at Oxford, he started publishing poetry in the late 1570s, but his main burst of writing seems to have been under the aegis of the Countess of Pembroke for whom he wrote lyrics, religious allegory and dialogues. She is the subject of some fulsome praise in the dedications to *Pilgrimage to Paradise* (1592), *The Countess of Pembrokes Passion* (?1592), *Auspicante Jehova, Maries Exercise* (1596), and *A Divine Poem* (1601). His other verse includes *A Small Handful of Fragrant Flowers* (1575) and *Britton's Bowre of Delights* (1591, 1597). He wrote mainly in pastoral and devotional modes, continuing later in his life to echo the musicality and courtly sophistication of the Sidneys.

> Grosart, Alexander B., ed., *The Works in Verse and Prose* (1879; reprinted, Hildesheim, 1969). (A collected edition.)
> Robertson, Jean, ed., *Poems (not hitherto reprinted)* (Liverpool, 1967). (Contains a useful introduction.)

CAMPION, Thomas (1567–1620), court poet and musician. Student at Peterhouse (1581–84), Gray's Inn, and also studied medicine in Europe. He wrote poetry as a student and some of his poems appeared in the unauthorized edition of Sidney's *Astrophil and Stella* (1591). In 1595, he published a volume of Latin epigrams, and his best-known work, for which he wrote the lyrics and most of the music, was a *Book of Airs* (1601). His prose treatise, *Observations on the Art of English Poesy* (1602) included a controversial defence of quantitative verse in opposition to Samuel Daniel's views. In the Court of James VI Campion wrote airs, music, masques, and was one of the most distinguished practitioners of the mixed art of music and poetry.

> Davis, Walter R., ed., *Works* (1969). (The standard edition)
> Hart, J., ed., *Observations in the Art of English Poesie* (1969). (A modern reprint.)
> *Observations in The Art of English Poetry* (Cheadle, 1976). (Contains a selection of poems.)

> See: Kastendieck, M. M., *Thomas Campion, England's Musical Poet* (New York, 1938; reprinted 1963).
> Lowbury, Edward, Salter, Timothy, and Young, Alison, *Thomas Campion: Poet, Composer, Physician* (1970). (The standard biography.)
> Eldredge, M. T., *Thomas Campion: His Poetry, and Music, 1567–1620* (New York, 1971).

Bryan Margaret, R., 'Recent Studies in Campion', *ELR*, 4 (1974), 404–11. (A useful survey of modern criticism).

Doughtie, Edward, 'Sibling Rivalry: Music vs. Poetry in Campion and Others', *Criticism*, 20 (1978), 1–16. (Raises the most interesting question in considering Campion's work.)

CHAPMAN, George (1559?–1634), poet, soldier, writer, translator. He was born in Hertfordshire, and may have studied at Oxford, despite his claim that he was self-taught. He travelled in Europe and may have served in the Low Countries War. He was associated with a number of intellectually avant-garde groups, and his friends included Christopher Marlowe. Among his patrons were the Earl of Essex, Prince Henry and King James's favourite, the Earl of Somerset. He became one of the major dramatists of the Jacobean period, with poetry playing a relatively minor part of his literary career.

Bartlett, P. B., ed., *Poems* (New York, 1941). (Standard edition.)

Zocca, L. R., ed., *Elizabethan Narrative Poetry* (New Brunswick, 1950).

See: Lord, G. de F., *Homeric Renaissance: The 'Odyssey' of George Chapman* (New Haven, 1950). (A study of Chapman's translation of Homer.)

MacLure, Miller, *George Chapman, A Critical Study* (1960). (An overview.)

Spivack, Charlotte, *George Chapman* (New York, 1967). (A basic introduction.)

Waddington, Raymond F., *The Mind's Empire: Myth and Form in George Chapman's Narrative Poems* (1969). (Concentrates on Chapman's interest in mythology.)

CHURCHYARD, Thomas (1520?–1604), poet, soldier, minor courtier and poetic hack. He may have started his 'literary' career in the reign of Henry VIII, and published poems and prose until the reign of James I. His poetical style remained the clumsy, repetitive, thumping lines of the worst of the 1540s and 1550s. He contributed poems to many miscellanies and his best work is probably the story of Shore's Wife which was added to the 1563 edition of *A Mirror for Magistrates*. His poetry includes *The Firste Parts of Churchyeards Chippes* (1575). Modern criticism is mainly confined to brief remarks, usually derisive. There is perhaps a case for a modern selection and introduction.

CONSTABLE, Henry (1562–1613), born into Warwickshire gentry, educated at Cambridge; became a Catholic and spent much of his time in Europe. Like Marlowe, was possibly a spy, even a double spy, for both the English and French governments, and was in touch with King James before 1603. Many of his poems circulated in manuscript or were published in miscellanies or other poets' collections. His religious sonnets, with their strong Catholic sentiments, were unpublished until the nineteenth century. His major collection of sonnets was *Diana* (1592, 1594).

Grundy, Joan, ed., *The Poems of Henry Constable* (Liverpool, 1960). (A modern edition, with a useful introduction.)

CROWLEY, Robert (1587–88), Protestant printer, propagandist and poet. An early Puritan leader whose verses were part of his propagandist campaign for the new ideas. He published the first printed edition, modernized and annotated, of Langland's *Piers Plowman*, seeing it unambiguously as hostile to Catholicism. His own poetry adapted traditional popular devotional and satiric styles to Protestant theology, and he was one of the earliest versifiers of the Psalms.

The Psalter of David newly translated into English (1549). (Psalm translation; not reprinted.)

See: Freer, Coburn, *Music for a King* (Baltimore, 1972). (Contains some brief references in Ch. 1.)

King, John N., *English Reformation Literature: The Tudor Origins of the Protestant Tradition* (Princeton, 1982). (Ch. 7 has a detailed discussion.)

DANIEL, Samuel (1562–1619), poet, courtier, diplomat, translator, teacher. He was born in Taunton, educated at Oxford. A typical professional writer of the period: his father and brother were both musicians and he spent some time at Court. He acted as a tutor and was employed by various aristocratic figures, including the Countess of Pembroke, and held minor court offices through such patronage. Under James I, he was employed to write court entertainments and masques. His poetry includes both sonnets, especially *Delia* (1592 and many other revised editions), and longer poetry, including the national epic, *The Civil Wars* (1595). His prose work includes *The Defense of Rhyme* (1603), opposing the Countess of Pembroke's and Campion's championing of quantitative verse.

Grosart, A. B., ed., *Complete Works* (5 vols, 1885–96; reprinted New York, 1963). (Long the standard edition.)

Himelick, R., ed., *Musophilus* (West Lafayette, 1965). (Edition of Daniel's minor epic.)

Michel, L., ed., *Civil Wars* (New Haven, 1958). (Modern edition of the long epic.) Sprague, A. C., ed., *Poems and A Defense of Ryme* (Chicago, 1905). (A useful collection for modern readers.)

See: Rees, Joan, *Samuel Daniel* (Liverpool, 1964). (A useful, well-organized introduction.)

Seronsy, Cecil, *Samuel Daniel* (New York, 1967). (Overview.)

Hulse, S. Clarke, 'Samuel Daniel: The Poet as Literary Historian', *SEL*, 19 (1979), 55–69. (Daniel's interest in history.)

DAVIES, Sir John (1569–1626), born in Wiltshire, educated at Oxford, then like so many other aspiring courtiers, at the Middle Temple. He became a courtier, poet, and under James I held a number of posts in Ireland including Solicitor-General and Speaker of the Parliament. 'Orchestra', his best-known poem, was published in 1596. He wrote epigrams, poetical praises of the Queen, and satires. Like Greville's or Chapman's his work tends to be serious and philosophical. *Nosce Teipsum*, like Greville's long poetical treatises, remains an interesting guide to some of the commonplace philosophical ideas of the late Renaissance.

Krueger, Robert, ed. *The Poems of Sir John Davies* (1975).

See: Sanderson, J. L., *Sir John Davies* (Boston, 1975). (A useful introduction.)

DE VERE, Edward, Earl of Oxford (1550–1604). Courtier, and favourite of the Queen in the 1570s. Nicknamed her 'Turk' by Elizabeth, he lost favour when an affair with one of her maids of honour was discovered. Some of his poems appeared in *The Paradise of Dainty Devices* (1576).

> May, Stephen, ed., 'The Poems of Edward de Vere, Seventeenth Earl of Oxford and of Robert Devereux Second Earl of Essex', *SP*, 77, no. 5 (1980), 5–132. (A fine modern edition.)

> See: May, Stephen, *The Elizabethan Courtier Poets* (Columbia, 1991).

DEVEREUX, Robert, Earl of Essex (1566–1601), nobleman, courtier, favourite of Elizabeth, husband of Sir Philip Sidney's widow Frances Walsingham, and incidental poet. One of the most brilliant figures in the Court, he gained increasing power over the ageing Elizabeth in the late 1580s and 1590s, until he was sent to Ireland, in part because he was becoming politically embarrassing and too obviously ambitious. His return in 1599 may have been designed to effect a coup, but he was not supported widely, was arrested and executed in 1601, with many of his supporters. Like most other highly placed courtiers, he played, danced and wrote incidental poems, many of which turn up in miscellanies and notebooks.

> May, Stephen, ed., 'The Poems of Edward de Vere, Seventeenth Earl of Oxford and of Robert Devereux Second Earl of Essex', *SP*, 77, no. 5 (1980), 5–132. (A fine modern edition.)

> See: May, Stephen, *The Elizabethan Courtier Poets* (Columbia, 1991).

DONNE, John (1571/72–1631), clergyman, politician, poet, Donne's career began with a reputation as a fashionable young libertine with great political ambition and ended with him as Dean of St Paul's. Born into a Catholic family, he was educated at Oxford, Cambridge and Lincoln's Inn though, because of his religion, he never took a degree. He drew himself carefully up the political ladder in the 1590s, was one of the most brilliant and fashionable young aspiring men about Court and became an MP in 1601. His elopement with his employer's niece meant the end of his public career and he languished unhappily for a few years until he gradually found employment under James I as a religious propagandist. Realizing he would find high office only as a clergyman, he was ordained in 1614 and thereafter developed into one of the Church of England's most brilliant preachers and divines. Late in his life he acquired a reputation for eccentricity and miserliness but continued to be highly regarded as a churchman. The poetry he wrote in the sixteenth century includes satires, elegies and the famous *Songs and Sonets* which were among the most admired poems of the last decade of the century, and well beyond. Donne's reputation grew enormously in the first half of this century and he remains perhaps the most accessible poet of the period for our time.

> Grierson, H. J. C., ed., *The Poetry of John Donne* (1912). (Still the most reliable edition, preferable textually to the Gardner edition.)
> Gardner, Helen, ed., *The Elegies and the Songs and Sonnets* (Oxford, 1965). (See also, for Donne's later poems, *The Divine Poems*, Oxford, 1952.)
> Milgate, Michael, ed., *Satires, Epigrams and Verse Letters* (Oxford, 1967). (Standard edition of the *Satires*.)

Smith, A. J., ed., *The English Poems of John Donne* (Harmondsworth, 1971). (A useful reader's edition with the *Songs and Sonets* alphabetically organized.)

See: Smith, A. J., *Donne: Songs and Sonnets* (1964). (An introductory reading.)

Empson, William, 'Donne in the New Edition', *CQ*, 8 (1966), 255–80. (Controversial, lively; see also 'Donne the Space Man', *KR* (1957), 337–99.)

Bald, R. C., *John Donne: A Life* (1970). (The standard biography.)

Sanders, Wilbur, *John Donne's Poetry* (Cambridge, 1971). (Still a most stimulating study; see also the review by Peter Dane in *AUMLA*, 37 (1972), 83–84.)

Everett, Barbara, *Donne as a London Poet* (1972). (Focuses on Donne's peculiarly brittle urban sensibility.)

Aers, David and Kress, Gunther, ' "Darke Texts Need Notes": Versions of Self in Donne's Verse Epistles', *Literature and History*, 8 (1978), 138–58. (A fine stylistic and semiotic study.)

Carey, John, *John Donne: Life, Mind and Art* (1981). (Argues for religious anxieties as a source for many of Donne's characteristics.)

Rajan, Tilottama, ' "Nothing Sooner Broke": Donne's Songs and Sonnets as Self-Consuming Artifacts', *ELH*, 49 (1982), 809–28. (Moderate and stimulating deconstructive treatment.)

Marotti, Arthur *John Donne, Coterie Poet* (Madison, 1986). (Pioneering essay on the political and patronage connections.)

John Donne Journal (North Carolina State University, 1982–   ).

DOUGLAS, Gavin (1474?–1522), Scottish poet, cleric, translator. Aristocratic background, and one of the leading writers of the Scots tradition in the Renaissance, known for his translation of Virgil's *Aeneid*. Educated at St Andrews and possibly in Paris, he took clerical orders and enjoyed court patronage all his life, rising to be Bishop of Dunkeld (1515).

Small, S., ed., *The Poetical Works of Gavin Douglas* (4 vols. Edinburgh, 1974).

Bawcutt, Priscilla J., ed., The Shorter Poems of Gavin Douglas (Edinburgh, 1967). (Useful introductory edition.)

Coldwell, Davis F. C., ed., Selections from Gavin Douglas (Oxford, 1964). (A brief selection.)

DRAYTON, Michael (1563–1631), writer, dramatist, friend of Shakespeare and Jonson. Born in Warwick into the gentry, attached to Sir Henry Goodyere's household and dedicated his *Idea* sonnets to Goodyere's daughter Ann. Other poetry includes longer poems in *Ideas Mirror* (1594). He also wrote in the epic vein, in *Englands Heroical Epistle* (1597 and many subsequent editions).

Buxton, John, ed., *Poems* (1953). (A useful collection in The Muses Library Series.)

See: Hardin, Richard F., *Michael Drayton and the Passing of Elizabethan England* (1961). (Deals with the nostalgia for the Golden Age of Elizabeth.)

Newdigate, Bernard H., *Michael Drayton and his Circle* (1961). (Literary friendships.)

Berthelot, Joseph A., *Michael Drayton* (New York, 1967). (A useful brief overview.)

Wrestling, Louise H., *The Evolution of Michael Drayton's Idea* (Salzburg, 1974). (An account of the revision of *Idea*.)

Johnson, Paula, 'Michael Drayton, Prophet without Audience', *SLitI* 1,2 (1978), 44–55. (Nostalgia, isolation, moral concerns.)

DUNBAR, William (1460?–1520?), Scottish poet and courtier. Educated at the University of St Andrews, and active at the Court of James IV of Scotland. His varied career as a poet grew directly out of his association with the Court; his poetry is arguably the best produced in Scotland between Henryson and Alexander Scott.

Kinsley, James, ed., *The Poems of William Dunbar* (Oxford, 1979). (A useful introductory edition.)

See: Scott, Tom, *Dunbar: A Critical Exposition of the Poems* (Edinburgh, 1960). (A fine study focusing on the socio-cultural milieu.)

DYER, Sir Edward (1543–1607), courtier, diplomat and poet, knighted in 1596. Had been educated at Oxford, and had grown up with Sidney and Greville, and was part of their group, sometimes referred to as the 'Areopagus', in the late 1570s and shortly thereafter. But he was never as prominent a figure as they, either as a courtier or poet. His poetry circulated at Court, but remained uncollected, even though it appears frequently in miscellanies and is referred to often in incidental references. The most famous lyric often attributed to him, 'My Mind to Me a Kingdom Is', is frequently anthologized.

See: Sargent, Ralph M., *The Life and Lyrics of Sir Edward Dyer* (Oxford, 1968).

May, Stephen, *The Elizabethan Courtier Poets* (Columbia, 1991).

ELIZABETH I (1533–1603), Queen of England (1558–1603), daughter of Henry VIII and Ann Boleyn, she came to the throne strongly supported by Protestants; by personal force and political cunning, she held together the warring factions of the age. She wrote verse occasionally, but it was never published or collected in her lifetime, although her learning was frequently mentioned, for example by Puttenham who speaks of how her 'noble muse easily surmounteth all the rest that have written before her time or since'.

Bradner, Lester, ed., *Poems of Elizabeth I* (Providence, 1964).

See: May, Stephen, *The Elizabethan Courtier Poets* (Columbia, 1991).

FOWLER, William (1560–1612), Scottish poet, attended St Leonard's College and St Andrews; and worked as a Protestant spy. Studied civil law in Paris. None of his poetry was published in his lifetime, but it included a collection of seventy-two sonnets, *The Tarantula of Love*, and a rather wordy and jumbled translation of Petrarch's *Trionfi*. He became a Protestant clergyman, came south with King James and helped in the preparation of the King's political treatise, *Basilikon Doron*.

Meikle, H. W., ed., *Works* (Edinburgh, 1914).

See: Jack, R. D. S., 'William Fowler and Italian Literature', *MLR*, 65 (1970), 481–92. (Continental influences on the Scots Renaissance.)

FRAUNCE, Abraham (1557–1633), schoolmaster, historian, translator, minor poet. Protege of the Countess of Pembroke, a member of her Wilton House Circle, and constant praiser of her bounty and talent. He was one of the most assiduous practitioners of hexameter verse, arguing for and exemplifying the adaptation of classical metre into English.

Snare, Gerald, ed., *The Third Part of the Countess of Pembroke's Ivychurch* (Northridge, 1975).

See: Attridge, Derek, *Well-Weighed Syllables* (Cambridge, 1974). (A judicious account which sees Fraunce as the period's best practitioner of classical metres.)

GASCOIGNE, George (1542?–77), soldier, courtier, poet, fiction writer. Born into Bedfordshire gentry, educated at Cambridge and Gray's Inn. Became courtier and MP for Bedford, but to escape being prosecuted for debt, fled to the Low Countries and became a soldier. One of the earliest professional writers in England. In the last thirty years or so, has become increasingly seen as the most interesting English poet and theorist between Wyatt and Sidney.

Cunliffe, J. W., ed., *Complete Works* (2 vols, Cambridge, 1907–10). Prouty, C. T., *A Hundreth Sundrie Flowers* (Columbia, Missouri, 1942). (Gascoigne's most important poems; see also the edition by B. M. Ward and R. L. Miller (Port Washington, New York, 1975.)
Notes of Instruction in English Verse, reprinted in G. Gregory Smith, ed., *Elizabethan Critical Essays* (Oxford, 1904–6).
The Steele Glas and the Complaint of Phylomene: A Critical Edition (Salzburg, 1975).

See: Johnson, Ronald C., *George Gascoigne* (New York, 1972). (A useful introduction in the Twayne Series.)
Mills, Jerry L., 'Recent Studies in Gascoigne', *ELR* 3 (1973), 322–26. (An account of recent criticism).

GOOGE (or GOUGE), Barnabe (1540–94), kinsman of Sir William Cecil, educated at Oxford and Cambridge. Primarily a translator or adapter of the classics, Googe translated moral and religious works in the 1560s and 1570s. His *Eclogues* (1563) are the product of a bright student of poetry, and are among the earliest example of pastoral eclogues in English. Like other mid-century poets, his work is conventional, alliterative, mainly written in fourteeners.

Kennedy, Judith, ed. *Eclogues, Epitaphs and Sonnets* (Toronto, 1989). Stephens, Frank, ed., *Selected Poems of Barnabe Googe* (Denver 1981). (A useful selection.)

See: Sheidley, William E., *Barnabe Googe* (Boston, 1981). (A Twayne survey, well indexed.)

GORGES, Sir Arthur (1557–1625). Courtier, ambassador, and cousin of Ralegh, he was close to the Queen in the 1580s.

> Sanderson, Helen, *The Poems of Sir Arthur Gorges* (Oxford, 1953).

> See: May, Stephen, *The Elizabethan Courtier Poets* (Columbia, 1991).

GREVILLE, Fulke, Lord Brooke (1554–1628), poet, statesman, landowner, friend of Sir Philip Sidney. Born in Warwickshire; educated at Shrewsbury with Sidney, and at Cambridge. Went to Court with Sidney in 1577, and remained closely associated with the Sidneys during his early career, an account of which he gave in a revealing life of Sidney, written about 1610, but not published until 1652. Greville served in many political positions, including a period as Lord Chancellor under King James, and was one of the longest-surviving public servants of the period. He was a generous patron of writers, but was himself reticent about his own poetry – except for the series of verse treatises and other public poems. His most significant work – one of the major collections of poetry in the period – was *Caelica*, a kind of poetic diary, written in quasi-Petrarchan manner over perhaps forty years. He died in 1623 from a wound inflicted by a servant who believed he had been cut out of Greville's will.

> Grosart, A. B., ed., *Works* (4 vols, 1870).
> Bullough, Geoffrey, ed., *The Poems and Dramas* (2 vols, Edinburgh, reprint. 1983). (The standard edition along with the next item.)
> Wilkes, G. A., ed., *The Remains* (1985). (Completes the standard edition.)
> Gunn, Thomas, ed., *Selected Poems of Fulke Greville* (1968). (A stimulating selection, superbly introduced.)
> Goews, John, ed., *The Prose Works of Fulke Greville, Lord Brooke* (Oxford, 1986) (Includes an authoritative edition of Greville's life of Sidney.)

> See: Rebholz, Ronald, *The Life of Fulke Greville* (Oxford, 1971). (A first-rate study.)
> Rees, Joan, *Fulke Greville Lord Brooke* (1971). (A useful overview.)
> Waswo, Richard, *The Fatal Mirror: Themes and Techniques in the Poetry of Fulke Greville* (Charlottesville, 1972). (A close reading of the poems.)
> Waller, G. F., 'Fulke Greville's Struggle with Calvinism', *SN* 44 (1972), 295–314. (Theological interests.)
> Warkentin, Germaine, 'Greville's Caelica and the Fullness of Time', *English Studies in Canada*, 6 (1980), 398–408 (Thematic)

HALL, Joseph (1574–1656), clergyman, satirist, poet. Born at Ashby de la Zouch and educated at Emmanuel College, Cambridge. He had Puritan affinities, and though his early literary career made him known as a satirist in verse and prose, he was intent on a clerical career and proceeded to a B.D. (1603) and then D.D. (1612). He later became Bishop of Norwich. His theological works, published from 1605, were mainly polemical, continuing the wit and learning with which he packs his satires. *Virgidemiarum* (1597) was a landmark in the satiric revival of the 1590s. In it he claimed to be the first English satirist.

Davenport, A., ed., *Poems* (Liverpool, 1949). (Standard edition.)

See: Huntley, Frank, L., *Bishop Joseph Hall 1574–1656: A Bibliographical and Critical Study*. (Cambridge, 1979). (Thorough, scholarly.)
McCabe, Richard A. *Joseph Hall: A Study in Satire and Meditation* (Oxford, 1982). (Satire, religious ideas.)
Cortell, Ronald J., 'Joseph Hall and Protestant Meditation,' *TSLL*, 20 (1978), 367–85. (Relates Hall to the Protestant devotional tradition.)

HARINGTON, Sir John (1560–1612), godson of the queen, and inventor of the flush toilet, he had a reputation as a court gossip, translator and epigrammist, but was a prolific, if incidental, poet and an informative letter writer. A modern edition of his poems is needed.

McClure, N. E., ed., *The Letters and Epigrams of Sir John Harington* (1930; reprinted 1977.)
Hughey, Ruth, ed., *The Arundel Harington Manuscript of Tudor Poetry* (1960).
Donno, Elizabeth Story, ed., *Sir John Harington's 'A New Discourse of a Stale Subject, Called the Metamorphosis of Ajax'* (1962).
Miller, R.H., 'Unpublished Poems by Sir John Harington,' *ELR*, 14 (1984), 148–58.

See: May, Stephen, *The Elizabethan Courtier Poets* (Columbia, 1991).

HAWES, Stephen (1475?–1523), courtier, poet in Henry VII's reign. Educated at Oxford, travelled on the continent, served as diplomat and civil servant. His poetry includes long allegorical and moral works, including *The Pastyme of Pleasure* (1509?).

Spang, Frank J., ed., *The Works of Stephen Hawes* (Delmar, 1975).
Gluck, Florence W., and Morgan, Alice B., eds, *The Minor Poetry of Stephen Hawes* (1974).

See: Edwards, A. S. G., *Stephen Hawes* (Boston, 1982). (An unusually good Twayne survey.)

LINDSAY, Sir David (1490?–1555), Scottish courtier and poet. Born into a prosperous family, and may have attended St Andrews University. By 1511, he was at the Court of James IV and closely associated with the King. Under James V, too, he was a courtier and diplomat. He wrote medieval dream allegories like *The Dreme* (1528) and much public poetry, including *An Pleasant Satyre of the Thrie Estaitis* (1540), and *The Monarchie* (1554).

Small, J. and Hall, F., eds, *Works* (New York, 1969).

See: Clewitt, Richard M. Jr, 'Rhetorical Strategy and Structure in Three of Sir David Lindsay's Poems', *SEL* 16 (1976), 3–14.

MARLOWE, Christopher (1564–93), a major dramatist as well as a poet. He was the son of a prosperous Canterbury shoemaker, attended Corpus Christi,

Cambridge, and probably became a member of Walsingham's secret service, spying for England on the continent. On his return to London, he worked for the Earl of Nottingham's theatrical company in the late 1580s. He was killed in a tavern brawl, possibly at the instigation of the government. His best-known poems are 'Hero and Leander' (1598) which was completed by Chapman, and 'The Passionate Shepherd to his Love' which has a companion piece by Ralegh.

> Orgel, Stephen, ed., *The Complete Poems and Translations of Christopher Marlowe* (Harmondsworth, 1971). (The best modern edition.)

> See: Bush, Douglas, *Mythology and the Renaissance Tradition in English Poetry* (revised edition, New York, 1963).
> Post, Jonathan F. S., 'Recent Studies in Marlowe (1968–1976)', *RES* 29, (1978), 36–61. (A useful survey.)
> Drew, Cynthia, 'Hero and Leander: A Male Perspective on Female Sexuality', *Journal of Women's Studies in Literature*, I (1979), 273–85.

MARSTON, John (1575–1634), one of the bright young satirists of the 1590s who, like Hall, later became a clergyman. Born in Oxfordshire, he was the son of a lawyer and attended Brasenose College, Oxford, and the Middle Temple. His 'Pygmalions Image' (1598) was a fashionable piece of erotic verse in the vein of 'Hero and Leander' and 'Venus and Adonis'. He published satires, which were banned in 1599 along with satiric writings by others. He became a dramatist, collaborating with Dekker and others, quarrelling and later reconciled with Jonson. In 1609 he was ordained, and became a country parson in Hampshire. His most important poems are the satires which, along with Hall's and Donne's, are the high point of the fashion in the 1590s. His major collections are *The Metamorphosis of Pygmalions Image* (1598), and *The Scourge of Villainie* (1598).

> Davenport, Arnold, ed., *Poems* (Liverpool, 1961).

> See: Ingram, R. W., *John Marston* (Boston, 1978). (A Twayne survey.)
> McGrath, Lynnette, 'John Marston's Mismanaged Irony: The Poetic Satires', *TSLL* 18 (1976), 393–408.

MONTGOMERIE, Alexander (1545?–98), Scottish courtier and poet who was active in James VI's Court in Scotland among the Castalian poets. He had Catholic sympathies and was banished from Scotland; he probably died abroad. His poetry combines religious allegory and complex lyrical grace.

> Shire, Helena M. ed. *Songs and Poems* (Edinburgh, 1960).

> See: Jack, Ronald D. S., 'The Lyrics of Alexander Montgomerie', *RES* n.s. 20 (1969), 168–81.

MORE, Sir Thomas (1478–1535), courtier, humanist, statesman and (to Catholics) martyr and saint. His greatest contribution to literature is *Utopia* (1516). His poetry plays a small but interesting part in his life and works, his best work being a collection of Latin epigrams and some English poems. They will be adequately edited in the forthcoming Yale edition of his complete works.

Campbell, W. E., ed., *The English Works of Sir Thomas More* (2 vols, 1931).

See: Willow, Mary Edith, *An Analysis of the English Poems of St Thomas More* (Nieuwkoop, 1974).

RALEGH, Sir Walter (1552?–1618), courtier, explorer, statesman, philosopher, historian, poet – a man of many roles and parts. Born into Devonshire gentry, his rough provincial speech and striking manners were legendary. By the mid-1570s he was a great favourite of the Queen at Court and seemingly inseparable from her. He led expeditions to Virginia and Guiana, and dominated the Court until he was found to have married one of Elizabeth's ladies-in-waiting without the Queen's consent. He was imprisoned and though eventually released, never regained his status. With James taking the throne, he was tried for alleged conspiracy, imprisoned in the Tower for over ten years and then released for a last expedition to South America, after the failure of which he was executed. His major work is the encyclopaedic, sombre *History of the World*. His poems were written incidentally, occasionally copied into miscellanies, but never published.

Works (8 vols 1829; reprinted New York, 1962).
Latham, Agnes, ed., *Selected Prose and Poetry* (1965).
—— *The Poetry of Sir Walter Ralegh* (1960).
Oakeshott, Walter F. *The Queen and the Poet* (1960). (Entertaining but suspect).
Ruddick, Michael, 'The Poems of Sir Walter Ralegh: An Edition' (unpublished doctoral dissertation, Chicago, 1970). The best discussion of the canon.

See: Greenblatt, Stephen, *Sir Walter Ralegh: The Renaissance Man and His Roles* (New Haven, 1973). (A pioneering study of Ralegh's shifting 'selves'.)
Tennenhouse, Leonard, 'Sir Walter Ralegh and the Literature of Clientage' in *Patronage in the Renaissance* ed. Stephen Orgel and Guy Fitch Lytle (Princeton, 1981) pp. 235–58.
May, Stephen, *Sir Walter Ralegh* (Boston, 1989).
—— *The Elizabethan Courtier Poets* (Columbia, 1991).

SACKVILLE, Thomas, Earl of Dorset (1536–1608), educated at both Oxford and Cambridge and later Chancellor of both. Attended the Inner Temple and became a leading courtier and statesman of the early part of Elizabeth's reign, serving eventually as Lord Treasurer. About 1561 he wrote, along with Thomas Norton, the play *Gorboduc*, the first blank verse tragedy in English. He collaborated with William Baldwin and others to produce *A Mirror for Magistrates* (1563 and subsequent editions), a collection of verse stories of prominent monarchs and statesmen. Sackville's Induction and the tragedy of Henry, Duke of Buckingham are probably the best parts of the work.

Campbell, Lily B., ed., *The Mirror for Magistrates* (Cambridge, 1946; New York, 1960).

See: Berlin, N., *Thomas Sackville* (New York, 1976). (A survey.)
May, Stephen, *The Elizabethan Courtier Poets* (Columbia, 1991).

SCOTT, Alexander (1525?–1584?), perhaps the most interesting poet of the
mid-century period in Scotland; his work circulated widely at the Scottish
Court and was collected in the Bannatyne Manuscript.

> MacQueen, John, ed., *Ballatis of Luve* (Edinburgh, 1970)
> ——— *Alexander Scott and Scottish Court Poetry of the Middle
> Sixteenth Century* (1968).

SHAKESPEARE, William (1564–1616), dramatist. Born at Stratford-upon-Avon
to a prosperous yeoman family, probably educated at Stratford Grammar
School. In London in the late 1580s, working for various theatre
companies, especially the King's Men. After a successful theatrical career,
retired to Stratford 1611. His poems were probably all written early in his
career, before the turn of the century.

> Booth, Stephen, ed., *Shakespeare's Sonnets* (New Haven, 1978,
> Second Edition, 1979). (The best modern edition.)
> Prince, F. T. ed., *William Shakespeare: The Poems* (1963).

See: Knights, L. C., *Explorations* (Harmondsworth, 1946). (Reprints an
earlier *Scrutiny* article on 'Time in the Sonnets'.)
Winny, James, *The Master Mistress: A Study of Shakespeare's Sonnets*
(1968)
Martin, Philip, *Shakespeare's Sonnets: Self, Love and Art* (1972).
Melchiori, Giorgio, *Shakespeare's Dramatic Meditations* (1976).
(Statistical and philosophical analysis of great suggestiveness.)
Fineman, Joel, *Shakespeare's Perjured Eye: The Invention of Poetic
Subjectivity in the Sonnets* (1986).

SIDNEY, Mary, Countess of Pembroke (1564–1621), sister of Sir Philip Sidney,
to whose ideals she devoted most of her adult life. Born at Penshurst
Place, she was educated at home, and became one of the most learned
ladies of the age. She married William Herbert, second earl of Pembroke,
set up what one of her followers termed a 'little court' at Wilton House,
and became a widely praised patron and, as well, a fine poet in her own
right. Her major works include a translation of Petrarch's *Trionfo della
Morte*, a verse translation of Garnier's play *Marc-Antoine* and other works.

> Rathmell, J. C. A., ed., *The Psalms of Sir Philip Sidney and the
> Countess of Pembroke* (New York, 1963).
> Waller, Gary, ed., *The Triumph of Death and Other Unpublished and
> Uncollected Poems* (Salzburg, 1977).

See: Waller, Gary, *Mary Sidney Countess of Pembroke* (Salzburg, 1979). (A
biographical and critical study.)
Roberts, Josephine A., 'Mary Sidney, Countess of Pembroke', *ELR*
(1985), 426–39. (A valuable, detailed annotated bibliography.)
Zim, Rivkah, *English Metrical Psalms: Poetry as Praise and Prayer,
1535–1601* (Cambridge, 1987). (Useful for the whole Psalm
metaphrase tradition.)
Hannay, Margaret P., *Philip's Phoenix* (New York, 1990).
Sidney Newsletter (Waterloo, Ontario 1980–83; Guelph, Ontario,
1983–   ).

SIDNEY, Sir Philip (1562–86), Elizabethan England's most celebrated courtier and poet whose death in 1586 created a legend even more powerful than his actual literary achievement. Born at Penshurst Place, he was educated at Shrewsbury and Oxford, went on a triumphant tour of Europe where he was befriended by monarchs, statesmen and literary figures. He returned to the English Court where he allied himself with the Earl of Leicester's Protestant faction and never quite gained the influence with the Queen he desired. Sent to the Low Countries as Governor of Flushing, he was mortally wounded in battle, and given a hero's funeral, mourned by friends and enemies alike. *Astrophil and Stella* (1581–82) is the first major Petrarchan collection in English; his treatise, *The Defence of Poesie* is the first major treatment of poetry in English in the period, and his *Arcadia*, a long prose romance written first for his sister and then revised, is the most important prose fiction in English before Richardson. None of his work was published in his lifetime, though it circulated widely at Court and among the members of his Circle, which included Greville, his sister Mary, his brother Robert, Dyer, and others.

Ringler, William A. Jr, ed., *The Poems of Sir Philip Sidney* (Oxford, 1962). (A landmark edition.)

Duncan-Jones, Katherine, and van Dorsten, Jan., eds, *Miscellaneous Prose of Sir Philip Sidney* (Oxford, 1973). (Contains the *Defence* and other works.) The letters will appear edited by Charles Levy and Roger Kuin.

Kimbrough, Robert, ed., *Prose and Poetry* (revised edition 1982). (A useful selection.)

See: Kalstone, David, *Sidney's Poetry: Contexts and Interpretations* (Cambridge, Mass., 1965). (Close analysis.)

Levao, Ronald, 'Sidney's "Feigned Apology"', *PMLA*, 94 (1979), 223–33. (A stimulating reading of the rhetoric of the *Defence*.)

McCoy, Richard C., *Sir Philip Sidney: Rebellion in Arcadia* (New Brunswick, 1979). (An exciting reading of the cultural politics of Sidney's career.)

Hamilton, A. C., *Sir Philip Sidney* (Cambridge, 1980). (The best modern overview.)

Sinfield, Alan, 'Sidney and Astrophil', *SEL*, 20 (1980), 25–41.

Sessions, William A., ed., *New Readings of Sidney: Experiment and Tradition* in *Studies in the Literary Imagination* 15 (1982). (Includes essays by Jane Hedley, Gary Waller, Annabel Patterson and Germaine Warkentin.)

Jones, Ann and Stallybrass, Peter, 'The Politics of Astrophil and Stella', *SEL*, 24 (1984), 53–68. (A brilliant essay on the interaction of literary and cultural codes.)

Waller, Gary F. and Moore, Michael D., eds, *Sir Philip Sidney and the Interpretation of Renaissance Culture* (1984). (Includes essays by Maurice Evans, S. K. Heninger Jr, Marion Campbell, Jacqueline Miller, Germaine Warkentin and Jon Quitslund. A collection of both traditional and revisionist views.)

Fienberg, Nona, 'The Emergence of Stella in "Astrophil and Stella"', *SEL*, 25 (1985), 5–19. (Feminist reading.)

Wayne, Don E., *Penshurst: The Semiotics of Place and the Poetics of History* (Madison, 1984). (An intriguing analysis of Jonson's poem on Penshurst and the Sidney family.)

Stillman, Robert E., *Sidney's Poetic Justice: the Old Arcadia, its
Eclogues, and Renaissance Pastoral* (1986). (Stimulating study of the
Arcadia poems.)
Sidney Newsletter (Waterloo, Ontario, 1980–83; Guelph, Ontario,
1983–).

SIDNEY, Sir Robert, Lord de L'isle (1563–1626), younger brother of Philip and
Mary. His career took shape under the shadow of his brother whom he
succeeded as Governor of Flushing. Returning to the Elizabethan Court
in the mid-1590s he enjoyed a moderately successful public career but
most of his commitment went to his estate at Penshurst Place, which is
celebrated in Ben Jonson's 'To Penshurst'. Sidney was not widely known
as a poet until the 1970s when his poetry was first identified by Peter
Croft.

Croft, Peter, ed., *The Poems of Robert Sidney Edited From the Poet's
Autograph Notebook* (Oxford, 1984). (A fine scholarly edition, rather
archaic in its critical perspective.)
Duncan-Jones, Katherine, ed., 'The Poems of Sir Robert Sidney',
English, no. 136 (1981), 3–72. (But see Deborah K. Wright,
'Modern-Spelling Text of Robert Sidney's Poems Proves
Disappointing', *SNew*, 3, no. 1 (1982), 12–16.)

See: Hay, Millicent V., *The Life of Robert Sidney Earl of Leicester*
(1565–1626) (Washington, 1985). (A rather pedestrian account).
Waller, Gary F., ' "The Sad Pilgrim": The Poetry of Sir Robert
Sidney', *Dalhousie Review*, 55 (1975–76), 689–705.
———' "My Wants and your Perfections": Elizabethan England's
Newest Poet', *Ariel*, 8 (1977), 3–14.
Wright, Deborah K., 'The Poetry of Robert Sidney: A Critical
Study of his Autograph Manuscript' (unpub. diss., Miami
University, 1980).
Sidney Newsletter (Waterloo, Ontario, 1980–83; Guelph, Ontario,
1983–).

SKELTON, John (1460?–1529), priest, courtier, and the most striking poet of the
early sixteenth century in England. Educated at Oxford and Cambridge,
and attached to the household of Henry VII and later Henry VIII, he
became rector of Diss, Norfolk, but spent most of his time at Court.
His verse is largely satiric and popular: in particular he attacked Cardinal
Wolsey, formerly a patron, and he had to take sanctuary with the Abbot
of Westminster until his death just before Wolsey's fall from power in
1529. His poetry was denigrated by most late Elizabethan courtly
commentators who found it rough in manner and uncourtly in
sentiment.

Kinsman, Robert S., ed., *Poems* (Oxford, 1969).

See: Fish, Stanley, *John Skelton's Poetry* (New Haven, 1965).
Edwards, A. S. G., ed., *Skelton: The Critical Heritage* (1981). (An
account of criticism since Skelton's time.)
Walker, Greg, *John Skelton and the Politics of the 1520s* (Cambridge,
1988).

SMITH, William (1546?–??). Little is known of his life: he was one of the many Petrarchan poets flourishing in the 1590s, and may have had or wanted some attachment to the Countess of Pembroke's household.

> Sasek, L. A., ed., *The Poetry of William Smith* (Baton Rouge, 1970).

See: Van den Berg, Kent T., 'An Elizabethan Allegory of Time by William Smith', *ELR*, 6 (1976), 40–59.

SPENSER, Edmund (1552–99) the sixteenth century's most outstanding public poet, whose *The Faerie Queene* made great claims for both English epic poetry and the Elizabethan regime. Born in London and educated at Merchant Taylors' School and Cambridge. As early as the late 1560s, in fact, he was writing poetry, and by 1579 published the *Shepheardes Calender* which was a milestone in the history of English poetry. He was employed by the Earl of Leicester and so came into contact with Sidney and his Circle. He went to Ireland in 1580, remaining there in various public posts until the year before his death, but had frequent contacts with the Court, notably in 1590, when he visited to oversee the publication of the first three books of his epic. Greatly disillusioned by the atmosphere at Court and especially by the treatment of his friend and patron Sir Walter Ralegh, the last books of the poem became less celebratory. But he remained a faithful servant of the regime: the Queen granted him a life pension in 1591, he advocated increased pressure upon the Irish in *A View of the Present State of Ireland* and finally he was forced to flee Ireland under the threat of a rising under the Earl of Tyrone. He returned to England in 1598 where he died a month later. There is a huge literature on Spenser; its monumentality is summed up by the *Spenser Encyclopedia* edited by A. C. Hamilton *et al.* (Toronto, 1990), in which the many (and varied) modern schools of criticism are represented. But until very recently, most scholarship and criticism on *The Faerie Queene* in particular has taken the poem very much at its face value. Goldberg's book (see below) marked the start of a new phase of criticism.

> Greenlaw, E. *et al.* eds, *Works: Variorum Edition* (10 vols, Baltimore 1932–58; reprinted 1966).
> Hamilton, A. C., ed., *The Faerie Queene* (1977). (The Longman Annotated Poets edition; the best annotated modern edition.)
> Oram, William, Einar Bjorvand, Ronald Bond, Thomas H. Cain, Alexander Dunlop and Richard Schell, eds, *The Yale Edition of the Shorter Poems of Edmund Spenser* (New Haven, 1989).
> Larsen, Kenneth J., ed. *The Amoretti* (Forthcoming).

See: Lewis, C. S., *The Allegory of Love* (Oxford, 1936). (A classic study.)
   Hieatt, A. Kent, *Short Times Endless Monument: The Symbolism of the Numbers in Spenser's Epithalamion* (New York, 1960). (Numerological reading of one of Spenser's more charming poems.)
   Fowler, A. D. S., *Spenser and the Numbers of Time* (1964). (A numerological analysis, but see W. Nelson in *RenQ*, 18 (1965).
   Roche, Thomas P. Jr, *The Kindly Flame – A Study of the Third and Fourth Book of Spenser's Faerie Queene* (Princeton, 1964).
   Cheney, Donald, *Spenser's Image of Nature: Wild Man and Shepherd in 'The Faerie Queene'* (New Haven, 1966).

Fowler, Alastair, ed., *Spenser's Images of Life* (Cambridge, 1967).
(C. S. Lewis's Cambridge lectures; a delightful introduction.)
Williams, Arnold, *Flower on a Lowly Stalk: The Faerie Queene VI*
(East Lansing, 1967).
Alpers, Paul J., *The Poetry of The Faerie Queene* (Princeton, 1967). (A
New Critical reading.)
Sale, Roger, *Reading Spenser* (New York, 1968). (Still one of the
best introductions.)
Evans, Maurice, *Spenser's Anatomy of Heroism* (Cambridge, 1970).
(Puritan elements in the epic.)
Tonkin, Humphrey, *Spenser's Curious Pastoral: Book Six of The Faerie
Queene* (Oxford, 1972).
Quilligan, Maureen, *The Language of Allegory* (Ithaca, 1979). (Fine
linguistically sophisticated approach to allegory.)
Goldberg, Jonathan, *Endlesse Worke: Spenser and the Structures of
Discourse* (Baltimore, 1981). (An important landmark in Spenser
criticism: the first deconstructive reading.) See also the 'new
historical' Spenser chapter in Goldberg's *James I and the Politics of
Literature* (Baltimore, 1983).
Shore, David, *Spenser and the Poetics of Pastoral* (Kingston, 1985).
Miller, David, *The Poem's Two Bodies: the Poetics of the 1590 Faerie
Queene* (Princeton, 1988).
Tonkin, Humphrey, *The Faerie Queene* (1989).
Waller, Gary, *Spenser: A Literary Life* (1994)

There is no collection of recent essays on Spenser equivalent in importance to the
Sessions and Waller/Moore volumes on Sidney; older collections include A. C.
Hamilton, ed., *Essential Articles for the Study of Edmund Spenser* (Hamden, 1972).
See also the *Spenser Newsletter* (1968–   ).

SURREY, Henry Howard, Earl of (1517?–47), aristocrat, soldier, courtier,
poet. Educated amidst the early Tudor humanists and learned in classical
and modern languages. In 1546, was convicted for treason and executed
in 1547. Had acquired a reputation for a quarrelsome, arrogant but
magnificent figure as a courtier. His poetry, which includes some of the
earliest Petrarchan verse in England, was not published in his lifetime,
but appeared in Tottel's *Miscellany* (1557), along with that of Wyatt and
others. In the sixteenth century, Surrey's poetry was generally praised
above Wyatt's, probably because he was an aristocrat but, although still
acknowledged for its technical pioneering, it has not continued to have
such a high reputation.

Jones, Emrys, ed., *Poems* (Oxford, 1964).

See: Sessions, William A. *Henry Howard, The Poet Earl of Surrey* (Boston,
1986).
——— *Sole Survivor: Henry Howard, The Poet Earl of Surrey*
(Forthcoming).

TURBERVILLE, George (1540?–1610), educated at New College and the Inns
of Court, and became a courtier and diplomat. In 1568 he went to Russia,
and some of his poems deal with what he saw there. Most of his verse is
lugubrious, moralizing and sing-song. There are some translations of Ovid

and Mantuan which are reasonably competent and he followed in Googe's footsteps by writing eclogues.

> See: Sheidley, William A., *George Turberville* (New York, 1981). (A Twayne survey.)

TYLER, Margaret (fl. 1578)

> See: Krontiris, Tina, 'Breaking Barriers of Genre and Gender: Margaret Tyler's Translation of The Mirrour of Knighthood', *ELR*, 18 (1988), 19–39.

WATSON, Thomas (1555–92), probably educated at Oxford, and a prolific translator from Latin and Italian. One of the earliest published Petrarchan collections, his *Passionate Century of Love* helped bring Petrarch into wider circulation in England.

> Heninger, S. K. Jr, ed., *Passionate Century of Love* (Gainesville 1964).

WROTH, Lady Mary (1586?–1653?) Daughter of Robert, and niece of Philip and Mary Sidney, she was at court by 1600, was married to Sir Robert Wroth, who died in 1615. She had two illegitimate children fathered by her cousin, William Herbert, third earl of Pembroke, and after the publication of *Urania* and *Pamphilia to Amphilanthus* in 1621, spent the rest of her life in relative retirement.

> Roberts, Josephine A., ed., *The Poems of Lady Mary Wroth* (Baton Rouge, 1983).
> —— *The Countess of Montgomery's Urania* (New York, 1994).
> Waller, Gary, ed., *Pamphilia to Amphilanthus* (Salzburg, 1977).

> See: Paulissen, May Nelson, *The Love Sonnets of Lady Mary Wroth* (Salzburg, 1982)
> Roberts, Josephine A., 'The Biographical Problem of *Pamphilia to Amphilanthus*', *Tulsa Studies in Women's Literature*, 1 (1982), 43–53.
> Miller, Naomi, 'Rewriting Lyric Fictions: the Role of the Lady in Lady Mary Wroth's *Pamphilia to Amphilanthus*', in *The Renaissance Englishwoman in Print*, ed. Anne Haselkorn and Betty Travitsky (Amherst, 1990), pp. 295–310.
> Miller, Naomi J., and Gary Waller, ed., *Reading Mary Wroth: Representing Alternatives in Early Modern England* (Knoxville, 1991). (Contains essays on biography, contexts, writings from a variety of critical viewpoints.)
> Waller, Gary, *The Sidney Family Romance* (Detroit, 1993). (A cultural/psychoanalytical study of Wroth and her cousin William Herbert.)

WYATT, Sir Thomas (1503–42), courtier, diplomat and probably one of Queen Anne Boleyn's lovers. His poems, along with some by Surrey, Vaux and others, first appeared in Tottel's *Miscellany* (1557) and constitute the first substantial body of poetry in English of real importance between Chaucer and Sidney. Wyatt's work is often seen as anticipating the seemingly realistic tones of Greville or Donne later in the century. He was born in Kent, educated at St John's College, Cambridge, and became a seasoned diplomat before he was twenty-five. Marshal of Calais 1528–32, knighted in 1536, imprisoned under suspicion of treason in 1536, but released, a pattern that was repeated in 1541. In 1542, he fell ill while on a diplomatic mission and died. His poems were widely circulated at Court. Some appeared in *The Court of Venus* (1540), but most waited until Tottel published them.

Daalder, Joost, ed., *Collected Poems* (1974).
Rebholtz, Richard, ed., *Collected Poems* (1978).

See: Southall, Raymond, *The Courtly Maker: An Essay on the Poetry of Wyatt and his Contemporaries* (1954). (Excellent on court background.)
Thompson, Patricia, *Sir Thomas Wyatt and his Background* (1964). (Old-fashioned but still useful.)
Leonard, Nancy S., 'The Speaker in Wyatt's Lyric Poetry', *HLQ*, 41 (1977), 1–8.
Kamholtz, Jonathan Z., 'Thomas Wyatt's Poetry: The Politics of Love', *Criticism*, 20 (1978), 349–65.
Greenblatt, Stephen, *Renaissance Self-Fashioning* (Chicago, 1980). (An important New Historicist study.)
Waller, Marguerite, 'The Empire's New Clothes: Refashioning the Renaissance' in *Seeking the Woman in Late Medieval and Renaissance Writings*, edited by Sheila Fisher and Janet E. Halley (Knoxville, 1989), pp. 180–3. (Feminist critique of Greenblatt).

Index